Disability, Civil Rights, and Public Policy

Stephen L. Percy

Disability, Civil Rights, and Public Policy

The Politics of Implementation

The University of
Alabama Press
Tuscaloosa and London

Copyright © 1989 by
The University of Alabama Press
Tuscaloosa, Alabama 35487–0380
All rights reserved
Manufactured in the United States of America

Percy, Stephen L.
    Disability, civil rights, and public policy : the politics of
implementation / Stephen L. Percy.
        p.   cm.
    Bibliography: p.
    Includes index.
    ISBN 0-8173-0444-4
    1. Handicapped—Government policy—United States.   2. Handicapped—
Civil rights—United States.   I. Title.
HV1553.P46   1989
362.4'0973—dc19   89-30317
                                                            CIP

British Library Cataloguing-in-Publication Data available

This book is dedicated
to the millions of Americans
with mental and physical
disabilities, who
struggle each day
to achieve an equal status
in American society.

Contents

Preface   ix

1. Disability, Public Policy, and
   Implementation   1

2. An Institutional Approach to
   the Study of Policy
   Implementation   21

3. Federal Laws to Assist Persons
   with Disabilities   44

4. From Symbolic Gestures to
   Implementation Guidelines:
   The Saga of Section 504   64

5. A Conservative Reaction to
   Section 504 Regulations: The
   Politics of Rollback   83

6. Barrier Removal and Facility
   Access for Disabled
   Persons   106

7. Access, Mobility, and Public
   Transportation   129

8. Access to Public and Higher
   Education   160

9. Employment Rights and
   Opportunities for Disabled
   Persons   193

10. Implementing Disability Rights
    Policies: Comparisons,
    Contrasts, and Dilemmas   221

Abbreviations   255

Notes   257

Select Bibliography   280

Index   301

Preface

Insufficient attention has been given to the creation, refinement, and implementation of disability rights policies in the United States. Following on the heels of other civil rights movements, disability rights laws emerged in the late 1960s and early 1970s. Often these antidiscrimination laws were more symbolic than precise in terms of objectives and strategies to guide policy implementation. The purpose of this book is to analyze and assess the process by which disability rights policies have been refined and then utilized to commence policy execution.

Policy refinement, the process of translating legislative mandates into strategies and procedures to govern administrative action, has proved to be dynamic and controversial. Recognizing the impact of implementation policies, those parties who benefit from them (program beneficiaries) and those whose behavior is regulated (regulated clients) seek to direct or redirect the flow of benefits and sanctions that arise from various public policies. When statutory language is vague, administrative authorities possess extensive discretion in fashioning strategies and procedures for implementation. They do not, however, formulate these strategies in a political vacuum. Instead, administrative policymakers, acting within the constraints of legislative intent, fashion strategies for implementation, while, at the same time, regulated interests and beneficiaries exert pressures to influence those strategies.

Dynamic decisions about policy refinement are made in several different institutions within the American political system. These institutions serve as the arenas where interested parties seek decisions to affect the content of implementation policies. The fragmented nature of our political system—resulting from a complex set of checks and balances among branches of the federal government and an intergovernmental system where governing powers are shared—presents a multiplicity of potential arenas for reaching decisions about implementation policy. Primary institutional arenas in implementation include administrative agencies, committees and subcommittees of Congress, and the federal courts. The principal theme of this book is that implementation policies are dynamic and changing, and that they result from protracted struggles by interested parties, waged within institutional arenas, to influence the form and direction of implementation policies.

The development of policies to implement disability rights laws documents the ever-changing nature of implementation strategies and the processes by which parties affected by the policies have sought to influence their content and scope. After presenting a theoretical framework for the study of implementation, one that follows an institutional approach, the book considers the development of administrative regulations for section 504 of the Rehabilitation Act of 1973, the legal linchpin of disability rights. The saga of section 504 demonstrates both the problems of translating vague legislative mandates into concrete regulations to guide implementation and the difficult value choices articulated through the regulations.

The book will subsequently examine the development and refinement of disability rights policies in four specific areas: removal of architectural barriers, urban transportation policy, public education, and employment practices. Implementation experiences are sufficiently common across these areas to allow for meaningful comparisons; they are also sufficiently unique to provide useful contrasts and insights into policy execution. The closing chapter endeavors to tie the book together by examining the politics of setting policies to implement disability rights protections and the competing equity conceptions that underlie these policies.

*　*　*

Oftentimes readers are interested in what stimulated the author's attention to and interest in the topic presented in his or her book. In my case, interest in disability rights issues was stimulated through a project I conducted through the Institute of Government at the University of Virginia upon the request of the Virginia Department of Rehabilitative Services. The purpose of this project was to trace and describe the current policy environment in the commonwealth of Virginia with respect to persons with disabilities and the state's vocational rehabilitation program. The heart of this project focused on examination of a major piece of disability rights legislation considered by the Virginia General Assembly in its 1984 and 1985 sessions. A significant component of the Virginians with Disabilities Act was a section that outlined the rights of and protections for persons with mental or physical disabilities. Much of the language of this section was taken from either federal laws or administrative regulations. The persistent connections between the proposed legislation and federal government policies stimulated my interest in the development of disability rights at the federal level.

My preliminary search for materials related to the question of how the federal government's disability rights policies evolved indicated that little scholarly work had been done in the area. To be sure, legal analyses of disability rights were prolific, as were advocacy pieces arguing for and against different policies. What was missing was a thorough examination of the political processes through which implementation policies for disability rights were formulated, translated into administrative guidelines, and executed. Three exceptions to this rule are excellent books on the following topics: (1) the legislative history of section 504 of the Rehabilitation Act of 1973 (*From Good Will to Civil Rights*, Richard Scotch, 1984); (2) the development of handicapped transportation policy (*Institutional Disability*, Robert Katzmann, 1986); and (3) the development of the full range of disability and rehabilitation policies (*Disability Policy: America's Programs for the Handicapped*, Edward Berkowitz, 1987).

Being trained as a political scientist and fascinated with disability rights issues, I decided to embark on a book-length project to explore political issues related to the development and implementation of handicapped rights policies. Upon this decision, I was faced with the significant question of what analytical or theoretical approach to employ as a tool to organize my study of disability rights. After consideration of different approaches, I have decided to employ a framework based upon policy implementation. This seems appropriate since I am interested more in explaining the refinement of disability rights policies as they are implemented than in their legislative origins. The problem with implementation as a theoretical approach is that, as yet, implementation studies do not provide a consistent or well-defined framework for analysis. Instead, these studies provide fascinating case insights into implementation and a myriad of related, but certainly not integrated, propositions about how a wide set of variables affects implementation outcomes.

Because a cogent implementation framework does not exist, I have made an effort in this book (and offered in chapter two) to develop my own organizing framework. It is based upon the notion of institutional analysis, namely that implementation policies are set and reset as relevant actors interact within institutional arenas so as to protect their own positions. My purpose is to devise a generic framework that is of value not only to my own study but also to other analysts working outside of the disability rights context. Like most implementation frameworks, mine remains more general than precise, with the intention that it might be applicable to many types of policies. Despite its generality, I find it a useful means to sort through and organize case materials, so as to understand the political processes and struggles that have shaped policies to implement disability rights protections in the United States. Only the test of time will indicate whether others will find the framework of use in studying implementation in other public policy contexts.

Preface

* * *

Like most authors, I find it appropriate to use the preface to express appreciation to those persons and organizations who have assisted me in preparing this book. Certainly, I shall invoke the standard disclaimer that while I am indebted to these persons for their insights, assistance, and support, I alone am responsible for any errors or omissions in analysis.

I would like to thank the University of Virginia for several types of support, especially for leave time to work on this project. This time was provided both by a sabbatical through the university's Sesquicentennial Program and Summer Grant Program. I also received a grant to cover supplies, reproduction, and travel from the univerity's Research Support Funds Program.

Several public officials supplied invaluable assistance through interviews and the provision of useful reports and other materials. I am particularly indebted to the following representatives of federal agencies: Robert Ashby (Department of Transportation), Clayton Boyd (Equal Employment Opportunity Commission), David Brigham (Department of Labor), and Dennis Cannon (Architectural and Transportation Barriers Compliance Board). I also learned a great deal through consulting projects with the Virginia Department of Rehabilitative Services. I am particularly indebted to Elizabeth Matthews for her support in this project, her insights into disability rights issues at the state level, and her sharing of personal experiences as the mother of a handicapped child.

Arlene Myerson and Pat Wright of the Disability Rights Education and Defense Fund were both of great help in providing both materials and insights into the development of section 504 policies. In addition, the Council for Exceptional Children also provided several useful materials.

One set of very important helpers is the usually unsung heroes of the Public Documents Section of the University of Virginia's Alderman Library. Walter Newsome and members of the Public Documents staff have shown relentless energy in tracking down strange and unusual sources and helping me effectively use a variety of research guides and indexes. To these library folks go my warmhearted thanks and my promise to eventually return the hundreds of documents I have checked out.

Two people were very helpful in proofing the endless drafts of this manuscript. Readers will never know how many errors, inconsistencies, and grammatical problems have been removed with their help. My thanks to Charles Eastwood and Katherine Percy.

To all of these people and organizations, I express my appreciation and thanks. I only hope they will judge that the final product ultimately merited their generous help and assistance.

S.L.P.

Disability,
Civil Rights,
and Public Policy

1

Disability, Public Policy, and Implementation

Citizens who experience mental or physical disability have traditionally represented a hidden minority in American society.[1] Literally through institutionalization, and subtly through negative attitudes and treatment, persons with disabilities have been isolated from the social mainstream and denied the benefits and opportunities available to nondisabled persons. This exclusion results, in part, from limitations in mobility, dexterity, and communication imposed by disabling conditions. But even greater barriers to the opportunities of modern society have been imposed by nonhandicapped persons, who have feared disabled people and have been preoccupied with that group's *inabilities* and problems rather than their *capabilities*. America's citizens and institutions—both public and private—have systematically ignored the needs of disabled persons when designing facilities, employment practices, educational programs, and the delivery of public services.

Disabled citizens no longer accept the barriers that have excluded them from consuming the benefits and opportunities that are so plentiful in American life. They are actively engaged in efforts on many fronts to overcome obstacles that impede access to the benefits that others take for granted. Some victories have been small in scope but significant in impact; the proliferation of specially designated parking places for handicapped persons is one example. Other efforts have been more far-reaching and represent a long-term strategy to remove limitations imposed on persons with disabilities. Relevant here are state and federal laws to protect the rights of disabled citizens in areas ranging from access to public buildings to accommodations in employment and public transportation.

This book is about people with disabilities and their struggle to achieve equal opportunity in America. Primary attention is given to their efforts to affect the development and implementation of public policies to advance and protect their own rights and opportunities. The book is also about *policy implementation*, that is, about the political and administrative processes in-

1

volved in carrying public laws into action. Public laws are in no way self-enforcing; instead, they must be executed by a wide variety of actors working in and through a number of institutional arenas. Understanding the dynamic process by which laws are translated into administrative guidelines and are then enforced is the key to understanding successes and dilemmas associated with implementing disability rights laws.

Implementation is a complex political and administrative process, which conceptually covers the period from legislative passage through policy evaluation. This process can be broken into components that are distinct conceptually but interact in practice. *Policy refinement* refers to those activities aimed at clarifying procedures, processes, and guidelines relevant to the administration of programs. Public laws set the statutory framework for implementation, but this broad policy outline leaves many questions about execution unanswered. For this reason, executive agencies are required to refine and clarify policy objectives and practices as a precursor to effective implementation efforts.

A second component of implementation is *policy diffusion*, the communication of the refined objectives and practices to the administrative agents charged with providing services, benefits, or protections. The outcomes of implementation are likely to closely match program objectives only if administrative agents understand policy intentions and the strategies and mechanisms selected for implementation. Diffusion is particularly important in an intergovernmental system, such as that of the United States, where both political and administrative authorities are widely distributed through thousands of public and private institutions.

Policy execution is the final component and represents the transformation activities performed by administrative agents for the purpose of distributing services, benefits, and regulatory protections. It is at this level that public and private agents interact with citizens, corporations, or other governments in an effort to achieve implementation objectives. Studies that focus on policy execution tend to take a ''bottom up'' approach to analysis of implementation, analyzing transformation efforts and influences on those efforts in order to understand how programs work to produce outcomes.

The analysis of disability rights policy pursued in this book will place heavy focus on the policy refinement phase of implementation. The reason for this emphasis is empirically based: in the roughly twenty-year period since the passage of disability rights laws by the federal government, the most prominent activity has been the development and refinement of guidelines, criteria, and obligations for implementation. Many of the laws raised more questions about implementation practices than they answered; they were heavily symbolic and thus imprecise as to strategies and objectives for policy execution. Public sector action to protect and advance the rights of handicapped persons is a relatively new responsibility, and as a consequence, significant effort has been consumed in policy refinement activities. This study will consider relevant issues of policy diffusion and execution where they are applicable, but considering the nature of implementation to date, most experience relates to policy refinement.

The fundamental question underlying this study of disability rights is: How did the federal government develop and refine policy objectives and strategies to carry out the legal mandates set in disability rights laws? The unfolding story presented in this book will document how the agencies of the federal government wrestled with controversial and confounding dilemmas and trade-offs in devising policies for implementation. Such policy development has not taken place in a vacuum; instead, it resulted from the frequent interactions of interested parties who wished to affect policy directions and the flow of program costs and benefits. The dynamic interactions among interested parties, in the context of institutional arenas, will be examined as a means to explain the development of implementation policies.

To understand the development and implementation of public policies to advance the rights and opportunities of persons with disability, it is necessary to consider the extent and sources of disabling conditions, the social and political position of disabled persons, and their long struggle to achieve equal social, political, and economic status in American society.

Disability: Diversity in Sources and Impacts

Disabililties result from a large variety of sources, including birth defects; occupational, traffic, and other accidents; drug abuse; military action; mental illness; and even the natural process of aging. When one reviews the extent and types of disabling conditions, it becomes apparent that this minority, while often hidden, is not small. Statistics to determine the number of disabled Americans demonstrate substantial range, depending upon the definition of disability used and the validity of measurement techniques.

Figures from several sources document the extent and costs of disability in America. The White House Conference on Handicapped Individuals (1977) estimated that as many as thirty-five million Americans experience some form of physical or mental disability. From the perspective of employment, a 1978 survey estimated that, of 127 million adults of working age, 21.9 million (17.2 percent) considered themselves as having work limitations resulting from health problems, and 11 million reported severe disabilities (Lando, Cutler, and Gamber 1982, v). And from the perspective of disability costs, the Institute for

Rehabilitation and Disability Management reported that in 1981 the cost of disability payments and health care services for handicapped Americans totaled over $184 billion—$114 billion for health care and $70.6 billion for wage replacement (Schwartz 1984).

These figures suggest that disability is not an isolated phenomenon but instead is prevalent throughout society. With a broad definition, one can estimate that as much as twenty to twenty-five percent of Americans experience some form of mental or physical handicap. These data also indicate substantial diversity in the nature and source of disability. Handicapped people are by no means a homogeneous group; they differ markedly in extent of impairment and range of potential abilities. This point is often missed by nondisabled persons, who tend to lump most types of disability into a single "handicapped" category. This tendency is not only frustrating to disabled people's sense of individuality but is also an impediment to development of enlightened policies to expand the opportunities afforded to handicapped persons.

The Hidden Minority

Persons with disabilities have been a neglected minority in American society, isolated from the mainstream. Those who have been able to succeed have generally been able to do so only by masking their disability. Certainly this was true of Franklin Roosevelt who, despite being confined to a wheelchair, attained the presidency. His political success was achieved, however, largely by downplaying and hiding his disabling condition rather than through any sense of enlightened understanding of the potential abilities possessed by disabled persons.

Disability has often been viewed as a form of social stigma, generating reactions of pity, helplessness, distrust, uneasiness, and even fear:[2]

> The attitudes we normals have toward a person with a stigma, and the actions we take in regard to him, are well known, since these responses are what benevolent social action is designed to soften and ameliorate. By definition, of course, we believe the person with a stigma is not quite human. On this assumption, we exercise varieties of discrimination, through which we effectively, if often unthinkingly, reduce his life chances. (Goffman 1963, 5)

Nonhandicapped people generally do not understand the problems and realities in the lives of persons with mental and physical disabilities. Instead, they tend to have views of handicapped persons that are unrealistic, negative, and paternalistic. Americans often desire to help handicapped persons yet, at the same time, see those persons as "different" and not equal to others in society.

4

Certain classes of disability, including drug abuse, alcoholism, and mental retardation, have frequently been misunderstood and viewed in a negative light. Until the past few decades, institutionalization was the primary form of treatment for mental illness. Once placed in institutions, mentally disabled persons were often sterilized against their own will, a practice that continued well into this century (Burgdorf and Burgdorf 1977). Only recently have noninstitutional forms of treatment, such as halfway houses and sheltered workshops, been made available to those with serious mental disabilities.

Many analysts contend that discrimination is rooted in inaccurate and limited conceptions, or paradigms, of disability and the needs and potentialities of disabled individuals:

> For many generations mainstream society's attempts to deal humanely with the disabled and the professional's vision of the nature of disability have been shaped by a host of mutually reinforcing paradigms. Starting from different intellectual premises, these frameworks have converged to produce a set of flawed assessments of the disabled person's needs and the place of disabled in American society. Indeed, despite their condemnations of prejudice toward the disabled, these models share far more with longstanding myths and stereotypes about handicaps than has generally been recognized. (Gliedman and Roth 1980, 17)

Breaking down these paradigmatic conceptions has been one of the most difficult tasks of handicapped rights advocates.

Researchers have examined the origins of social attitudes about disability and handicapped persons and have found that negative and inaccurate perceptions arise from many sources. One source has been literary and media depictions of disabled people. Thurer (1981) describes how literary characters with disabilities, from Captain Hook to the Hunchback of Notre Dame to Captain Ahab, have been depicted as evil, vengeful, and freakish. In a review of other research studies, Elliott and Byrd (1982) reach a similar conclusion about the negative images of disabled persons as portrayed in literature and television.[3] One analyst sums up the literary depiction of handicapped persons as narrow and typical of society's purposeful neglect of and distaste for disability: "Handicapped people are not especially important to writers. . . . In the area of the handicapped it turns out that writers have not so much led as reflected what they have found around them, and what they have found around them, of course, has been general neglect" (Trautmann 1979, 1).

The development of negative and unrealistic attitudes toward persons with handicaps is attributed to other sources besides literature and the media. Livneh (1982) presents a thorough review of studies that examine the formation of attitudes toward handicapped people. Among the sources of negative attitudes described are social customs and norms, child-rearing practices, and psychological fears and anxieties. Livneh (1982, 344) argues that these attitudes are "learned and conditioned over many years," and that efforts to change them require substantial effort.

In their analysis of attitudes toward disability, Bogdan and Biklen (1981) argue that negative views lead to discriminating attitudes against handicapped persons, or "handicapism," similar in nature to racism or sexism. In a provocative article, Kriegel (1969, 421) makes a similar connection between racial discrimination and prevailing public attitudes toward persons with disability, and the struggle of both groups to achieve a more equal position in society: "The condition of the Negro is imposed from outside. Obviously, this is not altogether true of the cripple. But while his physical condition is not imposed from outside, the way in which he exists in the world is. His relationship to the community is, by and large, dependent upon the special sufferance the community accords him."

Straus (1966, 5) suggests that negative views of handicapped persons result from fears and anxieties of nonhandicapped individuals about their own vulnerability to disability: "Such anxieties may well reflect the distressing thought that we too are vulnerable, a need to avoid identification with the disabled, an inability to tolerate helplessness, discomfort with the ambiguities which are often associated with disability, and even the embarrassment that many people feel because they do not know what to say or do in the presence of those whose condition makes them feel anxious." These fears and anxieties about interaction with disabled persons are commonplace, often magnified by unrealistic portrayals and by social and physical barriers that reduce the frequency of interpersonal contacts between disabled and unimpaired persons.

Researchers have considered the extent as well as the source of public attitudes toward handicapped people. English (1971, 2), in reviewing empirical research on this question, argues that "the attitudes of the general public toward physically disabled persons in general suggest that nearly half of the non-disabled public have primarily negative attitudes toward physically disabled persons." Other research shows these negative attitudes to extend to many aspects of the lives of disabled persons (Siller et al. 1967; Nathanson 1980). For example, a study of college students by Having and Meyerson (1981) showed that otherwise sexually liberated college students had disapproving attitudes about the sexual activity of disabled persons.

Public attitudes about and perceptions of disabled individuals arise, then, from many sources, ranging from personal fears and anxieties to inaccurate media and literary portrayals. These attitudes appear to be deeply based and difficult to change. *Their impact cannot be overstated, for it is clear that these attitudes have generated behaviors and decisions that have limited the opportunities and life-styles of disabled persons.* Often the most damaging effects have arisen from prejudices against disabled persons and misunderstandings about their plights and potential *abilities*. This point is made clear by Frank Bowe (1978, viii), a tireless advocate for disabled citizens:

> We have created an image of disabled people that is perhaps the greatest barrier they face. We see the disability—the chrome and the leather, the guide dog, the hearing aid, the crutches—and look the other way. Just as we cannot seem to see the man in the policeman, so imposing are the uniform and the cultural expectations that go with it, so we cannot see the woman in the wheelchair. We do not see, nor do we look to find, her abilities, interests, and desires.

Because of these perceptions and attitudes, society as a whole has not been open to the idea that disabled individuals can meaningfully participate in most life activities. As Isbell (1977, 62) has argued, "Society invariably perceives the disabled in terms of their disabilities, for what they cannot do, not for what they can do. This almost universal view is far more handicapping than any particular disability." Because of its blindness to those potentialities, society has erected many barriers, tangible and intangible, which impede the ability of disabled persons to participate in many facets of contemporary life. It is against this background that disabled citizens have struggled to change society so as to increase their opportunities and end their segregated status.

A Profile of Disabled Individuals

A survey of disabled individuals conducted by Louis Harris and Associates for the International Center for the Disabled in late 1985 presents data that profile the current status and perceptions of persons with physical and mental handicaps.[4] An overview of findings from this study is presented in table 1-1.

The portrait provided by the study shows that forty-four percent of those interviewed experienced some form of physical disability; thirteen percent suffered sensory impairment (e.g., blindness, deafness); six percent reported mental disability; five percent had respiratory ailments; and sixteen percent suffered from other disabling diseases (e.g., heart and blood diseases). Compared to nondisabled persons, handicapped individuals received much less education, were far more likely to be unemployed, and earned less income when employed.

The impact of disability on the lives of handicapped persons is clear from survey questions about social interactions and ability to reach personal potential. Over half of the respondents reported that their disabilities prevented them from achieving full potential in life, and fifty-six percent said that their hand-

7

Table 1-1 A Profile of Disabled Americans, 1985

Personal Characteristics

—Nature of disability: physical disability (44%), sensory impairment (13%), heart or blood disease (16%), mental illness/limitation (6%), respiratory illness (5%), other debilitating disease (11%).

—40% of disabled persons aged 16 years and older did not finish high school (compared to 15% of nondisabled population).

—50% of disabled persons aged 16 and over have household incomes of $15,000 or less (compared to 25% of nondisabled individuals).

—57% of interviewees said that their disabilities have prevented them from reaching their full potentials as persons.

—56% said their disabilities prevent them from getting around, attending cultural and social events, and socializing with friends outside of the home.

Employment Situation

—66% of disabled individuals aged 16 to 64 were not working.

—65% of nonworking disabled respondents said that they would like to be working.

—84% of those working full- or part-time were satisfied or somewhat satisfied with their jobs.

Barriers to Entering the Mainstream

—49% of those interviewed said that they were not able to use public transportation, get special transportation services, or get a ride when they needed one.

—40% said mobility and activities were limited because they could not enter public buildings/places or that such places lack bathrooms they can use.

—47% of working-age disabled persons, not working or working part-time, said employers would not recognize that they are capable of performing full-time jobs.

—28% of those not working cited lack of accessible or affordable transportation as an important reason for not working.

—35% of working-age disabled persons who are working or who have worked said employers made accommodations for their disabilities; 61% said no such accommodations were made.

—25% of working-age disabled persons said that they have encountered job discrimination because of their disabilities.

Source: The International Center for the Disabled and the National Council on the Handicapped, *Bringing Disabled Americans into the Mainstream* (Washington, D.C., 1986). Survey of 1,000 disabled persons conducted in November and December 1985 by Louis Harris and Associates.

icaps prevented movement in the community, attending cultural and sports events, and socializing with friends outside of the home.

Respondents were asked about barriers that prevented them from entering the mainstream of society. The most frequently cited impediment was fear that their disabilities might cause them to get hurt, sick, or victimized by crime if they left home more frequently. In addition to health and safety concerns, respondents also pointed to physical obstacles to their mobility. Forty-nine percent of those interviewed said that they were not able to use public transportation or gain access to specialized transportation services; forty percent said mobility was limited by buildings that were inaccessible or unequipped with restrooms they could use; and forty-seven percent of working-age respondents stated that employers would not recognize that they were capable of performing full-time work. While those interviewed indicated that significant progress had been made since the 1960s to improve the position of disabled persons, these persistent barriers were identified.

Public Policy and Disability

With the exception of schools for handicapped children, particularly those serving hearing- and sight-impaired students, and the creation of public institutions providing custodial care, public policy efforts on behalf of persons with disabilities have largely taken place during this century. Policy initiatives can be categorized into at least three types: rehabilitative services, income supports, and civil rights protections.[5] One set of policies centers on services to help disabled persons deal with and overcome their disabling conditions. Vocational rehabilitation programs originated in the United States immediately following the First World War, largely in response to the number of veterans who returned home with combat injuries. Programs were expanded to all physically disabled persons, with the expectation that vocational rehabilitation would return them to the work force and remove them from public assistance programs. Later, mental disabilities came to be included within the set of conditions that made individuals eligible for rehabilitative services.

Next came a series of public programs to provide income supports to persons whose disabilities prevent gainful employment. Revelant here are Social Security Disability Insurance and Supplemental Security Income. These programs, which were begun in the mid-1950s and were expanded in scope and eligibility during the 1970s, were designed to ensure that disabled citizens and their families receive financial support.

The third policy initiative has centered on efforts to legislate and enforce legal protections for those who experience mental or physical handicaps. Disability rights legislation includes sections 501 through 504 of the Rehabilitation Act of 1973, the Education for All Handicapped Children Act (1975), and the Architectural Barriers Act (1968). These laws, following a half century of federal programs to provide rehabilitation services and income supports to citizens with handicaps, represent a new and bold direction in public policy for disabled citizens.[6] With these laws, emphasis shifted from "treating" and "supporting" disabled individuals to creating legally protected opportunities and rights. The advocates of these policies recognized that most handicapped people can adapt to their disabilities and pursue meaningful and productive lives, if social and governmental barriers to their participation in society are removed.

With passage of this legislation, the move to ensure the rights of persons with disabilities shifted to the implementation arena. Getting rights protections stated in public laws is one thing; having them effectively and regularly enforced is another. The disability rights legislation was significant in symbolic value, committing the public sector to protecting and aiding mentally and physically handicapped citizens. At the same time, these laws did not provide clear direction as to the appropriate mechanisms or strategies for implementation. In the period since the passage of disabled rights laws, much of the implementation effort has centered on interpreting laws and developing guidelines for administrative action.

Without question, significant gains have been made as the result of the new rights-oriented laws. Some changes, including the provision of specially designated handicapped parking spaces proximate to commercial enterprises and public buildings, have been smoothly implemented with little uproar. The American public, which seldom has paid much attention to the needs of its disabled citizens, has become accustomed to handicapped parking spaces, as well as to special entry ramps and door entrances, curb cuts, elevators with braille floor designations, and specially designed restroom facilities. These modifications, so important to the mobility and access of disabled citizens, have become commonplace, and many have been achieved at relatively small cost.

Yet advancing the opportunities of disabled citizens involves more than "toilets and ramps." It requires systematic review of social practices and public policies in order that discriminatory actions can be identified and eliminated. Some policy initiatives taken for the purpose of extending the opportunities of handicapped persons have generated substantial controversy in the course of implementation. In the late 1970s, the U.S. Department of Transportation moved to require localities to purchase buses that "kneeled" or were equipped with lifts. These buses were expensive, prone to mechanical failure, and unpopular with transit drivers. They came to symbolize the handicapped rights movement to many urban citizens, who witnessed mechanical failure by the vehicles and low participation by wheelchair riders. Questions about costs and benefits arose from the controversy about specially designed buses, including ones about who should pay the cost of accommodation, the extent of benefits received by the disabled community, and ultimately the most difficult question, how far the public sector *must* go (and how much it must spend) to accommodate the needs of an identified minority group.

Arguments about disability policy are not limited to public transportation. Employers, bound by section 504 protections to reasonably accommodate handicapped workers, have questioned the type and extent of accommodations they must make. Public officials, worried about budget crunches and federal government cutbacks, wonder how extensive structural changes to government buildings and facilities must be to meet accessibility requirements. And in a similar vein, public and private educators have been and remain concerned about the types of special education services that are mandated for handicapped children, as well as the financing of these services.

Perplexing questions also remain about the criteria that define disability and determine who is eligible for protection under federal laws.[7] Recent controversies have surrounded the questions of whether unborn babies or those individuals who have contracted acquired immune deficiency syndrome (AIDS) fall within the class of individuals protected by disability rights laws. These and other difficult questions must be faced by policymakers and public administrators charged with enforcing rights protections for disabled Americans.

The primary objective of this book is to examine these unanswered questions by tracing the implementation process for disability rights policies. In order to explain development in implementation, a theoretical framework for the analysis of implementation will be developed. This is the primary task of the next chapter. At this point, it is useful to consider briefly the recent literature on policy implementation, a literature that has proliferated since the early 1970s. The insights of this literature will contribute to the development of the theoretical framework and the examination of disability rights policies undertaken by the federal government.

Prevalent Themes in Implementation Studies

Analysts and researchers of many stripes have conducted studies about the execution and conduct of public policies. Some analyses have explored the execution of particular policies as they are carried out in the "field." Far more have been broader studies of the policy process "in action," following the development of particular programs from inception through enactment and administration.[8] For any student of politics or administration, these studies of

11

policy implementation can be truly fascinating. They document the complex, often frustrating, process by which public policies enacted into law move into action, sometimes quickly, more often after substantial debate, delay, and controversy. One can see from these studies how political debates and intrigues carry over from the legislative consideration stage into policy execution, despite the common myth about the separation of politics and administration. One can also see the struggle that implementation authorities have in developing strategies for clear administrative action, given only broad objectives in legislative mandates. Studies also document the all too frequent problems, disappointments, and even failures of policy implementation efforts.

While implementation studies are individually fascinating, they are cumulatively frustrating in that there exists to date no prominent theoretical framework with which to organize and comparatively assess implementation experiences. Most analysts would concur with Alexander (1985, 404) that a consistent analytic framework "is needed for the development of a coherent and convergent body of theory capable of explaining relations between deliberations, actions, and outcomes." In addition to there being no consistent theory or model for the study of implementation, there is also no mutually agreed upon methodology.[9] Some case studies take a "top down" or macro perspective, comparing nationally defined objectives with what transpires in program performance at the local level. Other studies are more micro or "bottom up" in vantage point, focusing on implementation at the local level, paying less attention to broadly stated national objectives and more attention to the experiences and realities of actually delivering programs in the local context. Elmore (1982) refers to these approaches as forward and backward "mapping."[10]

One means of sorting through and organizing a review of the policy implementation literature is to identify the principal themes that emerge from empirical analyses of implementation. This is a bold task because of the wide-ranging set of factors that have been postulated or empirically demonstrated to affect implementation. Still, I venture such boldness and suggest four primary themes found in studies of implementation of public policy: implementation as political process, administrative process, intergovernmental relations, and the interplay of rational actors seeking to manipulate policy outcomes in their favor. Often multiple themes are found in individual studies, as a result of the complexity of human efforts to design and carry out public programs.

Implementation as Political Process

Several studies of implementation document the recurrent interplay of political actors, factions, and pressures in the execution of public programs. If *pol-*

12

itics is defined as the process by which governments make allocative decisions about the distribution of public costs and benefits, there is no question but that political factors continue to influence policy as it moves through the implementation phase. Despite exhortations by Woodrow Wilson (1887) and other progressive reformers, it has not been possible to make a meaningful separation of politics and administration. Political struggles to influence allocative decisions continue into the implementation phase. From this perspective, the different stages of the policy process represent institutional forums in which affected parties may seek to pressure for or against public policies. If an interest group loses in the legislative enactment phase, it can then organize tactics to enhance or impede policy during the implementation process.

The role of politics is clearly evident in the policy refinement phase of implementation, where legislative mandates are translated into more precise guidelines and strategies for carrying out the law. At the federal, and often state, level, this translation phase takes place during a rulemaking process conducted by administrative agencies. Rulemaking is political in that it allows executive agencies to develop and refine guidelines for administrative action, with such guidelines ultimately affecting the flow of government-sanctioned costs and benefits. In essence, legislatures delegate to executive agencies the authority to work out "the details" of administration; the expectation here is that agencies have the experience and expertise to develop appropriate administrative rules to carry out the law effectively. The political nature of making and revising administrative rules to govern programs is clearly depicted by Berry (1984) in his study of the federal food stamp program. He describes how political pressures, mainly from Congress, led to several changes in allocation rules, first to enhance coverage, and later, during Republican administrations, to restrict the flow of food stamp benefits.

The theme of politics in implementation continues beyond rulemaking to the process of activating and operating public programs. Acting within administrative rules, implementation authorities, such as municipal governments and single-purpose authorities, often have discretionary latitude in carrying out public programs. This discretion may be used to the political or administrative advantage of the implementing authorities. In a biting study of urban renewal in San Francisco, for example, Hartman (1984) describes how local officials, dominated by business interests, pursued urban renewal following local, rather than federal, priorities. According to the author, the U.S. Department of Housing and Urban Development (HUD) "evolved essentially as a conduit of funds to local agencies. As its legislative mandate to control projects developed, its philosophy and staff capacity did not keep pace . . . HUD staff subordinated themselves to local initiative" (Hartman 1984, 46). Since HUD tended to share a preference for large-scale downtown development with the dominant local co-

13

alition, it did not actively intervene, even after charges that local authorities did not adhere to provisions concerning displacement and relocation, until the deficiencies became so blatant as to embarrass the department publicly. Federal involvement was spurred not for administrative reasons but instead as the result of political pressures related to the displacement of former residents.

Implementation as Administrative Process

A second theme is the view that implementation is primarily an organizational process of administration, and not surprisingly, the approach is common within the field of public adminstration. Analyses using this perspective explain implementation in terms of traditional questions of administration, including tensions between centralization and decentralization, the structure of authority relationships, problems of communication and information flow, and the divergent expectations, skills, interests, and commitments of administrative personnel.[11]

Pressman and Wildavsky's (1984) widely cited study of an economic redevelopment program in Oakland, California, directs attention to the administrative process. The authors examine difficulties encountered by administrative authorities in getting the program off the ground, and the greater problem of targeting program benefits to intended beneficiaries, the poor and unemployed. A fundamental finding of this study is that implementation is often impeded by the complexity of joint action: "When a program is characterized by so many contradictory criteria, antagonistic relationships among participants, and a high level of uncertainty about even the possibility of success, it is not hard to predict or to explain the failure of the effort to reach its goals" (Pressman and Wildavsky 1984, 90).

One important set of administrative variables, considered in some fashion in most implementation studies, concerns the qualities of public officials, in particular, their skills, interests, commitment, and experiences. It is evident from empirical work that lack of commitment to policy objectives can impede effective implementation efforts, as can insufficient technical and political skills (see, for example, Mazmanian and Sabatier 1983; Sabatier and Mazmanian 1979; Levin and Ferman 1985). Similarly, various administrative skills can enhance implementation efforts. Notable in this regard is the "fixer," identified as the individual capable of spotting implementation problems and initiating strategic responses, often through coalition building and other interventions in the administrative process (Bardach 1977; Levin and Ferman 1985). The importance of staff to implementation suggests that administrative processes of personnel recruitment, task assignment, and evaluation have many potentially important linkages to the outcome of implementation programs.

Implementation as Intergovernmental Relations

A third theme crosscuts the previous two, framing implementation in terms of continuous interaction of federal, state, and local governments. From this perspective, implementation is seen as the manifestation of ongoing questions about which level of government should determine the allocation of public resources and the direction of policy execution. This intergovernmental issue clearly emerges in consideration of the form of federal aid transferred to state and local authorities, who are charged with implementing federally defined policy objectives (Goodrich 1981; Murphy 1976). Categorical grants, for example, tend to retain allocative decision power in Washington, whereas block and formula grants devolve substantially more allocative decisions to state and local governments.

Studies of American public policy have also documented administrative issues and problems in intergovernmental implementation, including the ongoing problems of communication, authority, monitoring, and accountability of federal programs as they are implemented by state and local authorities. Studies have shown, for example, that federal authorities and regional field offices often lack the capacity for stringent supervision or involvement in implementation, thus limiting federal control even in categorical grant programs, where fiscal transfers are, in theory, closely related to federal requirements about program operations. In this regard, Hargrove (1985, 35) contends that implementing policy through an intergovernmental system is problematic because "we do not know enough about the political and administrative incentives of state and local government officials to use them as instruments in federal policy."

Van Horn (1979) is among those who stress the importance of intergovernmental relations in comprehending the implementation of public programs sponsored by the federal government. At the outset, he argues that "federal programs embodying national goals but administered by state and local elected officials inevitably create tensions among levels of government over the shape and content of policy" (1). Van Horn explores these tensions in terms of three federal programs—general revenue sharing, the Comprehensive Employment and Training Act, and Community Development Block Grants—finding that "unclear public policies and vague national goals, along with the fundamental autonomy that state and local governments enjoy in the federal system, are the principal explanations for the minimal impact that public laws and federal implementing agencies have on intergovernmental policy implementation'' (163).

Difficulties in implementing policy changes in an intergovernmental system have also been described in the area of federal education policy, where analysts have shown the power of local and state authorities to impede and influence federal initiatives. In his study of Title 1 of the Elementary and Secondary Education Act of 1965 (aimed at increasing educational services for children of poor families), Jerome Murphy (1971, 60) identifies problems of implementation as central to ineffective implementation: "The federal system—with its dispersion of power and controls—not only permits but encourages the evasion and dilution of federal reform, making it impossible for the federal administrator to impose program constraints; those not diluted by Congressional intervention, can be ignored during state and local implementation."

Implementation as a Game between Rational Actors

Still another and potentially important theme in analyzing and understanding implementation identifies it as a set of interactions among rational actors involved in executing public policy. While similar in some respects to viewing implementation as a political process, this more micro approach emphasizes that outcomes are the result of regularized interactions, or "games," among rational actors, who have clear and identifiable stakes in implementation. Eugene Bardach (1977, 56), a prominent proponent of this approach, argues that the game metaphor

> directs us to look at the players, what they regard as stakes, their strategies and tactics, their resources for playing, the rules of play (which stipulate the conditions for winning), the rules of "fair" play (which stipulate the boundaries beyond which lie fraud or illegitimacy), the nature of the communications (or lack of them) among players, and the degree of uncertainty surrounding the possible outcomes.

Using this game-theoretical approach, analysts focus attention directly upon the resources and strategies of actors who seek to affect the outcome of public programs through their interactions with other relevant actors. This approach stresses not only the political nature of implementation actions, but also the processes through which interacting persons attempt to manipulate outcomes in their favor.

Montjoy and O'Toole (1979, 466) are among those who have employed the rational actor approach to explain the results of policy implementation. Beginning with the assumption that "agencies are populated with individuals who have their own values and seek to attain these within human limits to absorb and process information," these analysts explain implementation difficulties in terms of competition within agencies between existing routines and the activities required by new legislative mandates.

A Synthetic Approach to the Study of Policy Implementation

The theoretical framework to be developed and utilized in this book is a synthetic one that draws upon concepts, insights, and propositions from previous implementation studies. The purpose of the framework is to organize the exploration of implementation of policies to advance the rights of persons with mental or physical disabilities, with the intent that the exploration will yield not only an explanation of the development of disability rights policies, but also more general propositions for application and testing in other policy areas. The framework should also enhance the comparative assessment of implementation experiences across policy areas or types of governmental units.

Borrowing from the game-theoretical approach, a key premise of this book will be that implementation is nothing less than an ongoing game, where affected parties seek to affect outcomes by influencing decisions in particular institutional arenas. In this sense, administration will always be "political," and never the simple application of "scientific methods." Rational individuals and organizations seek to maximize benefits and minimize costs as distributed through public policy. This "politicization" of the administrative process is neither good nor bad but is predictable in light of the fragmented nature of our political system and the magnitude of benefits and sanctions distributed through public programs.

As previous implementation studies document, the politics of implementation are played out within a wide set of governmental arenas, each of which provides participants the opportunity to seek changes in implementation strategies and mechanisms. To some extent, the decisions reached within individual arenas are the result of the unique set of decision rules employed within the arena, including rules about who can participate and the nature and scope of decisions that can legitimately be made in the arena. In addition to unique institutional rules, there exist other general processes and factors that affect implementation decisions across all arenas. The cross-arena processes are the subject of the next chapter, which outlines an institutional approach to the study of implementation. These processes include *agenda setting*, that is, how issues come to the active attention of decision makers; *organizing principles*, which serve as the conceptual underpinnings of implementation policy; the *decision premises* of parties affected by implementation decisions; and the *political environment* in which such decisions are formulated and reached.

Outline of the Book

A framework for systematic examination of the implementation of public policy will be developed and illustrated in chapter two. The framework and the theoretical propositions derived from it will serve to organize the subsequent analysis of disability rights policies. This chapter will also consider the unique questions and issues that arise in the implementation of regulatory policy.

To set the stage for the study of policy implementation, the third chapter describes the development of federal laws to protect the rights of persons with disabilities. Beginning with the Architectural Barriers Act of 1968, and including the Rehabilitation Act of 1973 and the Education for All Handicapped Children Act (1975), the number of federally mandated protections for handicapped persons has grown dramatically. Examination of the legislative histories of these laws provides insights into the motivations and strategies of groups proposing legal protections, as well as those of the regulated parties who, while proclaiming support for persons with disabilities, frequently moved to weaken the laws so as to avoid costs and governmental interference.

The linchpin of rights protections for disabled citizens is section 504 of the Rehabilitation Act of 1973, a provision which states that no recipient of federal funds shall discriminate against persons with disabilities. While sending a strong symbolic message, this section, which received little legislative attention, provided no information about implementation. This meant that important policy decisions devolved to administrative agencies. Chapter four considers the lengthy and controversial process of administrative rulemaking that surrounded section 504, and the important policy mandates set through devised regulations, notably the missions of "reasonable accommodation" and "full accessibility." Chapter five explores initiatives taken by the Reagan administration to pursue regulatory relief by modifying and weakening the disability rights policies contained in section 504 regulations.

The next series of chapters, six through nine, explore implementation of disability rights laws in four policy areas: access to public facilities, public transportation, education, and employment practices. There are similarities and differences in implementation across these areas. While implementation in all cases concerns enhancing the opportunities of persons who experience disability, the strategies for implementation, and incumbent controversies, are unusual. In transportation, major controversy surrounded the full-accessibility

18

criteria, which required costly retrofitting or purchase of lift-equipped buses. Here the political influence of public transit authorities was instrumental in blocking a full-accessibility policy and substituting a modified approach that allowed greater local flexibility in implementation.

While access to public facilities and buildings, including polling places, medical facilities, and governmental offices, is taken for granted by most Americans, it is definitely a problem for many handicapped citizens. Various federal laws, and some state counterparts, mandate that the design of new and renovated public buildings provide access to handicapped persons. Some modifications are easy and relatively cheap, such as braille markings on operating controls in elevators to designate floors. Other changes are more costly, particularly the installation of elevators in multistory buildings. Implementation questions in the context of facility access center largely around when such modifications must be made and in what form.

While implementation generated immediate and powerful reaction in public transportation, and to a lesser extent in facility access, the story in the area of employment is much different. Here the regulated interests number not in the hundreds, as in the case of transit authorities, but in the hundreds of thousands of businesses and governmental units that receive federal financial assistance. The rules of reasonable accommodation in employment are more vague than the rather clear-cut requirement to make buses accessible. Given the dispersion of employers, and the ambiguity of accommodation rules, implementation has moved more slowly and, in many ways, has relied on disabled persons to initiate enforcement efforts in cases where they perceive discrimination.

Provision of "free and appropriate" educational services has been the persistent rallying cry for parents of handicapped children. Groups who represent disabled children and their parents have proved fierce fighters for handicapped education, and their efforts culminated in the passage of the Education for All Handicapped Children Act in 1975. Historically, education has been a service of prime importance to Americans, and it has been difficult to defend failure in educating handicapped children. The opposition to federal efforts to implement rights protections in education revolved less around whether such a policy was justifiable, than on who should pay for it and what types of services should be rendered. These questions remain as implementation efforts move into a second decade.

The concluding chapter of this book, chapter ten, synthesizes and contrasts implementation experiences across the four cases of transportation, facility access, employment, and education. Implementation of disability rights protections across these cases is sufficiently similar to allow for meaningful comparisons and contrasts but is also adequately varied to provide multiple perspectives from which to explore the institutional arena framework. This study of disability rights laws, pursued through case study analysis using a theoretical framework for organization, is intended to satisfy Hargrove's (1985, 75) admonition that "it is not clear how broad knowledge about implementation can be achieved without many case studies . . . which are performed with 'theoretical alertness' to the possibility of developing more general propositions." This alertness—to explaining developments in individual cases and to devising more general propositions about influences on implementation—serves as the motivating principle behind the analysis presented in this book.

2

An Institutional Approach to the Study of Policy Implementation

The enterprise of devising a generalizable framework for the study of public policy implementation might be viewed as a bold, if not foolhardy, endeavor. Providing an accurate and relatively complete description of the implementation experiences of specific public programs is in itself an arduous and often confounding task. Public programs vary so widely—in terms of the forces that pushed them onto the legislative agenda, specificity of enacting legislation, strategies and criteria devised for implementation, and nature and skill of authorities charged with execution—that it is difficult to develop a framework universally applicable to disparate policy cases. In their full complexity, programs appear unique in historical development, legislative enactment, and implementation experiences.

Yet despite inherent difficulties, there is a definite advantage to developing general frameworks for studying implementation. They enable researchers and analysts to transcend the infinite details and seemingly particularistic experiences of specific policies so as to devise and explore more general propositions about the workings of implementation. In this way, researchers work not only to comprehend implementation of a particular policy or set of policies, but also to craft theoretical hypotheses useful for understanding implementation in other policy contexts. If frameworks are widely applicable, then many types of meaningful contrasts and comparisons can be made across policy studies. Drawing such comparisons is difficult in the current situation, where analysts have approached policy studies from varied perspectives, reflecting their own interests, data sources, biases, and understandings of the policy process. As Van Horn and Van Meter (1976, 43) argue, the purpose of conceptual frameworks should be to "assist those seeking to derive generalizations from the findings of seemingly disparate case studies, and to provide a general blueprint for scholars wishing to embark on the study of implementation."

The theoretical framework to be developed here, and subsequently employed to study the implementation of disability rights laws, focuses on institutional

21

decision points, and the decision-making processes at these points. The primary contention is that *implementation ultimately results from a dynamic sequence of decisions made in institutional arenas.* Implementation outcomes are seldom the automatic results of the objectives and mandates set out in legislation. Instead, they are the complex consequence of repeated decision making, occurring within arenas, as groups seek to affect decisions in their favor.

The Building Blocks for a Conceptual Framework: Arenas, Actors, and Environments

Arenas

Given the pluralistic nature of the American system of governance, characterized by a complex set of intergovernmental relationships and a fluid system of checks and balances among governmental branches, it is evident that implementation occurs through multiple institutional arenas.[1] These arenas include Congress and legislative committees, federal administrative agencies, regional field offices, state and local authorities, and the courts.

One of the primary arenas for policy implementation rests within executive agencies, where the drafting and revision of administrative regulations take place. The primary input into the rulemaking arena is the public law created through legislative consideration and enactment. During rulemaking efforts, agencies develop guidelines and standards to use in executing public laws, generally providing the public the opportunity to consider and comment on proposed rules prior to their final issuance. From this point, decision making regarding implementation typically shifts to other arenas. For some policies, regional field offices become an important locus for implementation, as they make decisions about awarding projects and monitoring compliance with program rules.

State and local governments also represent important arenas. Various state agencies serve as intermediaries between the national and local governments and are responsible for setting guidelines, distributing funds, and undertaking evaluations. Local authorities, of both general and special purpose nature, undertake the actual provision of services through federally authorized programs. It is at the local level that policies generate actual benefits and regulatory sanctions.

The courts represent another important arena affecting the execution of public programs, and there is evidence that they are playing a growing role in implementation (Gambitta et al. 1981). Individuals or groups dissatisfied with the methods or outcomes of public programs can protest through the courts, appealing to constitutionally defined rights, including due process and equal protection provisions, and to the intent of the legislation that initially created programs in question. Judicial decisions can have significant impact both on policy refinement, where administrative rules are developed and revised, and on policy execution, the activities associated with operating public programs.

Legislatures serve as institutional arenas not only where laws are passed, but also where key decisions about funding, program authorization, and changes in laws are made. Legislators may seek to influence implementation by changing funding flows, modifying laws to clarify appropriate means of policy execution, and engaging in oversight activities.

Implementation as a Dynamic, Nonlinear Process

The discussion of institutional arenas is not intended to suggest that implementation is consistently a linear process whereby policies move predictably or easily through arenas to the point where benefits or regulatory sanctions are distributed. Indeed, the empirical studies of policy implementation suggest the opposite, that implementation is neither predictable nor regularized. Douglas Yates's (1977, 93) characterization of policy implementation as a pinball game seems applicable. The pinball itself represents the policy being implemented, the various channels and alleys signify the arenas where decisions are made about implementation, and the bumpers represent the various political pressures exerted on decisions. This analogy is apt in that it recognizes the process by which implementation takes place as dynamic, nonlinear, and unpredictable.[2] Policies bounce back and forth between arenas, as interested actors seek to affect the ultimate distribution of policy benefits and sanctions.

This interactive and multiarena nature of policy implementation has important implications relevant to the achievement of implementation outcomes. First, it is safe to assume that in practically no case does any one arena consistently dominate policy implementation. There are always other arenas to which disgruntled program beneficiaries or regulated parties can turn to exert pressures for changes in policies or implementation strategies.

Second, the *linkages* between arenas are important, for they affect the way policy decisions move through governmental institutions. Such linkages in the American political system tend to be weak, because of the relative autonomy of governments in the intergovernmental system, the separation of powers across branches of government, and the dispersion of policy authority across a large number of executive departments and independent commissions. Given the practice of implementing policy through an intergovernmental system, ''would-be innovators must induce policy actors across the country to change their behavior and must do so with little or no authority to require such changes'' (Weiss and Gruber 1984, 226). Characterization of the linkages between arenas as "loosely coupled systems" is an apt description (Berman 1978, 165). Moving a policy through the set of authorities charged with implementation does not resemble the flow of commands through a hierarchical organization (Weiss and Gruber 1984; Ingram 1977). Instead, implementation "is a complicated program assembly process involving numerous (usually independent) actors and decision points in an interactive process of bargaining rather than one of hierarchical command" (Levin and Ferman 1985, 2).

A third consideration associated with the multiplicity of policy arenas concerns differences in the preferences, aspirations, and policy preferences of actors within particular arenas. Administrators of local public housing or public transit systems are likely to have preferences for and visions of policy actions that differ from those of the national and state government authorities. Persistent differences in policy preferences and visions suggest ongoing tensions between arenas as policy implementation proceeds, tensions which on occasion will thrust the focus of decision making from one institutional arena to another.

The Actors

The institutional framework being developed in this chapter has close connection to the works of Bardach (1977), Montjoy and O'Toole (1979), Thompson (1981), and others, which consider policy implementation as a "game" whereby interested parties interact within institutional arenas in an effort to "win" the game. Winning generally means receiving an optimal level of the public benefits distributed through a program and/or avoiding costs and sanctions. A central assumption of this approach, one to be accepted here, is that actors in the implementation process are basically "rational"; that is, they have preferences about the distribution of program outputs, and they act in a self-interested manner to obtain benefits and to shirk costs. Thompson (1981) refers to this rational action as strategic behavior. Being rational does not preclude mistakes or misguided decisions, for errors can be made as the result of imperfect information or limited cognitive abilities. It is assumed, however, that individuals are capable of learning; that is, information about previous decisions can be used to make "better" decisions in the future.

Legislators. Legislators, of course, play important preimplementation roles, by considering and adopting legislation that becomes the primary policy input into the implementation process. Legislators may engage in oversight once implementation has begun to clarify ambiguities or modify implementation strate-

24

gies that are unpopular or seen as exceeding legislative intent. In terms of the U.S. Congress, the conventional wisdom, backed up by substantial empirical work, is that oversight tends to be sporadic and of relatively low priority to legislators. The low volume of oversight is attributed to the perceived low political reward for engaging in oversight, insufficient resources with which to monitor the expansive federal bureaucracy, acceptance by legislators of the technical competence and relevant experience of administrators, and subgovernment politics in which congressional committees develop consensual ties to corresponding executive agencies and interest groups.[3]

Some analysts see or forecast greater legislative oversight, although given the breadth of federal government programs, it is impossible to undertake close and persistent oversight over the full range of executive responsibilities. Ethridge (1985) argues that the growth of public interest lobbies and citizen concerns about issues such as the environment may change the political "profitability" of oversight activites. Certainly, dramatic public problems, depicted rapidly and in full intensity by the media, create opportunities where the public expects oversight. These occasions can make legislators public "heroes" overnight through their investigation of governmental actions, or failures to act, that are of public concern. Aberbach (1979) argues that congressional oversight activities will likely increase as the result of a post-Watergate concern about abuse of executive authority and increased committee staffs.

It is clear that congressional staffers often play significant roles in implementation activities. These staffs work for either individual legislators or standing and special committees. As a result of assignments, staff members become directly involved in specific policy areas, and given this experience and expertise, they are sometimes called into the implementation process. Implementers may call upon such staff as a means of checking questions about the intent of authorizing legislation or the likely reaction of legislators to proposed rules and strategies to govern implementation. In this way, congressional staff members serve as mediators between legislators and agency administrators.

Interested Publics. Two other sets of actors might be termed the "interested publics" of implementation. Ripley and Franklin (1986) call these actors the program beneficiaries and the regulated clients. The former are individuals and groups who receive and consume the direct benefits of public programs, including financial transfers (e.g., social security payments), in-kind benefits (e.g., excess commodities), vouchers (e.g., food stamps), facilities (e.g., public housing, parks), and services (e.g., public hospitals, police protection). Beneficiaries have a direct stake in public programs, whether it be in obtaining new benefits not previously provided by public authorities or in maintaining benefit flows generated by ongoing programs. In the analysis of disability rights to follow, the program beneficiaries are the physically and mentally disabled individuals expected to benefit from rights protection laws. These individuals are represented in the policy process by a diverse set of interest groups, each of which typically concentrates attention on persons with specific types of disabling conditions (e.g., National Association for the Blind, Paralyzed Veterans of America).

The other interested public is those individuals, associations, or organizations who experience costs and regulation as the results of public programs: the regulated clients. Costs include taxation and user fees, limitations on private rights (both individual and collective) for the benefit of broader society (e.g., zoning, traffic regulation, antitrust regulation), and affirmative action and other compensatory programs. Sometimes these costs are deemed necessary for the orderly operation of society (e.g., obeying traffic and public order rules), but in other contexts, they are perceived, at least by the restricted clients, to be unwanted intrusions upon private actions. Behaving rationally, regulated clients seek to weaken or eliminate restrictive policies during legislative consideration and policy implementation. In the context of disability rights programs, regulated clients include federal agencies, state and local governments, transit authorities, local school systems and universities, and private companies that have government contracts.

Both sets of interested publics, the beneficiaries and the restricted clients, have direct stakes in implementation, more so than other segments of society. When studying implementation in a given policy area, it is important to recognize both sets of actors and the strategies employed to affect policy implementation and outcomes. Often groups of beneficiaries or regulated clients have found it effective to work collectively to influence policymaking in both the legislative and implementation processes. Sometimes their coalitions are stable but more often are shifting, with such swaying indicating various preferences for outcomes and strategies for influencing the policy process.

Administrative Actors. Another set of actors in the implementation process is the administrative officials and personnel charged to carry policy into action. These administrative actors, at different intergovernmental levels, have different aspirations, needs, and preferences about implementation strategies and outcomes. Administrators at the national level develop general rules to guide implementation, and once implementation has begun, they strive to ensure that actions taken at the state and local levels are consistent with objectives and rules devised at the national level. State and local officials are caught in the bind of wanting the fiscal transfers available from the federal government, but simultaneously wishing to use the funds in ways and for purposes defined at a decentralized level. Attention to the administrative personnel involved in policy

26

implementation points directly to ongoing tensions in an intergovernmental system characterized by program funding and policy development at the national level and implementation carried out at lower levels of government.

Judicial Officials. If the courts represent an important institutional arena associated with implementation, then judges represent another important set of actors. Court decisions, made in response to individual disputes about policy implementation (and the process used to devise rules for implementation) can have significant bearing upon the direction that implementation takes. If laws are judged unconstitutional, or if administrative rules are assessed as inconsistent with legislative intent, then implementation typically halts or enters a holding pattern, awaiting court appeals, the development of new policy, or revised rules to govern implementation.

Despite traditional perspectives that the role of courts in implementation is primarily a reactive one, judges have increasingly become direct actors in implementation processes. The most noted example is Judge Arthur Garrity, who became actively involved in directing and enforcing the desegregation of Boston schools through an aggressive busing plan (Radin 1977; Nakamura and Smallwood 1980). Unlike other interested publics, whose roles in the policy process date back to legislative consideration of proposed laws, judicial personnel become involved in the process only after implementation efforts have begun. Yet despite their relatively late entry, judges have played major, even dominating, roles in certain policy areas, most notably those dealing with desegregation. As Johnson and Cannon (1984, 2) note, "Few areas of the American political system remain unnoticed by judicial decision making . . . judicial policies are also public policies: they too must be implemented before disputes or problems can be resolved, and they have an impact on the public."

Actors and Issue Networks. When studying the development and execution of public policy, it is important not only to identify the actors engaged in decision making, but also their interconnections with each other, both formal and informal. Heclo (1978) has offered the notion of "issue networks" as a means of describing the constellation of actors who concentrate attention on and regularly participate in decisions about specific policy issues. Earlier writers directed attention to a three-sided model of interested parties who exercise significant control over public policy. These three-way constellations—called variously "subgovernments," "cozy triangles," "policy communities," and "community of policy experts"—include bureaucrats in executive agencies, legislative committees and subcommittees, and interest groups, all concerned with particular issue areas.[4] Heclo (1978, 88) seeks to expand the notion of a triangular relationship to a richer conception of the diverse set of actors who affect public policy: ''Looking for the closed triangles of control, we tend to miss the fairly open networks of people that increasingly impinge upon government.''

Given the widening expanse of governmental activities and burgeoning technical information relevant to policy execution, issue networks take on great importance, since the actors in the network are among the few who understand the technical issues and likely consequences of implementation efforts. It is difficult for actors outside of the network to intervene because they often lack awareness that policy decisions are being made, the technical competence to understand complex policy issues, and the resources to tactically intervene. By studying the characteristics of actors in the network, including information about their talents, political experience, and policy preferences, one can gain insight into both legislative enactment and implementation decisions.[5] If, as postulated, actors behave in a self-interested manner to affect policy outcomes, then understanding the interests and concerns of actors in the issue network, as well as their political strategies, can shed light on the decisions that guide policy implementation.

To foreshadow arguments to be made later in the book, it is clear that the administrative rules governing section 504 of the Rehabilitation Act of 1973 took a strong civil rights posture largely as a result of the individuals in the Department of Health, Education, and Welfare who were assigned to draft them, and the issue network that formed around them (Scotch 1984). These staff members had extensive experience with civil rights policy but were relatively inexperienced in issues related to mental or physical disability. Given their experience and expectations, they framed section 504 rules from a strong advocacy position associated with civil rights law. Despite efforts to weaken the advocacy approach, the staff remained firm and the regulations, as ultimately published, bore the clear mark of these actors. They were able to sustain their position subsequently with the support of advocacy groups for disabled persons, although the agency staff had first to convince the disabled community of the importance of section 504 provisions. The issue network, including agency staff and disability interest groups, evolved during the rulemaking period and worked effectively to keep the rules from being watered down.

Leadership and Policy Entrepreneurs. At many decision-making junctures within the policy process, leadership is an important variable affecting policy outcomes; this is as true of implementation stages as it is of legislative passage. One type of leadership is exercised by *policy entrepreneurs*, whose ''defining characteristics, much as in the case of a business entrepreneur, is their willingness to invest their resources—time, energy, reputation, and sometimes money—in the hope of a future return . . . in the form of policies which they

approve, satisfaction with participation, or even personal aggrandizement''
(Kingdon 1984, 129). In the legislative arena, policy entrepreneurs introduce
and keep issues ''alive,'' with an eye toward creating new programs or expanding existing ones (Wilson 1980; Murphy 1971). During implementation
periods, entrepreneurs pressure agencies to move aggressively in both policy
refinement and execution, that is, to move efficiently to develop operational
rules and carry them out.

The entrepreneurs who guide issues to legislative consideration and through
enactment may continue their ''watchdog'' function during implementation, or,
as is more often the case, they may turn their entrepreneurial roles over to others. The second-generation entrepreneurs tend to be groups of or representatives for program beneficiaries, groups whose existence and growth have more
or less paralleled the development of the public programs from which they benefit. Both first- and second-generation entrepreneurs are effective to the extent
that they are able to keep their policy on the active agenda of implementing
agencies and to utilize other actors or policy arenas to rejuvenate implementation when agencies slack off.

Political and Policy Environments

Neither institutional arenas nor the actors who interact within them operate
in a vacuum. They exist and function within environments that may be favorable, neutral, or opposed to policy issues or implementation practices. The *political environment* concerns the basic ideological perspectives of the public
and political elites (the active participants in the policy process). Such environments are fluid and changeable and reflect predominant ideological views
about the appropriate size and functions of the public sector. The changeability
of political environments is demonstrated through a comparison of the basically
conservative 1980s—characterized by negative attitudes about ''big government,'' tax increases, and expansive social welfare policies—with the much
more liberal 1960s, when social innovations were launched on many fronts.

Of direct relevance to implementation is a subset of the political environment, the *policy environment*. This environment includes attitudes and opinions about specific policy issues or their implementation. Media coverage,
dramatic events, or negative implementation experiences can influence policy
environments and work to advance or impede policies. While crises or studies
can generate support for new or expanded policies, unfavorable information on
program performance and costs can create pressures for reforms in or elimination of public policies. Clever policy entrepreneurs may be able to use such
information to increase support for existing policies, push for new policy ini-

tiatives, or press for the dismantling of troublesome programs (Weiss and Gruber 1984).

Public attitudes may also be attuned to the *instrumentalities* of implementation. The public may support general policy objectives but may be opposed to strategies for achieving the objectives. A notable case in this regard is the use of busing to achieve racial integration of public school systems. Even among those who favor integration as a policy goal, many have come to question busing as an implementation method, in that it can destroy neighborhood schools and prolong bus rides by young children.

The policy environment may, of course, be closely tied to the political environment. As ideological moods swing, the popularity of particular sets of policies and the strategies for carrying them out may similarly change. The two are not perfectly correlated, however. Preferences for individual policies and implementation strategies can swing on their own, often as the result of dramatic events or exposés. Both environments are important to implementation because they set the parameters of political acceptability of policy innovations and execution strategies.

Decision Making in Institutional Arenas

Given the description of institutional arenas, the actors who regularly participate in them, and the environments in which arenas exist and function, it is useful to consider the processes by which decisions affecting implementation are made. It is difficult to discuss these processes generically, considering the variety of policy issues, actors, and arenas associated with implementation. One can, however, specify general influences affecting implementation decisions, including agenda setting, organizing principles, and the decision premises associated with arena participants.

Agenda Setting

One interesting implementation question concerns how issues and policies are brought to the attention of arenas associated with policy implementation. Many analysts have examined this question in the context of congressional politics; foremost here is the work of John Kingdon (1984, 3), who has analyzed how issues are raised to the legislative agenda. He defines an agenda as "the list of subjects or problems to which governmental officials, and people outside of government closely associated with those officials, are paying some serious attention at any given time." Cobb and Elder (1983a, 85) make a further distinction, in this regard, between ''systematic agendas'' (all issues perceived by members of the political community as meriting public attention) and ''governmental agendas'' (the set of items explicitly up for the active and serious consideration of authoritative decision makers).

From Kingdon's perspective, several factors can affect agenda setting. Severe problems or crises, for example, jar policymakers into paying attention to issues, often with the expectation that problem solutions be rapidly generated. Nuclear power accidents and the imminent financial collapse of major corporations or local governments are relevant examples. These problems require quick action so that problems can be alleviated and removed from the policy agenda. Polsby (1984, 150) terms policies of this type ''acute innovations.''

Not all issues rapidly accelerate onto legislative agendas; some reach the agenda only after slow public recognition of problems relevant to solution through public policy initiatives. The issue of hunger in America, gradually recognized in the 1960s, is illustrative of cases where issues are only slowly acknowledged as legitimate for legislative consideration. Only after long years of protracted discussion and widespread media portrayals of the poor was Congress sufficiently mobilized to commence the war on poverty (Berry 1984). In Polsby's (1984, 153) language, issues such as poverty represent ''incubated'' innovations, slow to bubble to the surface.

Agendas can also be influenced by changes in political and policy environments. Changes of administration and feedback from elections and referenda are examples of signals from the political environment that can move issues onto the policy agenda. For example, the impetus for deregulation, begun under the Ford and Carter administrations, was given greater boost by the election of conservative candidate Ronald Reagan, who campaigned against the costs and constraints imposed by excessive governmental regulation (Eads and Fix 1984; Miller and Eisenach 1981). Once legislative enactments have been made, issues may move off the agenda, only to return if policy implementation generates negative ''feedback,'' such as high costs, low achievement, unintended and negative consequences, or controversy about implementation mechanisms.

Pertinent to agenda setting is Kingdon's (1984, 174) concept of ''policy window'': ''opportunities for action on given initiatives, [which] present themselves and stay open only short periods.'' These opportunities become available for several reasons, including changes in administration or leadership posts, shifting of the ideological base of the legislature, turnover of political actors, or pressing problems or crises that citizens expect government to alleviate or solve. A salient feature of policy windows is that they are not open for long, largely because the intensity of policy issues tends to be transitory. Downs (1972, 40) makes this point in his analysis of ''issue-attention cycles,'' arguing that interest in policy issues declines ''as more and more people realize how difficult, and how costly to themselves, a solution to the problem would be." Walker (1977, 432), in an analysis of the agenda setting in the U.S. Senate, makes a similar point about the transitory and cyclical nature of public and legislative attention to issues:

> Once a topic like pollution control or mass transit has achieved the status of a "chosen problem" and it becomes clear that the votes are there for passage of bills on the subject, powerful forces are unleashed that press for action. As the surge progresses, the relative importance of succeeding legislative proposals tends to decline and the case for their passage seems weaker. . . . Competition mounts for space on the discretionary agenda from other aspiring problems and the surge comes to an end, leading eventually to new cycles of debate and legislation.

Analysts also need to be aware that the opposite of agenda setting, preventing issues from receiving attention and consideration, can be a political ploy of those who favor status quo conditions. Parties satisfied with the existing situation may seek to prevent new policy initiatives or changes in existing programs from achieving agenda status. Bachrach and Baritz (1979) refer to this activity as "nondecision making." The foreclosure of policy consideration can, in some instances, be as strong an impact on policy development and implementation as the power to place issues on the decision-making agendas of institutional arenas.

Organizing and Operating Principles

The wording of public laws enacted to initiate, expand, and fund public programs is generally lengthy and technical, and the bills themselves are often complex in terms of the breadth of program activities authorized. Somewhere along the line, either during legislative enactment or policy implementation, one or a few principles develop that serve as symbolic guidelines to carrying out public policies. These symbols, which serve to structure further thoughts about policy refinement and execution, may be termed *organizing principles*. The symbolic importance of these principles should not be underrated, for they serve to organize discussion and action related to policy implementation.[6] Kingdon (1984, 200) makes a similar point about principles that emerge through policy windows: "with the passage of landmark legislation or the adoption of a precedent setting presidential decision . . . public policy in that arena is never quite the same because succeeding increments are based on the new principle, people become accustomed to a new way of doing things, and it becomes as difficult to reverse the new direction as it was to change the old."

32

Organizing principles can emerge from other sources besides legislative enactments and presidential decisions, including the rulemaking activities of administrative agencies.

Organizing principles are translated into administrative action through an intermediate level of *operating principles*. These principles are the central mechanisms or strategies for executing public policy. Like organizing principles, operating ones take on symbolic importance; yet, in comparison, operating principles are more specific and instrumental. One clear example, in this regard, is the area of school desegregation, where integration has been the primary organizing principle and busing the operating principle.

In some policy contexts, organizing and operating principles work in tandem, where the latter are seen as the means to activate the former. In other contexts, multiple operating principles may compete to become attached to popular organizing principles. As but one example, the 1980s have been characterized by bipartisan support for balancing the federal budget and eliminating huge deficits; however, various operational strategies have been proposed for achieving this objective.

Both organizing and operating principles, once legitimized through legislation or administrative policy, can serve as important resources to those who benefit from policies based upon those principles. The political force of these symbolic principles rests in the way they capture the attention of policymakers and administrators and serve to frame and organize policy debates. Supporters can hark back to these principles, which often become part of the decision premises of policy actors, to regenerate support within the political system (Sabatier and Mazmanian 1979, 487).

The policy area to be explored in this book, programs to protect the rights of persons with disabilities, offers many examples of organizing and operating principles and illustrates the different sources from which such principles arise. One key organizing principle in the area of educating handicapped children is the notion of a "free and appropriate education." The Education for All Handicapped Children Act (PL94–142) includes language stating that public elementary or secondary schools that receive federal funds for handicapped education shall provide a free and appropriate public education to each qualified handicapped person in its jurisdiction, regardless of the nature or severity of the handicap.

While the question of a free education raised some questions, the issue of guaranteeing an "appropriate education" was even more troublesome, especially because of the diversity of debilitating problems and causes. Recognizing this, Congress moved to further delineate the notion of an "appropriate education" by developing an operating principle, the "individualized education program," or in the parlance of educational specialists, the "IEP." The

Policy Implementation

IEP stipulation requires schools to develop a specialized educational program for each handicapped student, taking into account the child's unique abilities and learning problems. The notions of a "free and appropriate education" and "individualized education programs" are coupled to organizing and operating principles formulated directly in authorizing legislation. They together have served as vibrant conceptual guides for efforts to enhance the educational opportunities of disabled children.

Organizing principles can also arise during the implementation process, again for the purpose of guiding the development of rules and the execution of policy. One example, directly relevant to the research at hand, is the concept of "balanced competing equities." This idea was developed by agency administrators struggling to draft regulations for section 504 of the Rehabilitation Act of 1973, which bans recipients of federal financial assistance from discriminating on the basis of handicap. The administrators decided that while costs were not germane to establishing discrimination, they were relevant to the fashioning of remedies for discriminatory actions. From this organizing principle, intended to balance the needs of beneficiaries and those of regulated clients, an important operating principle was devised: reasonable accommodation. This principle calls for public agencies and private companies to make accommodations in the workplace so that "otherwise qualified" disabled persons can work and advance in employment. Accommodations need be undertaken only if they conform to criteria for "reasonableness," intended to limit accommodations to those that do not impose substantial costs. While the question of what constitutes "reasonable" remains troublesome, the notion of required modifications by the public and private sectors has been a powerful symbol underlying efforts to activate the protections outlined in section 504.

Decision Premises

Decisions made within arenas are also influenced by the decision premises held by participants. Identification of such premises provides insights as to how the decisions made in institutional arenas afffect the range of policy actions considered by decision makers. Decision premises differ from organizing principles in that the former serve as broad constraints on the way decision makers approach policy problems and their solutions, while the latter concern symbolic images and models used to organize the implementation of particular policy objectives.

The roots of decision premises are many. Some are unique to individuals and arise from their personal preferences, aspirations, and experiences. Others result from professional education and training. Civil servants, for example, receive training in some professional field, training that affects worldview, technical knowledge, and perspectives on appropriate methods for achieving public policy objectives. Decision premises can also be rooted within organizations and arenas themselves. Organizational participants, for example, often have incentive to protect their organization from the outside environment (Thompson 1967), in order to maintain or expand the flow of salaries, benefits, and other compensations associated with organizational functioning (Downs 1967; Niskanen 1971). In this context, the survival and growth of the organization provides positive returns to members.

While "survival" and "benefit expansion" impulses are typical to most organizations, other decision premises are more subtly linked to life within organizations. One set of premises relates to what Downs (1967, 237) terms "bureaucratic ideology," an image generated within the organization about what the "good society" should be and how organizational practices can contribute to realizing this ideal state. An agency charged with civil rights enforcement might, for example, have as its image of the good society, one in which discrmination is greatly reduced or eliminated. This agency would probably have preferences as to the most appropriate means with which to reach objectives, including positions on the relative merits of affirmative action, quota plans, and other instrumentalities.

Decision premises also may be related to what might be termed "organizational culture," the perceptions of members about the mission of the agency and its ability to advance social or economic welfare. This culture, at one extreme, can be positive, with internal perceptions that the agency is vital, technically competent, and critical to the accomplishment of salient policy objectives. At the other extreme, organizational culture can be negative and protective in character, as when morale is low (perhaps due to budget cuts or reductions in staff), objectives pursued by the organization are deemed unimportant, or the outside environment is seen as hostile or threatening.

Many decision premises are likely transitory, reflecting changes in political administration, the political and policy environments, policy objectives, and personnel who lead and staff public organizations. More "basic" premises, such as organizational survival and efforts to sustain growth, are likely more immune to outside pressures, since they are more directly linked to the personal aspirations of organizational members.

Pulling the Pieces Together

The components of a framework to analyze public policy implementation have now been identified. The central presumption of this approach is that *the results of implementation can best be understood by tracing the flow of policy decisions across and through institutional arenas, where interested parties in issue networks interact, in a self-interested manner, to affect the distribution of costs and benefits in their favor.* From this perspective, implementation policy and activities are evolving, never final; dynamic, not hierarchical; more politically than technically based; and adaptive rather than isolated (Berman 1978; Stone 1980; Browne and Wildavsky 1984; Majone and Wildavsky 1984). Implementation results from decision making dispersed across multiple and different institutional arenas. "The outcome of the resulting chain of implementation decisions cannot be predicted or measured according to indicators of formal, top-down hierarchies of control. The analytical onus is better placed on the decentralized, sometimes informal, and often unanticipated points of decision" (Browne and Wildavsky 1984, 208).

Malcolm Goggin (1987, 27), in his study of child health care in the United States, takes a similar view to policy implementation, recognizing that implementation involves both politics and policymaking: "Rather than being merely a case of administrative routine, implementation is an integral part of political decision making. It is a series of goal-oriented decisions and actions that takes place in the context of public bureaucracies." The approach taken here would extend relevant decision making beyond public bureaucracies to other institutional arenas in the political system.

Those who receive program benefits and regulatory sanctions are aware of the impacts of public sector activity, and their response, being rational actors, is to use the political process to adjust distributional flows. While one policy or coalition of actors may predominate for a time, their dominance is seldom permanent. New problems, information, crises, or changes in the political environment can act to displace the existing balance, provide opportunities to dissatisfied parties, and generate new skirmishes and battles to affect policy outcomes.

The conceptual framework outlined above provides some triangulation points from which to study and explain decision making within institutional arenas. These include agenda setting mechanisms and the development and use of organizing principles. In addition, the decision premises of participants in institutional arenas provide clues about the preferences of policy actors and the conceptual "blinders" they possess when thinking about strategies for implementation practices and answers to implementation problems and failures. By recognizing the key place that institutional arenas play in determining implementation, and by understanding the decision-making processes and results associated with these arenas, we can gain a richer comprehension of why implementation takes place as it does, sometimes with gratifying results, and often with outcomes that fail to match anticipated results.

Regulation: Policy and Implementation

As we move to apply an institutional framework for studying implementation, it is appropriate to narrow the focus, to examine the policy type of most relevance to disability rights: regulation. Simply put, regulation may be conceptualized as efforts by the public sector to modify behaviors of individuals and groups in the private sector, the public sector, or both.[7] In Mitnik's (1980, 9) words: "Regulation is a process consisting of the intentional restriction of a subject's choice of activity, by an entity not directly party to or involved in that activity." Regulation, therefore, is the process of modifying individual and organizational behaviors to achieve broader social and economic objectives.

There is no question that regulatory activity has burgeoned in the last two decades. While earlier regulation efforts by the federal government centered on controls in the economic sphere—promoting fair competition and controlling the activities of monopolies, banks, and brokerage firms, among other things—more recent regulatory activity has been concerned with "social regulation" (Meier 1985, 3). The initiatives of social regulation include efforts to enhance occupational safety, protect the environment, advance civil rights, and protect consumers (see, for example, White 1981). The origins of the regulatory explosion of the 1960s and 1970s has been traced to such factors as the growth of federal intergovernmental transfers (providing the opportunity to exert regulatory controls as a condition of receiving financial transfers), the proliferation of public interest lobbies, the recognition of various problems as "national" in character, and the willingness of Congress to take strong and affirmative stances on social issues (through regulatory provisions) without having to commit new funds or create new administrative units (Kettl 1983; Meier 1985; Bardach and Kagan 1982; Congressional Quarterly 1982).

One interesting aspect of the explosion in social regulation was that the federal government placed mandates not only upon those who receive federal financial assistance, but also upon itself. This effort at self-regulation represented a departure from earlier regulatory initiatives, which placed mandates upon the private sector and state and local governments. In many areas of social regulation, Congress created roughly parallel mandates, requiring federal agencies to fall in line with regulatory requirements placed on other units of government. For example, the Architectural Barriers Act mandates that federal agencies take action to enhance the accessibility of federal government buildings and facilities. In a similar fashion, Congress stipulated, through section 501 of the Rehabilitation Act of 1973, that the executive branch take affirmative action to employ and advance in employment persons with disabilities.

As we shall see, mandates to achieve federal self-regulation raise interesting questions about enforcement, questions that to date have received little attention. In essence, the executive branch must enforce compliance of its own actions. Congress has created a variety of administrative bodies to oversee compliance; these include the Architectural and Transportation Barriers Compliance Board, the Equal Employment Opportunity Commission, and the Office of Federal Contract Compliance Programs. As described in chapters to come, these bodies have varied enforcement powers and uneven track records in enhancing compliance with regulatory mandates.[8]

The "rush to regulate" has lost steam in the 1980s, evidenced by growing calls for movement in the opposite direction, deregulation. Proponents of deregulation fault the rapid growth of regulations for unnecessary interference in the conduct of market and other private transactions, imposition of substantial costs on regulated interests and taxpayers with little evidence of positive results, and delays in the issuance of administrative rules and the implementation of programs (Tolchin and Tolchin 1983; Miller and Eisenach 1981; Daneke and Lemak 1985; White 1981). Yet despite these concerns, and some policy changes that have affected deregulation in such industries as the airlines and banking, substantial regulatory activity remains in effect.

Types of Regulation

Analysts of regulatory policy have documented the diversity of forms that public regulation can take. The Advisory Commission on Intergovernmental Relations (1984, 7–10) classifies regulation in terms of four types: direct orders, crosscutting requirements, crossover sanctions, and partial preemptions. In the context of disability rights laws, both crosscutting requirements and crossover sanctions are relevant. The former type of regulation requires compliance with federal rules across a wide range of federal programs, whereas crossover sanctions require compliance with regulations within the context of a specific program.

The antidiscrimination provisions of section 504, placed upon recipients of federal funds, are crosscutting requirements, which apply across the full range of federal programs and to both public and private entities. Crossover sanctions are used to implement the Education for All Handicapped Children Act; in this context, states and school systems receiving special education funds are required to provide "free and appropriate" educations, in the least restrictive environment possible, to all school-age children who experience disability. The enforcement mechanism in both cases is the cutoff of federal funds. While the threat exists, such cutoffs are infrequent, given the preference of administrative agencies to negotiate rather than penalize and the difficulty in monitoring dispersed administrative authorities so as to be able to establish noncompliance. However, the persistent threat of cutoff remains a potent weapon during negotiations, and in some instances, such power has been activated.

The Politics of Regulation

The politics surrounding regulatory policies tends to vary according to the nature of the regulation. James Q. Wilson (1980, 366–72) characterizes regulatory politics in terms of the magnitude and the breadth of distribution of the costs and benefits associated with the regulation. He describes four types of politics likely to emerge in the implementation of regulatory policy; these types are classified as follows:

		Breadth of Benefits Distributed through Policy	
		Narrow	Wide
	Narrow	Interest Group Politics	Entrepreneurial Politics
Breadth of Costs Distributed through Policy			
	Wide	Client Politics	Majoritarian Politics

Where either costs or benefits are narrowly distributed, the recipients have both the potential and incentive to organize so as to affect the policies that determine cost and benefit distributions. In the case of interest group politics, both sides have an incentive to organize so as to press policymakers—both during lawmaking and implementation—to affect the distribution of costs and benefits resulting from regulation. In situations where the costs are narrowly distributed but benefits are widely distributed (entrepreneurial politics), those who receive the costs, usually regulated clients, have strong incentive to organize to limit or reduce the cost burdens. Just the opposite is the case in client politics, where benefits are narrowly targeted but costs are widely dispersed. Here the benefit recipients have incentive to coalesce so as to maintain the benefit stream.

In terms of disability rights laws, most implementation policies fall into the interest group politics category. Policies to increase the transportation opportunities of physically disabled persons represent a classic case in this regard. The beneficiaries are those physically disabled individuals who cannot otherwise achieve access to means of public conveyance, particularly those who use wheelchairs. The regulated clients, public transit operators, are required to make accommodations to serve the physically disabled. As we shall see, the controversy that emerged in implementing full accessibility rules was largely one of public transit authorities on one side and groups representing physically disabled people on the other. The situation is similar in education for handicapped children, where groups representing disabled youths, often staffed by parents, have been diligent fighters for legal protections and active enforcement. School districts and state education agencies, the regulated clients, have actively participated too, not so much so to press for eliminating protections, but more to request greater financial assistance and longer time to effect implementation.

One final point relevant to the politics of regulation concerns the use of symbols to manipulate regulatory efforts. Edelman (1964, 22–43) has explored the use of symbols in regulatory policy and claims that symbols can provide reassurances to what otherwise might be seen as threatening regulatory action. As one example, he describes how the creation and extension of the federal income tax has repeatedly been defended in terms of the popular symbol of its progressiveness, despite the fact that special tax treatments severely restrict the actual progressiveness of the tax system. Symbols that reassure can have major impact on public perceptions of and reactions to policies and implementation. In subsequent analysis, we shall see how the symbol of "goodwill" initially made disability policies laws attractive; only when this symbol was peeled away to reveal real cost issues did significant political controversy arise.

The Behavior of Regulatory Agencies and the Potential for Co-optation

The perceived cozy relationships that develop between agencies charged with enforcing regulations and those they seek to regulate has been a concern of many policy analysts. The capture theory—advanced by Huntington (1952), Bernstein (1955), Stigler (1971), Peltzman (1976), Green et al. (1972), and others—views regulatory officials as "industry oriented, as reluctant to jeopardize their postgovernment careers by being too tough, or as gradually co-opted by informal contacts with representatives of regulated firms" (Bardach and Kagan 1982, 44). To the extent that agencies are seen as being captured, it is expected that they will effectively work for the interests of their clients instead of those of the broader public. One means seen for clients to exert influence over regulators is through control of technical information about the source of problems, likely consequences of implementation strategies, and actual experiences with policy execution (Mitnik 1980; Kettl 1983). Agencies need this information to formulate effective rules for implementation; using it may beholden them to their clients, but ignoring it may generate serious mistakes in implementation.

More recent studies question the universality of the capture phenomenon (Wilson 1980; Katzmann 1980; Derthick and Quirk 1985; Gormley 1983; Quirk 1981; Regens and Rycroft 1986). While analysts acknowledge some blatant cases of capture, such overriding control by regulated interests is seen as more the exception than the rule. Capture has become more difficult given the development of public interest lobbies, which pressure administrative agencies in directions different from those preferred by regulated interests (Berry 1977). Wilson (1980, 373) argues that the behavior of regulatory agencies is "complex and changing; it cannot easily be summarized as serving the interests of either the regulated sector or the public at large." Noll and Owen (1983, 158–59) suggest that a variety of factors mitigate against a fully captured agency, including political entrepreneurs who owe no debt to special interests, scrutiny by academics and other analysts, and lack of incentive for administrators to operate as efficient cartel managers.

While some analysts are concerned about capture, others raise the question of the discretion available to regulators and their lack of political accountability. Recognizing that regulatory responsibility has been dispersed across a number of different statutes and executive agencies, Litan and Nordhaus (1983, 3) contend that "decisions of fundamental political importance—how much the nation should spend to pursue its various regulatory objectives, which of these objectives deserves the highest priority, and, therefore, which groups in society deserve to benefit more—are left to unelected agency officials or not decided at all."

The Aggressiveness and Speed of Regulatory Enforcement

The aggressiveness of regulatory action has been another behavioral dimension on which regulatory agencies have been examined. When describing the aggressiveness and dispatch with which agencies move to enforce regulations, two predominant, and contradictory, views emerge. One perspective holds that agencies often act slowly and cautiously in enforcing regulations, generally as the result of close relationships with regulated clients. In the other view, regulatory agencies are depicted as "expansionistic," "imperialist," and autonomous in developing and implementing regulations. From this latter perspective, regulation is seen as "out of control" and insufficiently subjugated to political accountability.

Some difference between these perspectives may result from whether one is considering regulation by administrative agencies, as opposed to that under-taken by relatively autonomous independent commissions. The latter, of course, is more immune to immediate political influence. But this structural difference, though important, does not completely explain such disparate views on the behavior of regulatory authorities. Variations in regulatory behavior—sometimes active and aggressive, other times more docile and reactive—may be explained as the reactions of administrative agencies to a changeable, and often threatening, environment.[9] Resting at the vortex of implementation activity, subject to recurrent pressures by relevant parties in the issue network, administrative agencies adapt with various coping strategies.

In this regard, Wilson (1980, 376) contends that regulatory agencies are typically risk averse: "they prefer security to rapid growth, autonomy to competition, stability to change." Risk aversion can be seen as a response to an environment that can expose problems and failures (White 1981, 219). Wilson (1980, 377) goes on to argue that risk aversion does not imply timidness: "their desire for autonomy, for a stable environment, and for freedom from blame gives these agencies strong incentives to make rules and exercise authority in all aspects of their mission." Agency response, therefore, may vary, as agencies select protective reactions to perceived activity in and threats from the policy environment.[10]

The growth of regulatory activity by federal agencies has been matched by the time required to develop administrative rules; this delay has stimulated concerns about the capacity of agencies to effectively implement regulatory policy. While agencies often receive the blame for the slow pace of regulation making, some analysts point the finger in other directions. It is charged, for example, that Congress often is responsible for difficulties in formulating rules for regulation, given the vagueness and ambiguity of legislative mandates and the rapid proliferation of regulatory provisions (Kettl 1983; Stone 1982; Bryner 1981). Some even go so far as to claim that the open-ended nature of regulatory mandates is purposeful, allowing Congress to take strong positions without having to create new programs, since most regulations are simply tacked onto existing federal programs through crosscutting requirements and crossover sanctions.

Regulation and Implementation: Insights and Foreshadowings

These perspectives on the politics and processes of regulation suggest a number of issues pertinent to the analysis of implementation of disability rights laws. Among the issues to be considered in the chapters to follow are ones which relate to: (1) comparison and contrast of crosscutting requirements and crossover sanctions as means of enforcing antidiscrimination policies; (2) the nature of regulatory politics; (3) relationships between administrative agencies and regulated clients, so as to test for possible capture of regulators; and (4) sources of delays in implementation and enforcement. With these specific questions about implementation of regulatory policy in mind, as well as the conceptual framework for institutional analysis, we now turn to the development and implementation of federal laws to protect persons with disabilities and to expand their opportunities.

3
Federal Laws
to Assist
Persons with
Disabilities

Early Disability Programs

Programs to assist persons with disabilities were initiated by the federal government in the early decades of this century. The first were designed strictly with vocational rehabilitation in mind, that is, with an emphasis on assisting disabled citizens to sufficiently overcome disabling conditions so as to join or return to the work force. Other programs were developed to provide income assistance to workers who were temporarily or permanently disabled and unable to earn income. More recently, and of direct interest to this study, the federal government has enacted laws to protect the rights of disabled Americans in such areas as employment, education, public transportation, and facility access. An overview of early federal programs to aid handicapped persons provides information useful to understanding the later development of laws and policies to advance their rights.

Vocational Rehabilitation

The earliest federal programs created to aid persons with disabililties date to the period following the First World War. The Smith-Sears Veterans' Rehabilitation Act of 1918 initiated a program to vocationally rehabilitate disabled veterans, many of whom had recently returned home from the war in Europe. The Smith-Fess Act of 1920 (the Civilian Vocational Rehabilitation Act) established the first broad-based federal program to provide vocational assistance to handicapped persons. The program provided federal funds, at a fifty-percent matching rate, to state rehabilitation agencies for counseling, vocational training, and job placement services for physically handicapped persons.

From its genesis in the 1920s, the federal vocational rehabilitation program has grown extensively in the realms of persons served and the breadth of services offered. The Social Security Act of 1935 provided permanent status to the program, while subsequent legislative changes expanded the program in many directions, including provision of medical services and prosthetic devices; creation of programs to serve mentally disabled individuals, migratory workers, and disadvantaged youth; and provision of assistance to families of disabled persons. The focus of the program remains clearly *service oriented*, with the objective of assisting disabled persons to enter or reenter the work force.

Worker's Compensation

Policies to compensate workers disabled as the result of injuries sustained on the job represent another form of assistance to persons with disabilities. Such programs were stimulated around the turn of the century by state governments as the result of the growing number of serious occupational injuries sustained in industrial and manufacturing firms. Worker's compensation programs represented a departure from traditional reliance on the courts for settlements to workers who could prove employer liability (Stone 1984, 97). The essence of these programs, structured by state governments but underwritten by private insurance companies, is to provide medical benefits, vocational rehabilitation, income supports, and death benefits to workers injured on the job. The plans are generally "no fault" in nature, meaning that liability issues are not the basis for compensation benefits.

Income Support Programs

Another form of federal assistance to handicapped citizens is provision of income support. The Social Security Act of 1935 gave states funds to assist indigent dependent children, elderly adults, and blind citizens.[1] While the act also initiated unemployment and old age insurance programs, it did not create a permanent program of disability insurance, although the idea was considered at the time. Sponsors of the act were concerned and unsure about the costs of a disability insurance program and sought to avoid making the act so far-reaching as to diminish support in Congress. Some states, however, did set up temporary disability programs using the apparatus of unemployment insurance.

After legislative debate and administrative study, a system of disability payments, Social Security Disability Insurance, for workers between the ages of fifty and sixty-four was enacted through 1956 amendments to the Social Security Act. Payments were set at the same amount the individual would receive if he or she were sixty-five years of age. No needs test was applied, but disabled workers were required to have had coverage for a minimum number of quarters. This legislation put the system of public income support to disabled workers on a firm footing.

As with other disability programs, amendments to the original legislation served to expand the program, in this case, by removing the age fifty limitation for eligibility and changing the definition of disability from one of "long, continued, and indefinite duration," to one where disabilities have lasted, or are expected to last, not less than twelve months. Amendments in 1972 hinged benefit payments to the cost of living and provided that persons who had been receiving disability benefits for two years or more could become eligible for Medicare assistance. In 1972, Congress created another federal income support program, Supplemental Security Income. This program authorized uniform national benefits for the needy, aged, blind, and disabled, regardless of geographic location. These benefits were made subject to a needs test, and benefit levels could be reduced by other sources of income. Amendments in 1973 extended coverage to a set of "essential persons," mostly spouses of those eligible for the program.

Educational Programs for Handicapped Students

Federal government involvement in the education of handicapped children generally parallels the development of federal support for elementary and secondary education. Until the 1960s, elementary and secondary education was viewed almost solely as a state and local function, in which the federal government had little role. Beginning in the mid-1960s, the intergovernmental balance began to shift as the federal government initiated educational programs. The Elementary and Secondary Education Act (ESEA) of 1965 (PL80-10) provided federal funds to states to distribute to school districts on the basis of the number of low-income children in the district. It also authorized grants for the purchase of textbooks and educational materials, provision of specialized teachers, and efforts to strengthen state departments of education. In its original form, the legislation said little about educating handicapped children.

Amendments to the ESEA in 1966 directly addressed the education of disabled children. They included a new Title VI, authorizing funds to assist states in the initiation, expansion, and improvement of programs for the education of handicapped children. The definition of handicapped included reference to mental retardation and emotional troubles as well as to physical disabilities. The bill also supported the creation of an Overall Advisory Council on the Needs of the Handicapped.

Further amendments to the ESEA in 1967 increased the scope of federal programs for children with handicaps. The amendments (1) made local education agencies, in conjunction with state agencies of higher education, eligible for grants for a program of national resource centers to improve education of the handicapped; (2) authorized grants to establish a limited number of service centers to assist children who are both deaf and blind; and (3) provided funds for demonstration and research projects in the field of education for handicapped students.

Throughout the late 1960s, Congress, under constant pressure from parents groups representing disabled children, expanded funding of programs to aid in the education of handicapped students. In 1968, Congress extended educational assistance to handicapped preschool children through the Handicapped Children's Early Education Assistance Act. This innovative legislation authorized twenty-three million dollars for experimental programs for handicapped preschool children. A 1970 extension of the ESEA included a significant section known as the Education of the Handicapped Act. This act established, in the Office of Education, a National Advisory Commission on Handicapped Children, authorized to review the administration and operation of educational programs for handicapped children. The act also expanded funding for educational programs for disabled students.

Over a five-year period, interest groups representing disabled children amassed major political support sufficient to initiate and expand federal involvement in the education of disabled children in America. This involvement, while appreciated, was not adequate to ensure that handicapped children would receive the special educational services they needed. Parents groups representing disabled children recognized that school districts received federal grants only if they chose to do so, and that there was no requirement that school systems provide special educational programs and assistance to the full set of handicapped youths. With this in mind, the interest groups pressed on, seeking a bill that would require those receiving federal funds for special education to provide adequate educational services for disabled children. Their success in this endeavor, the Education for All Handicapped Children Act, is discussed in a section to follow.

An Incomplete Agenda

Once federal programs to assist persons who experience mental or physical disabilities were established, the tendency was to expand them incrementally in terms of persons eligible and served, budget allocations, and range of services provided. This trend has recently been reversed somewhat, as programs have experienced budget cuts as part of the Reagan administration's plan to reduce budget deficits by cutting back domestic social programs.

While groups representing the disabled community achieved significant policy objectives by the 1960s, their agenda remained incomplete. There was a recognition, particularly in the area of education for handicapped children, that society needed to do more than provide programs, many of which were perceived as ''entitlements'' similar in nature to welfare (Bowe 1980b). |Advocates saw the need for an attitudinal change, whereby persons with disabilities would be viewed as individuals with a wide set of abilities as well as one or more physical or mental impairments.| Handicapped persons increasingly sought to be identified in terms of potential skills and talents, rather than in terms of an affliction or problem that impeded fulfillment of individual capacities.

Another theme that began to emerge during this period was recognition that society itself imposed barriers, physical and social, to the pursuit of opportunities by disabled citizens. Some barriers erected by society were tangible in nature, including a variety of architectural designs and features that impeded the access of physically impaired persons to employment, social services, and even voting. Architects and building contractors constructed buildings with an implicit model of the able-bodied adult in mind. Given their absence from most social settings and the lack of political and economic power, disabled persons were disregarded by those who designed buildings and public facilities.

Civil Rights Movements

By the early 1970s, the American political system had witnessed several types of civil rights protests by disadvantaged groups who sought to improve their social, economic, and political positions through public policies. Notable results of the social protest movement waged by black Americans were the Civil Rights Acts of 1964 and 1968 and the Voting Rights Act of 1975. These landmark pieces of legislation, following upon years of protest and civil disobedience, were intended to outlaw discrimination on the basis of race in programs receiving federal funds, employment, voting, and public housing. Of particular relevance to the study at hand is Title VI of the Civil Rights Act of 1964, which states that ''no person in the United States shall, on the grounds of race, color, or national origin, be denied the benefits of, or be subjected to, discrimination under any program or activity receiving federal financial assistance.'' As we shall see, this antidiscrimination language was borrowed a decade later and applied to protections for disabled citizens.

There is no doubt that the civil rights movement demonstrated the impact that collective organization and protests can have on the political system, even for groups who traditionally lacked power in the political process. Civil rights protections were extended to women in the context of education through Title IX of the Education Amendments of 1972. This title prohibits discrimination on the basis of sex in educational programs receiving federal assistance. And while the Equal Rights Amendment was never ratified by a sufficient number of states to become part of the Constitution, it kept alive the ongoing question of civil rights for disadvantaged groups in American society.

Civil Rights and New Directions

By the late 1960s, the direction of public policies to assist persons with mental or physical disabilities began to take a new direction, one that focused more on rights and protections than on services and income supports. In the 1960s and 1970s, a series of advocates fought for policies to remove physical and social barriers that restrict the access of disabled persons to mainstream society. Initially, these policies were popularly received and little opposed; symbolically, almost everyone was in favor of greater opportunities for handicapped persons. Only when it became apparent that significant compliance costs would be mandated by the policies did substantial opposition arise. Groups representing disabled individuals proliferated during this period and grew in strength, partially in response to laws they perceived as taking significant steps to enhance their opportunities and provide them with civil rights. The most relevant public laws in terms of civil rights for disabled persons are the Architectural Barriers Act of 1968, the Rehabilitation Act of 1973 (especially section 504), and the Education for All Handicapped Children Act of 1975.

The Architectural Barriers Act

The origins of federal legislation to remove architectural impediments to the mobility of physically disabled persons date back at least as far as the late 1950s, when an ad hoc group was formed to study possible federal government efforts to increase the accessibility of handicapped people to public buildings.[2] The group, which included members of the President's Committee on Employment of the Handicapped and of the staff of the Veterans Administration, prepared a guide for access to public buildings that was subsequently distributed by the Labor Department to state employment agencies.

The push for barrier removal continued in 1965, when a provision of the Vocational Rehabilitation Amendments called for a study to determine what needed to be done to make facilities and buildings available to handicapped Americans. This report, prepared by the National Commission on Architectural Barriers to the Rehabilitation of the Handicapped and issued in June 1968, concluded: "More than 20 million Americans are built *out* of normal living by unnecessary barriers: a stairway, a too-narrow door, a too-high telephone. At the right moment, their needs were overlooked."[3] It also optimistically concluded that, "in time, the last vestiges of such thoughtlessness will disappear from the American scene."[4]

Armed with the commission's report, and its strong recommendations for legislative and administrative changes, the movement to remove physical barriers continued. Policy entrepreneurs moved to enact a law that would require all federal buildings used by the public to be accessible to physically handicapped individuals. The origins of this legislation, eventually to become the Architectural Barriers Act of 1968, has been attributed to Hugh Gallagher, a legislative aid to Senator E. L. Bartlett of Alaska (Katzmann 1986, 20–22). Gallagher, physically disabled and wheelchair-bound as the result of polio, witnessed firsthand the problems of accessibility in the offices and facilities of the federal government. In conjunction with Gallagher, Senator Bartlett introduced legislation intended to be considered by the Senate Committee on Public Works.[5] This brief bill (1) authorized the administrator of the General Services Administration (GSA) to devise regulations for the design and construction of public buildings to ensure accessibility by physically disabled citizens and (2) required that grants and loans by the federal government to construct public buildings be made upon the condition that the design and construction be in compliance with GSA accessibility regulations.

The Senate Subcommittee on Public Buildings and Grounds held hearings on the proposed legislation in July 1967, five months before the National Commission on Architectural Barriers to Rehabilitation of the Handicapped issued its final report. The bill's sponsor, Senator Bartlett, testified: "This may be considered by some as an unimportant bill since it contains no seeds of controversy, carries with it no appropriation, and will cost the taxpayers of this country only a nominal amount."[6] He also argued that the bill was long overdue: "I would characterize it more as a very belated attempt on our part to catch up, to discharge a long-overdue responsibility."[7]

Mary Switzer, the commissioner of Vocational Rehabilitation Administration, testified that architectural barriers work to impede the effectiveness of rehabilitation programs: "We are not getting the full benefits from this investment because of unnecessary architectural barriers in public and other buildings which the disabled must use in order to support themselves and live productively in the community."[8] This position provided a cost-effectiveness rationale for the proposed law.

While testifying in support of the bill, the chairman of the National Commission's committee on federal and state buildings suggested an important wording change to expand the scope of the accessibility mandate. He proposed employing the word "useable" along with "accessible" to ensure that interior features as well as entrances be designed with consideration of the needs of handicapped persons.[9]

Another suggested revision focused on an agency turf question. At the hearings, a representative of the Department of Housing and Urban Development (HUD) argued that each agency should oversee compliance with the public buildings it finances; for HUD, this would be responsibility for public housing units.[10] For their part, representatives of disability interest groups—including the Easter Seals Society, National Association of the Physically Handicapped, Paralyzed Veterans of America, and National Federation of the Blind—testified in strong support of the bill, reiterated the extent of needs of physically disabled individuals, and recited the important advantages to result from implementation of the bill.

The subcommittee made a few revisions in the bill and reported it to the Senate.[11] The revisions, reflecting arguments made in testimony, (1) narrowed the definition of public buildings to "nonresidential" buildings, (2) authorized the administrator of GSA to devise regulations in conjunction with the secretary of the Department of Health, Education, and Welfare (HEW), and (3) included the wording "accessible and useable" by the physically handicapped persons. A provision was also added to allow the administrator of GSA to grant modifications or waivers if it could be clearly shown that such regulations were not necessary. The bill, as amended, was passed by voice vote in the Senate on August 25 with little discussion or debate.

The House Subcommittee on Public Buildings and Grounds held hearings on the Senate bill in March 1968.[12] Testifying at the hearings, Senator Bartlett described the bill and its impacts. Consistent with the beginnings of other rights-related laws, Bartlett argued that compliance with the law would not entail new costs: "At a time when tremendous emphasis is being placed on reducing federal spending, this bill has an extremely attractive feature. It entails no significant cost."[13]

The House hearings in many ways reflected those in the Senate. Interest groups testified in support of the bill. Turf questions continued; HUD again voiced concern with the lead implementation role of GSA. In separate communication, the Department of Defense (DOD) expressed questions about the application of accessibility rules to military installations.

The House Committee on Public Works made revisions in the proposed legislation, some reflecting work that had been done in the Senate and others reacting to concerns expressed in hearings and other communications.[14] As passed in July 1968, the House version: (1) provided for a new definition of "public buildings," which included all residential units (public and private) of four or more units but excluded facilities under the jurisdiction of DOD; (2) exempted GSA authority over residential units; and (3) authorized HUD, in consultation with HEW, to prescribe regulations for accessibility in residential units. The House version thus differed from the Senate's counterpart in breadth of buildings to be covered by the law.[15]

Differences in the Senate and House versions were worked out in conference.[16] The definition of "buildings" was again modified, this time to include all buildings and facilities intended for public use, but excluding privately owned structures and military facilities designed for able-bodied men. The conference report was accepted by both houses and signed into law as the Architectural Barriers Act by President Lyndon Johnson, in August 1968, with the statement that "it will assure that architectural barriers to the handicapped are eliminated in all buildings constructed with public funds from this day on—and will correct many errors of the past."[17]

With this legislation, public policy of a rights-oriented nature—in this case to ensure accessibility in federally financed buildings—was enacted, moving policy away from a service orientation. The bill's supporters and sponsors appeared confident that this relatively simple piece of legislation would work effectively to eliminate physical barriers encountered by handicapped citizens in federal buildings. However, difficult questions were soon to emerge, questions not adequately answered in the 1968 act. Within two years, controversy was to unfold as to the ramifications of accessibility in public transportation. Soon too the issues of modifying existing buildings and the use of waivers would arise and generate implementation difficulties. Despite these persistent tensions, the Architectural Barriers Act was a significant step in the direction of policy to actively enhance the opportunities of the nation's handicapped citizens. This law, and its counterparts, signaled a new awareness of mainstream society of the needs and frustrations of disabled persons.

Section 504: The Linchpin of Rights Protections

Despite the political storms that it would eventually stimulate, section 504, the central linchpin of public policy efforts to advance the rights of persons with mental and physical disabilities, was "born" very quietly as a relatively unnoticed paragraph in a bill designed to reauthorize and expand the Rehabilitation Act. After holding extensive hearings and expressing support for expanding the program, Congress passed the Rehabilitation Act of 1973. This act extended the authorization for the program, provided $800 million for fiscal year 1973 and $917 million for fiscal year 1974, established an Office of the Handicapped within HEW, created other policy councils, required that first priority be given to the most severely handicapped, and moved from strict emphasis on vocational rehabilitation to broader programs to promote independent living. Also included was section 504, an antidiscrimination provision initially seen as innocuous but one that would eventually generate a powerful mandate.

The origins of section 504 have been attributed to a small set of policy entrepreneurs in Congress, notably Representative Charles Vanik (D-OH) and Senator Hubert Humphrey (D-MN), the latter of which had become an advocate for disabled citizens as the result of experiences with his mentally retarded granddaughter (Katzmann 1986, 45–47). These two legislators introduced bills in Congress, in the early 1970s, to amend the Civil Rights Act to include persons with mental or physical disability within the classes protected by the act. These bills, among the first to recognize the need for civil rights protections for persons with disabilities, stalled in committee and never made it to floor consideration.

As a result of an inability to amend the Civil Rights Act, a different strategy was taken in 1972, including an antidiscrimination clause within the Rehabilitation Act. Section 504 was not considered to be a major part of the Rehabilitation Act of 1972, legislation to reauthorize the vocational rehabilitation program, and in fact, it was not included in the original draft of the bill. Richard Scotch (1984), who in *From Good Will to Civil Rights* provides a detailed account of the development of section 504, traces the language of the section to staff members in the Senate and House of Representatives. These individuals, working on the staffs of the Senate Committee on Labor and Public Welfare and House Committee on Labor and Education, met in August 1972 to discuss revision of the marked-up rehabilitation bill. By Scotch's (1984, 51–52) account:

> Staff members were concerned that, when disabled individuals completed their training in the VR [vocational rehabilitation] system and were ready to enter the workplace, many employers appeared reluctant to hire them. Staff members felt that the final goal of the VR program, getting disabled people into the mainstream of society, was being blocked by negative attitudes and discrimination on the part of employers and others.

In order to overcome biases on the part of the business community, it was suggested that language be included in the Rehabilitation Act prohibiting discrimination against disabled persons in programs of the federal government:

> Such a provision would be comparable to the provisions of Title VI of the Civil Rights Act and Title IX of the Education Amendments of 1972, but would not

involve amending those statutes. Roy Millenson of Senator Javits' staff had been involved in the development of the Education Amendments, and he ran out to his office and brought back language from Title VI. The language was adapted and inserted at the very end of the Rehabilitation Act. In the version that was ultimately enacted, that provision became Section 504.

Hence, section 504 was created, in the minds of staff members, some with experience in the disability field, others in civil rights legislation. Out of their concerns, a brief statement was added to the bill, one with unprecedented consequences for the disabled community and the nation. The statement quite simply read: ''No otherwise qualified handicapped individual in the United States, as defined in Section 7(6), shall, solely by reason of his handicap, be excluded from participation in, be denied the benefits of, or be subjected to discrimination under any program or activity receiving federal financial assistance.''[18] Section 7(6), the definition of ''handicapped individual'' in the vocational rehabilitation program, was the existing one that made reference to employment: ''The term 'handicapped individual' means any individual who (A) has a physical or mental disability which for such individual constitutes or results in substantial handicap to employment and (B) can reasonably be expected to benefit from vocational rehabilitation services.''[19] This employment-limited definition was modified and expanded by an amendment to the Rehabilitation Act of 1974, in which ''handicapped individual'' was redefined as a person who ''has a handicap, has a record of handicap, or is regarded as having a handicap.''[20]

Despite the impact that section 504 would have, it was barely noticed during legislative consideration of the Rehabilitation Act.[21] The committee and conference reports issued for the Rehabilitation Act of 1972 gave practically no attention to the section, and no floor debates raised any questions about the provision. Members of Congress either failed to notice the provision or simply viewed it as a symbolic statement of goodwill toward persons with disability.

President Richard Nixon pocket vetoed the Rehabilitation Act of 1972 as passed by Congress for reasons having nothing directly to do with section 504. Nixon argued that authorized expenditures were too large and that the bill would create numerous committees and commissions that would waste taxpayers' dollars. The next year, a determined Congress reconsidered the bill, now the Rehabilitation Act of 1973, and made a few revisions, namely to reduce authorized expenditures and to decrease the number of new commissions.[22] After further wrangling, Congress approved the bill and President Nixon signed it in September 1973. Despite revisions meant to reduce the likelihood of a presidential veto, the bill had many significant provisions, including the requirement that state rehabilitation agencies give primary attention to their most seriously handicapped clients.

In addition to section 504, the Rehabilitation Act of 1973 had other provisions relevant to rights issues. Section 501 required the agencies of the federal government to take affirmative action in employing persons with disabilities. Section 502 established the Architectural and Transportation Barriers Compliance Board to oversee compliance of federal agencies with the Architectural Barriers Act. And section 503 stipulated that any contract by the federal government in excess of $2,500 contain a provision requiring that contracting parties engage in affirmative action to employ, and to advance in employment, handicapped workers.

Civil Rights and Education:
The Education for All Handicapped Children Act

In the period from 1965 to 1974, groups representing disabled children, including the National Association of Retarded Children and the Council for Exceptional Children, successfully lobbied for several federal policy initiatives in regard to the education of handicapped children. These initiatives together symbolized the growing awareness of policymakers about the educational needs of disabled children and the paucity of programs to provide them with an effective instruction. The laws enacted during the ten-year period ending in 1974 had created a Bureau for Education of the Handicapped within the Office of Education, initiated research programs concerning means to effectively educate disabled students, and created training programs to increase the skills of special education teachers. These gains were no small achievement, considering the long neglect of handicapped persons in general and, more specifically, of the educational needs of disabled children.

A report by the Rand Corporation on federal programs to assist disabled citizens, prepared in the early 1970s, summarized federal efforts to educate handicapped students:[23]

1. "Since the Federal Government supplies only 12 percent of the total special education funds, the present Federal role is not a dominant one, but appears to be a hybrid mixture of rules with primary emphasis on innovation and stimulation—the catalytic role."
2. "Estimates of the percentage of handicapped youth unserved by any special education program vary widely depending on assumptions made, but all point to the same conclusion: A very large proportion of those needing special education are unserved."
3. "Extremely large variations in the percentage served exist across the states and across the types of handicaps."
4. "Expansion of special education services to those now unserved will require

much more than dollars. Incentives must be built in to alter the mix of types of handicaps served.''

Overall, the report indicated that federal programs had stimulated state education agencies and local school districts to recognize the needs of and commence serving handicapped children. This stimulus, however, proved uneven, since the progress of states and school districts in developing special education programs varied dramatically across the nation. Many school systems did not even know the number of handicapped students in their jurisdictions, and some were afraid to initiate a count, since once identified, the students would need specialized educational services.

Early implementation of programs to provide more educational services to handicapped children led states and school systems to recognize the enormity of the task at hand. Pressures were mounting by parents groups to begin or improve special education programs, while at the same time, funds for the task were far insufficient to the task. These pressures lead Congress to consider new legislation to deal with the growing costs of education programs for handicapped children and mechanisms for advancing their educational rights.

Court Decisions: Right to a Free and Appropriate Education

Efforts to push for rights protections in education were greatly advanced by two court cases of the early 1970s. One case, still a landmark in the area of handicapped education, was the *Pennsylvania Association for Retarded Children [PARC] v. Commonwealth of Pennsylvania*.[24] In this case, the plaintiffs, acting on behalf of fourteen mentally retarded students and others of similar condition, brought a class action suit against the state of Pennsylvania, arguing that their due process and equal protection rights had been violated by state laws that (1) included no provision for hearings before a retarded child was excluded from public education, (2) assumed that retarded children are uneducable, and (3) arbitrarily and capriciously denied retarded children the right to an education (Burgdorf 1980, 75–92).

The litigation was settled in 1972 through a consent agreement in which the state agreed that ''it is the Commonwealth's obligation to place each mentally retarded child in a *free, public program of education and training appropriate to the child's capacity*.''[25] Seen as a victory by advocates of mentally disabled persons, the case received widespread publicity and generated similar legal action in other states. ''As one of the first statewide, federal, class action lawsuits brought on behalf of handicapped persons, it is often considered the cradle of the whole legal rights movement for handicapped people'' (Burgdorf 1980, 90).

In a second case, *Mills v. Board of Education of the District of Columbia*, parents and guardians of seven retarded children sued the Board of Education in the nation's capital, charging that the defendant denied them publicly supported education. Given that this case was heard in federal district court, its decision was seen as having widespread implications. The district court ultimately ruled in favor of the plaintiffs and ordered, among other stipulations, that

> the District of Columbia shall provide each child of school age a free and suitable publicly-supported education regardless of the degree of the child's mental, physical, or emotional disability or impairment. Furthermore, defendants shall not exclude any child resident in the District of Columbia from such publicly-supported education on the basis of a claim of insufficient resources.[26]

Following on the heels of the *PARC* case, the *Mills* case served to strengthen legal foundations of handicapped children to a free and appropriate education, primarily on the grounds of due process and equal protections rights: "The overriding implication of the 1971–72 court decisions is the right of equal access to education opportunity for all children'' (Lippman and Goldberg 1973, 59). The *Mills* case was additionally important, for it extended protection to all forms of disability, not just mental retardation, and stated that lack of funds was not a sufficient rationale to justify not providing equal and appropriate education to handicapped children.

Legislative Consideration of Education Bills

By the mid-1970s, the climate in Congress was generally favorable to the development of stronger efforts to ensure handicapped children educations tailored to their individual needs. Members of Congress and the disability community were aware of the *PARC* and *Mills* decisions, as well as of problems with implementing widespread special education programs.

The Education Amendments of 1974. In 1973, Congress considered bills to extend the Education of the Handicapped Act, initially passed in 1970. The House Subcommittee on Select Education held hearings in March on a bill to extend the Education of the Handicapped Act for three years. The hearing before the House subcommittee indicated the growing concerns about rights issues related to education of disabled children. Witnesses at the hearings strongly supported extension of the act and testified regarding cases where programs funded under the act had aided handicapped children. At the same time, witnesses (1) reiterated the extent of children who as yet received no educational assistance, (2) argued that the severely handicapped need attention first, and (3) supported a federal government role in coordinating special education efforts.[27]

In March 1973, the Senate Subcommittee on the Handicapped held hearings on the extension of the Education of the Handicapped Act, as well as other bills concerned with the education of disabled children. The recurrent themes expressed at these hearings were similar to those voiced in the House hearings, namely that current programs were a step in the right direction but woefully inadequate to the needs of handicapped children. Witnesses also decried the plan of the Nixon administration to lump programs into a new revenue-sharing program. In the words of one witness: "If they are going to just transfer programs . . . and just transfer dollars, in my opinion, as it has historically proven, the handicapped will come out on the bottom of the list."[28]

The Education Amendments of 1974, as passed by Congress, pushed states to provide educational services to handicapped children by requiring that states (1) submit comprehensive plans for providing full educational services to handicapped children, (2) develop a plan for providing due process to all handicapped children, (3) give top priority to serving children not enrolled in educational programs, and (4) educate children in the "least restrictive environment" possible.

Educational Rights Legislation in the Senate. In 1973, Senator Harrison Williams (D-NJ), chairman of the Senate Committee on Labor and Public Welfare, introduced a bill titled the Education for All Handicapped Children Act (S. 6). This far-reaching and comprehensive bill stated that its purpose was

> to insure that all handicapped children have available to them not later than 1976 a free appropriate education, to insure the rights of handicapped children and their parents or guardian are protected, to relieve the fiscal burden placed upon the states and localities when they provide for the education of all handicapped children, and to assess the effectiveness of efforts to educate handicapped children.[29]

This language directly followed from the *PARC* and *Mills* decisions of 1972. The bill's financial assistance component authorized the federal government to contribute seventy-five percent of the excess costs to educate handicapped children (costs above those for educating nonhandicapped children).

The Senate Subcommittee on the Handicapped held hearings on this bill from 1973 to 1975, including "field" hearings in Newark; Boston; Columbia, South Carolina; St. Paul, Minnesota; and Harrisburg, Pennsylvania. Throughout these hearings, sentiment within the committee strengthened in support of a strong rights bill. Hearing testimony also indicates the impatience of interest groups representing disabled children to have a rights bill passed by Congress. One example is a statement by a representative of the Council for Exceptional Children:

> The Council for Exceptional Children believes that it is time for Congress to take one more step to get the schoolhouse door open, and keep it open, once and for all . . . we feel this legislation, having undergone continuing refinement since the beginning of the decade, having been analyzed and debated in innumerable public forums over the years, having gathered to itself the endorsement of a wide array of organizations and hundreds of thousands of parents and other concerned citizens—should now be moved and moved immediately. Quite bluntly, every day of continued delay may mean that one more exceptional child may not be able to turn that corner to freedom and fulfillment.[30]

After three years of hearings, the subcommittee reported the bill to the full Committee on Labor and Public Welfare, which, a few days later, reported the bill to the full house. By a vote of eighty-three to ten, the Senate passed S. 6 in June 1975.

Educational Rights Legislation in the House. One bill, H.R. 70, "A Bill to Provide Financial Assistance to the States for Improved Educational Services for Handicapped Children," was considered in the House of Representatives in 1974. As the bill's title suggests, its primary emphasis was to increase federal assistance to states and localities for special education programs. Dual themes, the commitment to provide special education to all handicapped children and the inadequacy of current state and local resources for this task, were stated time and again during the hearings on H.R. 70. The need of states for more federal funds was reiterated by several of those giving testimony, including Francis Sargent, the governor of Massachusetts, who argued: "In Massachusetts we are finally beginning to realize the extent to which handicapped and retarded children have been neglected. Only you [Congress] can provide the major financial assistance that will guarantee the success of our efforts."[31]

Like state governments, interest groups representing handicapped children sought more federal money for special education, but another issue was of even greater significance: provision of mechanisms in public policy to require states and local school systems to provide an appropriate education to *all* disabled children. In the hearings on H.R. 70, for example, the representative of the National Advisory Committee on Handicapped Children reiterated its principal recommendation: "We affirm the right under the U.S. Constitution of all hand-icapped children to a tax-supported and appropriate education regardless of their physical or mental capabilities."[32]

During hearing testimony, major concerns about the proposed increase in federal financial assistance for the education of disabled children were raised by representatives of the Nixon administration. Charles M. Cooke, Jr., deputy assistant secretary for legislation at HEW, expressed the administration's con-cerns that the bill would exaggerate the federal role in educating the handi-capped: "We feel that such a massive shift toward Federal financial and administrative involvement in education for handicapped children, with its far-reaching implications for the heretofore complementary roles of Federal, State, and local governments, is extremely unwise and unnecessary."[33] Clearly, the Nixon administration's position was that H.R. 70 would represent an overex-pansion of federal government into state and local affairs; the administration preferred maintaining the present federal role of stimulus, as opposed to a more involved role of providing substantial financial assistance. While this House bill never passed, many concerns raised in the bill and in hearing testimony were reflected in a new bill, H.R. 7217, introduced in the House of Represen-tatives in 1975.

The House of Representative's version of the Education for All Handicapped Children Act, H.R. 7217, was similar in many regards to S. 6. Like its Senate counterpart, the bill's central purpose was to ensure all handicapped children a free and appropriate education and to provide increased funding for states to pursue this objective. Hearings were held by the Subcommittee on Select Ed-ucation in April and June 1975. As in the Senate hearings in 1975, those rep-resenting disabled children demonstrated irritation that an education rights bill had yet to be passed. The president of the National Education Association, for example, testified: "We urge the subcommittee to move as expeditiously as possible. . . . The handicapped youth of our affluent society should not be made to suffer the pains of despair and educational neglect due to counterpro-ductive political hangups."[34] Interest groups continued to stress the number of disabled children as yet receiving no specialized education, the importance of strong rights protections, and the need for expanded federal funding.

Consistent with a theme repeated by the Nixon and Ford administrations, the commissioner of education, Terrel Bell, expressed concern about expanding the federal government's role in providing educational services to handicapped youths: "We believe that enacting legislation such as H.R. 7217, with its pro-found and undesirable expansion of Federal responsibilities, is not war-ranted."[35] Giving the Ford administration little heed, the subcommittee reported an undiluted H.R. 7217 to the Committee on Education and Welfare, which in turn reported it to the full house. By a vote of 375 to 44, the House of Representatives passed the landmark bill.

PL94-192: The Education for All Handicapped Children Act

The Senate and House bills, S. 6 and H.R. 7217, were referred to a conference committee, which worked to rectify differences. There were many similarities in the bills, particularly in the primary objective of providing a free and appropriate education to all handicapped children. Three major issues on which the bills differed were resolved in the conference committee: expenditure authorizations, the level of government to receive federal funds, and a mechanism to ensure compliance with legislated requirements (Levine and Wexler 1981, 93–100).

The Senate bill based federal contributions on three hundred dollars for each handicapped child served and would expire in September 1979. The bill passed by the House authorized expenditures based on fifty percent of the national average per-pupil cost of education times the number of handicapped children served. Interest groups, as one would expect, preferred the more liberal House version, while the Ford administration signaled its displeasure with what it saw as generous funding arrangements (Levine and Wexler 1981, 94). The conference committee resolved these differences by making the bill a permanent authorization and developing a sliding scale of federal contributions, with the maximum amount of funds a state could receive being equal to the average number of handicapped children being served times an increasing percentage of the national average per-pupil expenditure for education. The percentage would start at five percent for fiscal year 1978 and rise to forty percent for fiscal year 1982 and after.

The second area of difference concerned the allocation of federal funds among levels of government. The House bill favored passing most funds directly to local education agencies (LEAs); state education agencies (SEAs) would receive only a five percent set aside. The Senate bill allocated funds directly to the SEA, with forty percent of funds distributed to the LEAs on the basis of number of children served. The remaining funds were allocated to the SEAs for carrying out provisions of the bill. This difference was resolved with a one-to-three ratio, whereby the SEAs received twenty-five percent of federal allocations and the LEAs received the remaining seventy-five percent on the basis of students served.

The conference report was accepted by both houses and reluctantly signed into law by President Gerald Ford on November 29, 1975.[36] The key provisions of PL94-142, the Education for All Handicapped Children Act, required states, as a precondition for receiving federal funds, to ensure that they provide a free and appropriate education to all handicapped children.[37] Such an education was defined as one that is provided at public expense, under public supervision and direction, and without charge, and which (1) meets the standards of the SEA, (2) includes preschool, elementary, and secondary education, and (3) is provided in conformity with the IEP established for each handicapped student. The IEP, an important guide to policy implementation, required that school systems provide a written statement for each handicapped child, indicating the child's present state of performance, future learning objectives, educational services needed, and the criteria for evaluation.

Conclusion: The Legacy of Legislative Consideration

By the end of 1975, Congress had enacted three important pieces of legislation that remain the foundation of public policies to protect and advance the rights of persons with mental or physical disabilities. Despite their common focus on rights, the bills are different in terms of their legislative histories. The Education for All Handicapped Children Act resulted from a protracted struggle by interest groups and concerned educators to see that all handicapped children, particularly those with mental disabilities, were ensured an appropriate education in public schools. The legislation was debated for several years, and the final bill was the result of long-term compromises and political wrangling.

Section 504 of the Rehabilitation Act of 1973 and the Architectural Barriers Act of 1968 experienced a very different legislative "birth." Section 504 was a "sleeper section" in a bill to reauthorize the long-standing vocational rehabilitation program. The section was seen as a symbolic "goodwill" statement toward those who experience disabling conditions. It is clear that the legislators who enacted section 504 did not understand the powerful impact this brief paragraph would ultimately have on public policies. While the Rehabilitation Act itself was involved in political pulling and hauling between Congress and the Nixon administration, section 504 was not part of the controversy. It is quite ironic that the Nixon administration, which favored limitation on federal government powers and responsibilities, would veto the bill on the grounds that it impeded executive authority but would miss the significance of section 504 in expanding the regulatory mandate of the federal government.

Both section 504 and the Architectural Barriers Act of 1968 originated from policy entrepreneurs who saw the need for public response to the needs of disabled citizens. These entrepreneurs had contacts among disabled citizens but initiated legislation more from their own sense of the importance of eliminating social and physical barriers than from political pressures from interest groups. For this reason, both measures were stronger on symbolic statement than guidelines for implementation. Just the opposite was true of the Education for All Handicapped Children Act, where interest groups foresaw implementation problems in advance and pushed for specialized language to clarify legal protections and mandate compliance activities. As Frank Bowe (1980b, 107) has commented: "It is unusual for a piece of legislation to be so detailed and explicit. Normally, such specificity is left for the administering agencies to develop. But in the case of PL94-142, the Congress was determined to protect the rights of children and the parents in the face of overt and blatant denial of these rights in the nation's sixteen thousand school districts."

Legislation relevant to disabled Americans did not stop with these important bills. We will trace changes in these laws as we turn to their implementation in later chapters. In addition to these laws, there was, by the 1980s, "a veritable avalanche" of other legislative initiatives relevant to persons with disabilities. Caveats and changes were made to several different federal programs to extend benefits, services, or protections to persons with disability, including such areas as public housing, transportation, health, employment, and social services. In terms of rights and protections for disabled citizens, however, the Architectural Barriers Act of 1968, the Rehabilitation Act of 1973, and the Education for All Handicapped Children Act remain the primary legislative bases. But legislation alone is insufficient to ensure that rights are acknowledged and that legal provisions are enforced; these remain the objective of policy implementation.

4

From Symbolic Gestures to Implementation Guidelines

The Saga of Section 504

Development of civil rights policies requires that five key questions be addressed: (1) *who* is to be protected from discrimination, (2) *what practices* constitute discriminatory action, (3) *whose discriminatory actions* are prohibited, (4) *what remedial action* is required to compensate for discriminatory practices, and (5) *what enforcement mechanisms* are devised to deal with persistent discriminatory action. To the extent that these issues are clearly described in public laws and their legislative histories, administrators are provided with a conception of legislators' views of the appropriate path of policy implementation. Ambiguity in legislative statutes, however, creates significant questions regarding implementation, questions which by default must be dealt with during rulemaking.

With the passage of the Rehabilitation Act of 1973, section 504 became law, following in the footsteps of other civil rights laws. The provision was strong on symbolic statement but short on guidelines for implementation. With practically no legislative history to serve as a guide, substantial and significant policy refinement was required by the executive branch as it commenced enforcement of antidiscrimination protections for persons with disabilities.

Who Is Responsible for Implementation?

Unlike other civil rights laws that designate which administrative authorities are responsible for implementing and issuing regulations, section 504 included no such provision. Since the execution of vocational rehabilitation was centered in the Department of Health, Education, and Welfare (HEW), it was generally perceived that this department would have lead responsibility for implementing section 504. By agency decision, the task of devising administrative regulations was vested in HEW's Office of Civil Rights (OCR).[1] In its first effort, HEW would design rules applicable to recipients of federal funds dispersed through the agency. Subsequently, HEW would be explicitly granted authority to coordinate section 504 efforts throughout the federal government; in this capacity, HEW devised a set of "coordinating" regulations for other agencies to follow in designing their own regulations for section 504 enforcement.

This assignment of primary responsibility for implementing section 504 in HEW's OCR, a decision apparently based more on administrative practice than political grounds, would have strong impact on the approach taken to implementation and the ultimate content of the regulations. The staff in OCR were individuals with extensive experience in enforcing civil rights policies, namely Title VI of the Civil Rights Act of 1964 and Title IX of the Education Act Amendments of 1972, as well as school desegregation. They were accustomed to taking affirmative positions and pushing aggressively for strong administrative measures and their enforcement.[2] This position contrasts markedly with the view of professionals involved in vocational rehabilitation, whose orientation focused on service delivery, cultivating community participation, and voluntary compliance (Scotch 1984, 62).

Early on, the OCR staff at HEW entered into discussions with congressional staff members affiliated with the Senate Subcommittee on the Handicapped.[3] These discussions represented the nascent stages of an issue network; both sides were committted to policy efforts to fight discrimination against handicapped persons.[4] The OCR staff members shared their concerns about the lack of legislative history, the ambiguity about authority to develop rules, and a definition of handicapped persons that was based upon employability. These issues were subsequently addressed in the Rehabilitation Act Amendments of 1974 (PL93-516), crafted in large part by the subcommittee staff in response to discussions with the OCR staff.[5] In addition to extending the authorization for the vocational rehabilitation program, the 1974 legislation modified the definition of handicapped individual, easing one concern of the OCR staff.

The definitional change was a significant one; it substituted for "employability" a far broader definition that included within the rubric of protected persons anyone who (1) has a physical or mental impairment that substantially limits one or more of such person's major life functions, (2) has a record of such impairment, or (3) is regarded as having such an impairment. Under the employability-based definition, many disabled persons were not entitled to section 504 protections, including severely disabled individuals, elderly disabled persons, and handicapped children. The change in emphasis on impairment of "major life functions" greatly expanded the set of persons protected under section 504. The new definition also included past impairments not currently causing problems and perceptions of impairments that do not actually exist (e.g., person incorrectly classified as mentally retarded).

The conference report issued in conjunction with the Rehabilitation Act

Amendments of 1974 was instrumental in establishing legislative history for section 504. The report directly linked the section to civil rights laws concerned with discrimination based upon race and sex: "The section therefore constitutes the establishment of a broad government policy that programs receiving Federal financial assistance shall be operated without discrimination on the basis of handicap."[6] The report also validated the issuance of regulations to implement section 504, stating that while the law "does not specifically require the issuance of regulations or expressly provide for enforcement procedures, it is clearly mandatory in form, and such regulations and enforcement are intended."[7]

Rule Writing and Delays

With the clarifications afforded by the Rehabilitation Act Amendments of 1974, passed in December, the OCR staff moved forward in devising regulations to govern implementation of section 504. This rulemaking process became protracted, subject to repeated delays; it would be another two and a half years until final regulations would be issued by HEW. The arduous rulemaking process has been chronicled elsewhere (Scotch 1984, 86–120; Katzmann 1986, 98–102), but a review of the key developments is helpful in understanding policy refinement relevant to implementation of section 504.

A final draft of rules for section 504 was finished by the OCR staff by the summer of 1975 and forwarded up the organizational chain to the secretary of HEW, David Matthews. The secretary, who has been described as cautious and indecisive (Scotch 1984, 87), questioned certain provisions of the rules, was reticent in moving forward with publishing the rules, and yet did not ask for major changes. He did request that an inflationary impact study be prepared, in line with President Ford's Executive Order 11821, requiring that programs expending more than $100 million be assessed in terms of their implications for inflation. Such an analysis was conducted twice, once in-house and once by an outside consulting firm. Both studies, while delaying publication of the regulations, concluded that section 504 rules would not generally entail large expenditures, and that whatever expenditures would result would be more than offset by benefits to disabled persons.[8]

With the inflationary studies completed, the draft regulations were again submitted to the secretary in March 1976, but again Matthews failed to order the regulations published in the *Federal Register*, the next step in the rulemaking process. Again he raised no specific objections but remained reluctant to move forward with the regulations. By this point, the secretary's delay was more than evident to the OCR staff that had devised the rules, the congressional staff that had close contact with OCR, and groups representing disabled citizens who were awakening to the potential importance of section 504 as a cornerstone for antidiscrimination policy.

The significance of rulemaking for section 504 was heightened by Executive Order 11914, issued by President Ford in April 1976.[9] This order designated the secretary of HEW as the coordinator across all federal government agencies of implementation efforts regarding section 504 and required agencies to issue regulations consistent with standards and guidelines set by HEW. The executive order also outlined enforcement practices.

Prodding from Other Arenas

As early as 1975, groups representing persons with disabilities had begun to recognize that section 504 offered a means to press for antidiscrimination measures in many areas of American society. As discussions ensued among the OCR staff members charged with drafting regulations and their contacts in the handicapped community, word began to spread among advocacy groups (Scotch 1984, 96). By late 1975, the issue network concerned about section 504 included the OCR staff, staff members of the Senate Subcommittee on the Handicapped, and key advocates for disabled citizens. Those to be regulated by section 504 were consulted little in the rule creation process and, at this point, were relatively uninvolved in regulation drafting.

The growing awareness of and interest in section 504 by groups representing disabled individuals is manifest in testimony given at congressional hearings held from 1972 to 1976 on the vocational rehabilitation program. As described in the last chapter, interest groups paid practically no attention to the section during legislative consideration of the Rehabilitation Act in 1972 or 1973; their concerns at this point centered primarily on continuing and expanding the rehabilitation program. In testimony given during hearings on the Rehabilitation Act Amendments of 1974 and in joint House-Senate oversight hearings in 1975, interest groups representing disabled persons pressed for extension of the act, greater federal funding, priority treatment of severely disabled persons (as stipulated in the Rehabilitation Act of 1973), and generally for more implementation efforts.[10] Little attention was given directly to section 504, with the exception of Roger Peterson of the American Coalition of Citizens with Disabilities, who argued: "We note that the regulations for Section 504 are still not published, and there is no executive order pertaining to its Government-wide implementation."[11] By the time congressional hearings were held in 1976, awareness of section 504 had grown substantially; groups representing handicapped citizens spoke far more frequently about section 504, noting its importance and decrying slow implementation.

Particularly active in pressing for action was the Action League for Physically Handicapped Adults. This group, coming to the center for advocacy on behalf of section 504, sued HEW and Secretary Matthews in federal court to issue section 504 regulations in June 1975 (*Cherry* v. *Matthews*).[12] The court subsequently ruled in favor of the plaintiffs in July 1976 and ordered the secretary of HEW to issue regulations, although no deadline for action was imposed. Advocates took more direct action to protest the delay in rule issuance in the spring of 1976, when they demonstrated in the office of Secretary Matthews as another means to press for action.

A second institutional arena, Congress, was also called upon to press HEW to move forward with rulemaking. In May 1976, the Senate Subcommittee on the Handicapped placed the question of section 504 on its agenda, at the behest of the committee staff and disgruntled advocates of disabled citizens, holding oversight hearings on the affirmative action and antidiscrimination provisions of the Rehabilitation Act of 1973. The HEW officials testifying at the hearing were among those at OCR who had been actively involved in drafting section 504 regulations. In testimony, they placed blame for the delay in issuing regulations on "the absence of substantive legislative history which would have provided us with greater insight into Congress' intent in enacting the provision" and on necessary deliberations concerning definitions of what conditions render a person handicapped and what practices constitute discrimination.[13]

The senators on the subcommittee were unimpressed by these explanations of delay, especially since they had moved to provide legislative history in their report accompanying the Rehabilitation Act Amendments of 1974. Their frustration was voiced by Senator Harrison Williams in his assessment of HEW actions to enforce affirmative action and antidiscrimination measures as outlined in the Rehabilitation Act of 1973:

> We have heard from many groups representing the handicapped and that these programs have so far been a failure. . . . We also know that the agencies have done little in the way of actual enforcement. . . . We know that the agencies have not hired the personnel which the Congress has mandated as necessary for enforcement of these laws. . . . Frankly, I think the time for excuses has now passed.[14]

These more or less simultaneous pressures in 1976 from the courts, Congress, and interest groups representing disabled citizens finally sparked action by Secretary Matthews. The draft regulations were first published on May 17 as a notice of intent to publish rules[15] and, with a few technical revisions, as a notice of proposed rulemaking on July 16.[16] Hundreds of comments were received in response to the proposed regulations. The diversity of comments, and the stridency of positions taken, demonstrated that many types of actors, including both beneficiaries and regulated clients, were aware of the potential impact of section 504. This short legislative provision was no longer a little-recognized symbolic gesture. The section 504 regulations signaled that behaviors would have to be changed and costs would be incurred. Recognizing these implications, the regulated clients—a diverse group including universities, public school systems, health providers, and state and local governments—moved to modify the rules so as to reduce or avoid costs and behavioral changes.

During the public comment period, the OCR staff conducted several regional hearings on the draft regulations. These provided further input into rulemaking efforts. The period for public comments on regulations for implementing section 504 ended in October 1976. By early December, OCR forwarded four issues to Secretary Matthews for his resolution; these included whether drug addicts and alcoholics were covered by the law, accessibility modifications required of existing structures, the applicability of minimum wage laws to institutionalized persons, and the role to be played by state agencies (Scotch 1984, 102). While these were troublesome issues, still being decided late in the rulemaking process, they were not the basic organizing principles that the OCR staff had used to devise implementation requirements.

In early January 1977, the final revised regulations were forwarded to Matthews for his signature, which would cause the rules to go into effect. But instead of signing the rules, he once again balked, this time by the unprecedented means of forwarding the revised regulations to the Senate Committee on Labor and Public Welfare, requesting verification that the rules were consistent with legislative intent. This move meant that the regulations would be passed on to the next secretary of HEW, since Matthews's term expired with the end of the Ford administration on January 20. Groups representing disabled citizens were not initially daunted, given their expectation that the Carter administration would be more favorable to their cause and would move expeditiously to issue section 504 regulations.

Such expediency, however, was not forthcoming under the new secretary of HEW, Joseph Califano. Upon taking office, he ordered a study of the implications associated with section 504. In his own words, ''From the moment I glanced at it I knew we were on the brink of another, though very different, civil rights revolution. I didn't want it to start from the dead-of-night posture in which Congress had acted, so I passed the word that I intended to take ample time to review the regulations and restructure them'' (Califano 1981, 259). His delay was not well received by interest groups, whose patience with rulemaking delays was wearing thin. Their response to Califano's failure to move immediately was to plan and mount public protests in April 1977. These publicized protests were staged at regional field offices, as well as at Califano's office and home. The OCR staff prepared yet another set of revised regulations, which, while basically unchanged, provided somewhat more flexibility in meeting regulatory requirements. Given these changes and mounting political pressures, Califano signed the rules on April 28, ending the long saga of administrative rulemaking.

The Content of Section 504 Regulations

The regulations for section 504 laid out the objectives and means of implementation of the antidiscrimination policy.[17] Included within the regulations are several organizing and operating principles that serve as the conceptual underpinnings of antidiscrimination policy for disabled citizens. These principles include program accessibility, reasonable accommodation, and free and appropriate education. In addition, the regulations sought to clarify the key definitional questions of who was entitled to protection under the law and whose behavior was to be regulated. The regulations were introduced by the statement that "Section 504 thus represents the first Federal civil rights law protecting the rights of handicapped persons and reflects a national commitment to end discrimination on the basis of handicap. . . . It establishes a mandate to end discrimination and to bring handicapped persons into the mainstream of American life. The Secretary intends vigorously to implement and enforce that mandate."[18]

Definitions of Handicapped Person: Who Is Protected

The regulations included the definition of handicapped person as outlined in the Rehabilitation Act Amendments of 1974; thus protections were extended to those with a mental or physical handicap that limits one or more major life activities, a record of such handicap, or being perceived as having such a handicap. "Major life activities" were defined as caring for one's self, performing manual tasks, walking, seeing, hearing, speaking, breathing, learning, and working. Disability, then, meant impediments to communication, mobility, learning, and earning a living.

These regulatory provisions did not answer all definitional questions, however. Throughout rulemaking efforts, the OCR staff debated the question of whether various groups, including alcoholics and drug addicts, homosexuals, and elderly persons, were entitled to protection under section 504. It was decided not to include homosexuals or elderly individuals simply on the basis of sexual preference or age. Neither factor, in and of itself, was considered to constitute a mental or physical disability. Drug abuse and alcoholism proved to be far stickier issues. Most health professionals characterized these conditions as mental and/or physical disorders and, thus, constituting eligibility for protection under section 504.

Many of the comments received in regard to proposed regulations expressed concern about including alcohol and drug abusers within the definition of disability. Characteristic of such concerns are the following public comments submitted during rulemaking, one by a local school system and the other by a department of local government:[19]

> If our school system is forced to admit to classes or provide a special teacher for a known dope addict, the Superintendent and the board members will be ridden out of town on a rail. (Public school system in New Mexico)

> Unlike other handicaps protected by the Act, drug addiction and alcoholism are conditions which the victims have the ability to cure. We find it highly inappropriate to require public employees to employ addicts using taxpayers' funds. . . . (City of Los Angeles, Personnel Department)

Wrestling with the issue, HEW requested the attorney general's office to prepare a legal opinion on whether alcoholics and drug abusers were appropriately considered as handicapped for the purposes of section 504. The opinion was in the affirmative, although many inside and outside of the administration were not comfortable with this position. The appendix to the published regulations, which discussed comments received by the agency during rulemaking, made direct reference to the attorney general's opinion and stated that, given the opinion, the secretary "therefore believes that he is without authority to exclude these conditions from the definitions."[20] To quell concerns strongly expressed in public comments, the regulations went on to state that protections would only be afforded to those drug users and alcoholics who were otherwise fit and qualified for the job in question.

Costs, Affirmative Actions, and Compensation

In designing section 504 regulations, the OCR staff had to come to grips with important issues related to compliance costs and remedial actions. In developing the rules, it was decided that implementation must be affirmative in pressing for remedial steps to provide greater opportunities for persons with disabilities.[21] Unlike other types of civil rights situations, a "cease and desist" requirement would not be enough. For example, telling an employer to stop discriminating, without simultaneously requiring some form of accommodation, would mean that implementation would have little, if any, impact. This approach is reflected in the first version of proposed rules that compared section 504 to other civil rights laws:

> There are no inherent differences or inequalities between the general public and the persons protected by these statutes [Title VI of the Civil Rights Act of 1964 and Title IX of the Education Amendments of 1972] and, therefore, there should be no differential treatment in the administration of Federal programs. The concept of Section 504, on the other hand, is far more complex. Handicapped persons may require quite different treatment in order to be afforded equal access to federally assisted programs and activities, and identical treatment, in fact, constitutes discrimination.[22]

The approach reflected in this statement recognizes that the neutrality principle applicable to the other civil rights law—which holds that race, sex, and national origin should be eliminated from decisions about rights, benefits, and services—does not translate well in an antidiscrimination policy based on handicap. The direction of the regulations was designed to include requirements that affirmative steps be taken to change behaviors and situations so as to increase the opportunities of handicapped persons. Greater equality of outcome was the ultimate goal, and to achieve this, remedial efforts were mandated.

A second issue dealt with compliance costs. The members of the OCR staff, possessing strong views in favor of civil rights, were less concerned with cost issues than other administrators might have been. They were not predisposed to consider the cost issue, based on the perspective that rights are fundamental, not subject to qualification on the basis of costs or other grounds. They did recognize, however, that crafting required accommodations to handicapping conditions would entail expenditures and be politically sensitive. In the first version of the draft rules, the concept of "competing equities" was introduced as a means of signaling the need for a balance between needed remedies for disabled persons and the mandated costs of accommodation to be born by regulated clients. The discussion in the regulations suggested this basic cost issue was the most difficult one to address in drafting regulations: "The most important problem which has hindered the development of the regulation is the constant need to weigh competing equities while resolving complex issues. . . . Implicit in this situation is the need to assess carefully the overall impact of a particular requirement both on the persons protected by the statute and those regulated by it."[23] Adroit interest groups were quick to pick up on this notion of "balanced competing equities," sensing that HEW might be backing away from stringent enforcement. If cost consideration could be weighed against ending discriminatory action, then, advocates for disabled persons feared, the strength of the mandate would be greatly diluted. A comment submitted during the rulemaking process by the United Cerebral Palsy Association highlights the concerns of disability groups in regard to the competing equities principle: "The balancing preoccupations of the regulations are overemphasized and lessen the impact of the regulations. The purpose of the Section 504 regulations is to define what constitutes discrimination, not to provide relief to federal recipients before discrimination is even defined."

In the second publication of the rules in July 1976, the OCR staff directly addressed questions about the competing equities principle. They noted, and accepted as accurate, the judgment of many commentors that prohibition of discriminatory action, as contained in section 504, was absolute and without exception. The rule writers noted at the same time that other commentors, especially public school systems and universities, had reiterated that they would be unable to bear the additional costs mandated by the regulations. The decision from HEW was to stick to a middle ground that accepted some notion of balance between the needs of handicapped persons and the compliance measures required of regulated parties. To achieve this balance, it was announced in the rules "that cost or difficulty are appropriate considerations, not in determining what constitutes discrimination, but in fashioning a remedy if a recipient has been found to be discriminating."[24]

Decisions on remedial action and cost considerations were basic to the regulations. The focus on remedial actions required to demonstrate compliance made the rules stronger than they might otherwise have been, since recipients of federal funds would be required to take positive steps to assist disabled persons. Compliance was to mean more than simply stopping discriminatory practices; it would entail performance of several types of behavioral modifications and new activities. Decisions related to costs, the "balanced competing equities" position, reflected a compromise stance. Disallowing cost issues from consideration of discriminatory behavior reinforces the provision as protecting rights, while the recognition that cost could figure into determining remedial actions provided some limitations on the extent of accommodations that regulated interests would have to perform. This competing equity approach was borne out in regulatory provisions developed for particular program areas, including employment, facility access, and education.

Section 504 and Employment

Subpart B of the regulations concerned protections for disabled persons in employment, stipulating that "no qualified handicapped persons shall, on the basis of handicap, be subjected to discrimination in employment under any program or activity to which this part applies.''[25] This provision required a definition of "qualified handicapped person": an individual "who, with reasonable accommodation, can perform the essential functions of the job in question.''[26]

Description of what types of accommodations are required under section 504, and which ones are "reasonable," entail specification of the types of compensatory action to be taken. Appropriate accommodations were defined with reference to examples that included making employee facilities readily accessible to and usable by handicapped workers, job restructuring, modifications in work schedules, changes in equipment, and provision of readers and interpreters. A limitation on mandated accommodations was included through the modifier "reasonable." Accommodations in employment were required only if they did not impose an "undue economic hardship." However appealing such a hardship provision might be, its definition in practice was far more difficult to fashion. The only guidance furnished by the rules in ascertaining undue hardship is that such determination should be made with reference to the overall size of the recipient's program (with respect to employees, number and type of facilities, and size of budget), the type of recipient operation, and the nature and cost of the needed accommodation. Only indirect guidance was thus provided for ascertaining when accommodation becomes "unreasonable" and no longer required.

The reasonable accommodation provision, serving as a key operating principle for implementing employment protections, generated several types of reactions during rulemaking. As might be expected, potential employers expressed concerns about the extent of required accommodations and their associated costs. Typical of such reactions was a comment by the administrative officer of York, Pennsylvania: "Federal Agencies presuppose that employers, be they private or public, have unlimited funds, unlimited power to institute sweeping personnel changes free of union interference, are unconcerned about productivity, and value the rights of the target group in question, whichever it is, above the rights of other employees." In similar responses to other principles in the section 504 regulations, some of those providing comments either misunderstood the boundaries of reasonable accommodation or purposely misstated their impact. A supervisor of a school system in Colorado argued in terms of reasonable accommodation that "the application of this principle is boundless. Financial costs will be exorbitant. It establishes a principle that it is the state's responsibility to provide another person to assist *every* handicapped person in every 'life function' from birth to grave."

On the opposite side of the issue, civil rights and handicapped groups expressed apprehension that the regulations were too lenient. Specifically, they were concerned that the ''undue economic hardship'' limitation on mandated accommodations would impede implementation of employment protections. Reflecting this sentiment, an attorney for the Center for Public Representation argued that ''the 'undue hardship' factors should be eliminated. Recipients may use these provisions to avoid compliance with the Act and cost should *not* be a factor in enforcing civil rights.'' Disability groups argued that the law itself contained no such provision limiting antidiscrimination on a cost basis and thus questioned the inclusion of the undue hardship criterion in the regulations.

Ultimately, HEW held firm in its position. In response to employers, it contended that many types of accommodations would not entail excessive cost, and that, in all cases, the disabled person must be otherwise qualified to perform the job task. While the undue hardship clause remained troublesome to some advocates of strong antidiscrimination measures, HEW reasoned that a balanced approach that kept the cost of accommodations within some reasonable bounds was more likely to be effectively implemented than an approach that was unyielding in consideration of accommodation costs.

This approach implies that determinations of undue economic hardship would be made on the basis of ''we'll know it when we see it.'' What is important to recognize in this regard is that reasonable accommodation requires a matching of individual handicapping conditions with changes in specific employment situations. In no way did the regulations prescribe a clear form of action required of all recipients. The ''individuality'' of remedial action makes enforcement more difficult because determination of compliance must always be made on a case-by-case basis. This is not the situation, as we shall see, with accommodations in public transportation, where more precise actions applicable to all transit conveyances were prescribed.

Section 504 and Accessibility

Another component of section 504 regulations dealt with the accessibility of handicapped individuals to public buildings and other facilities. The rule writers, recognizing that facility access would be controversial because of the substantial costs potentially associated with building restructuring, adopted a second operating principle: *program* accessibility. Rather than stipulate that all buildings be completely accessible, the regulation required that recipients of federal funds operate a program that ''when viewed in its entirety is readily accessible to and useable by handicapped persons''; it goes on to specify that this ''does not require a recipient to make each of its existing facilities or every part of a facility accessible'' to disabled persons.[27] Structural modifications are thus not required if other sorts of accommodations could be made; examples included rescheduling of classes or service delivery to accessible locations, redesign of equipment, and home visits by health care workers. In choosing such strategies, however, recipients were required to give priority to methods that offer programs and services to handicapped persons in the most integrated setting possible. The latter provision reflects the persistent demand by disabled persons that mainstreaming—integrating handicapped and nondisabled persons—be pursued to the fullest extent possible.

The regulations were more stringent in terms of newly constructed buildings financed with federal funds; here buildings were required to be designed and constructed so as to be "readily accessible to and useable by handicapped persons."[28] It was also stipulated that alterations made to existing facilities should include modifications to enhance accessibility by disabled individuals. In both cases, the standards of the American National Standards Institute (ANSI) were specified as standards for achieving accessibility in construction.

The program accessibility criterion for existing buildings was certainly a compromise. It was intended to enhance the accessibility of handicapped individuals and required changes by recipients of federal funds. But at the same time, it fell short of requiring complete accessibility. The accessibility question was clearly one of major concern to public school systems and institutions of higher education, both of whom consistently complained about the high costs of achieving accessibility in educational settings, where most of the physical plant had already been constructed. It is clear from the comments submitted by educational institutions during rulemaking that section 504 was perceived as requiring very extensive and costly modifications of structures. Many of the comments seemed to miss the point that program accessibility provided recipients with means other than structural modification to meet requirements of the section 504 regulations.

The rule writers responded to the concerns of local schools and universities by trying to clarify the extent of mandated compliance activities. The appendix to the regulations discussed the university case in some detail. It stated that universities would be in compliance if they had accessible buildings and were able "to reschedule or relocate enough classes so as to offer all required courses and a reasonable selection of elective courses in these buildings."[29] One has to wonder, however, about what constitutes a "reasonable selection of elective courses"; the rules go no further in spelling out this criterion.

The accessibility rules also stipulated a time period for implementation. Program accessibility was required within sixty days of the effective date of the regulations (June 3, 1977), except where structural changes were needed, in which case a three-year compliance period was mandated.

Section 504 and Education

The next two subparts of the regulations concerned the application of section 504 provisions to education services from preschool through university level. The section 504 regulations for education were developed closely with those relevant to the Education for All Handicapped Children Act passed in 1975. Given the persistent delays in section 504 rule-making, the regulations for both acts were considered simultaneously within HEW, even though section 504 predates the education act by about two years.

The influence of the Education for All Handicapped Children Act (PL94-142) is clear, in that the statutory provisions of the act are reflected in the section 504 regulations. They require, for example, that handicapped children receive a free and appropriate education, to the greatest extent possible, in settings with nondisabled students. These provisions were stipulated in PL94-142, so in this context, the rules mostly mirror the education law itself. This is the one situation where legislative guidelines were available when crafting rules for implementation of antidiscrimination on the basis of handicap. Development and execution of individualized education programs, an important operating principle to guide implementation, are listed as one means of satisfying the "appropriate education" requirement. The rules also require that other nonacademic services, including extracurricular activities and counseling, be provided to handicapped children at a level comparable to services provided to nondisabled students.

The most relevant regulations concerning higher education are the rules concerning program accessibility already discussed. The section 504 regulations also provided discussions of admissions and recruitment policies, academic requirements, provision of auxiliary aid (e.g., braille texts, interpreters), housing, and financial assistance, as they apply to providing persons with disability.

Colleges and universities were the most prolific writers of comments during section 504 rulemaking. Their concerns beyond facility restructuring centered on the costs of providing special education services to disabled students; they objected primarily on the grounds of the costs associated with such services. Typical in this regard was a comment by the dean of students of George Fox College in Oregon:

> When will the government learn that to expand services/dollars to include a newly protected group *without increasing the available pool of dollar resources* is really nothing more than taking from one group in order to provide for another? The idea that colleges and universities can always spend a "little bit more" to add an additional protected class when in fact the pool of available resources is not increased one penny, should be labeled a fiction and destroyed, once and for all.

In the final rules, HEW replied to these cost concerns, arguing that recipients could meet obligations of auxiliary aids by using existing resources, such as those of vocational rehabilitation agencies and charitable organizations.[30]

The HEW Coordination Guidelines

Moving to implement Executive Order 11914, which specifies HEW as the lead agency in coordinating section 504 across the federal government, Secretary Califano issued, in June 1977, proposed rules to be followed by other agencies as they devised their own section 504 regulations.[31] These guidelines, known as "coordinating regulations," echoed HEW's own regulations, using the same definition of "handicapped person" and calling for reasonable accommodation in employment, program accessibility in existing buildings, and ready and usable access to newly constructed facilities. Thirty days were allotted for comments from other federal agencies and the public. Final coordinating regulations were issued by HEW in early 1978.[32] They served to stimulate the rulemaking agendas of other federal agencies and provided guidelines as to the content of regulations to be created by the agencies to implement section 504.

Analysis of Section 504 Rulemaking

The implementation of section 504 lurched forward, slowly and unevenly, during the four-year period of administrative rulemaking. This period was characterized by growing awareness inside and outside of government that this originally little-noticed provision, tacked onto the Rehabilitation Act of 1973, was to have far-reaching impacts on the lives of persons with disabilities and a variety of institutions across the nation. In a clear sense, policymaking regarding nondiscrimination on the basis of handicap was made during rulemaking; seldom has Congress provided so little guidance about policy objectives or strategies for implementation. It was left to the executive branch to set the course for implementation of section 504.

Organizing Principles and Section 504

Several central organizing principles devised by the regulation writers in HEW's OCR set the general direction for policy implementation. Two such principles were considered top priority in laying the fundamental groundwork for translating a symbolic statement of purpose into a workable implementation strategy. These two were the principles of "remedial action" in overcoming discrimination and "balanced competing equities" for fashioning remedies.

As described above, the first principle of "remedial action" indicated that handicapped persons were to be treated differently than other classes protected by civil rights. To overcome discrimination against disabled persons, accommodations to remove obstacles to participation in many spheres of contemporary life were required.

The second fundamental principle organizing implementation strategy was that of "balanced competing equity," the notion that while costs are not relevant to determining discrimination, they may be considered in ascertaining remedies appropriate to overcome discriminatory practices. This approach reflected an awareness on the part of rule drafters that some cost limitation was required in order to avoid "massive resistance" to the regulations. This balancing concept, in turn, lies at the heart of two operating principles. One is the hardship clause used to limit accommodations in employment to those that are "reasonable." The section 504 regulations offered little guidance as to how hardship was to be determined but clearly signaled to employers that there are limits to the extent of modifications they must make. The second operational principle related to cost balancing is program accessibility, which differs from a full-accessibility criterion by requiring that only basic programs or services be made accessible to handicapped persons. This more limited conception of accessibility prevented recipients of federal funds from being required to make all areas in public buildings available to physically disabled persons.

Ultimately, the regulations represented a balance between the competing interests of persons with disabilities and those judged to be discriminating against them. The balance is probably tilted toward handicapped persons, in that section 504 was fashioned largely in a civil rights mold, and because efforts to backtrack on rights are generally much more difficult than retrenchment in other areas of social policy. Still, the rights did not unleash unlimited obligations on the part of those found to be discriminating. Their responsibilities to take affirmative action are limited by economic hardship, program versus full-facility accessibility, and the time periods allowed for meeting compliance with the regulations.

Issue Networks and Section 504

Issue networks played an important role in the development of section 504 regulations. One network developed between the staff at the OCR and the Senate Subcommittee on the Handicapped during the early period of rulemaking.

Both groups were committed to developing a strong antidiscrimination policy to protect handicapped persons. Their initial interaction focused on clearing up some basic ambiguities through enactment of the Rehabilitation Act Amendments of 1974. The network subsequently expanded as the OCR staff entered into informal discussions with contacts in groups representing persons with disabilities. This network shared commitment to strong regulations and communicated information about what was happening at HEW as rulemaking progressed. The interest groups and Congress thus had inside information about rulemaking delays and developed strategies to push HEW from the outside to move forward with issuing regulations. Their strategies focused in the main on keeping the rulemaking for section 504 on the active decision agenda of administrative leaders in HEW.

The regulated clients—universities, public school systems, local and state governments, hospitals, welfare offices, and private and public employers—entered the political fray later than other groups. They were not often consulted by the OCR staff drafting regulations and thus were slower to recognize the potential impact of section 504. With the publication of proposed rules, their attention was quickly garnered. They responded actively through submission of comments during rulemaking, but by this time, the basic parameters of implementation strategies for section 504 had been set.

OCR's Control over Rulemaking

One of the most interesting conclusions about the whole rulemaking saga associated with section 504 is how little the regulations actually changed during the four-year period in which they were devised, debated, revised, and issued. The organizing principles created by the rule writers were set relatively early on and remained basically intact despite many pressures exerted during rulemaking. After recognizing the potential of section 504, groups representing handicapped citizens pushed consistently for the strongest possible rules, while regulated interests pushed in the opposite direction for rules that were less stringent and more flexible. Despite these pressures, HEW rule writers remained firm, although they endeavored to explain their positions in greater detail as rulemaking progressed.

What, then, accounts for the ability of HEW to stick to its own principles in the face of conflicting pressures? Several explanations likely account for this result. First, by the nature of the rulemaking process, administrative agencies retain the upper hand in drafting rules. Substantial thought by policy experts goes into drafting rules, and often informal discussions are pursued with affected interest groups at the same time drafting takes place. These discussions provide useful input and suggest probable areas of conflict and disagreement. By the time rules are published, the agency has substantial commitment to them, especially given agencies' perceptions of their own expertise and the investment they have made to draft the rules.

While public comments are required during rulemaking and agencies are instructed to consider the comments, administrators are by no means required to change rules to conform with opinions and concerns expressed in the comments. As West (1985, 88) argues, the intent of "notice and comment" rulemaking, as prescribed in the Administrative Procedures Act, is to *expose* agencies to relevant views, not necessarily to set the course of rulemaking. Public comments are often perceived by agencies as more important in tightening problem areas than in setting basic directions for policy implementation.

In the case of section 504, regulation writers were also in the unique situation of drafting administrative rules of substantial consequence, which few parties inside or outside of government initially recognized as important. In the early stages, they were able to move relatively freely, since no watchdog groups were closely scrutinizing rulemaking or pushing particular perspectives.[33] This low visibility, coupled with practically no legislative history, gave regulation writers the widest possible ground in crafting guidelines for implementation. They were free in this environment "to follow their professional and political ideologies to craft a very strong regulation" (Scotch 1984, 80).

It is also clear, in retrospect, that the assignment of responsibility for section 504 rules to OCR and thus to a set of individuals ingrained with legal training and commitment to advancing civil rights, had major impact on the drafting of regulations. Very different regulations would have emerged from HEW had rulemaking responsibility been handed to officials who oversee vocational rehabilitation services. Their perspectives and experiences were different, and it seems unlikely that such rights-oriented rules would have emerged from offices more attuned to service delivery.

The concern of Congress at this point was primarily to prod the executive branch to fulfill its overdue responsibility for issuing the regulations. The key legislators who were involved in handicapped issues grew more and more frustrated with HEW's procrastination in promulgating regulations. The battle on this front therefore rested more on getting the rules published than on their content. Congress too was under growing pressure from handicapped groups to push for action from the executive branch.

Once the basic approach to the section 504 regulations had been set by OCR, it was hard for opponents to throw them offtrack. It was difficult to argue against eliminating discrimination against handicapped persons, who, most participants realized, had been denied participation in many facets of economic and social life. Thus those advocating strong rights protections for mentally and physically disabled persons had "moral prestige" as an asset in their cause (Rabkin 1980, 335). Especially before the less popular issue of compliance costs became evident, one would have been hard-pressed to mount an effort against strong guidelines. By the time cost issues arose, the basic groundwork had been set, and derailment would have been far more difficult.

The ability of HEW to press forward with its preset organizing and operating principles, therefore, is explained by a constellation of factors that is somewhat unique. With little public visibility and no legislative history, the regulation drafters, already of a strong civil rights mold, had relative freedom in determining guidelines for implementation. They could stick to their guns during rulemaking because they were more immune to political pressures than the legislative branch and could indirectly appeal to the moral prestige of aiding handicapped citizens. This immunity to political pressures was in no way permanent, however. Regulated interests, who remained concerned about bearing the costs of accommodations, did not give up upon issuance of the regulations but, instead, moved, as we shall see, to other institutional arenas to press their case. Both Congress and the courts would be called upon as a means to challenge section 504 regulations. But for the moment, in the spring of 1977, when final regulations were issued, the staff at HEW, with the help of interest groups supporting disabled Americans, proved capable of designing and issuing a strong set of antidiscrimination regulations that would ultimately change the way the nation views and treats its disabled citizens.

5

A Conservative Reaction to Section 504 Regulations

The Politics of Rollback

No sooner were the administrative regulations for section 504 issued in final form in 1977, than Congress, in reauthorizing the Rehabilitation Act, enacted legislative changes affecting the section's scope and implementation. With these legislative modifications, the political scene remained quiet until the Reagan administration assumed office in January 1981. At this time, section 504 was identified by a vice presidential task force on regulatory relief as a prime target for reexamination, with an eye toward reducing federal influences upon the operation of state and local governments.

The change of presidential administration prompted a change in the policy environment regarding federal regulatory activity, providing an opportunity for regulated clients and their contacts in the new administration to pursue a campaign to roll back the impact of federal regulations. The campaign for "regulatory relief" was waged in several institutional arenas and included an initiative to redirect policies to implement section 504 and, as described in later chapters, in other areas of handicapped rights policies.

The predominant arenas used to pursue regulatory relief were the executive agencies, where major efforts to revise administrative regulations were undertaken. The process of reexamining and redrafting regulations for section 504 took place during the first two years of the Reagan administration, generating strong lobbying efforts on the parts of groups representing disabled citizens. After protracted negotiations, political fallout, and numerous redrafting efforts, the proposed regulatory revisions were abandoned, leaving the original coordination regulations that had been drafted by the Department of Health, Education, and Welfare (HEW) intact. Also during this period, the courts began to issue decisions reflecting judicial interpretation of the scope of accommodations mandated by section 504, with these decisions subsequently affecting implementation practices.

Legislative Changes to Section 504

The year following the publication of HEW's final rules for section 504, Congress considered legislation to reauthorize the Rehabilitation Act. As part of this legislation, the Comprehensive Rehabilitation Services Amendments of 1978 (PL95-602), the only change to date in the language of section 504 was made. Also included were amendments relevant to the definition of persons protected under the act and the award of attorneys' fees to parties taking legal action under the handicapped rights provisions of the act.

The House version of 1978 legislation reauthorizing the Rehabilitation Act expanded the wording of section 504 to include the agencies of the federal government. The Rehabilitation Act of 1973 did not include language clearly placing the federal government under section 504; given ambiguity about coverage, HEW, in 1977, requested the Department of Justice (DOJ) to rule on the applicability of section 504 to federal agencies. In September 1977, DOJ ruled that, according to the statute, section 504 applied to recipients of federal funds but not to the programs conducted directly by federal agencies. While the failure to include federal agencies under the nondiscrimination provisions of section 504 was basically an oversight, the federal government was assailed for what was seen as a hypocritical stance. The bill, therefore, directly included federal agencies under the section 504 rubric and specified that these agencies develop regulations to implement section 504 in programs they themselves conduct. The Senate agreed to these legislative changes in conference committee.

The 1978 legislation also included an alteration in the definition of "handicapped person" for the purposes of sections 503 (the affirmative action requirement for those who contract with the federal government) and 504. The definitional change concerned drug addicts and alcoholics, a class of disabled persons whose coverage under section 504 had generated controversy during the drafting of administrative regulations. As described in the previous chapter, HEW's Office of Civil Rights included drug addicts and alcoholics under the provisions of section 504 after receiving an interpretation from the attorney general that these individuals suffered a handicap and could not be omitted from antidiscrimination protections. Worries about protections being afforded to drug users and alcoholics remained after the final regulations were issued, especially among employers. Representative of their concerns was a statement by the Air Transport Association made at hearings on the Rehabilitation Act held by the Senate Subcommittee on the Handicapped: "The airline industry does not believe that Congress intended the law to require affirmative action in recruitment and advancement in employment of persons in an active state of alcoholism or drug addiction."[1]

Congress responded in 1978 by amending the law so that, for the purpose of employment, sections 503 and 504 were not applicable to those individuals whose drug or alcohol use prevents performance of work requirements or constitutes a direct threat to the property or safety of others. This provision originated in the House Committee on Education and Labor, where Representative John Erlenhorn (R-IL) added wording to the rehabilitation bill to restrict protection of drug users and addicts. While the amendment made no direct reference to employment, the committee report stated that the restriction was intended primarily to protect employers.[2] When the House bill was considered on the Senate floor, concerns were expressed by Harrison Williams (D-NJ) that this class of handicapped individuals would be denied protections against discrimination in health and social services.[3] The Senate adopted a compromise amendment whereby protections were denied to drug addicts and alcoholics in employment when their condition rendered them unable to perform ''essential job functions.'' In conference committee, the House accepted the Senate's approach.[4]

Another important change contained in the 1978 amendments was inclusion of a new section, 505, which provided that the remedies, procedures, and rights set forth in Title IV of the Civil Rights Act of 1964 be available to those seeking redress for discrimination under section 504. Through this measure, persons with disabilities were given a private right of action to pursue legal remedies to suspected discrimination on the basis of handicap. This addition to the Rehabilitation Act clarified the legal procedures appropriate for enforcing section 504 and forged closer linkage of handicapped rights legislation to other civil rights laws. Section 505 also stipulated that courts may award to prevailing parties, other than the government, reasonable attorney's fees. The provision of these fees, added by Congress in response to interest group concerns, was seen as enhancing the ability of aggrieved parties, particularly poorer ones, to seek legal redress for violation of the nondiscrimination provisions of section 504.

Other Developments during the Carter Administration

During the time that Congress was reviewing its authorization of the vocational rehabilitation program, HEW was initiating programs to educate handicapped citizens about the rights and protections afforded by section 504. The department developed and awarded grants for the development of educational materials and seminars for instruction on the meaning and implications of section 504. Contractors in this program included the Berkeley Center for Independent Living, the Disability Rights Education and Defense Fund (DREDF), the Public Interest Law Center of Philadelphia, and Barrier Free Environments of Raleigh, North Carolina. The effect of this program was to increase the awareness of persons with disabilities across the nation of the protections afforded by section 504 in education, facility accessibility, public transportation, employment, and other areas. The instruction they received through the program worked to enable persons with disabilities to monitor and participate in compliance efforts.

Another important consequence of the training programs was the development of a network among the organizations conducting the section 504 outreach program and local agencies and disabled persons across the nation. For example, DREDF developed a network of individuals and groups with whom they had worked during training and information sessions.[5] This network, newly educated on the extent and nature of protections afforded by federal law, would prove an important political force as the Reagan administration moved to eliminate or restrict federal programs assisting disabled Americans.

Other developments during the Carter administration ultimately affected the implementation of section 504. In 1979, Congress passed legislation to create a new Department of Education (DOE) by separating educational programs and offices out of HEW and other agencies and placing them in a new department. Creating the DOE had been a long-standing objective of President Carter, who perceived a need for a cabinet-level department to deal with federal education programs.

Administration of the rehabilitation program was shifted to the new DOE, while lead-agency responsibility for coordinating section 504 regulations was retained by the new Department of Health and Human Services (HHS). Soon afterward, however, President Carter, by Executive Order 12250, transferred lead-agency responsibility for section 504 to DOJ.[6] The rationale for this move of coordinating responsibility was to place authority for implementing section 504 in the agency responsible for other civil rights laws. Disability interest groups generally applauded this action, which they felt emphasized the rights nature of section 504 and its relation to other civil rights laws.

An Important Supreme Court Decision on Section 504

The first major case to examine section 504 and its provisions for reasonable accommodation in education was *Southeastern Community College v. Davis*.[7] This case centered on a hearing-impaired licensed practical nurse who sought admission to a nursing program provided by Southeastern Community College. Davis's admission was denied on the basis that she could not successfully complete the nursing program, which included both academic and supervised clinical work, because of her hearing impairment. The school claimed that the only means for Davis to satisfactorily complete the clinical component of the program would be to substantially modify the program or lower its standards. Davis sued the school in federal court, contending that her denial of admission violated the nondiscrimination protections afforded by section 504. The case worked its way through the federal courts, with HEW's regulations for section 504 being published during judicial consideration.

The *Davis* case reached the Supreme Court in 1979 and received widespread attention, since it was the first ruling of the nation's highest court on section 504. The Court examined the history and structure of Southeastern's nursing program and found that the type of modification sought by Davis in order to pursue the nursing program—individual faculty supervision—went beyond the reasonable accommodation mandate of section 504, as articulated in HEW regulations. The Court noted the language of the regulations, which state that, while auxiliary aids may be required, "recipients need not provide attendants, individually prescribed devices, or readers for personal use or study."[8] From the Court's view, individualized faculty supervision was analogous to affirmative action; it argued that there was no language in section 504 or its regulations to support affirmative action type remedies.

Without the provision of individual supervision, the Court argued that the respondent could not satisfactorily complete the requirements of the college's nursing program. While she could successfully undertake academic work, she would be unable to complete the clinical requirement. "Whatever the benefits respondent might realize from such a course of study, she would not receive even a rough equivalent of the training a nursing program normally gives."[9] And in wording that would later take on importance, the Court opinion held that "such a fundamental alteration in the nature of a program is far more than the 'modification' the regulation requires."[10]

Finally, the Court acknowledged that it may be difficult to clearly demarcate the point where failure to accommodate is legal under the law and where it becomes discrimination: "We do not suggest that the line between a lawful refusal to extend affirmative action and illegal discrimination will always be clear."[11] The Court threw this difficult determination back to the executive branch, stating that "identification of those instances where a refusal to accommodate the needs of a disabled person amounts to discrimination against the handicapped continues to be an important responsibility of HEW."[12]

Legal analysts continue to debate the long-term impact of the *Davis* decision.[13] On the one hand, the Court's decision and analysis suggest an individualized approach to determining the presence of discrimination and the extent of requisite accommodations (Bell and Burgdorf 1983, 111). The *Davis* decision was reached primarily on the basis of the specific elements of the Southeastern nursing program, and hence its impact on other situations is not immediately clear. At the same time, the Court ruling reaffirmed the notion that there are limits to the extent of accommodations that must be made for disabled persons; if an educational system can show that an accommodation negatively effects its standards or ''fundamentally alters'' the program, then *Davis* would suggest that reasonable accommodations need not be made.

Reagan, Regulatory Relief, and Section 504

Very early in the Reagan administration, it was made clear that one important initiative to be aggressively pursued was a systematic review of federal regulations. The deregulation effort was centered in a Task Force on Regulatory Relief, chaired by Vice President George Bush. This task force, from its start, developed close connections with the Office of Management and Budget (OMB) and accepted OMB's list of regulations for review. The OMB list included section 504, which was seen by the administration as prescribing an expansive responsibility on state and local education agencies. Handicapped regulations concerning public transportation and architectural barriers were also targeted by the task force, as well as other regulations concerning environmental protection, occupational safety, and many others.[14]

The Reagan administration carried forward its deregulation plan as it began, in 1981, drafting new coordination guidelines for federal agencies to follow in designing their regulations for implementing section 504. At this point, the coordination regulations devised by HEW, and released in 1978, remained in force, although responsibility for coordination had been transferred to DOJ. Given its responsibility for coordination, DOJ took the lead role in rulemaking efforts to revise section 504 regulations so as to provide regulatory relief to recipients of federal funds. Simultaneously, as DOJ undertook regulation redrafting, OMB also engaged in rule writing. While not specifically charged with this responsibility, OMB's regulation drafting activities resulted from the regulatory reform ethos of agency leaders and Executive Order 12291, which authorized OMB to perform a cost-benefit review of all proposed regulations.

Controversy and political battle surrounded these regulation drafting efforts, despite the fact that the administration never moved so far as to publish a notice of proposed rulemaking. Instead, the drafting and redrafting took place internally, as interest groups, who became aware of each draft, pressed the administration for changes and as executive agencies scrutinzed the implication of successive drafts. One central actor in this process was the Disability Rights Education and Defense Fund, an outgrowth of the independent living movement in California. Because it sensed the Reagan administration was moving forward with an effort to roll back both laws and regulations that protected handicapped persons against discrimination, DREDF decided to open a Washington office in 1981. Soon afterward, DREDF organized a meeting of key interest groups concerned with disability policy, including the Paralyzed Veterans of America and the National Center for the Deaf. At this meeting, the more established groups agreed to let DREDF undertake oversight and lobbying on behalf of section 504; these groups were, at the time, fighting against budget cuts in their ''own'' disability programs.

In late 1981 and early 1982, drafts of new coordination regulations for implementing section 504, written both by DOJ and OMB, were circulated within federal agencies for comment. It did not take long for these drafts to be leaked to the relevant interest groups and the press. Throughout 1982, DOJ continued to redraft the section 504 regulations while it continued discussions with DREDF and other interest groups.

The Congressional Research Service performed a legal analysis of early proposed changes in section 504 regulations drafted by OMB and DOJ (Jones 1982).[15] By contrasting the OMB and DOJ drafts with the coordination regulations promulgated by HEW in 1978, the magnitude and direction of regulatory changes being proposed by the Reagan administration can be illustrated. Generally, the section 504 drafts prepared by DOJ and OMB represented a constriction of regulatory requirements, compared to the original HEW rules. Furthermore, careful analysis indicates that the OMB rules weakened regulatory provision more than the approach presented in the regulations drafted by DOJ.

The imposition of a new organizing principle, cost-benefit analysis, was the primary means by which both the OMB and DOJ regulations sought to lessen nondiscrimination requirements related to handicapped persons. The origin of this cost-benefit principle is attributed to Executive Order 12291, issued with the intent ''to reduce the burdens of existing and future regulations, increase agency accountability for regulatory actions, provide for presidential oversight of the regulatory process, minimize duplication and conflict of regulations, and insure well-reasoned regulations.''[16] The cost-benefit principle was articulated as follows: ''Regulatory action shall not be undertaken unless the potential benefits to society for the regulation outweigh the potential costs to society.''[17] Implementation of the cost-benefit objective was, according to the executive order, to be performed in a two-pronged approach, first by each agency through a Regulatory Impact Analysis and subsequently by a task force within OMB.[18]

Prohibitions against Discrimination

The original section 504 coordination regulations, as promulgated and issued by HEW, provided that ''no qualified handicapped person shall, on the basis of handicap, be excluded from participation in, be denied the benefits of, or be otherwise subjected to discrimination under any program or activity that receives or benefits from federal financial assistance.''[19] After this general declaration, the HEW regulations proceed to describe several types of discriminatory actions that are prohibited, including a less effective provision of services to handicapped persons than for other citizens.

The DOJ draft regulations roughly parallel the HEW ones, except that the phrase ''or benefits from'' is deleted. This three-word deletion is very significant, because it would restrict the range of programs affected by the regulations to only those units that *directly* receive federal aid. The DOJ regulations also deleted several of the specific types of discriminatory actions that are prohibited. OMB's discussion of prohibited actions is even shorter than the one proposed by DOJ and lists few activities that are clearly prohibited.

Another change proposed by DOJ was to delete from the HEW regulations the provision that recipients may not perpetuate discrimination against handicapped persons by giving ''significant assistance'' to any person, agency, or organization that discriminates on the basis of handicap.[20] While other provisions prohibit recipients from engaging in contracts, licensing, or other arrangements that discriminate against persons with disabilities, the significant assistance language was aimed at preventing discrimination being fostered through less formal relationships between recipients of federal aid and other firms and organizations. Deletion of this principle tended to restrict the reach of the antidiscrimination provision in relationships such as those between a school and the employees engaged in internship programs sponsored by the school.

Still another deletion of language from the HEW regulations in the DOJ draft concerned actions that have ''the effect of'' discriminating against disabled persons. The HEW rules forbid actions that have the effect of discrimination, as well as those purposefully intended to discriminate. The DOJ rules, moving to narrow the breadth of section 504's impact, removed the ''effects'' language. The narrowing of interpretation was consistent with the approach of the Reagan administration in other civil rights areas.

Definition of ''Qualified Handicapped Person''

An important component of any set of regulations for implementing section 504 protections is that defining which persons are afforded protections under the law. One key definition concerns ''qualified handicapped person.'' The HEW regulations defined such a person as one who (1) with respect to employment, can perform the essential functions of the job in question, and (2) with regard to services, meets the essential eligibility requirements for the receipt of such services.[21]

The DOJ draft regulations kept these provisions and added two more, one regarding education and the other regarding programs that have requirements concerning academic standards or levels of accomplishment. With regard to education, the DOJ rules stated that a qualified handicapped person is one who is of an age (1) during which nonhandicapped persons are provided services and (2) during which education is mandatory under state law. In terms of other programs that have requirements concerning academic performance or levels of accomplishment, a qualified handicapped person is one who meets ''essential program requirements'' and can achieve ''the purpose of the program.'' This language reflects wording from the *Davis* decision, which stated that recipients must be able to meet basic program requirements to be eligible for section 504 protections.

The regulations proposed by OMB were briefer than the HEW and DOJ rules and have no reference to employment or education. This version stated that a qualified handicapped person is one who, in spite of his or her handicap, (1) meets the essential eligibility requirements, if any, for participation in the covered program and (2) is able, given reasonable accommodation on the part of the recipient, to realize the benefits of, or to perform the functions required by, participation in the covered program or activity.

Reasonable Accommodation

The concept of reasonable accommodation, while not clearly defined and applied only to employment, is a primary operating principle in the HEW regulations.[22] It acknowledges that eliminating discrimination against handicapped persons may require positive action or compensation to place these individuals on equal footing with other citizens. The DOJ regulations provide a definition of reasonable accommodation as ''steps taken by a recipient to enable handicapped persons to perform the essential functions of a job or service or achieve the purpose of a program under which a beneficiary is required to meet academic standards or to achieve a level of accomplishment.'' After giving some examples of reasonable accommodation, the DOJ regulations caution that it does not require modifications in the fundamental nature of the program or steps that would impose an undue hardship on a recipient or beneficiary.

In the DOJ draft regulations concerning reasonable accommodation, we see both the language of the *Davis* decision and the emphasis on a cost-benefit approach. Echoing the language of *Davis*, the DOJ draft stated that section 504 did not require the alteration of fundamental program requirements or the lowering of academic standards. Retention of the undue hardship principle was consistent with the administration's effort to emphasize cost-benefit analysis in federal regulations.

The DOJ regulations also contained a section applying reasonable accommodation beyond employment. The same language as the HEW rules is used, except that the clause limiting accommodations to those that do not impose undue hardship is deleted. In the place of this clause, the DOJ regulations stated that recipients will be deemed to have made reasonable accommodation if, in good faith, they (1) have provided an opportunity to object to the requirements and practices and to propose reasonable accommodations, (2) have notified other persons of such objections or proposals and provided opportunity to comment, and (3) have made, taking the standards of the regulations into account, a written determination, accepting, rejecting, or modifying the objections and proposals and then have taken steps consistent with the regulations. Thus, a process for compliance is laid out, and if the process is adhered to, the recipient may be able to avoid rendering accommodations.

As with other areas, the OMB draft regulations went even further in limiting required accommodations by recipients of federal assistance. OMB's regulations deleted any reference to employment in defining reasonable accommodation, thus spreading the undue hardship principle more broadly to other service areas. This version also added several considerations that recipients might use in determining when accommodations would pose undue costs or burdens. Among these considerations were "competing demands for scarce resources" and the value of the accommodation to the handicapped person and society. In another section, OMB's version states that accommodations are not required if they impose "unreasonable burdens on beneficiaries."

Without question, the DOJ and OMB proposed revisions in the section 504 regulations represent a constriction of reasonable accommodation provisions. The DOJ rules at first glance appear to expand protections by applying reasonable accommodation to areas beyond employment. Yet while "this approach allows for flexibility in determining reasonable accommodation on a case by case basis, it does not take into consideration the fact that, although a decision may be made in good faith, it may well be based on invalid premises that render it discriminatory" (Jones 1982, 11). The OMB approach guts reasonable accommodation even further, allowing costs and burdens of others to be figured into calculations to determine when accommodations are required. The number of limitations on reasonable accommodations, in both versions, suggest that recipients of federal funds would have multiple means to avoid compliance with the nondiscrimination protections of section 504.

Requirements for Accessibility

The original HEW regulations for section 504 outlined a two-part strategy for removing physical barriers for handicapped persons. For existing facilities, the regulations put forth the principle of program accessibility, requiring that programs, when viewed in their entirety, be accessible to handicapped persons.[23] For new facilities, the regulations required that building designs incorporate accessibility standards as described by the American National Standards Institute (ANSI).[24]

The regulations proposed by DOJ incorporate the program accessibility concept as the primary responsibility of recipients for existing facilities. This version added a section on historic preservation programs and provides for waivers for accessibility in some historic buildings and landmarks. For new construction, the DOJ draft regulations stipulated that such construction must conform with accessibility standards. However, exceptions to this rule are allowed in circumstances where (1) bids for construction were received before the effective date of the regulations, (2) construction or alteration is done to a building that does not need to be accessible to the physically handicapped because of its intended use, and (3) alterations are structurally impracticable. These exceptions weakened the regulations, as compared to their original version, by expanding circumstances under which accessibility standards can be waived. The DOJ regulations did add sections providing for coordination with the Architectural and Transportation Barriers Compliance Board (ATBCB).

The regulations posed by OMB regarding accessibility were far weaker than those offered by DOJ. The OMB rules dropped sections relating to program accessibility as ''unnecessarily prescriptive'' and the section on ATBCB for its ''attempts to lock the Administration into the continued existence'' of the board.[25] With regard to existing structures, the OMB regulations indicate that recipients will be in compliance if they conform with the retrofitting guidelines contained in the Uniform Accessibility Standards.[26] These standards were, at this point, being designed as a guide to accessibility by the four federal agencies heavily involved with facilities and property: the Department of Housing and Urban Development, the Department of Defense, the General Services Administration, and the Postal Service.

Education and Transportation Services

The DOJ proposals for regulatory reform included sections on education and transportation.[27] While there are many similarities between the DOE rules for enforcing section 504 (drafted by HEW in 1978) and those drafted by DOJ in its interagency coordinating role, there are also some differences. For one thing, the DOJ version included a new section related to cost-benefit calculations, namely that when more than one appropriate method is available to achieve the free and appropriate education requirement, then recipients must select the least burdensome method consistent with their obligation to educate in the most integrated setting possible. The education section of the DOJ rules also dropped the requirement for a due process hearing when parents or others wish to challenge the educational plans developed for handicapped children.

It should be noted that DOE was, during 1982, reconsidering a revision of its regulations for implementation for the Education for All Handicapped Children Act (PL94-142). As will be described in chapter eight, section 504 and PL94-142 served as a joint and reinforcing mandate, requiring local school systems to provide a free and appropriate education to handicapped children. Groups representing disabled children feared that a weakening of section 504 regulations would allow DOE to more easily weaken its rules for implementing PL94-142. Hence, the importance, in their view, of maintaining strong standards in section 504 coordination regulations related to education.

In terms of transportation, the regulations proposed by DOJ reflected recent developments in the transportation field related to section 504. The HEW coordination rules included strong accessibility language, which was subsequently reflected in the Department of Transportation's (DOT's) section 504 regulations mandating accessibility in all modes of public transportation. This full-accessibility position was challenged in the courts in the case of *American Public Transit Association v. Lewis*, in which the federal courts eventually ruled that the DOT accessibility rules exceeded statutory authority. In response, DOT issued a new set of regulations, requiring only that local transit systems provide ''special efforts'' to serve handicapped persons.

The DOJ regulations proposed in 1982 went further than DOT's ''special efforts'' ones, requiring that transit services to disabled persons be ''as effective as'' those provided to other users. Comparative effectiveness was to be determined in reference to geographic area and hours of operation, fares, restrictions on trip use, and response time. With this comparative effectiveness position, DOJ moved to clarify and, to a degree, strengthen the accommodation mandate in public tranportation. At the same time, this position was more lenient than the full-accessibility approach initially undertaken by DOT under the Carter administration.

Overview of Changes Proposed by DOJ and OMB

It should be clear that the OMB rules represented a significant pullback from the section 504 regulations in place in 1982. The DOJ rules, while not as drastic as the OMB ones, still represented a much looser set of requirements for compliance with the nondiscrimination mandate. The constriction of requirements was based upon two approaches. One was the incorporation of language from the *Davis* decision, which the administration perceived as limiting the reach of section 504 protections. Wording to the effect that accommodations do not require a lowering of standards or modification of fundamental program requirements has its origins in the *Davis* decision. The other justification for reduced regulatory power was based upon the cost-benefit principle, which generally works to waive compliance efforts where benefits are perceived to exceed costs.

The Politics of Regulatory Reform

One may ponder why the Reagan administration moved forward with an initiative to constrict the impact of section 504 and, as we shall see in later chapters, other handicapped rights programs. Generally, these initiatives were based more upon the premise that the federal government had gone too far in directing the actions of state and local governments, than on any ill feeling against handicapped persons. Many of the persons in DOJ and OMB who participated in drafting rules were young lawyers, strongly conservative in their convictions, yet inexperienced in disability policy.

It also seems clear, in retrospect, that the administration underestimated the political strength of interest groups and issue networks related to disability policy. Certainly, the history of strong handicapped groups that focused on rights issues was far shorter than that of other civil rights groups, such as those representing blacks and women. Still, the passage of section 504 had awakened many hearts and minds and, at the same time, encouraged a strong new political force. While the administration may have felt that it was easier to roll back handicapped rights than other civil rights, this proved to be a false assumption. Handicapped groups were growing and coalescing and were able to generate political support on their own behalf. They also had strong moral suasion on their side.

It comes as no surprise that groups representing handicapped Americans were none too pleased with efforts at regulatory reform. With the blessing of other interest groups, DREDF took the lead in challenging the Reagan administration on its effort to weaken section 504 protections. With each successive draft of the regulations, and many followed the ones described above, DREDF requested meetings with William Bradford Reynolds at DOJ and C. Boyden Gray of the Task Force on Regulatory Relief.[28] The position of DREDF and other interest groups was that no change should be made in the section 504 regulations; while they recognized that beneficial changes might be made, they felt that opening the door to regulatory changes would offer an opportunity for the Reagan administration to weaken the regulations.

During meetings between various administration officials and DREDF, discussions ensued regarding the regulatory changes. DREDF used a two-pronged approach that emphasized legal analysis of the regulatory changes on the one hand and the implicit threat of political protest on the other. The administration became aware of DREDF's network of disabled people around the nation, and by 1982, efforts on other fronts to reduce federal regulations pertaining to handicapped persons were producing a major political liability.

Under protracted pressure, and sensing that the fallout was greater than potential benefits, the administration eventually abandoned its efforts to reform the coordination regulations for section 504 in early 1983. In a letter addressed to DREDF, dated March 21, 1983, Vice President Bush informed the group that the Task Force on Regulatory Relief, the umbrella for regulatory reform, had concluded its review of section 504 coordination regulations and had decided not to undertake any revisions. This decision was explained as follows:

> A full evaluation of all the information brought to bear on this subject prompted the conclusion that extensive change of the existing section 504 coordination regulations was not required, and that with respect to those few areas where clarification might be desirable, the courts are currently providing useful guidance and can be expected to continue to do so in the future. In these circumstances, the Administration has decided not to proceed with its planned issuance of a revised set of proposed coordination regulations.[29]

While acknowledging that the administration had lengthy discussions with handicapped groups and with Congress, the letter did not note the role that political pressures had played in the administration decision. Given extensive political flack and checks from the legislative branch, the administration decided to rely on another institutional arena, the federal courts, as a means to constrict the reach of section 504. This was not altogether an unpromising strategy for the administration, considering the generally conservative and restrictive nature of decisions by the federal courts in regard to section 504.

The "Federally Conducted" Regulations

In the spring of 1983, DOJ, in its position as lead agency for coordinating section 504 implementation, undertook rulemaking efforts. The purpose of the rulemaking was to create coordinating regulations for federal agencies to follow in designing section 504 regulations to cover programs operated by the agencies themselves. While the proposed coordination regulations for federally conducted activities paralleled those for recipients of federal financial assistance, there were substantial differences between the two. The regulations proposed by DOJ for the federal government itself were weaker in several regards than those imposed on recipients. When DOJ distributed drafts of the federally conducted rules on April 15, the brief euphoria of disability groups over their victory in retaining the 1978 regulations for federal recipients was ended. Once again, they saw an effort by the Reagan administration to roll back the protections afforded by section 504—this time in rules governing programs conducted by the federal government itself (Stanfield 1983; Buress 1983).

Disability groups reacted quickly once they became aware of the content of the federally conducted rules, spreading the word through their network of contacts. Once again, DREDF requested meetings with William Bradford Reynolds and the rule drafters at DOJ; again they reiterated their concerns about any effort to lessen the impact of nondiscrimination regulations.

After about six months of regulation drafting and redrafting, review by executive agencies, and discussions with disability groups, DOJ issued a notice of proposed rulemaking for federally conducted activities.[30] The key components of these regulations concerned the definition of persons protected against nondiscrimination, employment, and facility accessibility. Despite some revisions during preliminary regulation drafting, the rules outlined in the notice of proposed rulemaking were, in certain areas, less stringent than those in effect for recipients of federal financial assistance.

The definition of "qualified handicapped person" in the proposed rules differed from the existing definition in the recipient rules. The proposed definition read: "With respect to any program or activity under which a person is required to perform services or to achieve a level of accomplishment, a handicapped person is one who meets the essential eligibility requirements and who can achieve the purpose of the program or activity without modifications in the program or activity that would result in a fundamental alteration in its nature."[31] In discussing the definition, the rules noted that it reflects the language of the Supreme Court in the *Davis* decision. The commentary stated that while the definition "allows exclusion of some handicapped people from some programs, it requires that a handicapped person who is capable of achieving the purpose of the program must be accommodated, provided that the modifications do not fundamentally alter the nature of the program."[32] In this way, the proposed rules added a new limitation on requisite accommodation of handicapped persons, the "fundamental alteration" rule.

For the employment section, the proposed rules contained a broad statement of nondiscrimination against handicapped persons in employment and then stated that the definitions, requirements, and procedures of section 501 of the Rehabilitation Act of 1973 apply to federally conducted programs. Section 501 stipulated that federal agencies take action to employ persons with disabilities. The administration of this section was placed upon an Interagency Committee on the Handicapped in consultation with the Civil Service Commission. Not included in the proposed rules was the organizing principle of reasonable accommodation that was included in the 504 regulations for federal grant recipients.

The regulations proposed by DOJ also included sections on accessibility. The principle of program accessibility was included in the proposed federally conducted rules, although qualifiers were added so that it (1) does not necessarily require the agency to make each of its existing facilities accessible to handicapped individuals or (2) does not require the agency to take any action that "it can demonstrate would result in a fundamental alteration in the nature of a program or activity or in undue financial and administrative burdens."[33] Unlike the rules for program beneficiaries, which place no limits on mandated accessibility (except those entailed in the program accessibility concept), the proposed rules added two limits, again based on the language and reasoning of the *Davis* decision. Federal agencies are not required to undertake accessibility modifications if those changes represent a "fundamental alteration" in the program or present an undue financial burden.

As expected, the proposed rules generated substantial reaction, especially from the handicapped community. In March 1984, DOJ published a supplemental notice in the *Federal Register* in reaction to the initial comments it received in response to its notice of proposed rulemaking.[34] The notice indicated that DOJ was inclined to make some changes on the basis of public comments. One of the proposed changes concerned the meaning of the "undue financial and administrative burden" provision, which DOJ agreed to clarify by adding wording to the effect that, given the extensive resources and capabilities of federal agencies, compliance in most cases would not result in undue financial and administrative burdens.[35] The supplemental notice also proposed that the burden of proof for determination of "undue financial or administrative burden" and "alteration of fundamental programs" be the responsibility of executive agencies, not handicapped persons.

The department issued the "federally conducted" regulations in final form in September 1984. The tone of the commentary presented with the regulations seems defensive in nature, which is not surprising in light of the three years of heated political battles that took place between the administration and interest groups. Although DOJ admitted that 902 of the comments received during the comment period argued that section 504 rules for federally conducted programs should be identical to those for recipients of federal financial assistance, the department stuck to its line that modifications in the new rules were justified according to the *Davis* and other recent court decisions.[36]

In the commentary, DOJ also responded to comments noting that the department had not adjusted its rules for recipients of federal funds in light of the *Davis* decision and, hence, had no reason to create different rules for federally conducted programs. In an interesting response, the commentary noted that DOJ "has interpreted its section 504 regulation for federally assisted programs in a manner consistent with this final rule. The Department believes that judicial interpretation of section 504 compels it to incorporate the new language in the federally conducted regulation." The commentary indicated that DOJ, while not admitting that it had tried and failed to modify the federally assisted regulations, was interpreting the federally assisted regulations in a manner congruent with the *Davis* decision.

There is extensive discussion of the "qualified handicapped person" definition, where DOJ reiterated the correctness of its reliance on *Davis*. The sections on employment, which simply referenced the rules and procedures of section 501, were defended in the final rules (as in the proposed ones) on the basis of the court decision in *Prewitt v. United States Postal Service*.[37] In terms of accessibility, the final regulations remain basically the same as proposed, except that the burden for demonstrating that compliance creates financial burden or fundamental alterations is clearly placed upon the executive agency.

Controversy over Section 504 Enforcement

During the first four years of the Reagan administration, political debate surrounded not only the efforts at regulatory reform, but also the actions of DOJ in enforcing section 504. Much of the controversy centered on William Bradford Reynolds, who headed the agency's Civil Rights Division. Dissatisfaction with enforcement was expressed in 1982 during hearings conducted by the House Subcommittee on Civil and Constitutional Rights. Concerns about section 504 implementation by DOJ were articulated at the hearing by Robert Funk of DREDF, who represented the American Coalition of Citizens with Disabilities. After reviewing the history of section 504, Funk contended: "Since the present [Reagan] Administration has taken office, Section 504 and its implementing regulations have been the subject of relentless attack that may undermine the meaningful civil rights protections it has begun to offer to disabled people."[38] Similar complaints were voiced at the hearing by representatives of interest groups concerned about discrimination against minorities and women. The common argument was that the Civil Rights Division was reluctant, under the Reagan administration, to maintain the aggressive enforcement position adopted by the Carter administration.

Appearing before the subcommittee, Reynolds defended DOJ's record in enforcing civil rights: "With regard to our enforcement activity of the past year, I would disagree with any of those that would characterize it as having been nonvigorous."[39] After reviewing cases initiated by the department, Reynolds contended: "This level of activity exceeds the track record of prior administrations.[40]

Concerns about the civil rights enforcement of DOJ were raised again in two separate hearings in 1983. One was held by the Subcommittee on Civil and Constitutional Rights of the House Judiciary Committee.[41] Tempers ran high at these hearings, as representatives of civil rights groups chastised the Reagan administration for its record on implementing civil rights protections. The general counsel of the National Association for the Advancement of Colored People went so far as to ask Congress to abolish the Civil Rights Division in DOJ, recommending that the division's funds be distributed to civil rights offices in other agencies because "the Department of Justice has become a department of injustice as it relates to victims of discrimination."[42] With regard to section 504, a representative of DREDF argued that Reynolds, as head of the Civil Rights Division, had adopted an unnecessarily narrow interpretation of the rights of the handicapped.[43]

Another hearing in 1983, held by the Subcommittee on the Handicapped, was prompted, in part, by a news report broadcast on a Washington, D.C., television station. The report focused on several lawyers who had left DOJ because of their concerns that the agency was not following its legal mandate to enforce civil rights.[44] The news story included a report about Timothy Cook, a disabled attorney who had resigned that day from the Department of Justice because, in his words, "the current leadership of the civil rights division is not truly adequately representing the American public in this regard. Congress passed these laws with the expectation that they would be forcefully and aggressively enforced. That's not being done."[45] He went on to add colorfully that "having the president appoint someone like Reynolds to the head of the civil rights divisions would be like appointing a pacifist as head of the Department of Defense."[46]

The powerful news report by the local channel generated substantial reaction and was a prime topic of the subcommittee hearings on the protection of institutionalized persons. In opening remarks, Reynolds referred to the report as a "one-sided media event" that was "complete with chorus of critical comments from other former employees."[47] He also argued that the published charges contained "some of the most distorted factual statements I have ever seen."[48]

After reviewing the television report, Senator Lowell Weicker (D-CT) disagreed with Reynolds's characterization, calling it "journalism at its best."[49]

In the subcommittee hearings, the senators heard testimony from Cook and another lawyer who had resigned from DOJ. The subcommittee requested, and placed in the record, the detailed resignation memorandum that Cook had submitted. The memo was a scathing indictment of the failure of the Reagan DOJ to enforce civil rights for disabled persons and others. One objective of the memo was to unveil what the author perceived as an inaccurate claim of the attorney general that, with the exception of busing and affirmative action quotas, the enforcement activities of the agency were congruent with those of previous administrations. Cook concluded his memo with the statement that "when the history of the Civil Rights Division is written, the chapter on this administration will be entitled 'The Deviant Years'. This assumes that civil rights enforcement will flower again. I believe it will; the hopes and dreams of those excluded from the American experience will not die quickly and easily."[50]

Senator Weicker, obviously moved by the testimony, promised two things: to immediately dispatch committee staff members to the field to bring back first-hand reports on mental institutions and to call the secretary of HHS to testify about what could be done with federal funds to press the institutions into positive changes. He concluded the hearing by stating, "I can assure those both within these walls, and those without, that the Congress will act to assure that those whose lives are in any way threatened, or endangered, will receive the advocacy and the help of the Federal Government."[51]

The controversy about the civil rights activities of DOJ and about the leadership of Reynolds as head of the Civil Rights Division was reignited in 1985 when President Reagan nominated Reynolds for promotion to the third-ranking position in DOJ. This nomination generated strong reactions from many quarters. Conservatives favored the nomination of someone they saw as constraining civil rights activism by the federal government. Most civil rights groups, including those concerned with disabilities, rose in strong opposition.

In June 1985, the Senate Judiciary Committee held three stormy days of hearings on the Reynolds nomination. The record of the Civil Rights Division was reviewed in such areas as school desegregation, voting rights, and enforcement of rights protections.[52] At the hearings, several senators accused Reynolds of laxness in civil rights actions, while he defended his record as one of effective enforcement. In the end, the committee voted ten to eight not to report out the nomination to the Senate floor, thus killing the nomination. While some strong opponents in the Senate suggested that Reynolds resign from his position as head of the Civil Rights Division, he announced he would stay on "to make sure that the progress we have made over the past four years will continue throughout the second term" (Kurtz 1985b).[53]

Judicial Interpretation of Nondiscrimination Statutes

While the Reagan administration endeavored to revise federal regulations governing the behavior of federal agencies and recipients of federal assistance relevant to section 504, the federal courts continued to examine disputes about the intent and scope of this statutory provision. One major decision raised very important questions for civil rights enforcement and served to raise the hackles of Congress.

In February 1984, the Supreme Court, in the case of *Grove City College* v. *Bell*,[54] made a ruling that weakened the impact of antidiscrimination laws. The case centered around a private Pennsylvania college that refused to sign a compliance statement, issued by DOE, promising that the college would comply with Title IX of the Education Act Amendments of 1972 not to discriminate on the basis of sex. Implementation of Title IX provisions requires the Department of Education to execute a compliance agreement with all educational institutions that receive federal funds. The department requested the statement be signed because the college received federal aid in the form of federally funded student loans known as Basic Education Opportunity Grants (BEOGs). The college refused to sign the assurance of compliance, arguing that it did not directly receive federal financial assistance. When it failed to sign, DOE moved to cut off financial aid reaching the college. In response, the college brought suit against the secretary and DOE to reinstate federal financial aid to students attending the school.

In rendering its decision, the Supreme Court ruled that the college was legally subject to the antidiscrimination provisions of Title IX. At the same time, the Court judged that antidiscrimination provisions were applicable only to those *components* of the institution's activity that actually received federal financial assistance. In the Court's words: "We conclude that the receipt of BEOG's by some of Grove City's students does not trigger institutionwide coverage under Title IX. In purpose and effect, BEOG's represent federal financial assistance to the College's own financial aid program, and it is that program that may be properly regulated under Title IX."[55]

This decision overturned a decade of administrative interpretation, which viewed a violation of antidiscrimination law as grounds to cut off funds to *all* programs of the organization or institution. In this way, *Grove City* was seen as a dramatic setback by civil rights advocates, on the grounds that it limited enforcement activities to programs of institutions. While the *Grove City* case concerned Title IX of the Education Act Amendments of 1972, its impact on other antidiscrimination laws was immediately evident. This precedent would mean, for example, that enforcement of legal protections afforded by section 504 of the Rehabilitation Act of 1973 would similarly be limited to institutional programs instead of entire institutions.

Congress reacted to this Supreme Court decision by considering legislation to overturn it through the amendment of various civil rights laws. The language of these amendments, included in the Civil Rights Restoration Act of 1985 (H.R. 700), focused enforcement activities on institutions rather than on programs within institutions. In congressional hearings, Representative Don Edwards (D-CA) articulated the purpose of the proposed legislation:

> Because of a Supreme Court ruling about a year ago, this Congress must once again reaffirm its commitment to the principles that Federal tax dollars cannot be used to subsidize discrimination. We must do so by amending four laws which, together, prohibit discrimination on the basis of race, color, national origin, sex, handicap, and age in programs receiving Federal financial assistance.[56]

One of the laws to which Edwards referred was section 504 of the Rehabilitation Act of 1973.

That the handicapped community saw a threat from the *Grove City* ruling is evident in testimony given at the hearings by groups representing persons with disabilities. The directing attorney for DREDF, Arlene Mayerson, argued, for example, that "a decade of tremendous progress for disabled people will come to a halt and the promise of equal citizenship extended by Congress in 1973 will be ripped away if H.R. 700 is not passed by this Congress."[57] This sentiment was echoed by a representative of the Developmental Disabilities Law Project, who stated in written testimony: "Without H.R. 700, prohibitions against discrimination would be limited to those specific programs to which federal money can be traced. Such a narrow application of Section 504 falls short of implementing the intent of Congress, is inconsistent with long-standing executive policy, and renders federal agencies and the courts powerless to reach even the most blatant forms of discrimination."[58]

William Bradford Reynolds, the Reagan administration's spokesman on civil rights, appeared before the joint hearings to present the administration's view on H.R. 700. Reynolds argued: "The Administration fully agrees that the Supreme Court's programmatic interpretation of title IX should be overturned by providing, through an amendment, institution wide coverage of colleges and universities."[59] At the same time, he objected to H.R. 700 as the vehicle for a statutory amendment, contending that the bill "uses the extension of Federal dollars as the excuse for opening virtually every entity in the country—public and private—to Federal supervision, regulation, and massive bureaucratic paperwork."[60] He also opposed the bill on the intergovernmental issue of over-extension of federal government activity into the affairs of state and local governments.

Despite strong support for the Civil Rights Restoration Act, Congress was unable to take definitive action on the legislation until 1988. Significant opposition arose to the bill, spearheaded by the U.S. Catholic Conference, which feared its passage would have the impact of expanding abortion rights. Their concern was based on the assumption that passage of the bill might require Catholic hospitals to perform abortions in order to receive federal funding. While the bill's supporters rejected this interpretation, lingering fears by the Catholic community contributed to congressional reluctance to move the bill to a vote on the floor of either house.

After several years of debate and controversy, Congress enacted the Civil Rights Restoration Act in 1988; the legislation restored the institution-wide interpretation of enforcement responsibilities for several antidiscrimination laws, including section 504. The bill passed the full Senate only after a controversial amendment was added, which stated that the law would in no way require hospitals or universities to perform abortions. The House of Representatives voted by a large margin to pass the restoration act as amended.

The restoration act was subsequently vetoed by President Reagan, who argued that in its current form the legislation would unjustifiably extend the power of the federal government in the affairs of churches, other private institutions, and state and local governments. Despite pressure from the president and conservative groups across the nation, both houses of Congress voted to override the presidential veto, thus establishing (or in the view of some, reestablishing) the institution-wide approach to enforcement of nondiscrimination policies.

Rollback Reconsidered

The early 1980s witnessed several initiatives by the Reagan administration to use the regulatory process to loosen the antidiscrimination protections afforded by section 504. With the election of Ronald Reagan and enough senators for the Republicans to take control of the Senate, the policy environment in the nation's capital moved to a conservative position. One hallmark of the new political environment was a preference for reduced federal regulations. Section 504 regulations represented one of many areas of civil rights and social policy where the influence of the federal government on subnational units was viewed as excessive and contrary to effective policy development and implementation. As documented in chapters to come, efforts to roll back civil rights protections for disabled persons were undertaken in many areas in addition to the rulemaking actions of DOJ.

The effort at regulatory reform was ultimately abandoned as the administration recognized it was in a losing battle with interest groups and Congress. Legislative leaders in civil rights and disability policy were unwilling to see their lawmaking successes felled by the newly installed Reagan administration. And in what may have been a political miscalculation, the administration failed to see in advance the strength and political skills of groups representing disabled Americans. These groups formed the core of an issue network that had become concerned not only with services, but also with legal protections; like their advocates in Congress, these groups were willing to aggressively fight regulatory reform. In light of this opposition, the administration conceded its effort to revise section 504 regulations.

In his letter acknowledging the administration's decision to cease regulatory changes for section 504, the vice president acknowledged that some issues yet unresolved were being considered by the federal courts. Given that cases such as *Davis* tended to restrict the reach of section 504, the administration likely saw advantage to letting the courts, serving as another institutional arena for policy consideration, make the tough and restrictive decisions. And from there, the adminstration could use judicial precedent in revising regulations and pursuing enforcement of section 504.

After the regulatory reform fight had ended, controversy continued to surround the implementation efforts of DOJ, generally, and the head of the Civil Rights Division, specifically. Handicapped groups and disaffected lawyers who had left the agency argued that DOJ ignored section 504 regulations as written and employed its own interpretation in the process of initiating and joining legal actions. Debate over the role of DOJ in enforcing section 504 and other civil rights protections continued during the second term of the Reagan administration, as interest groups voiced concerns that civil rights enforcement was languishing.

6
Barrier Removal and Facility Access for Disabled Persons

Efforts to advance the opportunities of persons with disabilities and to enhance their entry into mainstream society have resulted in many policy initiatives, including laws and protections relating to education services, public transportation, and employment. The forerunner of these initiatives, however, dating back to the mid-1960s, was the push to remove and eliminate architectural barriers that impede mobility and access to public facilities. The barrier removal initiative was politically controversial, caused widespread misunderstanding, and generated resistance on the part of regulated parties. At first, architectural accessibility was perceived to mean simply "toilets and ramps" for handicapped persons, modifications that most affected parties would agree to provide, albeit reluctantly in some instances. An accurate understanding of mandated responsibilities under barrier removal policies, however, indicates a far broader requirement to make architectural changes so as to provide disabled persons with access to areas within most public buildings and not just to "toilets and ramps."

Upon recognizing broader responsibilities to make physical accommodations, many parties affected by accessibility requirements, including organizations in both the public and private sectors, overreacted, forecasting the need to spend millions upon millions of dollars to accommodate a small segment of the population. This emotional and often vitriolic outpouring occurred in spite of policy provisions that allowed, in many instances, alternative means to comply with accessibility mandates besides undertaking major reconstruction. The evidence that many forms of accessibility modifications could be performed relatively inexpensively, and that the costs of building accessibility features into new buildings was negligible, did little to mitigate claims that excessive costs and unlimited responsibilities were being unleashed by accessibility policies.

The development of implementation policies for architectural accessibility—whose statutory bases lie with the Architectural Barriers Act (ABA) of 1968 and section 504—is examined in this chapter. It will be shown that the creation and refinement of implementation policies evolved through struggles waged in several institutional arenas, including all three branches of the federal government. Disability interest groups, some relatively new to the political scene, pressed with diligence to see that implementation policies afforded strong requirements for accessibility. The regulated clients, including the agencies of the federal government, resisted strong regulations, which they perceived would require extensive architectural modifications and costs.

Playing a central role in refining accessibility policy was the Architectural and Transportation Barriers Compliance Board (ATBCB), created by Congress in 1973 as an instrument to coordinate implementation of the ABA. ATBCB served as the principal arena for the Reagan administration to pursue its objective of regulatory relief in the context of barrier removal policy. Congress played a recurrent role both through statutory changes and oversight activities, providing an arena for disaffected parties to voice their opposition to existing policy provisions. The General Accounting Office (GAO), one of Congress's investigative arms, also played a key role through two studies that documented widespread problems with implementation. As we shall see, implementation policy as of the late 1980s reflects a compromise position between the policy preferences of disability groups and regulated parties. The policy has resulted from the persistent struggle of both sides to influence the direction of and obligations mandated for implementation.

Legislation to Remove Architectural Barriers

The origin, consideration, and passage of the ABA were described in chapter three. As passed by Congress, the act required that all buildings constructed, leased (after construction or alteration in accordance with federal government supervision), or financed by the federal government be accessible to physically disabled persons.[1] For the purposes of the act, "building" was defined as any building or facility intended for use by the public, with the exception of privately owned structures and facilities on military installations intended for the use of able-bodied personnel.

As the result of tensions between executive departments, the responsibility for issuing compliance regulations was split among three "standard-setting" agencies: the Department of Housing and Urban Development (HUD) was given responsibility for federally funded residential units; the Department of Defense (DOD), for facilities on military installations; and the General Services Administration (GSA), for all other federal buildings. All three agencies were instructed to consult with the secretary of the Department of Health, Education, and Welfare (HEW) in devising regulations. Finally, the agencies were granted authority to waive or modify standards in particular cases if it could be shown that waiver or modiciation was clearly necessary.

Regulations to Implement the ABA

One year after the ABA was enacted by Congress, GSA issued final rules to guide implementation.[2] It is not clear why the rules were published as final rules, without the typical period for public comments.[3] The GSA regulations filled less than a page of the *Federal Register* and mostly reflected the provisions of the ABA itself. The definition of buildings covered by the act mirrored the one set out in the act and, like the act, excluded privately owned residential buildings and facilities on military bases intended for able-bodied personnel. Included under the definition were those buildings leased by the federal government after being constructed or altered under federal supervision.[4]

The regulations required that the design, construction, and alteration of buildings covered by the act be undertaken according to standards devised by the American National Standards Institute (ANSI) in 1961. Exceptions were allowed to these requirements for (1) new and altered buildings whose intended use made accommodations unnecessary, (2) existing buildings where changes did not involve "facilities susceptible to installation or improvements to accommodate the physically handicapped," and (3) construction or alterations of buildings completed or substantially completed by September 2, 1969.[5] Thus, the rules for the most part were quite simple: ANSI standards were required in the design, construction, and alteration of public buildings covered by the act. The troublesome points, from the vantage of implementation, were those related to permissible exemptions to the standards.

Creation of ATBCB

In a further effort to effect the removal of physical barriers that impede the access of handicapped individuals to federal buildings and facilities, Congress in 1973 created the Architectural and Transportation Barriers Compliance Board to coordinate implementation efforts within the federal government. The origins of ATBCB can be traced to Senate consideration of the extension of the vocational rehabilitation program in the early 1970s. The provision creating the board was included as one of the "miscellaneous" amendments of the Rehabilitation Act, as passed by Congress in 1972.[6] The bill, however, was vetoed by President Richard Nixon, who objected on several grounds to the proposed bill. One of his objections was that "the bill also would establish numerous committees and independent commissions which are unnecessary, would waste taxpayers' dollars, and would complicate and confuse the direction of this program."[7]

With some modifications, the Rehabilitation Act was passed in 1973 and signed by the president; it included section 502, creating ATBCB. The law specified that ATBCB be composed of the heads (or their designees) of eight cabinet departments and agencies, including the Departments of Transportation, Labor, and the Interior, HEW, DOD, HUD, GSA, and the Veterans Administration. The functions of the board were to:

1. Insure compliance with standards set by GSA, HUD, and DOD pursuant to the ABA of 1968 (as amended in 1970).

2. Investigate and examine alternative approaches to the architectural, transportation, and attitudinal barriers confronting handicapped individuals, particularly with respect to public buildings and other public facilities.

3. Determine measures taken at the federal, state, and local level and by other public or nonprofit agencies to eliminate barriers.

4. Promote use of the international accessibility symbol.

5. Report to the president and Congress on results of studies and investigations of barrier elimination.

6. Make recommendations to the president and Congress for legislation and administration as deemed necessary to eliminate barriers.

Provisions of section 502 called for ATBCB to investigate the extent to which transportation barriers impede the mobility of handicapped persons.

In the following year, Congress passed several amendments to the Rehabilitation Act, including some related to ATBCB. One amendment resulted from concerns about leadership among the agencies on the board. The 1974 amendments designated the secretary of HEW to be chairman of ATBCB on the grounds that most programs dealing with disabled persons were located in HEW. Another problem identified with ATBCB was that it provided no mechanism for direct input from handicapped citizens or groups. In the 1974 amendments, Congress empowered the board, upon recommendation of the secretary of HEW, to appoint a Consumer Advisory Panel, a majority of whose members would be disabled persons. The purpose of the advisory panel was "to provide guidance, advice, and recommendations to the Board in carrying out its functions."[8]

Implementation of the ABA

With the issuance of its 1969 regulations, GSA began to implement policies to remove architectural barriers in public buildings. Other agencies specifically named in the act, DOD and HUD, also issued regulations. In the early 1970s, when queried by Congress, GSA stated that implementation was going smoothly.[9] To check this assertion, Congress asked GAO to investigate the implementation of the ABA.

The GAO Report

The report on implementing the ABA, issued by GAO in July 1975, was critical of implementation efforts and served to spark the interest of Congress in strengthening barrier removal efforts.[10] In contrast to GSA's assurances that implementation was progressing smoothly, GAO found in its survey of 314 federally financed buildings that: (1) none of the buildings was completely free of architectural barriers; (2) buildings currently being designed were only slightly more barrier-free than the buildings designed and constructed before passage of the ABA; and (3) there had been about a ten-percent decrease in noncompliance with ANSI guidelines.

Three primary deficiencies in the ABA of 1968 were identified in the GAO report. The first concerned the definition of "building" as covered in the act. The report noted that the definition was narrow and did not include *leased* buildings whose construction or alteration was done without federal government supervision. This included most privately owned buildings leased by the federal government. Second, the implementing agencies had not proved creative in developing accessibility standards unique to their agencies and facilities. And third, the report noted that the Postal Department was not covered under the act, thus unintentionally exempting a major service provider from compliance with the barrier removal mandate.[11]

Congress Reacts to the GAO Report

Several members of Congress were displeased to learn of the implementation problems uncovered through the GAO report. In October 1975, the House Subcommittee on Investigations and Review held hearings on the effectiveness of the ABA. At the start, Representative James Cleveland (R-NH) testily commented:

> I find it is a shocking commentary on our system of values that more has not been done to make public buildings accessible to the physically handicapped. Further, I find it is also a sorry commentary on the responsiveness of the Federal Agencies involved that we must hold these hearings today. This GAO report . . . describes something of a horror story of agency inaction and confusion which I find hard to believe.[12]

A representative of the National Paraplegic Foundation commended the GAO report for "telling it like it is; or perhaps, more appropriately as it is not."[13] He argued that there was a long distance to go before a barrier-free environment is created and that Congress should give ATBCB more muscle and resources to get the job done.

Walter Meisen, as assistant commissioner of GSA, appeared before the subcommittee to provide a response to the GAO report. He described steps that GSA had already undertaken in response to the report, including (1) commissioning the design of new accessibility standards related to the types of facilities handled by GSA and (2) requiring surveys of federal buildings so as to determine the extent of barriers to the access of physically disabled persons.[14] Meisen also defended GSA implementation actions, while admitting that more could be done. He also questioned the strictness of criteria used by GAO in determining compliance, arguing that they tended to understate the extent of accomplishments that had been made in barrier removal. Representatives of HUD and DOD also testified in support of their agencies' implementation activities.

During the next year, the House Subcommittee on Public Buildings and Grounds held hearings on legislation that would become the Public Buildings Cooperative Use Act of 1976, the second title of which was an amended form of the ABA. The amendments to the ABA (1) included the United States Postal Service (USPS) under the act's provisions,[15] (2) included all leased buildings and privately owned residential units used for the purpose of public or federally subsidized housing, and (3) changed the wording about agency development of accessibility standards from "is authorized to prescribe" to "shall prescribe." The intention of this wording change was to remove the discretionary authority of agencies in issuing accessibility standards, while the first two changes extended the act to federal buildings not directly covered under the original act. These amendments to the ABA stimulated the rulemaking agendas of various federal agencies, and particularly that of GSA.

Another Round of GSA Rulemaking

Responding to the 1976 modifications to the ABA, GSA embarked on a four-teen-month period of rulemaking to update its regulations on accessibility in public buildings and facilities. Two sets of proposed rules were published, one in February and the other in September 1977.[16] Both sets of regulations were similar to those promulgated in 1969. The definition of "buildings" covered by the act was extended to include all buildings leased by the government after January 1, 1977.[17] The ANSI standards, revised in 1971, were designated as the accessibility requirements to be followed in making accommodations. Finally, a variety of exceptions to accessibility requirements were specified, including cases where (1) the building, by its use, was not to be usable by the public or handicapped persons, (2) alterations were not structurally possible, (3) no available leased property meeting accessibility requirements was available in the area.

GSA received many comments in response to proposed rules, most of which voiced concerns about permissible exemptions to compliance.[18] GSA responded in the final rules that waivers to ANSI standards are provided in the standards themselves if alternative modifications yield levels of accessibility equivalent to those provided through ANSI specifications. The most frequently received reaction concerned the provision that exempted leased space where it was determined that no otherwise legally acceptable lease proposal met the accessibility standards. Interest groups representing physically handicapped persons argued that there was no statutory basis for this exemption. GSA argued, in response, that the wording "whenever possible" in the law established the intent of Congress not to force requirements in cases where accessibility could not be achieved.[19] The agency also attempted to reassure interest groups that "responsible and judicious action by the administering agency will preclude any unwarranted liberal interpretation of this policy."[20]

Congress, ATBCB, and Policymaking

Revisions in Structure and Mission

While GSA was undertaking rulemaking efforts, Congress shifted attention to reauthorization of the Rehabilitation Act, including revisions to the structure and operation of ATBCB. While not the primary item of interest or controversy during the 1977 hearings held by the Senate Subcommittee on the Handicapped, concerns were expressed about ATBCB and its ability to achieve its mission. The first executive director attributed implementation problems to several factors, including

> the reluctance of the executive branch of Government to focus attention and support on the Board and its program sufficiently to allow for its timely and effective implementation; the inadequacy of funding support and assistance both from the administration in its budget requests and from Congress in its appropriation; the difficulties associated with the design and implementation of a new program with all of the attendant problems related to that process; insufficient oversight to insure the timely implementation of the statute; and perhaps most importantly, in my view, basic structural deficiencies in the Board which require congressional review and perhaps statutory change.[21]

The former executive director went on to argue that "the Board has never developed a quasi-independent status. Rather, those individuals representative of the nine agencies composing the Board for the most part insist upon representing their own interests and those of their agency with a desire to protect individual agency turf and programs."[22] Other testimony questioned whether there was a conflict of interest in agency members overseeing compliance in federal agencies including their own.[23]

Responding to concerns about board membership, Congress, through the Rehabilitation, Comprehensive Services, and Development Disabilities Amendments of 1978 (PL95-602), changed the structure of the ATBCB.[24] The House-Senate conference committee on the bill accepted a plan whereby eleven public members would be appointed to the board, at least five of whom would be handicapped. With eleven members, the public representatives would have a majority position on the board. The president was authorized to appoint the first board chairman, with subsequent chairmen elected by majority vote. The law also authorized technical assistance to public bodies seeking to comply with the ABA and required the board to issue minimum guidelines and requirements for compliance with the ABA as amended. The latter charge, promulgation of minimum standards, represented an effort to clarify and coordinate the guidelines being devised and issued by various agencies of the federal government.

Rulemaking and ATBCB

Implementation of legislated changes in the structure and mission of ATBCB moved slowly in the year following the passage of the 1978 revisions to the Rehabilitation Act. Although he signed the bill, President Carter had reservations about the majority position of public members of the reconstituted board.

Through his legislative liaison, Carter signaled interest in modifying some of the changes; for one thing, the president preferred an equal vote between public and governmental representatives on the board. Given reservations, Carter was slow to appoint public members, finally doing so in December 1979. This delay more or less paralyzed the board's actions during 1979, since without the public representatives being appointed, the board could not achieve a quorum. When selecting members, Carter exceeded the legislative mandate by appointing handicapped persons to nine of the eleven public positions on the board. This move proved significant, at least in the eyes of many observers, since it contributed to a strong advocacy position by many board members (Clark 1981a).

With the public members finally appointed, the reconstituted board moved to implement its mandate to devise and issue minimum guidelines for implementation of the ABA. Board staff had already begun work on the guidelines prior to appointment of the public members. In February 1980, the board issued a notice of intent to undertake rulemaking in regard to developing minimum guidelines for accessible design.[25] The notice posed several questions related to the guidelines and solicited public reactions about exemptions from compliance with design specifications and the application of accessibility standards to leased facilites.

Congressional Oversight of ATBCB

Congressional interest in the operation of ATBCB continued into the early 1980s, as evidenced by oversight hearings held in 1980 and 1981. The 1980 hearings focused on the activities of the recently reconstituted board and its efforts to advance barrier removal efforts.[26] The chairman and vice chairman, Max Cleveland and Donald Elisburg, respectively, testified about the activities of the reorganized board, including rulemaking efforts.

The Subcommittee on Select Education also heard testimony from an official of GAO who had reviewed a recently completed second study of barrier removal efforts and ATBCB. The GAO study was commissioned by Congress to determine whether the implementation problems identified in its 1975 study had been rectified.[27] Once again, GAO identified major problems in implementation of barrier removal policies. This report focused directly on the role of ATBCB in policy implementation and found, among other things, that:

1. The board was hampered in fulfilling its mission by dependence upon HEW for budget and resources.

2. Standards devised for implementation of barrier removal in construction and renovation were insufficiently detailed and not uniformly applied in administrative agencies.

3. Systems within agencies to ensure that architectural guidelines are followed were not sufficiently comprehensive.

4. The primary authority for the oversight of implementation of barrier removal policy was scattered across multiple agencies, including ATBCB and GSA.

In concluding its study, GAO recommended that Congress amend the ABA to (1) establish ATBCB as the principal authority to provide leadership and ensure compliance, (2) require the board, not GSA, to provide annual reports to Congress on waivers of standards, and (3) require other administrative agencies to confer with the board and obtain concurrence with accessibility guidelines. The recommendations were tantamount to placing the board in the administrative center of efforts to implement barrier removal policies; this would, in turn, reduce the fragmentation of authority currently characteristic of policy implementation.

Rulemaking Continues

Throughout 1980, ATBCB continued efforts to devise minimum guidelines for compliance with provisions of the ABA. In August, following its February notice of intent to devise administrative rules, the board issued a detailed set of proposed rules.[28] They contained two important components, technical criteria and scoping requirements. The former resembled, but also went beyond, the ANSI standards, in that technical design criteria were presented in words and in diagram form and included specifications about restroom and entrance ramp designs.

The proposed rules also included "scoping" conditions; these stipulated under what circumstances technical designs must be implemented and the extent of design features that must be included in facility design or modification. Scoping requirements are what made the ATBCB rules more stringent than ANSI standards and are what generated significant controversy. There was little quibble with stipulations about features to be included in new construction, but many questions were raised about scoping requirements in building additions or modifications. For example, the proposed rules stated that if an addition was added to a building, but no new doors were included, then it was still required that one of the doors in the existing building be made accessible according to technical guidelines. The rules also required that if a portion of a building was modified, then all features of accessibility must simultaneously be performed in that portion. Thus, if a lobby were substantially restructured, then all features of the lobby—including restrooms, commons areas, entrances, drinking fountains, public telephones—must be simultaneously made accessible.

One portion of the administrative rules, which soon would generate political battle, concerned application of minimum accessibility guidelines for leased space. As described above, the 1976 amendments to the ABA extended applicability to all space leased by the federal government. The final ATBCB rules interpreted the act to require that accessibility be undertaken at the time when leases are entered into or renewed by the federal government, whether or not any structural alterations were otherwise planned. Where no accessible space was offered for lease, the government would be allowed to rent space only where certain conditions were met; these included conditions that at least one entrance and each "essential feature" be accessible according to technical standards described in the rules. Sensing some confusion on this point, the board requested both its own general counsel and the Department of Justice (DOJ) to evaluate its interpretation of coverage of leased facilities. Both judged the board's position that leased facilities should be made accessible at the time of lease creation or renewal to be a correct interpretation of the ABA as amended in 1976.[29]

While ATBCB moved forward with rulemaking, heading toward publication of final rules, the Carter administration expressed concerns to the board about the far-reaching scope of the rules and their expected implementation costs and requested that issuance of final rules be delayed while further impact analysis was undertaken. The board was undaunted and argued that, in light of its independent status, it was not bound by White House instructions.

The decision to publish the rules in final form was considered by the board at its meeting in early January 1981. The final rules closely resembled the proposed ones, with a few minor modifications. Three federal agencies, USPS, HUD, and GSA, opposed the minimum guidelines in their current form, arguing that they were too broad and required extensive modification not mandated by the ABA. Roger Craig, representing USPS, described the sentiments of the opposition: "I believe this is a classic case of pushing so far, so fast, on so skimpy a base, in so much disregard of legal and practical limits, that to support the rule would harm, rather than help, the interests we are called to serve here."[30] One key point that led Craig and others to oppose the rule regarded the provision requiring accessibility modifications at the point any lease is entered into or renewed. On this matter, Craig stated that "the leasing situation demonstrates one of the most regrettable features of the Board's thrust, at least until very lately: A push for the maximum coverage without regard to cost or getting the most accessibility for the dollar."[31]

Following heated debate, the board voted to approve the minimum guidelines by a vote of fourteen to four, with USPS, GSA, HUD, and one public member voting against the regulations. No doubt recognizing the impending change of presidential administration, the board moved quickly to finalize its rules, ordering them published in the *Federal Register* and setting an immediate date for compliance with no phase-in period.[32] Subsequent to the board meeting, USPS announced that it would not abide by the new ATBCB rules and instead would follow its own less stringent rules.[33]

Deregulation and Reconsideration of the ATBCB Rules

Clearly, the election of Ronald Reagan changed the political environment of the federal government. Early in the new administration, ATBCB was targeted as an example of excessive regulations by the vice president's Task Force on Regulatory Relief, which claimed the board's new minimum guidelines would cost taxpayers $800 million or more. In fact, the task force recommended that the board itself be eliminated and its responsibilities shifted to GSA. This position was made official when the Office of Management and Budget (OMB) officially proposed to Congress in early March that the ATBCB be terminated, effective October 1, 1981.

In an unusual turn of events, the board moved within three months to reconsider its own rules, reflecting, in part, the spirit of "regulatory relief" being fostered by the new Reagan administration. Growing during this time was concern about the cost of implementing the minimum guidelines. A move to rescind the minimum guidelines, only finalized three months earlier, was initiated by Roger Craig of USPS at ATBCB's meeting in May 1981, where he presented a draft notice of rescission of the minimum guidelines. He moved at the meeting to have the notice published in the *Federal Register*. Chairman Mason Rose ruled the motion out of order, arguing that the materials had not been received sufficiently prior to the meeting for proper consideration.[34] After substantial parliamentary haggling, the rescission proposal was referred to the board's Standards Committee and a special meeting was scheduled to consider rescission in June (later scheduled for July).

At its summer meeting, the board returned to consideration of rescinding its minimum guidelines for accessibility. The Standards Committee, citing the board's intent that the "guidelines should be a living tool, responsive to broad needs, and easily changeable," recommended that an advance notice of proposed rulemaking be published in the *Federal Register* to solicit comments on how the guidelines could be improved or modified.[35] This motion was defeated by a twelve to ten vote, with all the federal agencies and one public representative voting no. This group wanted to take stronger action in the form of publication of a notice of proposed rulemaking in the *Federal Register* to rescind the minimum accessibility guidelines published in January.[36]

In response to a motion offered by USPS representative Roger Craig that the board initiate action to rescind the minimum guidelines, chairman Mason Rose removed his hat as chair and made an impassioned plea against rescission. The plea included an attack on the USPS, which had consistently directed moves to rescind the guidelines.[37] Craig rose to defend his agency, noting that USPS "has a laudable record in the area of access to the handicapped. . . . So, I will not accept any charges that the Postal Service worships the almighty dollar and won't do anything for the handicapped."[38]

After heated discussion, a vote was called on the motion to initiate rescission action by publishing a notice of proposed rulemaking in the *Federal Register*. The agency representatives and one public member again voted as a bloc in favor of rescission, resulting in a twelve to ten vote in favor of the motion. The bloc voting of the agency representatives came after a recent meeting with C. Boyden Gray, counsel to the vice president's Task Force on Regulatory Relief.

The board's chairman, in no hurry to publish the rescission notice, called for a cost-benefit analysis of the rescission, in keeping with Reagan administration practice to study the costs and benefits of regulatory actions. When given a green light by the White House to forgo the cost-benefit study, Rose insisted that the waiver be made in writing. In the notice of rescission, published in the *Federal Register* on August 4, it was argued that the decision to rescind the minimum guidelines was based upon "new" cost estimates and concerns about "excessive" regulation:

> Recent cost estimates provided by the standard-setting agencies indicate that the rule may be more costly to comply with than previously believed. Because of these new cost estimates and publicly expressed concerns about the effectiveness of excessive regulatory compliance costs upon the economy, the Board considers it appropriate to initiate this rulemaking.[39]

The shifting position of ATBCB resulted in large measure from the changed presidential administration, whose representatives now reflected a conservative, antiregulation position. Within the board, the move against the minimum regulations was headed by USPS, whose primary objection centered on stipulations about leased property. In its own rules, USPS interpreted the mandate of the amended ABA concerning leased property to mean that modifications to enhance accessibility were required *only* when structural modifications were

118

made in leased property, not whenever leases were renegotiated or renewed. This was not an inconsequential issue to USPS, since over seventy-five percent of its facilities were leased. USPS argued that minimum guidelines were excessively costly and that rescission would provide a new opportunity for federal agencies to cooperatively develop new and consistent guidelines.

The notice to rescind rules generated extensive comments, with over one thousand received by the time of the board's meeting in September. A review of the public comments is instruction.[40] A large proportion were from private individuals, most of whom argued simply that the board should retain its minimum guidelines. The efforts of interest groups representing disabled people were also apparent, since the rulemaking file contained many preformatted letters opposing rescission; these were distributed by the groups, simply signed by individuals, and forwarded to ATBCB. A comment from the Disabled American Veterans Association exemplifies the sentiments of many handicapped groups: "It has been more than 13 years since the initial legislation on barriers and almost 2 years since the Board was mandated by public law to establish the guidelines. For the Board to take action to rescind these guidelines at this time is, in our opinion, unconscionable."[41]

The rescission move also generated reactions from Congress. On the floor of the Senate, Alan Cranston, a longtime advocate of disability rights, criticized the efforts of the Reagan administration to weaken ATBCB and its mandate to enforce the ABA. Cranston, while noting that members of Congress had seen some problems with minimum guidelines, stated that the rescission move "orchestrated by the administration through its representatives on the Board—with only one public member joining a united Federal agency phalanx marching in lockstep—is a blatant example of this administration's lack of concern for the requirements of laws designed to guarantee basic civil rights for this significant segment of our citizenry."[42]

The board returned to the issue of rescinding the minimum guidelines at its September 1981 meeting.[43] The chairman noted that ninety-three percent of the comments supported retention of the minimum guidelines and stated that many requested more time to respond to the notice. As expected, the USPS representative motioned that the minimum guidelines be rescinded. A new member from DOJ, William Bradford Reynolds, made a motion to amend the rescission motion; the substitute motion called for the board to suspend its guidelines and provide for an extended public comment period through November 6. The chair ruled that the suspension element of the substitute motion was out of order, because it was not part of the established agenda and would require a separate rulemaking process. After lengthy discussion, ATBCB voted to extend the comment period to November 6 and to take no action to enforce the minimum guidelines.[44]

One interesting development reported at the September meeting was a report by Chairman Rose of a meeting held the previous day with C. Boyden Gray of the vice president's office and counsel for the Task Force on Regulatory Relief. Rose reported that consensus had been reached at the meeting that controversy surrounded only about five percent of all accessibility problems, the hard and expensive cases. Also discussed at the meeting was the best approach to dealing with the difficult cases, including whether it was better to rescind the existing rules or to seek their modification. The chairman reported that Gray had agreed that the public and federal agency members of the board should be brought together at the bargaining table for good faith negotiations.

Another Round of Congressional Oversight

The House Subcommittee on Select Education conducted oversight hearings in November 1981, prompted by the unusual developments surrounding the ATBCB accessibility guidelines. The chairman of the subcommittee, Austin J. Murphy, stated that hearings were undertaken not because the board had failed to meet its mandate to devise minimum guidelines, but instead because "having met the mandate in January of this year, the Board—specifically, the administration appointees—reversed itself in July, and is now attempting to rescind its earlier decisions on accessibility standards. We are here today to find out why."[45]

The chairman of ATBCB, Mason Rose, gave a bitter account of recent activities of the board to rescind rules. He recounted the leadership role taken by USPS to retract the rules over the objection of all but one public member. The chairman acknowledged that "the mood of the administration is to eliminate unnecessary layers of regulations and we have been pointed out in this controversy as being an unnecessary layer."[46] He responded, however: "We are exactly the opposite. Our minimum guideline was developed for the purpose of creating uniformity in the Federal system . . . we are really going to eliminate different layers of regulation and make one regulation."[47] Rose recommended that the board be reorganized and streamlined to five public members. He objected to the regulated agencies' being represented on the board and argued for a more independent regulatory body.

The subcommittee also heard from USPS and groups representing disabled Americans. The representative from USPS testified at the hearings that "prior rulemakings were primarily put forward by the Board staff and there has been a general feeling that cost is not a substantially relevant issue in the area of accessibility, that this is a matter of civil rights and that cost is no object. We disagree with that position."[48] Interest groups representing disabled persons

120

expressed alarm about and vehemently opposed the board's decision to withdraw its minimum accessibility guidelines. For example, a representative of the Open Doors for the Handicapped expressed the sentiments of most handicapped groups, stating: "It is absolutely essential that the Architectural and Transportation Barriers Compliance Board regulations not be rescinded. Any action taken to rescind the guidelines or reduce funds of the Compliance Board would be disastrously regressive."[49]

Despite the heated rhetoric expressed at the hearings, there was evidence that the seeds of a compromise had been planted. In his testimony, Chairman Rose, while chastising the administration for backing away from the board's minimum guidelines, praised William Bradford Reynolds of the Civil Rights Division, with whom Rose and his staff had engaged in discussions about possible compromises in the minimum guidelines.[50] Rose also reported on his discussion with C. Boyden Gray of the vice president's Task Force on Regulatory Relief.[51]

Rulemaking Continues

Rulemaking regarding ATBCB's minimum guidelines took another turn in late 1981, as the board at its December meeting voted to undertake a revision of existing regulations.[52] This was a compromise that moved away from total rescission. The public members recognized the strength of the agency representatives, as manifest in the twelve-to-ten vote to rescind the minimum guidelines, and saw that negotiation and compromise were needed to prevent rescission. For its part, the administration-backed position was increasingly unpopular. ATBCB received an avalanche of thousands of comments in response to the rescission notice, ninety-three percent of which supported keeping the existing rules. The administration also received extensive negative press as the result of its move to weaken regulations related to the education of handicapped children (see chapter eight). Given these pressures and recognitions, all sides saw advantage to compromise. By unanimous decision, the board agreed to the route of amending existing rules through a new rulemaking effort.

A notice of proposed rulemaking, offering amendments to the 1981 minimum guidelines, was published in the *Federal Register* in January 1982. The notice included a copy of existing regulations, along with proposed additions and deletions.[53]

One change concerned the sticky issue of accessibility modifications in leased facilities. The proposed amendments deleted the rules governing leased facilities, noting the ongoing debate about the intent of the ABA in this regard:

In view of the continuing controversy over the point at which the Architectural Barriers Act applies to leased buildings and facilities, this Part no longer specifies at which point the accessibility standard must apply to leased buildings and facilities. This change has been made solely in recognition of the fact that the issue concerning the applicability of the Architectural Barriers Act to leased buildings is a legal one on which the Board expresses no position.[54]

With this declaration, the board moved to distance itself from the troublesome point, designating it as a "legal issue." This issue was being addressed in the courts by the suit brought by Mason Rose and the Paralyzed Veterans of America against the USPS in the Ninth Federal District (*Rose v. U.S. Postal Service*).

Changes were made in other areas of the minimum guidelines, in response to extensive pressure from administrative agencies. Rules governing building entrances and handicapped parking spaces were modified as compromise positions were reached. For example, while the original ATBCB minimum guidelines called for accessible entrances on each building exposure (where multiple exposures existed), the amendments dropped this provision and set forth the less stringent rule that only one building entrance be accessible. Efforts were also made to increase the compatibility of the ANSI standards and the technical specifications in the ATBCB regulations.

Other Administrative Actions

The Reagan administration took other actions to circumvent ATBCB and its accessibility guidelines. One was an initiative by OMB, undertaken in June 1982, to bring the four standard-setting agencies—GSA, HUD, DOD, and USPS—together to design a unified set of accessibility guidelines. The efforts of the "uniform task force" took place during the latter half of 1981 on into 1982. The draft versions of the uniform standards showed them to be weaker than the ATBCB guidelines, particularly in terms of scoping requirements.

In other, more drastic action, the administration continued to advocate that the board be dissolved and included no appropriation request for ATBCB in the fiscal year 1983 budget. The administration's position was voiced by William Bradford Reynolds during appropriations hearings: "The Administration views this as the appropriate time to recommend that there be no further appropriation for the ATBCB in fiscal year 1983. The principal Board activity has now all but concluded. . . . To retain the Board 'in being' so as to permit it to perform what would largely be a duplicative role serves neither the handicapped community nor the public at large."[55] Reynolds went on to describe how other governmental agencies could perform the remaining tasks of ATBCB.

Despite his need to reflect the administration's position, it appears that Reynolds personally continued to see merit in ATBCB. It was at his request that public members of the board also appeared at the hearings; predictably, their sentiments were in opposition to those voiced by the administration. As an example, public member Carol Grant responded to the administration's position that ATBCB had basically finished its primary tasks: "Has the Board completed its mission? No. We must ensure that accessibility standards issued by the four standard-setting agencies are consistent with the minimum guidelines and requirements."[56] Public members also argued that the OMB-directed efforts of the standard-setting agencies to devise uniform, yet weaker, guidelines had basically "ignored the Congressional mandate that requires conformity with the [ATBCB] guidelines. This effectively negates the consumer and federal input that went into the development of the guidelines."[57]

There were also rumors that the president might fire the public members and replace them with individuals more receptive to the administration's preference for regulatory restraint. Ultimately, Congress rejected the administration's position and appropriated about $2 million for the board, thus allowing its continued operation.

Completion of Rulemaking and the New Minimum Guidelines

The rulemaking docket on the ATBCB's plan to amend the minimum regulations closed on March 15, 1982. Minor revisions were made, and the rules were prepared for final consideration at the board's meeting in May. Political conflicts climaxed again in May, as the uniform task force prepared to publish its guidelines for accessibility to govern the four standard-setting agencies. At the behest of C. Boyden Gray, the agencies held off publishing the uniform rules until the board made its final decision on minimum guidelines. At the board's meeting on May 4, the amended rules were accepted, with efforts by GSA and HUD to relax certain provisions rebuffed. While hailed by some as a victory for handicapped individuals,[58] the action represented a compromise whereby both groups yielded some ground. The final rules were published in August 1982.[59] After eighteen months of controversy and debate, ATBCB had a new set of minimum guidelines with which to direct the regulatory activity of the standard-setting agencies.

With the acceptance of the revised guidelines, the four standard-setting agencies went back to the drawing board with their uniform guidelines, while the task force worked with the ATBCB staff to develop uniform standards in accordance with the new minimum guidelines. A proposed version of the uniform standards was revised and published in the *Federal Register* in April

1983.[60] The standards claimed to meet or exceed the technical specifications contained in the ATBCB minimum guidelines. Only sixty-five comments were received in response to the proposed guidelines, and these were divided in terms of those who wanted more stringent standards and those who wanted more lenient ones. Final uniform standards were published in August 1984,[61] with the standard-setting agencies stating their belief that ''the standards in this document will result in buildings and facilities that uniformly will provide ready access and useability for handicapped people.''[62]

The Politics of Implementing Accessibility Policy

For people with disabilities, the physical world began to show significant signs of change by the mid-1980s. The ABA, coupled with similar state laws, have torn down and eliminated physical barriers that have impeded the access of physically handicapped persons to public buildings and facilities. Yet despite gains, progress has been slow. The ABA was a strong statement of congressional intent, but federal agencies were generally slow in implementation efforts, as documented by two GAO reports.

The stormy development, near rescission, and revision of minimum guidelines by ATBCB documents, in a nutshell, the recurrent tensions and problems associated with policy implementation. Federal agencies, led by USPS, balked at certain provisions of the original guidelines, especially those that entailed significant costs and those where legislative intent was not clear. While pledging to aid the access of disabled persons, the agencies argued that their responsibilities were not unlimited. Handicapped groups and their representatives on ATBCB fought to keep the accessibility guidelines as stringent as politically feasible, seeing the guidelines as an important cornerstone in mainstreaming the disabled population of America.

Multiple institutional arenas participated in the creation and refinement of policies to implement the ABA, as illustrated by table 6-1, which lists the key decisions and actions taken in the development of implementation policy. Congress took the lead by creating the ABA, but it fell to administrative agencies to determine the specifics and to establish procedures to enhance accessibility. ATBCB was imposed upon the bureaucracy, as Congress sensed insufficient implementation efforts and saw need for a centralizing force to orchestrate barrier removal efforts across agencies of the federal government. Congress also intervened in 1976 to strengthen the ABA as its investigative arm, GAO, documented implementation problems and delays.

The federal courts also played a role, as dissatisfied advocates for disabled citizens challenged the implementation practices of USPS, particularly their rules governing accessibility in leased facilities. This issue had divided ATBCB, which sidestepped the question of leased facilities in its revised rules, citing the pending court case *Rose v. U.S. Postal Service*. The plaintiffs in this case charged that USPS was in violation of the ABA and the program accessibility provision of section 504, in that the agency had not moved more rapidly in achieving accessibility in its offices, particularly in those that were leased. USPS argued that it made accessibility modifications when so required, but that modifications in leased facilities were required only when new leases are created.

The plaintiffs lost in federal district court, where the judge ruled that "the words of the statute are clear. Buildings existing at the time of the lease are subject to the standards prescribed by the [ABA] only when they are altered."[63] This decision was reversed in federal circuit court, where the judge reviewed legislative intent and found that "Congress intended that the alterations be done by the private lessor as a condition of doing business with the Postal Service."[64] While this ruling technically pertains only to the California District Court's jurisdiction, the precedent set by the ruling is far-reaching.

Responding to the *Rose* case, USPS relinquished its interpretation of ABA requirements pertaining to leased space and accepted the notion that modifications are required at the point of lease renewals. USPS issued a notice of interim standards in the spring of 1986 for the large set of facilities leased by USPS.[65] For its part, ATBCB began drafting a section on leased facilities for inclusion in its minimum accessibility guidelines. In early 1987, the board issued a notice of proposed rulemaking, which outlined accessibility requirements for leased space.[66] With minor revisions, ATBCB approved these as final regulations at its meeting in May 1988, finally completing this multiyear debate about the requirements imposed by the ABA relevant to leased buildings and facilities.

The minimum guidelines and their counterpart, the uniform standards, today reflect a policy compromise regarding accessibility, a compromise crafted through multiple institutions. The original guidelines, published in early 1981, were a relatively strong interpretation of congressional intent. They were challenged by federal agencies who felt the guidelines surpassed legislative mandate; the challenge intensified as a change in the political environment resulted in initiatives to reduce regulatory activity by the federal government. While the deregulation fever was at its pitch, early in the first Reagan administration, forces nearly succeeded in revoking the minimum guidelines. Such action was not taken, however, as the various sides moved to accept a compromise solution, whereby some weakening of the guidelines was accepted, but the overall thrust and objective were retained.

With the last remaining significant area of controversy—accessibility re-

Table 6-1 Decisions and Actions within Institutional Arenas Affecting the Development of Implementation Policy for Barrier Removal

Institutional Arena/Date	*Decision/Action Taken*
National Commission on Architectural Barriers to Rehabilitation of the Handicapped (1967)	Released report detailing the extent of architectural barriers in public buildings and the mobility needs of persons with disabilities
Congress (1968)	Passed the Architectural Barriers Act (ABA) requiring accessibility in most federal and federally assisted buildings
General Services Administration (GSA) (1969)	Issued final regulations for implementing ABA, with language closely paralleling the statute
Congress (1970)	Amended ABA to include federally funded transit facilities
Congress (1973)	Created, through section 502 of Rehabilitation Act, the Architectural and Transportation Barriers Compliance Board (ATBCB) to ensure compliance with ABA
Congress (1974)	Section 502 amended, with secretary of HEW named as ATBCB chair; Consumer Advisory Panel created
General Accounting Office (GAO) (1975)	Released report critical of practices to implement ABA
Congress—House Subcommittee on Investigations and Review (1975)	Conducted oversight hearings on effectiveness of barrier removal policies; critical testimony presented
Congress (1976)	Amended ABA to include USPS and leased property; required agencies to issue regulations to implement ABA
GSA (1977–78)	Revised regulations for ABA, based on statutory changes made in 1976
Congress (1978)	Revised section 502, adding public members to ATBCB; required ATBCB to issue accessibility guidelines for implementing ABA
President (1979)	Carter delayed a year in naming public members to ATBCB
Congress—House Subcommittee on Select Education (1980)	Conducted oversight hearing on ATBCB and its implementation of ABA

126

Table 6-1   (Continued)

Institutional Arena/Date	Decision/Action Taken
ATBCB (1980–81)	Undertook rulemaking efforts to develop minimum guidelines for agencies to follow in complying with ABA; final rules issued in last days of Carter administration
GAO (1980)	Issued second report outlining deficiencies in implementation of ABA
Vice Presidential Task Force on Regulatory Relief (1981)	Targeted regulations for ABA as place for review, with eye toward regulatory relief
ATBCB (1981–82)	Internal battle over whether to rescind or weaken the existing minimum guidelines; eventually, a revised set of guidelines issued, which loosened some requirements and omitted reference to leased property
Congress—Senate (1981)	Senator Cranston attacked administration on effort to have minimum guidelines revised
Congress—House Subcommittee on Select Education (1981)	Conducted oversight hearings on ATBCB action to rescind or revise minimum guidelines
Office of Management and Budget (OMB)/Administration (1982)	Recommended all funding for ATBCB be eliminated; Congress maintained current level funding
OMB/Administration (1982–84)	Encouraged standard-setting agencies—HUD, GSA, DOD, USPS—to issue uniform guidelines for implementing ABA; at early point, this effort intended to create alternative to ATBCB minimum guidelines
Federal Courts (1984)	Federal circuit court ruled, in *Rose v. U.S. Postal Service*, that USPS has duty to provide handicapped access to leased buildings under ABA
Congress (1984)	Passed law to make facilities used for voting in federal elections accessible
Congress (1986)	Amended section 502, adding additional public member to ATBCB and other changes
ATBCB (1986–88)	Drafted and approved regulations to cover accessibility requirements for leased facilities

quirements for leased space—finally settled in 1988, attention begins to focus on enforcement activities. For its part, ATBCB continues to perform its central tasks of handling complaints about accessibility, responding to requests for technical assistance, and serving as a clearinghouse for accessibility information. ATBCB's annual report for 1987 notes that the number of accessibility complaints received by the board rose in most years during the 1980s; most of those where the board had jurisdiction were resolved through voluntary action.[67] It is interesting to note, however, that a large proportion of complaints lacked jurisdiction because they were not covered by provisions of the ABA. This would include buildings constructed prior to 1969 and those operated by state and local governments. These cases show that despite its reach, the ABA and its administrative regulations do not yet cover a large number of buildings in which the federal government conducts business.

7

Access, Mobility, and Public Transportation

Major political controversy has continually surrounded implementation policies to remove transportation barriers to handicapped citizens, and these policies have changed directions several times. Multiple institutional arenas have been used by the interested publics, both the regulated clients and the beneficiaries, to affect transportation policy for disabled Americans. Examination of policies to remove barriers to the use of public transportation highlights many of the tensions and dilemmas associated more generally with implementation of disability rights laws.

At least four distinct phases of transportation policy for handicapped citizens can be identified, each with its own basic organizing principle (Fix, Everett, and Kirby 1985). These include: (1) a "special efforts" phase, stipulating that efforts be made in the design and construction of transit facilities to accommodate handicapped individuals; (2) a "full-accessibility" phase, requiring that all modes of public transportation accommodate physically handicapped persons; (3) a "local option" phase, providing that local governments and transit systems take the initiative to achieve accessibility, and (4) a "comparable standards" phase, allowing flexibility in achieving accessibility but simultaneously requiring that services for disabled persons be comparable to those provided to other transit users. The current comparability standard is a rough compromise between policies that gave local units primary responsibility for implementation and those that required full accessibility with little local discretion in policy execution.

Transportation Needs of Disabled Persons

Early debates on alternative means of providing transportation services for physically handicapped persons were hampered by imprecise knowledge about (1) the number of persons unable to use public transportation because of phys-

129

ical barriers and (2) the potential demand by disabled individuals for such transportation if barriers were removed. To answer these questions, the Urban Mass Transportation Administration (UMTA) twice commissioned studies on the transportation needs of the nation's handicapped citizens. The first report, issued in 1973, estimated that about thirteen and a half million elderly and handicapped persons were unable to use existing mass transportation systems because of travel barriers.[1] These barriers included those related to vehicles, terminals, and transit stops. The report noted that no large community had undertaken a comprehensive, barrier-free transit system, although some efforts to accommodate handicapped and elderly persons had begun through the use of special services such as Dial-a-Ride. An estimate was made in the report on the latent travel demand of the elderly and handicapped; it was found that removal of travel barriers would nearly double trips by these groups.

The second study, issued in 1978 and based on interviews with handicapped persons across the nation, provided the following findings:[2]

1. There were 7,440,000 "transportation-handicapped" citizens, including five percent of urban dwellers and twenty-one percent of nonurban residents.

2. Compared to nontransportation-handicapped persons, transportation-handicapped persons took fewer trips in general, more medical/therapy-related trips, and fewer trips for commercial and recreational purposes.

3. Nineteen percent of transportation-handicapped persons could not use public transportation at all, and thirty percent could use such transportation only with substantial difficulty.

4. Twenty-nine percent of transportation-handicapped persons would take more trips if the ideal transportation type were available (representing an additional twenty-nine and a half million trips per month).

The study also describes the nature of physical barriers to each type of transportation mode, including those related to buses, subways, and taxis.

Early Legislation Regarding Public Transportation and Disabled Persons

The original legislation mandating attention to the needs of physically handicapped persons in public transportation has been aptly termed a "hodge-

130

podge'' (Katzmann 1986).[3] Policies concerning transportation accessibility came in short, somewhat unrelated bursts in the early 1970s but together stimulated efforts to enhance the mobility of physically disabled persons.

The Washington Metro and the Architectural Barriers Act

The first legislative attention to transportation policy and the needs of handicapped people occurred as the result of the Architectural Barriers Act (ABA) of 1968. This act mandated accessibility in newly constructed buildings and facilities financed by federal funds but did not specifically mention public transportation.[4] Within a year and a half after passage of the act, controversy arose about whether the act applied to the Washington, D.C., Metro system, a costly subway system being built in part with federal funds. The authority constructing the Metro claimed that it was exempt from compliance with the ABA because it was a regional authority funded by state as well as federal funds and whose plans were not subject to approval of the federal government. At hearings on this issue, groups representing handicapped citizens challenged this position and pushed Congress to clearly include the Metro system within the rubric of the ABA.[5] Congress responded by amending the ABA in 1970 so as to include the Washington Metro system.

Amendments to the Urban Mass Transportation Act of 1964

The Urban Mass Transportation Act of 1964 provided federal funding for the development of comprehensive and coordinated mass transportation systems in urban areas. The original act made no mention of handicapped persons. This was changed in 1970 through amendments to the Urban Mass Transportation Act. Section 16 of the 1970 act stated: ''It is hereby declared to be the national policy that elderly and handicapped persons have the same right as other persons to utilize mass transportation facilities and services.''[6] The act went on to stipulate that ''special efforts shall be made in the planning and design of mass transportation facilities and services so that the availability to elderly and handicapped persons of mass transportation which they can effectively utilize will be assured; and that all Federal programs offering assistance in the field of mass transportation should contain provisions implementing that policy.''[7]

The origins of the special efforts provisions are interesting because they were not included in the original versions of the 1970 act, nor were they added by the committees that considered the bill. Instead, the provisions were added by a floor amendment offered by Representative Mario Biaggi (D-NY), who

131

served as a policy entrepreneur on behalf of handicapped persons. It has been argued that the freshman legislator was in search of a policy issue to call his own and had become concerned about the mobility limitations experienced by physically disabled persons (Katzmann 1986, 28–29). The basic substance of the Biaggi amendments was to declare as national policy the commitment to make public transportation accessible to handicapped persons and to provide grants and loans to assist state and local authorities in meeting this objective. There was, however, no prescription that accessibility was *required* as a condition of receiving mass transit funds, nor was any federal agency given responsibility to promulgate accessibility rules and regulations.

Federal-Aid Highway Act of 1973

Still another piece of legislation in the transportation field is the Federal-Aid Highway Act of 1973. While the primary policy debate in this legislation concerned use of the Highway Trust Fund to finance urban mass transportation projects,[8] some provisions of the bill concerned the handicapped. One provided funds to the Washington, D.C., Metro system to subsidize construction of elevators to enhance access to the system by physically handicapped individuals. This funding resulted from hearings held in 1972 on the accessibility of the Metro.[9] Despite the 1970 amendments to the ABA, disability groups argued that the Metro was not moving actively forward to ensure accessibility.

Also included in the Federal-Aid Highway Act of 1973 was a provision authorizing grants and loans to private nonprofit organizations capable of providing transportation services to the elderly and handicapped, including paratransit or demand-responsive systems (e.g., Dial-a-Ride programs). This provision resulted from an amendment by Representative Bella Abzug (D-NY), who, in testimony before the House Subcommittee on Housing, suggested that such services would aid the immediate needs of handicapped and elderly persons.[10] The amendment was included in the committee report on the bill and the version passed by Congress. Still another provision, similar to that in the 1970 amendments to the Urban Mass Transportation Act, required that the secretary of transportation ensure that transit projects receiving federal funds be planned and designed so as to be accessible to the elderly and handicapped who could not otherwise use such systems.

Overview of Early Legislation

In a piecemeal fashion, Congress began to address the mobility needs of handicapped persons in the 1970s. Through the efforts of a few policy entre-

132

preneurs, some who were looking for an issue to champion, a series of legislative initiatives were introduced to increase the accessibility of public transit systems to elderly and disabled persons. Initially, attention was focused on the Metro subway system in the nation's capital, a large and visible project with substantial federal funding. Groups representing disabled citizens argued persuasively that this highly touted, state-of-the-art system was not, despite all of its technological sophistication, being built so as to be accessible to physically disabled people. Appealing to the powerful symbols of equity and fairness, these groups were able to persuade Congress to intercede to make the Metro accessible; Congress even agreed to allocate an extra $65 million to pay for vertical elevators.

Throughout the early 1970s, Congress grew progressively more aware of the needs of handicapped Americans, including their mobility problems and difficulties in using public transportation. The initial legislative response was to require that "special efforts" be taken to enhance accessibility, while allowing such efforts to be designed at the local level. By 1974, the emphasis began to shift to stronger measures that would go beyond requiring special efforts and providing limited funding for research and paratransit alternatives.

Phase One of Rulemaking: Special Efforts Regulations

Responding to transportation-related legislation of the early 1970s, UMTA moved to issue regulations concerning handicapped needs in public transportation. Both internal and external factors motivated rulemaking activity. Internally, UMTA realized that it would eventually be required to issue some type of regulations or standards related to access of the handicapped, in light of the legislative activity in this area. According to Katzmann (1986, 91–94), UMTA, in devising rules, was concerned that its own authority would not be unduly restricted and that it would be protected as much as possible from legal challenges. An external stimulus to rulemaking was a court suit against the Department of Transportation (DOT) and other parties concerning purchase of buses that were seen as inaccessible to physically handicapped persons (*Disabled in Action of Baltimore v. Hughes*). As part of the out-of-court settlement, DOT agreed to issue regulations concerning the design of mass transportation facilities usable by the elderly and handicapped.

In 1974, UMTA devised an initial draft of the rules[11] and, in November of that year, sponsored three informal hearings held in Washington. One can see from what transpired at these hearings that the goodwill and fairness symbols that had made handicapped legislation acceptable to Congress had begun to fade, as cost concerns emerged as a controversial issue. A key question began to emerge about *who* would be responsible for paying the costs of accessibility, given general consensus on the importance of the accessibility objective. The battle between groups representing handicapped persons and the regulated clients (public transit authorities) began to take form at this stage. During the hearings, representatives of disabled persons objected to the creation of a separate transportation system, which would work against their overall aim to mainstream.[12] The transit authorities, represented by the powerful American Public Transit Association (APTA), argued for local flexibility in meeting accessibility objectives. Another set of participants at the hearings were manufacturers of mass transit equipment, who argued for performance standards over precise design specifications, stating that the former would generate more creative responses to accessibility needs.

Apparently, UMTA took the hearing testimony seriously, for it revised regulations and issued the new ones as proposed rules in February 1975. The regulations cited provisions of the Federal-Aid Highway Act of 1973, the Urban Mass Transportation Act as amended, and section 504 of the Rehabilitation Act of 1973 as the authority for promulgating rules.[13] Among the provisions spelled out in the regulations were requirements related to planning transportation systems and purchasing equipment:

1. All transportation improvement programs and plans submitted to UMTA would include an element intended to meet the transportation needs of the elderly and handicapped persons (including identification of the location and projected travel needs of elderly and handicapped).

2. Each applicant for capital assistance would provide a definite plan and program for meeting the needs of the elderly and handicapped.

3. Fixed transportation facilities would be accessible to the physically disabled and would be designed, constructed, and altered in accordance with minimum standards set by the American National Standards Institute (ANSI).[14]

The focus of the proposed rules, then, was on special efforts by implementing authorities to plan, design, and construct facilities so as to be accessible to persons with disabilities and to plan services usable by these citizens. Transit authorities were given the flexibility they wanted to plan transportation services.

During the period of public comments on the regulatory proposals, several hundred responses were received by UMTA, in addition to testimony given at hearings in Los Angeles, Denver, Chicago, St. Petersburg, Boston, and Washington. Final rules were issued in April 1976.[15] The phrase "special efforts," derived from the Biaggi amendment to the Urban Mass Transportation Act, runs rampant throughout the final regulations (while not in the proposed ones). Such special efforts requirements, designed to enhance the accessibility of elderly and handicapped individuals to transit systems, were attached to planning and capital assistance grants made by UMTA. The key concept of special efforts was not, however, defined in the regulations, although some examples were provided of the "level of effort that will be deemed necessary to satisfy this requirement with respect to wheelchair users and semiambulatory persons."[16] These examples included:

1. A program for wheelchair users and semiambulatory handicapped persons that would involve the expenditure of an average annual dollar amount equivalent to a minimum of five percent of the section 5 apportionment to urbanized areas.

2. Purchase of new wheelchair-accessible fixed-route equipment until one-half of the fleet was accessible, or the alternative provision of service that would provide comparable coverage and service levels.

3. A system that would ensure that every wheelchair user in the urbanized area would have public transportation available if requested for ten round-trips per week at fares comparable to those charged on standard transit systems.

The regulations stated that these examples were "not regulatory standards or minimums," nor did they "exhaust all valid approaches."[17] The examples highlight the flexibility designed into the rules, for they allow transit providers to use such options as accessible buses, paratransit systems, and others to satisfy regulatory requirements. Such a flexible approach with local options, UMTA argued, was justifiable, given that

> the comments on the proposed regulations revealed substantial disagreement over the best type of service for wheelchair users—accessible fixed route service, with or without accessible feeder service, demand-responsive van or small bus service, subscription service, subsidized shared-ride taxi service, or some combination of these services. Given present knowledge, we cannot say that one of these services or even one combination is best for all communities. In fact, it is likely that site-specific planning and tailoring of appropriate services will always be necessary.[18]

The last sentence of this argument is interesting in that, within a few years,

DOT would reject the site-specific approach to providing accessibility to handicapped persons.

Phase Two of Rulemaking: Section 504 and Full-Accessibility Regulations

The long-term impacts of the special efforts regulations will never be known, since the 1976 regulations were practically obsolete when they were issued. Within two years, DOT was engaged in another major round of rulemaking regarding accessibility. This effort, and the abandonment of the special efforts approach to implementation, resulted from section 504 of the Rehabilitation Act of 1973.

As described in chapter four, the Department of Health, Education, and Welfare (HEW) issued final rules regarding guidelines for federal agencies to follow in implementing the nondiscrimination provisions of section 504 in early 1978.[19] Included in these coordination regulations were provisions concerning program accessibility in public transit systems. In applying the program accessibility principle to transportation, a key decision had to be made as to whether ''program'' referred to the transit system *as a whole* or to the component programs *within* the system. Some comments on the proposed rules had suggested that the ''system as a whole'' conception of ''program'' be employed. Had this interpretation been accepted, then compliance with program accessibility could have been achieved through parallel paratransit systems, since these would have enabled the system ''as a whole'' to provide transportation services accessible to handicapped persons. This interpretation was not much different from the special efforts approach to accessibility. The final HEW regulations came down firmly and succinctly on this point, requiring accessibility in *each* of the component programs within the transportation system.[20] The importance of this decision should not be understated. The selected definition of ''program'' as each component of transit systems meant that modifications would have to be made in practically all components, most notably in bus and rail transportation. These required modifications would certainly cost substantial dollars, and no longer could anyone claim that the antidiscrimination measure would entail no new costs.

Generally, the Department of Transportation accepted the lead of HEW in setting policy directions for section 504, even though it had recently completed an extensive rulemaking effort on its own. This acceptance of HEW guidelines, which might have been challenged by DOT, has been attributed to a significant change in the policy environment.[21] In January 1977, the Carter administration took office and Brock Adams became secretary of transportation. The new secretary was generally sympathetic to the mobility plight of disabled citizens and, given his basically liberal ideology, was not opposed to using governmental regulation to increase accessibility of handicapped persons to public transportation.

Writing the Full-Accessibility Regulations

As a result of HEW guidelines and the change of political leadership, DOT began the process of drafting regulations relevant to section 504 in early 1978. The department began by reviewing its special efforts rules and determined that these would not fulfill the mandate set out in HEW guidelines for implementing section 504. With this determination, DOT set out to devise another set of regulations. In a notice of proposed rulemaking, DOT issued proposed regulations in June 1978, along with a detailed economic impact statement listing expected costs and benefits of the regulations.[22]

Central to this discussion were the rules covering program accessibility. Following HEW guidelines, the proposed regulations required that new buildings and facilities, and alterations to existing facilities, be accessible to handicapped persons and that minimum ANSI accessibility standards be followed.

Two areas would prove more troublesome: modification of existing buildings and stipulations regarding the purchase of fixed-route buses. While program accessibility did not require that each part of each transportation program be accessible, it did mean that *some* parts of *each* program would be accessible. The proposed rules prescribed a strong definition of program accessibility for fixed facilities, requiring that "all public mass transportation stations and other fixed facilities be accessible to handicapped persons, including those that cannot use steps, except that in unusual circumstances, where compelling reasons exist, a small portion of stations or other fixed facilities may be exempted."[23] These were strong words. Program accessibility meant, under the regulations, that accessibility would be required in *most* fixed facilities, not half or some small percentage. As DOT recognized, such modifications would entail substantial costs, estimated at approximately $1.6 billion and representing the "great bulk of costs of implementing the regulation."[24]

The other issue that generated widespread concern centered on regulations for the purchase of new buses for fixed-route service. The regulations required that fixed-route systems be made program accessible within three years (within six years for extraordinarily expensive changes), so that the system, when viewed in its entirety, would be accessible to handicapped persons who cannot use steps. The regulations stipulated that all new fixed-route buses purchased with UMTA funds would be accessible to the handicapped and that after October 1, 1979, such buses would meet the Transbus design standards devised by DOT.[25]

In total, these full-accessibility regulations represented a major departure from the special efforts rules issued only two years before. No longer would local transit systems have substantial flexibility in designing accessible transportation systems, nor could they rely on separate paratransit systems by themselves to meet compliance with federal regulations. Instead, they would be mandated to modify all components of the overall transit network.

Reactions to the Full-Accessibility Regulations

The reactions to the proposed regulations were swift and strong. Over six hundred comments were received during the rulemaking period, in addition to testimony given at five regional hearings. These comments concerned a wide variety of issues, some being narrow and technical and others questioning the basic organizing principles underlying the rules. The broad issues expressed in the comments concerned the costs of compliance, distribution of benefits, workability of technology, and use of paratransit systems.

The Costs of Compliance. Many comments, and particularly those from transit authorities and their representative, APTA, concerned the costs of meeting the DOT requirements for full accessibility. In particular, these commentors recited the costs required to modify existing transit stations and facilities and to purchase accessible buses. APTA repeatedly articulated its cost concerns in extensive communications with DOT during the rulemaking period, arguing that the agency had underestimated compliance costs and the inflationary impact of the regulations.[26] The Ohio Public Transit Association concurred with APTA, arguing that "the costs of compliance with the proposed 504 regulations are immense and the inflationary impact almost incalculable."[27]

Distribution of Benefits. Several issues relating to the distribution of benefits under the full-accessibility regulations were raised during rulemaking, some directly and others more subtly. One salient issue concerned whether fully accessible transit stations and vehicles would significantly enhance the mobility of physically handicapped persons, since such individuals may not have a means to travel to the accessible stations. DOT's own study, released in 1978, found that handicapped persons showed greater interest in door-to-door service and subsidized ride programs than in accessible fixed-route buses.[28] This issue—of how much accessible bus systems would enhance the mobility of handicapped persons—was to continually plague the advocates of full-accessibility regulations.

It was also noted that full accessibility would aid only a small fraction of the total pool of physically disabled persons. Accessibility was modeled on making transit systems available to wheelchair users, as mandated by federal laws. The wheelchair image was sometimes invoked to stress the limited number of individuals who would be accommodated through full accessibility, and this number, when coupled with costs, generated very high cost-per-wheelchair-rider figures. One set of such figures showed the costs of accessibility per wheelchair user to vary from $59 to $1,440 per trip (Fielding 1982, 271); another estimated the thirty-year cost of making public transit accessible to be $38 per user.

Even more subtly, critics began to raise a very basic issue, never satisfactorily resolved during legislative consideration, of whether there were bounds on the needs and rights of citizens with disabilities. This issue was subtly raised when the Ohio Public Transit Association compared the needs of handicapped individuals with those of its traditional riders:

> Often overlooked in discussions of transporting the severely handicapped on regular transit services are the effects such provisions would have on the quality of the service as experienced by regular riders. It is these steady patrons who are the principal justification for public transit, those who ride daily to work or education. Transit, and indeed national energy policy, cannot afford any action which would impair the major market.

Not so implicit here is the perception that transit services are designed primarily for "regular" (i.e., nondisabled) riders, and that they have "rights" to quality service that should not be impaired through pursuit of accessibility objectives.[29] While not all critics were as open about their concerns that the needs of handicapped persons were eclipsing those of others, it is clear that such sentiments were not uncommon during this period.

Questions about Technology. Several comments received during rulemaking questioned the technology associated with accessible buses, in general, and DOT's Transbus, in particular. APTA and other transit authorities argued that the lift technology on accessible buses was unproved, and that it was thus questionable to include requirements for such buses in the regulations. Their arguments were backed up by reports from authorities who were using lift-equipped buses with less than complete success. A transit authority in the St. Louis area reported, for example, that on any given day fifty to sixty percent of its lift fleet was inoperable. Problems of operating and maintaining the lifts raised many questions about the "technological fix" as a means of achieving accessibility.

Paratransit and Specialized Transportation Services. Numerous commentors suggested that demand-response systems such as Dial-a-Ride, jitney services, and taxi vouchers would be both more cost-effective and more responsive to the transportation needs of handicapped persons than fully accessible systems. The DOT regulations suggested that such systems could be employed while longer-term efforts to modify transit facilities and vehicles were undertaken. Many commentors, including transit authorities and some handicapped individuals, argued that paratransit should be used on a permanent basis. The handicapped community was divided on this issue, as it remains today, because paratransit, while more responsive and usable by disabled individuals, represents a separate and segregated transportation system (Clark 1980). In this regard, paratransit violates the long-standing effort of handicapped groups to integrate disabled citizens into the mainstream of society. On this basis, other groups representing disabled persons challenged the paratransit approach for its segregating impact (e.g., Cannon and Rainbow 1980).

The Final Accessibility Regulations

DOT basically stood firm on its positions regarding accessibility in the final regulations, although it responded in detail to many of the comments received during rulemaking, as it issued final regulations in May 1979.[30] The introduction stated: "The Department is convinced that the rule responds to the needs of handicapped persons in compliance with the law and in a prudent and financially responsible manner."[31] The regulations retained the important concept of accessibility in all transit programs operated in a community, the requirement that new transit facilities be built according to ANSI standard, and the stipulation that new buses bought with DOT funds be accessible to wheelchairs. In a move to appease transit authorities, DOT extended, from six to ten years, the time for authorities to have half their buses accessible. To clarify concerns, the final regulations also stipulated that the regulations did not require any lift-equipping of buses for which a solicitation was issued on or before February 15, 1977. The regulations reviewed the costs of making bus systems accessible, as reported in comments submitted during rulemaking, disputed some cost estimates, and argued, in conclusion: "While not denying the reality of increased costs for operators, the Department is not persuaded that the financial impact, in absolute or relative terms, is as high as some commentators assert."[32]

In the hotly debated area of modification of existing facilities, DOT kept its requirement that key stations become accessible within three years, with possible extensions if extraordinary costs were involved (twelve years for rapid rail, twenty years for light rail, and thirty years for commuter rail). These key station requirements were to be the most expensive of the regulations promulgated by DOT.[33]

Controversy over the Full-Accessibility Regulations

Controversy about full-accessibility objectives in public transportation did not end with the issuance of DOT's final rules; instead, it intensified. APTA, other regional associations, and individual transit authorities sounded off long and loud about the excessive costs they were required to bear under the regulations. Their complaints did not fall on deaf ears, as many members of Congress began to question the wisdom of the full-accessibility rules that derived from the short and symbolic section 504. Transit officials voiced their concerns to Congress during various hearings on vocational rehabilitation and urban mass transportation held during and immediately after rulemaking.

The themes reiterated by APTA and the transit authorities at the hearings were that full accessibility was very costly (and they provided extensive data to back up their claim) and that local flexibility was the best means of meeting the transportation needs of physically disabled people. One example of these arguments is the testimony of the executive director of APTA, presented at hearings before the House Subcommittee on Surface Transportation:

> While we believe that it is desirable to provide strong national guidance as to the role of public transit systems in providing mobility for the elderly and handicapped citizens, we also believe that local communities must have the ability to decide for themselves the specific ways in which a nationally determined goal will be met. . . . local decisions as to the choice of alternative transportation services must be premised on local needs.[34]

For their part, groups representing disabled persons continued to press Congress for strong efforts to remove physical barriers that impede access to public transit. In testimony before the Subcommittee on Surface Transportation, John Lancaster of the Paralyzed Veterans of America testified in favor of the accessible Transbus and argued against the local option idea: "That [the Transbus] only makes sense to me, pure, simple logic, and we do not think that, whether it is the county in Iowa, or Burlington, that they should have any choice as to whether or not they are going to buy this bus."[35]

Negative reactions were expressed in other arenas. Public leaders, particularly local government officials, used the media to complain about the compliance costs associated with implementing section 504 in public transportation. One critical opponent of DOT's accessibility regulations was Mayor Edward Koch of New York City, who argued:

> The Departments of Transportation and Health and Human Services (the erstwhile Department of Health, Education, and Welfare) have issued regulations that set as a mandate total accessibility for the handicapped to transit *systems*, instead of dealing with the *function* of transportation: mobility. In rejecting numerous appeals for modest exemptions and waivers, these regulations impose a restrictive and inflexible interpretation of the basic mandate of section 504. Ironically, in focusing on accessibility the regulations fail to benefit a significant portion of the severely disabled. Subways and buses may ultimately be made fully accessible, but a disabled person may not be able to get to the system to enjoy its accessibility. (Koch 1980, 45)

Koch's statement echoes the two themes made by transit and other local government officials: full accessibility is too costly and does not represent the most effective means of enhancing the mobility of physically disabled persons.

The media remained actively attuned during this period, presenting news stories on debates about the regulations and the compliance costs likely to be incurred by transit authorities. Even the more liberal press raised tough questions about the full-accessibility requirement. The *New York Times*, for example, argued in an editorial in early 1980: "Want a textbook example of how good but vague intentions can balloon into exorbitant programs? Consider the regulations that require Federally funded mass transit systems to make buses, subways, streetcars, and commuter trains accessible by wheelchairs."[36] The editorial went on to voice a notion that was gaining increasing acceptance, namely, that the needs of disabled persons should be balanced against the costs of meeting those needs: "Let [Congress] do what it should have done in the first place: balance its laudably humanitarian instincts with some notion of what the program will cost and who will have to pay."[37]

Unfavorable Reports on Full-Accessibility Regulations

At least two reports issued in late 1979 and early 1980 generated further controversy about DOT's full-accessibility regulations. One study was conducted by the Congressional Budget Office (CBO) upon request of the Senate Budget Committee and the Transportation Subcommittee of the House Committee on

Public Works and Transportation.[38] Among the findings of this report, subsequently challenged by DOT analysts, were the following:

1. The DOT full-accessibility regulations would cost $6.8 billion to implement over thirty years.

2. Enactment of DOT regulations would serve no more than seven percent of all severely disabled persons.

3. Spreading the cost of implementation of DOT regulations across the limited number of wheelchair users would result in costs of $38 per trip, compared to average per-trip costs of 85¢ for the general public on mass transportation.

4. An alternate taxi plan offering door-to-door service would cost thirty-five percent less than the full-accessibility plan, serve twenty-six percent of severely disabled, and have an average per-trip cost of $7.62.

Given these and other data, the CBO report concluded: "The rules issued by DOT in implementing section 504 of the Rehabilitation Act of 1973 would prove extremely costly and would benefit a relatively small number of handicapped persons. . . . If the Congress wishes to offer handicapped persons transportation services that they can and will use, door-to-door services and specially equipped automobiles appear most promising."[39]

A second report was issued by the Subcommittee on Oversight and Review of the House Committee on Public Works and Transportation, subtitled "Do We Know What We're Trying to Do?"[40] The report, based on hearings held in the previous year, was critical of what it saw as DOT's overreliance on technological developments in pursuing its objectives, particularly of the workability and cost-effectiveness of the Transbus scheme. The report also questioned the full-accessibility principle, noting that it "found it significant that there apparently is a difference of opinion within the handicapped community, just as there have been differences within DOT, as to the preferred strategy—full accessibility or special local services."[41] The report recommended that further thought and discussion should be given "regarding the issue of full accessibility versus local option to provide special services."[42] In a minority opinion at the end of the report, a group of committee members directly endorsed the local option position.

These reports, critical of full-accessibility rules as an effective means to increase the mobility of physically handicapped persons, were widely circulated and used by opponents of full-accessibility objectives to criticize DOT's regulations. In addition, two other studies commissioned by DOT to evaluate the Transbus system were released during 1979. Both questioned whether the current Transbus technology was sufficiently developed and suggested that the purchase of buses with the existing lift technology might be a financial risk.[43] These studies added further fuel to doubts about technological developments as a prime basis for pursuing full-accessibility objectives.

Transit Authorities Take the Offensive

APTA and the transit authorities reacted to the DOT regulations by reaching out to other institutional arenas in an effort to overturn full accessibility as the basic organizing principle. One effort was to challenge the DOT rules in the federal courts, charging that they went beyond section 504's authority (*APTA v. Lewis*). In essence, the plaintiffs claimed that section 504's brief statement of antidiscriminatory policy provided no statutory authority to require full accessibility in public transit systems. While APTA lost the first round at the district court level, they would eventually fare better in the circuit court.

Congress Considers Full Accessibility and Alternatives

APTA and other regulated clients also turned to Congress to press for relief from full accessibility. These efforts came to a head in 1980 as both houses of Congress considered measures to limit the impact of the DOT regulations. The measures were considered as part of legislation dealing with urban mass transportation systems. Action in the Senate began as Representative Edward Zorinsky (D-NB) introduced an amendment to the transportation act that would allow local governments to comply with full-accessibility regulations by spending five percent of their mass transit money on transportation services for elderly and handicapped persons; determination of how the money would be spent would be determined locally. In essence, the plan would resemble the special efforts approach with a five-percent spending requirement.

The amendment was opposed in this form by traditional Senate advocates of disabled citizens, including Senators Harrison Williams (D-NJ) and Alan Cranston (D-CA). These senators and others negotiated a compromise with Zorinsky. Transit systems could provide transportation services to physically handicapped persons through means other than fully accessible buses and transit facilities if they (1) spent five percent of transit money for handicapped persons, (2) provided transportation services no less beneficial than the DOT rules required, and (3) developed alternative programs that met specified service criteria. The service criteria, which would place constraints on local options, included provisions that (1) transportation service be supplied throughout the recipient's service area, (2) no waiting lists or advance registration requirements be used, (3) fare rates be comparable to those of the transit system in general, (4) minimum waiting periods be reasonable, and (5) there be no restrictions on travel purpose.[44] The amendment further required that alternative plans could not be approved by DOT until the views of the handicapped persons who would use the service were solicited. The Zorinsky amendment, as modified through negotiation, passed by voice vote.

The House considered a similar local option proposal during consideration of the Surface Transportation Act of 1980 in the Subcommittee on Surface Transportation and the Subcommittee on Oversight and Review (both of the Committee on Public Works and Transportation) and on the House floor. As in the Senate, there appeared to be growing support for some form of local option plan, although legislators disagreed on the extent that local flexibility should be coupled to service requirements. The House finally accepted a compromise amendment offered by Representative James Howard (D-NJ). This amendment allowed for local flexibility in meeting accessibility objectives but went further than other proposals in that it specified minimum service criteria.

In drawing up the Howard amendment, the staff on the Subcommittee on the Handicapped conducted informal negotiations with key interest groups, including APTA, Paralyzed Veterans of America, the American Coalition of Citizens with Disabilities (ACCD), DOT, and CBO.[45] Howard hoped that the amendment that resulted from these negotiations would appease the various groups who were so bitterly divided over the question of stepping away from full accessibility toward greater local flexibility. The service criteria contained within the negotiated amendment paralleled those in the Zorinsky amendment in the Senate and included provisions about waiting time, not making restrictions in regard to travel purpose, and hours of operation.[46] After further compromise, the Howard amendment was accepted by voice vote.

In the end, the debate, negotiation, and compromise in both houses yielded little result, for the mass transportation act was never passed by Congress. There was substantial disagreement over various components of the bill other than the handicapped transit policies. But while the bill never became law, the conception of local flexibility in designing accessible transit systems, coupled with requirements about minimum standards of service quality, would later reemerge as a principle to organize transportation policy for physically handicapped people.

The Unraveling of Full-Accessibility Regulations

By 1980, the conceptual threads of the full-accessibility regulations, issued by DOT in 1979, had begun to unravel. Congress demonstrated through amendments added to mass transportation bills that it was willing to forsake the full-accessibility rules, which had generated substantial pressure from the transit industry for relief. Implementation was proving difficult as city after city applied for exemptions from regulations, arguing that such conditions as climate and topography made accessibility unworkable in their communities.[47] While DOT did not consider most of the exemption requests legitimate, processing the requests did consume agency resources. The volume of requests indicated that many transit agencies were not willing to move aggressively to implement the regulations.

Once the unraveling began, it was hard to stop. The death blow to the regulations came in 1981, when the U.S. Court of Appeals for the District of Columbia overturned a lower court decision in the *APTA v. Lewis* case and ruled that the full-accessibility regulations exceeded statutory intent as spelled out in section 504. At the same time, significant changes had occurred in the political environment, as Ronald Reagan, elected to office by a wide margin, and his administration took office. One of Reagan's campaign pledges had been to aggressively pursue deregulation. Early in its first year in office, the administration signaled its intention to review many federal regulations, including several concerned with nondiscrimination on the basis of handicap (Clark 1981c). The new administration did not find the *APTA* decision particularly troublesome, since conservatives had not been pleased generally with the full-accessibility regulations.

Another factor to further defuse the full-accessibility approach was a 1981 decision by the Department of Justice (DOJ), reflecting its new position as coordinator of federal government efforts to implement section 504. When HEW was split into two separate departments, President Carter initially assigned section 504 coordinating responsibility to the new Department of Health and Human Services. Soon afterward, however, Carter transferred coordinating responsibility to DOJ, where enforcement of other civil rights laws were centered, through Executive Order 12250.[48] Using its newly appointed authority, DOJ in August 1981 suspended the section 504 guidelines (as outlined in the original HEW implementation guidelines) for mass transportation, citing the *APTA* decision.[49]

Phase Three of Rulemaking: The Local Options Regulations

Recognizing the *APTA* decision and the ideological change associated with the new administration, and anticipating DOJ's suspension of implementation guidelines for mass transportation, DOT entered its third phase of regulations. In July 1981, DOT issued what it termed an "interim final rule," which amended the 1979 rules by deleting the regulations covering mass transportation.[50] The *APTA* decision was listed as the reason for the change in regulations. In place of the full-accessibility principle, DOT adopted the original principle of special efforts, which provided local flexibility in determining how to make transportation systems usable by the physically handicapped. In terms of program accessibility, the rules mandated that transit authorities "certify that special efforts are being made in their service area to provide transportation that handicapped persons can use. This transportation shall be reasonable in comparison to the transportation provided to the general public and shall meet a significant fraction of the actual transportation needs of such persons within a reasonable time."[51] One may note some ambiguity in the special efforts requirement, especially as regards to "reasonableness" in comparing handicapped and general public transportation and the time frame for implementation. The closing date for comments was set for sixty days after issuance of the interim rules. No further rules were issued, however, until 1983, as still another organizing principle had come into play.

Certainly, as could be predicted, interest groups representing disabled persons were quite dissatisfied with the interim final rules. They declared the rules were backtracking, tossing determination of system accessibility back into the laps of local governments. They expressed their concerns to DOT through comments offered on the interim final rules, most of which supported a return to the full-accessibility approach.[52]

The American Coalition of Citizens with Disabilities was one of the lead groups to challenge the return to the special efforts approach to implementation. ACCD prepared a report in response to the CBO report (described above), which had raised questions about the cost-effectiveness of full-accessibility regulations. The report argued that "local option as currently practiced by the transit industry has resulted in the design of a variety of systems highly discriminatory against disabled people in that they provide a much lower level of service than that which is provided to the general public, even though they may provide a symbolic, 'superior', door-to-door feature" (Cannon and Rainbow 1980, ix).

The legislators who had customarily supported strong measures to enhance accessibility reacted to the interim final rules and the concerns of groups representing physically disabled persons. Five senators on the Banking, Housing, and Urban Affairs Committee requested, in January 1982, that the General Accounting Office (GAO) conduct a study of the special efforts being undertaken by localities to accommodate the transportation needs of elderly and handicapped citizens. The GAO report, based on a survey of eighty-four transit systems in thirty-three states, found that while accessibility efforts had been performed or initiated, many mobility barriers remained.[53] One report finding was particularly interesting: only thirty of the eighty-three bus systems and six of the fourteen rail systems intend to reach the level of accessibility as required by the 1979 full-accessibility rules, now that the rules have been removed.

Phase Four of Rulemaking: Comparable Standards Approach

The Senate took the initiative in 1982 by adopting a legislative provision calling for DOT to promulgate rules establishing minimum service criteria for transit authorities to follow in serving physically handicapped people. The provision took the form of an amendment to the Surface Transportation Assistance Act of 1982, an extensive law covering many aspects of transportation policy. The amendment, offered on the floor by Senators Alan Cranston and Donald Riegel (D-MI), sought to toughen the local option, special efforts approach to accessibility by requiring the secretary of transportation to establish minimum service criteria for transit authorities to follow in designing services for elderly and handicapped citizens. The amendment stipulated that services should be "the same as or comparable to those which such recipients provide to the general public."[54] Unlike previous measures, however, the amendment did not list any minimum criteria, leaving such determination to DOT. The Cranston-Riegel amendment was eventually passed by Senate vote and became part of the Surface Transportation Assistance Act of 1982. It was subsequently accepted by the House-Senate conference committee with substitute wording that deleted the "same as or comparable" service language.

Proposed Rules for Comparable Standards

In September 1983, DOT issued a set of proposed rules in response to the Cranston-Riegel amendment, signaling another round of rulemaking activity.[55] The purpose of the regulations was to establish minimum service criteria for the provision of transportation services to handicapped and elderly persons, to provide for public participation in establishing such services, and to create a mechanism for enforcement. The regulations repeated the special efforts provision included in the interim final rules and stipulated three means by which localities could make services available to elderly and handicapped people: (1) make fifty percent of fixed-route buses used during peak and nonpeak hours accessible, (2) provide a paratransit or special service, or (3) provide some mixture of both.

The regulations also listed a set of minimum criteria for the provision of transportation services to elderly and handicapped persons. These included stipulations that:

1. Service would be available through the same geographic areas as served by transportation to the general public.

2. Service would be offered on the same days and during the same hours as services provided to the general public.

3. The cost of trips would be comparable to the cost of a similar trip (in length and time of day) provided to the general public.

4. Use of the service would not be restricted by priorities or conditions related to trip purpose.

5. Users of the service would not be required to wait for the service more than a reasonable length of time.

6. There would not be a waiting list for the provision of service to eligible users.

The origins of these criteria date back to 1980 and were proposed in a similar form in the Zorinsky amendment. With the Cranston-Riegel amendment purposely avoiding any listing of service criteria, the rulemakers went back to earlier legislation as a guide for devising minimum service guidelines.

The proposed regulations also included a cost-cap provision stating that no recipient of DOT funds would have to spend more than a ceiling amount in any fiscal year to meet the service requirements for elderly and handicapped persons. The proposed rules offered two alternative cost-cap formulas and invited comments on which alternative, or other formula, would be appropriate. One plan was to base the cap on 7.1 percent of the average annual amount of financial assistance expected in the current fiscal year and received in the two previous fiscal years. The other approach was to require no expenditures in excess of three percent of the average of the recipient's operating budget for the current fiscal year and the previous two fiscal years. Thus, one approach would set the cost-cap in reference to federal dollars received and the other in reference to operating budgets.

Consideration of Proposed Rules

As had been the case in its other rulemaking efforts, DOT received many comments in response to the rules proposed in 1983. The comments were predictable, with the transit industry arguing that the rules were too stringent and would impose substantial costs on transportation providers. Taking the opposite position, the disabled community pushed wherever possible for strict rules and expressed concern that the cost-cap provision would weaken efforts to achieve a more accessible public transit system. Overall, however, the comments demonstrated less strident and divisive positions; debate centered more on refinement of the rules than on broad differences in philosophy about the need to pursue accessibility so as to enhance the mobility of physically handicapped persons.[56]

Debate about the proper extent of local discretion in fashioning transportation services to serve handicapped persons reemerged in the comments about the rules. Typical of comments received from the transit industry was a submission from the Knoxville/Knox (Tennessee) Metropolitan Planning Commission, which argued for greater local discretion: "Our staff is convinced that the local community is in a better position to make decisions on how best to serve the transportation needs of local handicapped and elderly residents."[57] Disability groups expressed the opposite view, worrying that local option would blunt accessibility efforts and allow proliferation of separate transit systems for the handicapped. A comment from the executive director of the Connecticut Office of Protection and Advocacy for Handicapped and Developmentally Disabled Persons made this point: "My initial objection to the proposed rule is that it contains no requirement for equal access to public transit by persons with disabilities, nor does it even make a minimal effort to encourage the development of integrated transportation services."

The several hundred comments received in response to the proposed rules also focused on the particulars of the regulations.[58] In terms of service options (i.e., fifty percent accessible buses, paratransit, or a combination), most commentors reacted favorably. There was greater controversy about the minimum service criteria. Advocates of persons with disabilities suggested that other criteria might be added, including, for example, those related to wait time, ride length, quality of phone service for scheduling paratransit rides, and training of transit personnel. Handicapped groups also favored public participation in determining service programs and argued that their participation should be strengthened.

The cost-cap requirement also generated a large number of comments for the rulemaking docket. The handicapped community objected in principle to the cap, arguing that it weakened the import of the rules by placing a limitation on the costs that would be incurred to provide service to serve elderly and disabled citizens. Just one example is a comment submitted by the Governor's Committee on Employment of the Handicapped, State of Washington:

These proposed rules would treat the transportation needs of people with disabilities as an optional service which will only be addressed if there is enough money left after basic services are provided. . . . Putting a dollar limit on the recognition of a person's civil rights subverts the whole tradition of civil rights protections in this country and no justification exists for such a limit in the proposed rules.

For its part, the transit industry, and its representative, APTA, voiced support for the concept of the cost cap but argued that the two formulas would result in excessive expenditures.

During this time, DOT prepared a regulatory impact analysis of the proposed rules.[59] This detailed document explored the costs and benefits of implementing the proposed regulations. One interesting finding, of many presented in the report, concerned a comparison of implementation costs under various alternatives, including the two cost-cap formulas listed in the proposed rules, as well as paratransit and fifty percent lift-equipped bus options. The nationwide, thirty-year present value cost for these plans were as follows:[60]

Paratransit (user-side subsidy):	$0.98 billion
50 percent of buses lift equipped:	$0.69 billion
7.1 percent DOT funds:	$2.72 billion
3 percent operating budget:	$2.37 billion

The results showed the formula based on operating budgets to cost less than the one based on federal funds received by the recipient. Interestingly, the paratransit and accessible bus options were seen as requiring less expenditure, in the long run, than either of the cost-cap formulas.

The Final Comparable Standards Regulations

After extensive discussion, review, and revisions, as well as approval by the Office of Management and Budget's Regulatory Analysis Group and DOJ, DOT issued final rules in 1986.[61] They echoed the proposed ones, with some technical and minor revisions made in response to the voluminous public comments received during rulemaking. The final regulations retained the six minimum service criteria, revising the wait time criterion from not waiting more than a reasonable length of time to receiving service within twenty-four hours of request. The cost-cap provision was retained, and the three percent of average operating budget criterion was selected, given that it was found in the regulatory analysis to be less costly in the long run than the alternative approach.

Analysis of Implementation of Transportation Policy for Handicapped Persons

The foregoing description of transportation policy shows that implementation has primarily involved efforts to define and set implementation directions; shifting policy directives have resulted in sporadic, rather than coordinated and effective, policy execution. The volatility of policy directions can be explained in terms of the theoretical framework developed in earlier chapters. Ultimately, shifting implementation strategies resulted from the actions of interested parties to influence transportation policy, and their actions led them to different institutional arenas as a means to influence that policy.

Institutional Arenas and Implementation

The array of institutional arenas utilized during efforts to develop and refine public policies governing handicapped access to public transit is outlined in table 7-1. Early efforts to enhance the mobility of the nation's disabled citizens commenced in Congress, as policy entrepreneurs pushed for legislation to meet their needs. From Congress, efforts to define and revise policy initiatives shifted to the executive branch, first to UMTA and then to DOT. The rulemaking agenda of DOT was influenced by HEW, as efforts were undertaken to implement section 504. In response, DOT devised its full-accessibility rules, which in turn provoked regulated clients (the transit industry) to push for relief in two other arenas, the federal courts and Congress. Both of these arenas responded, Congress in an abortive attempt to pass legislation allowing local flexibility with minimum service criteria, and the courts by eventually striking down the full-accessibility rules.

In the lurch, DOT initiated two more rulemaking phases. One was the interim final rules, which provided for special efforts to be set by local option. Congress again reacted, this time in response to concerns from the handicapped community that the local option policy would cause a major withdrawal from objectives of enhanced mobility of disabled persons. Through legislation in 1982, Congress required DOT to set minimum service criteria; DOT did this and introduced a cost cap on the extent of expenditures to be undertaken to comply with federal rules to increase the accessibility of mass transportation systems.

Implementation and Organizing Principles

Each phase of transportation policy was guided by a major organizing principle, with policies shifting between three such principles: (1) special efforts requirements that gave local governments substantial discretion in designing transit systems for handicapped people; (2) full-accessibility requirements that set clear guidelines for achieving accessible transit, with little room for local autonomy; and (3) special efforts requirements coupled with minimum service criteria. The third principle, applicable since May 1986, represents a compromise between the first two approaches and balances local direction in designing systems for handicapped transit with nationally determined criteria for basic service levels. The cost cap included with the third and most recent principle serves a purpose similar in nature to the "reasonableness" limitation attached to required accommodations in employment of persons with disabilities. The cap served as a signal to the political environment that DOT recognized there were financial limits to the extent of mandated accommodations in public transportation systems.

Throughout the controversy about transportation policy, the various organizing principles served as the symbolic focus of debate and as the target for policy changes. To a great extent, organizing principles derived from the basic decision premises of the various parties concerned about transportation policy, most notably the transit industry (regulated clients) and those representing physically disabled Americans (policy beneficiaries). Local option approaches favored by the transit industry were compatible with its view that individual transit systems should be able to devise and operate their own systems, with a minimum of federal government intrusion. (Of course, this did not necessarily imply operation with a minimum amount of federal funds, monies which the industry repeatedly sought.)

The decision premises of handicapped groups included the recognized need for greater mobility for disabled persons and the view that services for handicapped persons should, to the greatest extent possible, be provided in settings integrated with the nondisabled population. From the perspective of these actors, mainstreaming in public transportation implied removal of barriers that prevented handicapped persons from using the public transit services available to the nondisabled. Achieving this objective was most likely, from the perspective of the disabled community, by a strong national policy tied to provision of federal funds to transit systems throughout the nation.

Issue Networks and Policy Implementation

In striking contrast to other civil rights policies, the beneficiaries, physically handicapped individuals and their families, were not initially the movers and

Table 7-1 Decisions and Actions within Institutional Arenas Affecting the Development of Policies to Implement Accessibility in Public Transportation

Institutional Arena/Date	Decision/Action Taken
Phase One: Special Efforts Policy	
Congress (1970)	Amended Architectural Barriers Act to include transit systems financed by federal dollars, including the D.C. Metro system
Congress (1970)	Amended the Urban Mass Transportation Act of 1964 to require special efforts to enhance accessibility of transit systems to elderly and handicapped persons
Congress (1973)	Passed the Federal-Aid Highway Act, which included funds for installing elevators in D.C. Metro system; provided financial support to organizations to provide transit services to elderly and handicapped persons
Congress (1974)	Amended the Federal-Aid Highway Act to include wheelchair-bound persons and prohibited approval of mass transit programs that do not provide access to physically handicapped persons
Urban Mass Transportation Administration (1974–76)	Undertook rulemaking to develop administrative regulations to implement accessibility in public transit; adopted special efforts approach, with local flexibility
Phase Two: Full-Accessibility Policy	
HEW (1978)	Issued coordination regulations for section 504, including strong accessibility language
Department of Transportation (DOT) (1978–80)	Undertook rulemaking to develop administrative regulations for section 504 applied to public transportation; adopted full-accessibility approach requiring all transit modes be made accessible
Congressional Budget Office (1979)	Issued report on the expected costs of complying with full-accessibility regulations
House Subcommittee on Oversight and Review (1980)	Issued report critical of DOT's reliance on technological solutions, particularly the Transbus plan

154

Table 7-1 (Continued)

Institutional Arena/Date	*Decision/Action Taken*
Congress (1980)	Attempted to redevelop implementation policy for accessibility in public transit through provisions of a transportation bill; an agreement worked out that would allow greater local flexibility but require minimum service criteria be met; ultimately, bill not passed
Federal Courts (1981)	Federal circuit court ruled, in *APTA v. Lewis*, that full-accessibility regulations exceed statutory intent of section 504
Department of Justice (DOJ) (1981)	In its role as lead agency for coordinating section 504, DOJ suspended coordination regulations as they apply to transportation
Phase Three: Local Options Policy	
DOT (1981)	Issued final interim rules to guide section 504 implementation efforts; returned to special efforts approach
General Accounting Office (1982)	Issued report showing some accessibility modifications taken, but many barriers remain; showed barrier removal slowing with rescission of full-accessibility regulations
Congress (1982)	As part of Surface Transportation Assistance Act, Congress required DOT to issue regulations to establish minimum service criteria for implementation of section 504
Phase Four: Comparable Service Policy	
DOT (1983–86)	Undertook rulemaking to develop administrative regulations to implement minimum service criteria mandate; included cost cap along with service criteria requirements
Federal Courts (1986–)	Suits initiated by handicapped groups, charging that cost-cap elements of 1986 DOT regulations exceed statutory authority

shakers behind policy innovation. Instead, a small set of entrepreneurs who had become aware of the plight of disabled persons started legislative action. Relatively quickly, the groups representing persons with disabilities became aware of the significance of legislation and attendant policy implementation. These groups grew both in number and strength during the 1970s, undoubtedly stimulated in part by increasing recognition of their needs by the federal government. The early antidiscrimination legislation proved of symbolic value, raising the low expectations of disabled persons about their participation in society. By the late 1970s, these groups had developed substantial expertise and political savvy, resources they would use to tactically intervene in the implementation process.

The issue network of the regulated interests, the transit industry and local governments, was organized and politically operative prior to debates about handicapped transportation policy. The transit industry had as its representative APTA. Throughout policy controversies and development, APTA was ready, presenting testimony, preparing reports, criticizing DOT studies, and often pressing Congress for policy changes. As its allies, local governments, forced to make changes in transit systems and other public buildings, moved to blunt full-accessibility rules and press for local flexibility in accommodating physically disabled persons. In the end, both sides, the regulated interests and the program beneficiaries, proved to be strong political forces in shaping the ultimate direction of transportation policy.

Political and Policy Environments and Implementation

An analysis of the development of transportation policy relevant to handicapped persons over the past decade shows that changes in the political and policy environments contributed to the repeated shifting of transportation policy. The movement of DOT away from special efforts policies to those requiring fully accessible services was enhanced by the change of presidential administration and the leadership of DOT. Secretary Brock Adams was generally more favorable to using the regulatory process to press for accessibility for handicapped persons than his predecessors. Much the reverse occurred in 1980, as the Reagan administration came into office, promising and moving to reduce the impact of federal regulations. The successful legal challenge of APTA to overturn the full-accessibility rules was no problem to the new administration, which had no commitment to the rules promulgated under the Carter administration. These key changes in leadership positions, therefore, contributed to the redirecting of transportation policy.

Conclusion

For its quiet beginnings, handicapped transportation policy grew to fierce political proportions; symbolic politics based primarily on goodwill did not last for long. This can be explained by the fact that Congress had been lax in considering and debating its antidiscriminatory policy. The cost and other ramifications of antidiscrimination laws only became apparent during the regulatory process. Thus, it was at this stage that significant policy debate began and relevant interest groups activated strategies to affect the parameters of implementation. Their strategies, employed in different institutional arenas, resulted in transportation policy that has been called ''chaotic'' and ''vacillating'' (Katzmann 1986, 188).

Overall, the two sides appeared to have been roughly equal in their impact on the policy implementation process. Some argue that handicapped groups have been powerful in affecting transportation policy to their advantage (Fielding 1982). For their part, handicapped groups argue that despite their efforts, there remains significant work to be done to mainstream disabled persons in public transportation as well as in other facets of social and political life. While the relative influence of the groups varied along with the changing political and policy environments—handicapped persons were most powerful in earlier periods dominated by fairness symbols, and the transit industry grew stronger when compliance costs raised concerns—both exerted major influence on current implementation policy.

While controversy over transportation policy regarding services to persons with physical disabilities appears to have calmed somewhat for the moment, the debate about the appropriateness of a cost cap continues. Soon after the final DOT regulations were issued, the cost-cap provision articulated in the regulations was challenged in federal court by the coalition group Americans Disabled for Accessible Public Transportation and the Eastern Paralyzed Veterans Association. These groups challenged that the statutes underlying handicapped accessibility in public transportation do not provide for cost limitations on accessibility mandates. The federal judge in the case concurred with the plaintiffs on this point, striking down the cost-cap measure as arbitrary and capricious.[62] This move returned the policy question of the cost cap to DOT, which, at the time this book went to press, was debating whether to appeal the decision.

While the controversy over the cost cap continues, it should not overshadow the point that the handicapped and transit industry groups were much closer in policy perspectives in 1988 than they were a decade before. The transit authorities had accepted, by the mid-1980s, that the federal government was committed to some form of handicapped accessibility as a requirement of federal

157

funds and that many accommodations were not as costly as anticipated. The handicapped groups remained committed to efforts to increase the mobility of disabled persons, although many realized that accessibility costs affected the political feasibility of various policy options. The first decade of implementation experience, then, documents a recurrent effort to devise a workable and acceptable policy outline for providing transportation services to disabled persons across the nation.

Questions remain about the appropriate direction for future public policies to advance the mobility of handicapped persons. Alternatives range across the board and include (1) shifting the focus away from public transit to greater use of specially equipped private automobiles (Meyer and Gomez-Ibanez 1981), (2) returning to accessibility in all forms of mass transit, (3) using more paratransit services (Fix, Everett, and Kirby 1985), and (4) providing subsidies to disabled users of transit services (London 1986). Paratransit, once a popular approach that offered a demand-responsive and cost-effective means to serve handicapped persons, has lost some of its allure. This has happened because transit officials have realized that fully developed paratransit systems, devised to provide service levels comparable to those provided to the general public, are quite costly.[63] This point has been brought out by studies that document the expense of comparable paratransit services.[64] Given recognition of the costs of paratransit programs, some transit systems are considering the use of subsidies, where more traditional transit modes, such as taxis, are used, with the transit authority subsidizing the travel costs of handicapped persons. No matter what alternatives are considered, it is clear that cost considerations will play a major, if not predominant, role in the development of future transportation policy.

Finally, there is evidence that the locus of policy debate and implementation is shifting away from the federal government to the state and local level (Clark 1986). With some consensus that policy at the national level has stabilized, at least for a while, interest groups representing disabled persons have moved their advocacy efforts to the local level. Their purpose, at the minimum, is to ensure compliance with federal comparable service regulations. Where possible, however, they will push their preference for greater accessibility in all public transit modes, for local transit authorities can choose to exceed federal requirements. As with other policy areas, implementation during the current period of federal budget cutbacks and deregulation fever has stimulated renewed interest by beneficiary groups in policymaking and implementation at the state and local levels.

The one fact that is clear, as the result of several years' experience with policy implementation, is that it is difficult to develop a consensus among the interested parties about the best strategy for improving the transportation options available to persons with disabilities. As London (1986, 21) has argued:

> devising transportation services and facilities to meet the mobility needs of a relatively small yet highly diverse disabled community has proven a complex and controversial problem. In attempting to find a solution, policymakers, planners, transit operators, and disabled citizens are realizing that agreeing on a transportation solution that is cost-effective for all disabled people is as difficult a balancing act as deciding how to cut the federal deficit.

Given the diverse preferences of the policy actors involved in assisting the transportation needs of handicapped citizens, difficulties in devising a "balanced" policy position, agreeable to all sides, may remain an elusive goal for some time. Yet the parties are, at this point, closer to a mutually acceptable solution than they were when implementation action began, for through political battles and negotiations, they have learned of each other's needs and constraints.

8
Access to Public and Higher Education

A persistent battleground between advocates for persons with disabilities and providers of public services has been the area of education, with skirmishes waged both in local public school systems and in colleges and universities across the nation. Advocacy groups, led by parents of handicapped children, have worked diligently to increase the educational services and opportunities available to children with mental or physical disabilities. Their efforts, combined with those of supporters in Congress, led to passage of legislation that serves as the linchpin of programs to advance the educational opportunities of handicapped citizens.

As with other disability rights policies, those concerning education were shaped by decisions made in multiple institutitutional arenas, including state and federal courts, Congress, and executive agencies. The primary beneficiaries of these educational policies, handicapped children and their parents, formed a well-organized issue network, in which parents devoted boundless time and energy toward the objective of enhancing the educational opportunities of their children. The diligence and political pressure of parent groups, coupled with continuous support from various policy entrepreneurs in Congress, resulted in strong legislation that, unlike other disability rights laws, contained language outlining both the responsibilities of school systems and the mechanisms to guide compliance.

The Education for All Handicapped Children Act, known simply within the education field as "PL94-142," along with regulations devised to enforce section 504 of the Rehabilitation Act of 1973, set the stage for a new phase of policy implementation. Through these laws and their regulations, recipients of federal funds for special education are mandated to provide each handicapped child with an education tailored to his or her individual education needs. This extension of federal influence into public education, traditionally viewed as a state and local responsibility, was welcomed by those who sought to pressure school systems to provide educational services to handicapped children. Fed-

160

eral involvement was much less welcomed by state and local education authorities, although they willingly accepted the financial assistance included as part of the act.

As described in chapter three, Congress was unusually careful in the statutory design of PL94-142; the language of this statute is uncharacteristically specific about state and local government responsibilities and implementation procedures. This specificity was by no means an accident; instead, it resulted from the concerns of parent groups that every effort be made to ensure compliance by state and local education agencies (SEAs and LEAs). Many of the parent-advocates had extensive experience in dealing with school systems, many of which had resisted their requests for the provision of special educational services.

Rulemaking for PL94-142

With the passage of the Education for all Handicapped Children Act in November 1975, the Department of Health, Education and Welfare (HEW) began the process of drafting regulations for the new law. Because of the widespread implications of the law, HEW decided to include several forms of public participation in the rulemaking process. Outreach efforts included (1) disseminating audiovisual presentations describing PL94-142 to state education agencies and national parent organizations, (2) holding twenty public hearings on both geographic and special interest bases, and (3) convening a national writing group to assist in drafting regulations.

These efforts culminated in a set of proposed regulations published in the *Federal Register* in late December 1976.[1] The proposed rules were prefaced with cautious remarks, indicating that HEW intended rulemaking to be an iterative process, with the current rules only a first step in designing regulations.[2] The rules also stated that because the statute is both comprehensive and specific on many points, HEW had decided to incorporate the basic wording or substance of the statute into the regulations.

Probably the most far-reaching component of the Education for All Handicapped Children Act was its requirement that handicapped students receive a free and appropriate education, which was defined in the regulations, following the statute, as education where services: (1) are provided at public expense, under public supervision and direction, without charge, (2) meet the standards of the SEA, (3) include preschool, elementary school, and secondary school, and (4) are provided in conformity with an individualized education program (IEP).[3] Central to implementation is the IEP, which must include such enumerated items as statements about the child's present level of educational performance, annual performance goals, short-term instructional objectives, and specific educational services needed by the child.[4] The regulations specified that the IEP be designed through meetings of the child's teacher, another representative of the LEA, parents, and, where appropriate, the child. It also stipulated that the IEP be developed each year, at the beginning of the school term.

Another important dimension of PL94-142 was its requirement that education services provided to handicapped students be provided in the "least restrictive environment" conducive to the child's needs and abilities. With regard to this operating principle, the regulations state that, to the maximum extent possible, handicapped children should be educated in settings with nonhandicapped students. The use of special classes, separate from nonhandicapped students, is allowable only when the nature or severity of the handicap is such that education in regular settings cannot be satisfactorily achieved. The obvious objective of the least-restrictive-environment provision was to mainstream disabled students into normal classroom settings to the extent that such activity does not impede their education and that of other students.

Administrative regulations for PL94-142 also followed statutory language in requiring that school systems provide various related services in order to achieve an appropriate education. Related services were defined as "transportation and such developmental, corrective, and other supportive services as are required to assist a handicapped child to benefit from special education."[5] A listing of potentially relevant related services included speech pathology and audiology, psychological services, physical and occupational therapy, recreation, learning disability assessment, counseling services, and diagnostic or evaluative services.

During the ninety days that HEW allowed for public comment on the proposed regulations, sixteen hundred comments were received. Many of these dealt with specific statutory requirements, such as concerns about provisions for a free and appropriate education, federal priorities for services, IEPs, due process procedures, and determining the population of handicapped children.[6] While acknowledging these concerns, the final rules stated that these comments were aimed at statutory provisions and were thus outside the decision parameters of agency rulemaking. The final rules, issued in August 1977, closely resembled the proposed rules, although a few technical revisions were made in response to comments.[7] The final rules became effective October 1, 1977, issuing in a new era in the education of children who experience mental or physical disabilities.

Section 504 and Education of Handicapped Students

The advancement of educational rights for students with disabilities results not only from PL94-142 but also from section 504 of the Rehabilitation Act.

Access to Public and Higher Education

The legislative history of section 504 was described in chapter four, and the rulemaking efforts to implement the section were examined in chapters four and five. Two elements of the section 504 rules, as devised and issued by HEW, bear upon education. First, the rules specify a requirement for program accessibility for all public services, and second, they outline regulations specifically for elementary, secondary, and higher education.

Program Accessibility

The rules issued by HEW for section 504 in 1977 included a requirement for program accessibility: a recipient of federal funds ''shall operate each program or activity . . . so that the program or activity, when viewed in its entirety, is readily accessible to handicapped persons.''[8] As described in chapter four, the program accessibility principle represented a compromise between complete accessibility in all programs (as advocated by some handicapped groups) and limiting accessibility to only those programs directly serving persons with disabilities. The rules clearly stated that program accessibility did *not* mean that recipients must ''make each of its existing facilities or every part of every facility accessible to or useable by handicapped persons.''[9] The rules also stipulated that priority be given to serving handicapped persons in the ''most integrated setting appropriate.''[10]

For school systems and educational agencies, program accessibility required that essential components of educational services be accessible to handicapped students. The regulations provide flexibility in achieving this objective, allowing service providers to develop ways of delivering key educational services to students with disabilities. The rules did specify, however, that future facilities constructed for service delivery, including schools and other classroom facilities, be readily accessible to handicapped persons. This mandate is similar to the one imposed by the federal government upon itself through the Architectural Barriers Act.

Local Public Education and Section 504

In addition to program accessibility regulations, germane to all public services, HEW's section 504 rules contained two sections directly concerned with education. One applied to preschool, elementary, and secondary education; the other, to college-level education. The influence of the Education for All Handicapped Children Act is clearly evident in the section 504 regulations; both sets of regulations were written at the same time and within the same agency. The section 504 regulations were written by the Office of Civil Rights and those for

PL94-142 by the Bureau of Education. There was direct consultation between the two groups of rule writers, who recognized the overlap of these two anti-discrimination programs for educational services.

Closely paralleling the PL94-142 regulations, those for section 504 required that elementary and secondary schools receiving federal funds must provide a free and appropriate education for all students designated as handicapped.[11] An appropriate education was defined as one designed to meet the individual needs of handicapped persons and developed through an IEP as described in the Education of the Handicapped Act. In this way, the language of section 504 regulations was directly coupled to the PL94-142 regulations.

Higher Education and Section 504

The regulations for section 504 were extended to higher educational institutions. The regulations stipulated that universities and colleges must avoid discrimination against otherwise qualified students in terms of admissions, educational services, housing, financial aid, and nonacademic programs.[12] They were also required to make "academic adjustments" to ensure that normal educational requirements do not have the effect of discriminating against qualified handicapped students. Sample adjustments listed in the regulations made reference to rules about length of time to complete degrees, substitutions for required courses, and adaptation in the manner courses are conducted.

The Cumulative Effect

The joint effects of the two sets of interrelated regulations by HEW, one for section 504 and the other for PL94-142, cumulatively have had a profound impact on the delivery of educational services to handicapped students. The regulations for the Education for All Handicapped Children Act made receipt of federal funds for special education contingent upon delivery of a free and appropriate educational service. School systems wishing to avoid these regulations could legally do so only by giving up their federal funds for handicapped education. But even doing this would not put them in the clear, since section 504 rules pertain to school systems receiving *any* form of federal funds. The joint effect was to place a very real and unavoidable mandate on public school systems and institutions of higher education to provide educational services to, and eliminate discrimination against, persons with disabilities.

Questions and Problems in Implementation

With the issuance of HEW's regulations for PL94-142 and section 504 of the Rehabilitation Act of 1973, local school systems and institutions of higher education began the process of assessing their new responsibilities for educating handicapped students. The regulations for the Education for All Handicapped Children Act, effective October 1, 1977, gave school systems eleven months to devise plans for providing a free and appropriate education to identified handicapped students. Section 504 regulations, effective in June 1977, required that program accessibility be achieved within sixty days, except where structural modifications were required; in the latter case, a phase-in period of three years was specified. Section 504 regulations for a free and appropriate education in elementary and secondary schools had the same September 1978 deadline as specified in the PL94-142 rules, while rules for postsecondary education implied that compliance began immediately upon the effective date of the rules.

Given ambitious compliance deadlines and the extent of change in existing practices required by PL94-142 and section 504, it was not difficult to predict problems and delays in implementation. Because many local school systems had long neglected the educational needs of disabled children, meeting the objective of a free and appropriate education was probably best seen as a long-term objective rather than a goal achievable in the short run. Yet despite predictable implementation difficulties, evidence from multiple sources indicates that the antidiscrimination laws had immediate and profound impacts. Without question, they raised the consciousness of educators and administrators about the needs of handicapped students.

Evidence from Congressional Hearings

Throughout the period 1977 to 1981, a substantial number of oversight hearings were held on the Education for All Handicapped Children Act by both the House Subcommittee on Select Education and the Senate Subcommittee on the Handicapped.[13] Examination of testimony provides insight into initial experiences with policy implementation.

The Issue of Costs. Public school systems and universities across the nation, as they assessed compliance activities and associated costs, recognized that meeting the dual mandates would require significant expenditures. At congressional hearings, concerns about costs were aired, along with repeated requests for greater federal financial assistance. At hearings in 1977 on the implementation of section 504, before the House Subcommittee on Select Education, a representative of the Council of Chief State School Officers applauded the objectives of enhancing educational services to handicapped children yet also complained about implementation costs: "We are concerned that state and local governments alone cannot absorb the enormous additional financial burden of compliance with Section 504."[14]

The position of higher education institutions, as voiced at the hearings, was that section 504 placed a heavy burden on universities, a burden that many lacked the resources to meet. Many expressed resentment at the federal government's creating the section 504 mandate without providing funds to assist in compliance. One example given at the hearing was that of Lawrence University, a small liberal arts school in Wisconsin. The university's vice president testified that section 504 compliance could mean expenditures of up to $3 million, for a school whose annual budget was $9 million. The witness concluded: "To the extent you feel that the HEW regulations as now published reflect fairly the intent of the legislation . . . the conclusion is clear, and that is, that the only option for funding is direct federal grants."[15]

Similar pleas for funds and dire predictions about compliance costs were voiced about PL94-142 at a series of hearings conducted by the Senate Subcommittee on the Handicapped and the House Subcommittee on Select Education in 1978, 1979, and 1980. Throughout these hearings, the persistent call from state education administrators, local school officials, and parents of handicapped children was for greater federal funds to assist state and local institutions meet the mandate set forth in PL94-142.

By 1980, while pleas for funds continued, attention shifted to the widening gap between program authorizations and appropriations. The act authorized the federal government to pay an increasing share of the "excess" costs of educating children with disabilities. Excess costs are those above the average for educating nonhandicapped students. The law authorized the federal government to pay up to five percent of excess costs in fiscal year 1978, rising to a maximum of forty percent in fiscal year 1982. Appropriations for handicapped education, however, consistently lagged behind authorized levels. As a representative of the Council for Exceptional Children colorfully noted, "We have reached a point now where, as some suggest, we can march an army between the authorization levels and the appropriation levels."[16]

Another cost-related concern expressed at the hearings was that fulfilling the mandate to advance the education of handicapped children would force school systems to divert money and programs away from other students. This sentiment was voiced not only at the hearings but also in the press. An editorial in the *New York Times* expressed worry about diversion of funds to handicapped children, arguing that "it is perverse for Congress and the courts to define an 'appropiate' education only for the handicapped and to write rules that result in the deprivation of other children.''[17]

The repeated message was that more federal dollars were needed to ensure that the full mandate defined by PL94-142 be effectively carried out. State and local officials from across the nation argued that they needed financial help from the governmental entity that required them to implement an aggressive new program to expand educational programs for the nation's handicapped children. Parents and advocacy groups, fearing slow implementations and incomplete services, joined the chorus for greater federal funding of handicapped education.

Concerns about Implementation Practices. Many issues and problems other than compliance costs were aired at the oversight hearings. Handicapped groups testified that implementation was progressing too slowly, and several instances of school systems not meeting the full guidelines were described. Complaints were also made about particular components of the Education for All Handicapped Children Act as they were carried into action. These included reference to individualized education plans, least restrictive environments, and the provision of related services.

The IEP, the heart of implementation efforts for PL94-142, received many favorable comments as a mechanism for structuring a free and appropriate education. Commentors noted the benefits of having several persons—including specialists, teachers, and parents—involved in preparing the IEP. For example, one witness noted: ''The IEP has enabled us to bring together people who are from very different backgrounds and professional specialties, to work together for that child. That never happened before, and that has been a marvelous breakthrough.''[18]

Despite identified benefits, representatives of educational agencies argued that the IEP generated substantial effort and paperwork that detracted from the rendering of services. Others noted that parents often remained uninformed about the provisions of PL94-142 and thus their participation in formulation of the IEP was hampered. Still another problem identified was that the pre-IEP evaluation was often time-consuming, generating delays in formulation of the IEP and commencement of educational services. Suggested remedies to these problems were to train and hire more specialized personnel to take the lead in formulating IEPs and to develop more public information programs to inform parents about their participation in the IEP process.

The drafters of PL94-142 recognized that the least-restrictive-environment provision, intended to mainstream handicapped children into regular school settings, had a potential downside. The intention was that mainstreaming be used only when handicapped students do not require the benefit of specialized education outside of regular classrooms. The problem arises if students are placed in regular settings in order to save costs, when actually they would be better served in specialized settings separate from nonhandicapped students. At the oversight hearings, some parents expressed concern that children were now being "dumped" into regular classrooms[19] in order to achieve "forced social integration."[20] Some teachers and administrators discussed the difficulty in determining when mainstreaming is beneficial and when it may detract from the learning of disabled students.

The requirement that local school systems provide related services to enhance the educational achievement of handicapped students was another implementation component that generated problems in execution. School officials repeatedly voiced concerns about the extent of their responsibility to provide related services, particularly in the realm of costly medical and health services. Some witnesses also questioned whether the requirements of PL94-142 would lead other social service agencies to shirk their responsibility to handicapped children by trying to foist the costs of service delivery upon educational institutions.

To sum up the positions voiced at the hearings, the following conclusions can be advanced. Parents and advocacy groups applauded the objectives of PL94-142 and provided evidence that things had started to change. Yet simultaneously, they voiced frustrations that program implementation was not moving more rapidly. The SEAs and LEAs applauded the overall mission but voiced concerns about the massive undertaking and costs involved. A balanced assessment was given by Senator Jennings Randolph (D-WV) at the start of one of the hearings, when he declared:

> A national commitment of the scope and magnitude suggested by Public Law 94-142 . . . is not realized overnight. While the enactment of the law may be accomplished by a pen stroke, implementation is necessarily a more arduous process. As with much new legislation, the early stages of implementation of Public Law 94-142 have been beset by problems which have been both substantial and numerous. Nevertheless, a high sense of commitment endures despite these challenges.[21]

Research Findings on Implementation of PL94-142

While Congress held oversight hearings in the late 1970s on PL94-142, a variety of research studies were undertaken to analyze implementation experiences. They provided preliminary information on implementation, much of which corroborated testimony presented at the oversight hearings. The studies provided good news and bad, finding that educational services to handicapped children were growing but that implementation problems were also being encountered. The research studies, many commissioned by the Department of Education (DOE) and two others by the General Accounting Office (GAO), documented many types of implementation experiences across the nation.

Students Served. A review of data collected by DOE in the years 1976–77, the year before PL94-142 was enacted, and 1980–81 showed a nearly thirteen-percent increase in the number of handicapped children served (Zettel 1982). This meant that over 450,000 more handicapped children were receiving education services by local school systems, an increase mostly attributed to the implementation of PL94-142. This figure is more impressive when it is recognized that the overall school-age population in the United States dropped six percent during this five-year period. The greatest growth was found in the preschool children and those between the ages of eighteen and twenty-one; these age groups were included in PL94-142 but had been neglected by many states prior to enactment of the federal law.

   Despite impressive gains in the number of children served and the range of services they received, research studies also demonstrated that many children remained unserved or underserved. This point was highlighted in a study conducted by the GAO in 1981, which found that the goal of providing a free and appropriate education, as mandated by PL94-142, would ''not be achieved until at least the mid-1980s.''[22] The most common reason cited for the delay by local education officials was lack of funds to meet their full responsibilities. A second GAO study found that while states had been active in isolating and beginning services for handicapped students who previously had not been served, many children currently in school were not receiving an adequate special education.[23]

Individualized Education Programs. Research findings on the effectiveness of IEPs were mixed. Studies showed that most school systems had moved forward to develop IEPs for handicapped children. One study found that nearly ninety-five percent of the sampled handicapped students had IEPs on file by the end of 1978, showing that educational systems recognized their responsibilities under the PL94-142 mandate (Research Triangle Institute 1980). Yet several studies found that even though the IEPs were being developed, there were many deficiencies in them. A report by the Research Triangle Institute (1980) found that about two-thirds of the IEPs lacked some of the eleven elements required by law, and that in only one-third were all three required participants—teachers, LEA representatives, and parents—involved in formulating the IEP. Much the

169

same evidence was found in a GAO study: eighty-four percent of IEPs lacked one or more required information items, and fifty-two percent lacked evidence that all three participants were involved in formulating the IEP.[24] Still similar results were reported in a study of three hundred IEPs in Connecticut (Schneck and Levy 1979). All of these studies called for greater in-service training for teachers in the proper preparation of IEPs for handicapped children.

Least Restrictive Environment. A report by DOE's Office of Special Education and Rehabilitative Services found that in the 1978–79 school year, over ninety-four percent of handicapped children were educated in regular schools, sixty-eight percent in regular classes, and twenty-six percent in special education classes.[25] Only about six percent were educated in separate schools for handicapped children or in other institutional settings. This represented an increase in students being educated in less restrictive settings. The DOE report also noted that the number of previously institutionalized children being served by LEAs increased by more than sixty percent during the three-year period from 1976 to 1979.

Another source of data on implementation of the least-restrictive-environment stipulation was supplied by the U.S. Office of Civil Rights.[26] According to its study, the percentage of handicapped students in full-time special education programs dropped by five percent to twenty-two percent between the 1976–77 and 1978–79 school years. A study by state affiliates of the United Cerebral Palsy Association (UCPA) noted that some schools had difficulty determining whether segregated or mainstreamed class instruction was most beneficial to handicapped children.[27] While noting the advantages of mainstreaming, some schools reported that disadvantaged children excel and feel more comfortable in settings segregated for special education.

Related Services. Preliminary evidence on the provision of related services to handicapped children was also presented in the UCPA study. The association's affiliates cited failure to provide related services as the foremost problem in implementation of PL94-142. Lack of adequate transportation services was noted as a major problem, particularly for students who had to travel to distant facilities for special education classes. The report also noted continued confusion and controversy about which social service agency should pay for related services and stated that this controversy had impeded the provision of related services in many school systems.

Individual and Institutional Participants. Research studies also examined the impact of the Education for All Handicapped Children Act on the individuals and educational institutions involved in policy implementation. A study by Education Turnkey Systems (1981) examined the impact of the law and its regulations on SEAs, which were given substantial supervisory roles in implementing PL94-142. Study findings indicated that implementation activities had required substantial resources and personnel, raising concerns about SEA neglect of other responsibilities. Implementation, it was found, created greater tensions within SEAs and between SEAs and other governmental agencies. Another study corroborated the burden that SEAs perceived as arising from implementation of the law (Management Analysis Center 1977).

The reaction of school administrators to their new mandate to provide a free and appropriate education to handicapped children was examined in a study of local education agencies in Missouri (Foster 1980). In an open-ended question, administrators identified the greatest impact of PL94-142 as expansion of programming efforts for handicapped education. This expansion was not seen as a great problem, except that school systems have insufficient funding to achieve totally their new mandate.

The question of teacher concerns with the execution of the objectives of PL94-142 was examined by another study (Roy Littlejohn Associates 1978). One finding indicated there was substantial variation in the involvement of teachers in handicapped education and in the pressures they experienced in assisting local schools to achieve compliance with PL94-142. In part, this variability was explained by differences in the amount of information about PL94-142 known to teachers and distributed by local school systems. The study also noted differences across school systems in terms of the priority given to educational services for handicapped students. Teacher concerns about implementation included time and work load pressures, changing educational roles and relationships, and organizational pressures. Research conducted by the National Association of State Directors of Special Education (Schipper and Wilson 1978) confirmed findings that teachers were concerned about the increased demands being placed upon them by implementation of PL94-142; teachers also expressed the opinion that they were being asked to perform tasks for which they had not been adequately trained.

Another research project examined the relationship of teacher job satisfaction and implementation of PL94-142 (Schwartz et al. 1979). This study of over three hundred regular education, elementary teachers found that about a half had not been told about their responsibilities in the mainstreaming process and that many had not had adequate input into the process. Another finding was that teachers who had been involved in the mainstreaming of handicapped students had more positive perceptions of their implementation role and higher job satisfaction than other teachers. Still another study demonstrated that imple-

171

mentation of a free and appropriate education was having an impact on collective bargaining activities, as teachers strove to negotiate their involvement in the implementation process (Alexander, Bond, and Soffer 1979).

A perspective on another participant, the parents of handicapped children, was provided by a survey of parents conducted by the National Committee for Citizens in Education in 1978–79.[28] Like other studies discussed above, this one found a large proportion of IEPs to be in place and parents to be aware of their child's IEP. These findings led the report writers to conclude that substantial progress had been made in implementation. However, the report also found that parents were often not participating as full partners in the development of IEPs. Over half of the parents reported that the IEPs were completed prior to their meeting with school officials, and a third said that the IEP did not state how much time their child would spend in regular classroom settings. Parents also reported being unprepared to participate in the IEP process, and forty-five percent said that annual goals set in the IEP did not fully meet their child's educational needs.

Implementation Costs. Preliminary evidence on the costs of complying with the free and appropriate education requirements of PL94-142 were gathered through a survey conducted by the National School Board Association (NSBA 1979). Among the findings of the project were that:

1. Local school district budgets for special education were rising at the rate of fourteen percent per year (twice as rapidly as instructional and operating budgets).
2. Nationwide, special education budgets were equivalent to about twelve percent of instructional budgets.
3. Most school districts had to place some handicapped pupils in instructional settings outside of the districts' own facilities (representing a cost four times greater than average per-pupil expenditures for nonresidential settings, and eight times greater for residential settings).

Coming as no surprise to LEAs, these figures provided preliminary estimates of the costs involved in implementing PL94-142.

Regulatory Reforms and the Carter Administration

Recognizing the realities of policy implementation, the Carter administration undertook action to review PL94-142 regulations for the purpose of enhancing policy execution. One effort focused on clarifying expectations about the preparation and execution of IEPs by LEAs. The result of this effort was the issuance of a departmental interpretation describing the IEP in greater detail than the original regulations had done.[29] This interpretation provided greater guidance to school officials in developing and administering IEPs that are consistent with the PL94-142 mandate.

Late in the Carter administration, DOE issued a notice of intent to develop regulations, interpretive rules, or policy statements relevant to the Education for All Handicapped Children Act and section 504 of the Rehabilitation Act of 1973 as it pertains to education.[30] The notice solicited comments on several issues related to policy implementation, including due process protections, out-of-state placement of handicapped children, extensions of the school year, services for handicapped students placed in private schools, least-restrictive-environment stipulations, and suspension and dismissal. By the end of the comment period, in early 1981, several hundred comments had been received. These comments presented ideas on many sides of each issue; heavily represented were reactions from public school systems across the nation.[31] Despite the outpouring of public reactions, DOE never made an official response, given that the Reagan administration took office in early 1981 and undertook different approaches to the education of handicapped children.

Enter the Reagan Administration

Only weeks into its first term of office, the Reagan administration announced a variety of plans to implement the new president's pledge to reduce the influence of the federal government in the conduct of state and local affairs. An early signal as to the new administration's position was given by Terrel H. Bell during the Senate hearing on his nomination as the new secretary of education. While expressing his commitment to a strong educational system, Bell declared his belief that the federal government was overly intrusive in the affairs of SEAs and LEAs. He stated this position with direct reference to the Education for All Handicapped Children Act, arguing that the law "specifies a bit too much. I think it directs and gets into the area even of instructional methodology to an extent that I do not think reflects good Federal policy. . . . I have heard an outcry from superintendents concerning this issue. They feel that it is a burden, that there is a heavy-handed direction from our office. I would want to do my best to give some relief there."[32]

The Proposal for Education Block Grants

In early May 1981, the Reagan administration's plans for federal education programs became clearer, as the administration introduced in Congress the Elementary and Secondary Education Consolidation Act of 1981. The thrust of this bill was to collapse forty-four existing categorical programs for education into two large blocks grants, with a corresponding twenty-five-percent reduction in funding across the programs. One block grant was designed to provide financial assistance to meet special education needs and would include the Education for the Handicapped Act and Title I of the Elementary and Secondary Education Act (ESEA). The appropriations for these programs in fiscal year 1981 were about $1 billion for handicapped education and $2.5 billion for Title I. As designed, the block grants would eliminate many of the requirements included in the categorical programs, including the requirements in PL94-142 for a free and appropriate education. In Senate hearings on the bill, Secretary Bell argued: "This proposed legislation is a logical next step in making further progress in providing Federal financial assistance to schools and to students. We believe that we can now move to delegate more responsibility and to encourage greater latitude in how State and local decisionmakers utilize Federal financial assistance in elementary and secondary schools."[33]

The administration's block grant scheme evoked immediate reaction, both from Congress and many education and handicapped constituent groups. In hearings before the Senate Subcommittee on Education, Arts, and Humanities, Secretary Bell was asked repeatedly about the fate of legal protections afforded handicapped children under PL94-142. In response, he stated confidently that, given section 504 and its regulations, school boards would "have the force of law that they cannot neglect the rights of these handicapped children."[34]

Several senators on the subcommittee, long supporters of programs for handicapped persons, responded angrily to the administration's proposal and Bell's defense of it. Senator Edward Kennedy (D-MA) challenged Bell's contention that the new bill would direct benefits to the same students with special needs as provided under current law.[35] In hearings the next day, public participants were invited to provide assessments of the proposed educational block programs. The president of the Children's Defense Fund, testifying at the hearings, recited the positive results of federally funded programs in education and argued that "they are proposing in these block grant and consolidation requirements to undermine these programs at a time when they are working."[36] She went on to argue that the administration was "ignoring the history and asking us to trust State and local officials, where we have a strong history of neglect and exclusion of these groups of children."[37]

Analysis of the statements made at the hearings by handicap advocacy groups makes it clear that their primary concern was that elimination of the legal protections of PL94-142—including requirements for a free and appropriate education in the least restrictive environment possible—would result in reduced attention to the education needs of handicapped children. They feared that the impetus for legally required special education programs and services might be blunted as state legislatures set different spending priorities for public education. These groups had perceived foot-dragging in many states in special education services prior to PL94-142 and now worried about a return to earlier conditions with the removal of the legal mandate for providing free and appropriate educations. The administration's position that section 504 protections would prevent a return to foot-dragging was no consolation to these groups.

A contrasting position on the proposed block grants was taken by representatives of SEAs, who favored greater state and local flexibility in spending federal grant funds. For example, the Delaware superintendent of public instruction argued:

> Probably the single most important advantage of program consolidation is the opportunity it offers to increase flexibility in the use of Federal funding for education. Existing Federal laws and regulations place undue limitations and burdens on State and local education agencies when one notes that nationwide the Federal Government will provide only about 9 percent of revenues for public elementary and secondary education during the current school year.[38]

Despite the support from SEAs and LEAs, the education block grant plan generated little enthusiasm in Congress. Eventually, one education block grant was formed out of a few small categorical programs, but the Education for All Handicapped Children and ESEA–Title I programs remained intact. The strong reactions of various handicapped groups, coupled with strong support by several members of Congress for handicapped rights, led to the protection of educational services for handicapped students as a categorical program.

Efforts to Revise Regulations for PL94-142

Recognizing that the effort to include the Education for All Handicapped Children Act in a special education block grant had failed in 1981, the Reagan administration took a different tack the next year through an effort to loosen the regulations for implementing the act. The effort, one more in a line using regulatory reform as a vehicle to reduce the involvement of the federal government in state and local government affairs, generated major controversy and ultimately was abandoned by the administration as it sensed defeat.

In August 1982, DOE issued a notice of proposed rulemaking to revise the regulations pertaining to the Education for All Handicapped Children Act. The proposed rules removed or weakened a variety of stipulations upon SEAs and LEAs. In prefacing the rules, Secretary Bell stated: ''The overriding purpose of the proposed revisions is to improve the process for ensuring a free appropriate education for handicapped children envisioned by the statute by removing excessive regulatory overlay that detracts from that purpose.''[39] The preface also stated: ''In streamlining and simplifying these regulations, care has been taken not to weaken the key procedural protections and rights of handicapped children and their parents.''[40]

The regulatory changes proposed by DOE would have, among other things, loosened requirements concerning (1) parental notification about IEP planning, (2) provision of related services and extracurricular activities, and (3) placing disabled children in the least restrictive environment conducive to their needs. Analysis of the regulatory changes and prefatory remarks indicates that the administration intended to reduce the regulatory impact on state and local governments while staying within the legal mandate of PL94-142. The streamlining and simplification of regulations was greatest in places where it was perceived that the regulations exceeded statutory provisions.

Regional Hearings on Regulatory Reform. As part of its rulemaking process, DOE sponsored a series of public hearings on the proposed regulatory changes in PL94-142. The public reactions expressed at the hearings were overwhelmingly negative, as parents groups and other advocates turned out in force to fight the changes. One of the rallying cries of parents groups concerned the ''stripping'' away of the parents' role in formulating IEPs. Few things generate as vociferous a reaction from parents as any suggestion that their direct role in educating their child be reduced.

The grass roots support for the existing PL94-142 regulations was not entirely spontaneous. It resulted in substantial measure from the networks that had developed between key national interest groups representing the needs and rights of disabled persons and their memberships across the nation. Particularly important was the network developed by the Disability Rights Education and Defense Fund (DREDF) and similar organizations engaged in educational outreach programs to inform disabled persons about their rights under section 504 and PL94-142. Individuals trained through these programs were not ready to back away from their newfound rights. Instead, they were ready to respond when signaled to do so by national groups, who sought to use grass roots pressure on Congress or the administration. The grass roots networks publicized the regional hearings on proposed regulatory reforms, worked to ensure the hearings were held in accessible locations, and encouraged participation. The vocal opposition to the proposed regulations generated press attention and powerful headlines.[41] The press coverage and the vocal opposition it displayed were not missed by members of Congress or the Reagan administration.

176

Congress Reacts to Regulatory Reform. Members of Congress reacted swiftly to DOE's effort to scale back regulations for PL94-142. Within a week of publication of proposed revisions in the *Federal Register*, the Senate Subcommittee on the Handicapped held hearings on the proposed changes. Senator Lowell Weicker (D-CT) opened the hearings, criticizing the administration's position on handicapped education programs and its initiatives for block grants, cuts in appropriations, and regulatory revision.[42] Other members of the subcommittee made similar opening remarks, voicing concerns about the regulatory proposals and skepticism about the administration's claim that such reforms would improve the education of handicapped children.

Appearing at the hearings, Secretary Bell outlined and defended the regulatory proposals, arguing that DOE had tried "to strike a good balance between the rights of local and State education entities and the rights of handicapped children, as is mandated in PL94-142."[43] Bell's defense of the proposed regulatory changes centered on the need to return flexibility and creativity to SEAs and LEAs.

Strong opposition to DOE's regulatory revisions was voiced at the hearings by interest groups, including representatives of the Association for Children and Adults with Learning Disabilities, the Association for Retarded Citizens, the National Education Association (NEA), and the Consortium Concerned with the Developmentally Disabled. Predictably, these individuals attacked DOE for backtracking and for threatening advances that had been made in providing quality educational services to handicapped children. Typical of their testimony before the subcommittee was a statement by the representative of NEA:

> By proposing the changes in regulations governing Public Law 94-142, the administration is actually abandoning the responsibility to the 10 million handicapped children and 30 million handicapped adults in the Nation . . . the Government this time is demonstrating its willingness to return to what I call an asylum attitude giving the States carte blanche to return these 10 million children to the closets from which society has been trying to liberate them for 100 years.[44]

On the same day as the hearing, action was taken in both houses of Congress to check the regulatory actions of DOE. In the Senate, Lowell Weicker proposed a floor amendment to the Supplemental Appropriations Act of 1982, which stated that it was the sense of Congress that the proposed regulatory changes relevant to PL94-142 should be delayed, allowing Congress to approve or disapprove the changes. In introducing the amendment, Weicker reviewed progress in educating handicapped children and argued that "just at a time when virtually everyone agrees the big job is getting done and done well, the

Department of Education dares to propose changes in the rules which govern the program. . . . As incredible as it may seem, what in fact is being proposed is to weaken kids' ability to join with their nondisabled peers."[45] The amendment was accepted by a vote of ninety-three to four, providing an early signal to the administration that Congress was concerned about possible dilution of its Education for All Handicapped Children Act.

Similar action was taken in the House of Representatives, where Mario Biaggi, long an advocate of federal programs for handicapped persons, introduced a resolution (H.R. 558) that expressed the sense of the House that the proposed regulatory changes to PL94-142 should not be permitted to take effect. The resolution, referred to the House Subcommittee on Select Education, was considered during three oversight hearings in late September to examine the regulatory changes being advanced by DOE.[46] At the hearings, witness after witness expressed concerns about the proposed regulatory changes. Even school administrators, who had in previous years argued for reduced federal control on local education, stated their assessment that more harm than good would be done by modifying the existing regulations for PL94-142.

On the third day of hearings, Secretary Bell appeared before the subcommittee and presented a surprise. He announced that in light of hearings held by the department about the regulations and other input, DOE had decided to "withdraw" several of the proposed regulatory changes.[47] The retracted provisions included the most controversial ones—those dealing with least restrictive environments, related services, timelines, attendance of evaluative personnel at IEPs, and others. Bell stated that the withdrawal of regulatory changes was undertaken "largely in response to the hundreds of parents of handicapped children who have dedicated their energies to these children."[48]

Initially, members of the subcommittee reacted favorably to what was seen as a conciliatory move by Bell and the administration. The spirit of good feeling lasted only for minutes, however, as subcommittee members questioned Bell about what was meant by "withdrawal" of the proposed regulations. The subcommittee wanted Bell to state that withdrawal meant that the administration would return to the existing regulations on those issues where it retracted changes. Bell was unwilling to go this far, stating that DOE wanted flexibility to make technical or clarifying changes, should it desire to do so after further study.

The discussion became more intense as Mario Biaggi informed the subcommittee of an internal memorandum written by a staffer in DOE regarding departmental response to controversy about its proposed regulatory changes. In the memo, the staffer, Joseph Beard, proposed that DOE send up its regulatory proposals in multiple packages so that controversial changes might not bring down less controversial ones. Unfortunately for DOE, the memo went on to state that this strategy might "divide the enemy" and suppress effective opposition to the proposed changes.[49] Secretary Bell immediately disavowed the memo, stating that it represented the ideas of one individual and that the staffer had been reprimanded. Bell argued: "I don't have a hidden agenda or intent here and I just plead with you not to read into that an intent that I do not have."[50] Yet despite the disavowal, some members of the subcommittee feared that the move to withdraw some regulatory proposals was part of a hidden political strategy to destabilize opposition to the proposed regulations.

At the end of the hearing, the subcommittee was not sufficiently satisfied with the pullback by DOE to hold off on a vote on the House resolution opposing the rules. In a meeting after the hearings concluded, the Subcommittee on Select Education voted unanimously to report the resolution to the full Committee on Labor and Education. The following day the full committee by voice vote unanimously reported the resolution to the full House, stating that the regulatory changes proposed by DOE for PL94-142 "should be rejected in their present form and should not be permitted to take effect while Congress is in recess."[51]

In response to the sustained negative reaction from Congress, pressures from handicapped interest groups, and unfavorable press reports, DOE and the administration eventually abandoned efforts to revise the PL94-142 rules. The political fallout from the regulatory revision was assessed by the administration to be too great to compensate for the potential benefits of reform. Since DOE had already retracted many components of regulatory changes, there seemed little to gain from action that generated such heated political debate and negative reaction.

The Furor Subsides, Implementation Continues

With the abandonment of regulatory reform efforts, the controversy and furor that surrounded the PL94-142 program abated, and implementation of the program to provide a free and appropriate education for handicapped children continued. Congressional appropriations for the programs continued to increase, but in amounts far short of the levels authorized by the law. Through the Education of the Handicapped Act Amendments of 1983 (PL98-199), Congress extended the authorizations for the Education of the Handicapped Act (EHA), of which PL94-142 is a part, and re-funded a National Advisory Committee on the Education of Handicapped Program. This advisory body was initially established as part of the EHA in 1966 and functioned until 1977, when its appropriations were not renewed. The 1983 law also created incentive grants for establishing programs for early childhood education from birth through five years of age.[52] The regulations for implementing these legislative provisions were issued by DOE in late 1984.[53]

Court Action and Congressional Response

While controversy raged between Congress and the executive branch over block grant proposals and regulatory changes, questions over implementation were also being raised in the courts. Since statutes and regulations never cover all issues potentially relevant to implementation, many questions about policy execution end up in the courts, as interested parties seek to clarify legal mandates and responsibilities. Many education cases were brought to the federal courts, with several reaching the Supreme Court. The cases focused both on section 504 of the Rehabilitation Act of 1973 and on PL94-142. The net effect of many of the Supreme Court cases was to constrict the mandate to provide a free and appropriate education.

Section 504 and Reasonable Accommodation in Education

The first major case to examine section 504 and its provisions for reasonable accommodation in education was *Southeastern Community College v. Davis*.[54] This case, described in chapter five, centered on a hearing-impaired nurse who sought admission to a nusring program provided by Southeastern Community College. Davis was denied admission on the basis that she could not successfully complete the nursing program, which included both academic and supervised clinical work, because of her hearing impairment. The school claimed that the only means for Davis to successfully complete the program would be to modify the program substantially or to lower its standards. Davis sued the school system in federal court, contending that her denial of admission violated the nondiscrimination protections afforded by section 504.

In 1979, the Supreme Court ruled against Davis, finding that the type of modification sought in order to pursue the clinical component of the nursing program—individual faculty supervision—went beyond the reasonable accommodation mandate of section 504, as articulated in HEW regulations. The court saw individualized faculty supervision as analogous to affirmative action and argued that there was no language in section 504 or itr regulations to support affirmative action–type remedies. The impact of the *Davis* decision, therefore, was to place some limits on the responsibility of federal recipients to reasonably accommodate the needs of handicapped individuals.

A Ruling on "Appropriate Education"

Other judicial cases concerned implementation of the Education for All Handicapped Children Act. One area of ambiguity in the act concerned exactly what constitutes an "appropriate" education. The act was not very clear on this point, defining an "appropriate" education rather circularly as "special education and related services which . . . include an appropriate preschool, elementary, or secondary education in the State."[55] Recognizing the diversity of handicapping conditions, Congress chose not to provide a precise listing of the educational components of an "appropriate" education, relying instead on the IEP process to devise a program individually tailored to the needs of a disabled child. The openness of the "appropriate" education provision raised questions in implementation, questions that were ultimately addressed in the federal courts through *Board of Education v. Rowley*.[56]

The *Rowley* case involved a child, Amy Rowley, who had minimal hearing but who demonstrated better than average performance in a regular classroom setting with the use of a special hearing aid and special tutoring instruction, both provided by the local school system. Amy's parents, feeling the child could perform even better with a sign language interpreter, requested this service for their child. The school system refused, and the Rowleys initiated legal action to obtain an interpreter; their case was upheld in the Federal District Court for Southern New York[57] and the Second Circuit Court of Appeals.[58] These courts ruled that the legislative intent behind the "appropriate" education stipulation of PL94-142 required provision of special services sufficient to maximize a handicapped child's potential commensurate with the opportunity provided to other students.

In its 1982 ruling on the *Rowley* case, the Supreme Court overruled the lower courts and concurred with the local school system that PL94-142 did not require provision of a sign language interpreter. In the majority opinion, authored by Justice William Rehnquist, the Court noted: "Noticeably absent from the language of the statute is any substantive standard prescribing the level of education to be accorded handicapped children."[59] To answer the question of the meaning of "appropriate" education, the Court turned to legislative history and earlier cases on education of handicapped children. The opinion reviewed the *Mills* and *PARC* cases (described in chapter three), noting that they held that handicapped children are entitled to equal *access* but not to any specific level of educational services. Since these cases had been discussed in detail in the legislative history of PL94-142, the opinion held that this standard was implied by Congress. The majority opinion thus held that the statute "does not imply Congressional intent to achieve a strict equality of opportunity of services."[60]

The Court's basic position in the *Rowley* case was that school systems are required to provide a "basic floor of opportunity" to all handicapped children, with such a floor consisting of access to specialized instruction and related services that are individually tailored to provide educational benefit to the handicapped child.[61] The Court argued: "Insofar as a State is required to provide a handicapped child with a 'free and appropriate education', we hold that it satisfies this requirement by providing personalized instruction with sufficient support services to permit the child to benefit educationally from that instruction."[62]

In its examination of the *Rowley* case, the Supreme Court also considered the appropriate scope of judicial review under the procedural safeguards section of PL94-142. Here the Court offered guidance to reviewing courts, stating that while they may base decisions on the "preponderance of the evidence," as so instructed by the statute, this was "by no means an invitation to the courts to substitute their own notions of sound educational policy for those of the school authorities which they review."[63] It was the Court's position that Congress intended such questions of "educational policy" to be handled at the state and local levels during the process of determining IEPs. The opinion identified two questions for reviewing courts to consider in regards to "appropriate" education: (1) has the state complied with the procedures set forth in the statute? (2) does the IEP designed for the handicapped student enable the child to receive educational benefit?[64] From the Court's view, should these two conditions be met, then the school system has adequately complied with its obligations to provide an appropriate education to handicapped children.[65]

The decision on this first major ruling related to the Education for All Handicapped Children Act was quite significant, seen as a victory for those concerned about the expansive mandate created by the act and as a serious defeat by the handicapped community. The Court opinion in *Rowley* both constricted the working conception of what constitutes an appropriate education under the act and suggested that courts show great deference to SEAs and LEAs in determining appropriate education programs for handicapped children. With this interpretation, the extent of services parents could seek on behalf of their child was reduced, while the discretionary power of school systems and SEAs to implement whatever educational programs they deemed appropriate for the education of handicapped children was enhanced.

The Award of Attorneys' Fees

Another case, *Smith v. Robinson*, centered on whether parents or others who undertake legal action under the protections afforded by PL94-142 are entitled to the award of legal fees if they prevail in their legal action. Unlike other civil rights laws, PL94-142 did not explicitly provide for the award of legal fees for parents who win their cases. In some previous cases, courts had allowed parents to recover legal expenses under other laws, including section 504 of the Rehabilitation Act. In *Smith v. Robinson*, the Supreme Court ruled in 1984 that where PL94-142 and the Education of the Handicapped Act are applicable to the complaint brought by the parent or guardian, only the provisions of that act can be used in determining the award of legal fees.[66] Since the act does not provide for such awards, the Court ruled that parents could not seek legal fees if they were successful in their case.[67]

Longtime advocates of handicapped citizens in Congress reacted in 1985 by introducing the Handicapped Children's Protection Act, designed in direct response to the Supreme Court decision in *Smith v. Robinson*. Provisions of both the House and Senate versions of the bill amended the EHA to allow judges to award attorneys' fees to prevailing parties. In its final form, the Handicapped Children's Protection Act of 1986 (1) provided for the award of reasonable attorneys' fees to parents who prevail in legal action under PL94-142; (2) stated that nothing in the EHA should be construed to restrict the rights, procedures, and remedies available through the Constitution, section 504 of the Rehabilitation Act of 1973, and other federal statutes protecting the rights of handicapped children; and (3) called for a study by GAO on the impact of the amendments to the EHA as contained in the new law.

Reimbursement for Private School Education

In 1985, the Supreme Court considered the question of whether parents who remove their children from a public school system, when dissatisfied with their handicapped child's IEP, are entitled to reimbursement by the school system for private school expenses. The case *Town of Burlington v. Department of Education* centered on the parents of a child with severe learning disabilities.[68] The child, Michael Panico, had been enrolled in the local school system in grades one through three, at which time it was apparent that the child's educational progress was unsatisfactory. After discussions with the school system over Michael's IEP, the parents, who remained displeased with the educational plan, filed for a hearing with the state's bureau of education and removed their child from the school system. He was then placed in a specialized school. Eventually, the hearing officer of the state education bureau ruled in favor of the parents' claim that the school system's IEP was inappropriate and that the specialized school was the least restrictive environment for educating the child. The hearing officer ordered the school system to pay for the education of

Michael in his new school and to cover the education and transportation costs for the period leading up to the hearing decision.

The school system then sued the state and parents in district court, arguing that since the parents had removed the child without prior approval by the school, the system was not responsible for Michael's educational costs. After several steps in the federal courts, the case reached the Supreme Court in 1985. The Court ruled that reimbursement to parents for expenses in private school placements is appropriate if the court determines that the placement is consistent with the terms of the statutory provisions of PL94-142. Because state authorities had ruled that the private placement was appropriate, the Panicos were entitled to reimbursement.

Reauthorization and Emphasis on early Education

In 1986, Congress considered reauthorization of the EHA and PL94-142. The Senate version extended the mandate to provide a free and appropriate education to children beginning at age three. Previously, the act provided grants to assist in educating children in the three-to-five age group but did not mandate free and appropriate education for these young children. The House did not respond favorably to expanding the free and appropriate education mandate. In a compromise move drafted by the House Committee on Education and Labor, the mandate was dropped and replaced with provisions that would increase grants for educating children in the three-to-five age group and that would create a new incentive grant program for educating children from birth through age two. This compromise was accepted by the Senate and the Education of the Handicapped Act Amendments of 1986 became law as PL99-506. This law also reauthorized a variety of discretionary programs related to research, training, and evaluation of handicapped education programs.

Implementation of Section 504 in Higher Education

While the controversy in handicapped education focused primarily upon PL94-142, significant implementation efforts were also under way in higher education. While not covered by the Education for All Handicapped Children Act, colleges and universities across the nation were required under section 504 to engage in program accessibility. This required them to make essential educational programs accessible to physically and mentally disabled individuals, as well as to have all new construction meet American National Standards Institute standards for handicapped accessibility.

One measure of the extent of compliance with the 504 mandate is provided through a study of higher education programs to assist handicapped persons. The study, conducted by the National Association of College and University Business Officers (NACUBO) in 298 colleges, documents the number of handicapped students enrolled and expenditures for facilities and programs for them (NACUBO 1981). The study found that, from the period 1976 to 1980, the percentage of students identified as handicapped had increased. This rise is explained both in terms of the impact of section 504 (more opportunities for higher education) and better accounting methods used by schools to ascertain the number of handicapped students enrolled. On the whole, more disabled people were enrolled in public, compared to private, institutions of higher education.

Among the distribution of handicapping conditions reported by colleges in the NACUBO study, mobility impairments were most frequent in number, followed in order by vision problems, hearing impairments, and learning disabilities. The remaining handicaps were scattered across many types of handicapping problems. In terms of service-related expenditures, over the five-year period from 1976 to 1981, total expenditures for facilities for handicapped students in the higher education institutions rose from $5.3 million to $22.9 million, an increase of 425 percent. On the average, institutional expenditures per school increased from $61,000 to $184,000 during the period. Expenditures on programs, far smaller than those for facilities, rose from $2.9 million to $6.4 million, or from an average of $41,000 per school to $76,000. Expenditures for both facilities and programs were consistently higher in public institutions, which educate a large percentage of all handicapped students.

Another empirical study, jointly conducted by the President's Committee on Employment of the Handicapped and the American Council on Education, provides a profile of entering college freshmen who identified themselves as disabled (Hippolitus 1985). The study shows that the number of self-identified disabled persons entering higher education increased from 2.6 percent in 1978 to 7.4 percent in 1985. The report argues that "such advances would seem to attest to the value of Section 504 of the Rehabilitation Act of 1973 and of other programs which encourage the participation of students with disabilities in higher education" (Hippolitus 1985, 2). After recognizing important gains, the joint study also argues that major challenges remain, since "the college freshman with a disability is older, less academically prepared for a higher education, from a lower high school class standing, possessing a lower level of self-confidence about himself or herself, and more dependent on outside funding" (Hippolitus 1985, 10).

As with implementation in other areas of disability rights programs, the case in higher education suggests that while significant gains have been made, substantial obstacles remain to achieving the objective of full educational opportunity. The two studies suggest, but cannot prove, that section 504 is responsible for the higher enrollments of persons with disabilities in college education. Yet while the data do not reflect the unique effect of section 504, it is clear that the statutory requirement and its administrative regulations have played some role in increasing the higher education opportunities available to students with disabilities.

An Assessment of Implementation Experiences

In 1985, PL94-142 celebrated its tenth anniversary, which was commemorated by Congress through a concurrent resolution. While many evaluations and assessment of PL94-142 have been made, perhaps the most eloquent one was made by the House Committee on Education and Labor in regard to the concurrent resolution:

> In comparison with the situation ten years ago, more handicapped children are now being identified, evaluated, and properly classified. In addition, more handicapped children are receiving appropriate services in the least restrictive environment.
>
> Equally impressive is the impact of Public Law 94-142 on attitudes. Handicapped children are learning self-respect and working to maximize their potential. Parents' expectations about the capabilities of their handicapped children have expanded. Teachers and administrators are treating handicapped children as individuals with individual strengths, weaknesses, and needs. Parents and school employees are working hand-in-hand. Handicapped children are befriending non-handicapped children.
>
> In sum, the Committee finds that in the past ten years the educational opportunities made available to handicapped children has been a significant improvement. These successes should make us proud.[69]

Yet given this positive evaluation of implementation, the committee went on to argue that "more remains to be done to ensure that the goals of the program are attained for all handicapped children, regardless of their socio-economic status and regardless of the nature and severity of their handicapping condition."[70]

The Cost Dilemma

Several ongoing implementation problems remain as PL94-142 continues into its second decade. Perhaps the most prominent one concerns acquisition of

186

financial resources in order to achieve compliance—a problem that has persistently plagued implementation. Without question, compliance with the legal protections afforded by PL94-142 requires the expenditure of substantial resources. This was recognized by Congress, which initially planned to provide up to forty percent of the excess cost of educating children with handicaps and learning disabilities. Congress, however, has been less generous when making appropriations, which, while increasing, remain far less than the forty-percent target.

In many ways, the cost dilemma contributed to strained relations between SEAs and LEAs and the federal government. From the state and local perspective, the federal government created a powerful mandate through PL94-142, one which required them to engage in and finance new services, modify educational practices, and conform to monitoring processes. The new mandate, at the same time, required substantial new expenditures, only part of which was federally subsidized. Creating such a powerful and expensive mandate without full funding generated resentment at the subnational level, especially since appropriations lagged behind planned authorizations.

The Joint Mandate: PL94-142 and Section 504

Given these burdens, Stark (1982, 487) ponders why state and local governments did not forsake federal grant monies and withdraw from the program. The response to the question is that the regulations for section 504 impose responsibilities similar to those for PL94-142, and even if states left the PL94-142 program, they would remain responsible for providing a free and appropriate education for handicapped children.[71] As recipients of federal funds, school systems and local governments can legally withdraw from section 504 protections only by forsaking all federal funds, an action that no state or local government can afford to undertake. The overlapping nature of the section 504 and PL94-142 regulations prevented implementation confusion and delays that might have resulted had the two sets not been coordinated during rulemaking.

Questions about Effectiveness of Educational Strategies

Policy questions persist about the most effective means of ensuring and providing an appropriate education to children with disabilities. Such questions, raised in many quarters, were highlighted in a major study conducted by the Commission on Education of the Deaf. One area of concern to the commission was the determination and delivery of an appropriate education to each deaf child. In this regard, the commission found that "many children who are deaf are receiving inappropriate and inadequate educational services. . . . What constitutes an 'appropriate education' for each child is too often determined by placement, rather than by educational and related services to meet the child's particular needs."[72]

The commission also identified the least restrictive environment provision of PL94-142 as a source of major difficulties: "Parents, deaf consumers, and professional personnel of all persuasions, have, with almost total unanimity, cited LRE as the issue that most thwarts their attempts to provide an appropriate education for children who are deaf."[73] At least part of the commission's concern focused on the overextensive use of regular classroom settings, which often are not seen as the most appropriate context for educating children with disabilities.

Key policy questions such as these—including determination of what constitutes an appropriate education, the relative utility of restrictive versus nonrestrictive settings, and the provision of related services—lie at the heart of efforts to provide quality educational services to children with disabilities. There are no universal answers to these questions; they must be answered in the context of the educational needs and abilities of individual children. The current challenge remains to develop effective strategies to make appropriate determinations on an individual basis.

Implementation in a Multiarena Context

Consistent with a theme articulated throughout this book, it is evident that policies to direct implementation of PL94-142 derived from decisions reached in multiple institutional arenas (see table 8-1). The law itself was enacted through pressures on the legislative system by parents and education interest groups, coupled with judicial decisions in the early 1970s that held that handicapped children have a right to public education. In designing the law, Congress went unusually far in spelling out processes and conditions for implementation, including such principles as free and appropriate education, IEPs, and least restrictive environment. Given the specificity of the statutory language, in its first effort to devise rules, HEW took the statute and largely incorporated it into federal regulations.

Subsequent policy decisions for implementation were made in different arenas as participants sought to affect the execution of handicapped education. With a change in the political environment, one which favored deregulation and reduced federal involvement in state and local affairs, initiatives were taken in lawmaking and rulemaking. These efforts, aimed at reducing federal involvement in providing educational services to children with disabilities, generated conflict in Congress, which took action to block the initiatives of the Reagan administration.

The courts too played a vital role, as implementing authorities and affected parties endeavored to understand the scope of compliance actions mandated by PL94-142. Parents and advocacy groups used the courts as a vehicle to press educational systems for greater action in educating handicapped children. Since these pressures generally meant more services and greater expenditures, state and local authorities answered the challenges in court, arguing that their responsibilities were not unlimited. Some judicial decisions in the 1980s worked to restrict state and local responsibilities. Where Congress disagreed with these interpretations of its intent, it took action to clarify laws in order to reinstate provisions overruled in the courts.

The final chapter remains to be written on the cumulative impact of the Education for All Handicapped Children Act and the education provisions of the section 504 regulations. Gains have been made, but not as quickly as expected by interest groups and Congress. Efforts to scale back the program were defeated, and a lull more or less exists in the late 1980s. Given fiscal retrenchment by the federal government in the 1980s, appropriations for handicapped education barely held their own, leaving states to pick up the balance. At the same time, handicapped education programs appear stronger in the sense that widespread political support has been demonstrated, and it is unlikely efforts will soon be proposed for either substantial cutbacks or weakening of the program.

The focus of implementation has shifted back to the state and local level as the second decade of policy execution takes place. Clearly, financial limitations remain and constrain the ability of school systems to meet the full range of handicapped education needs. Yet as a report by the National Education Association (1978, 13) notes, money problems are likely not the most severe:

> The barriers that will be hardest to bring down are those that involve human attitude and bureaucratic inertia. No amount of money is going to cure the human ailments of prejudice against and withdrawal from those who do not fill some vague standard of normalcy. No amount of money is going to infuse state departments of education, public schools, and other related agencies with the flexibility, openness, and responsiveness necessary to work effectively with each other, with parents, and with students, in meeting the mandates of the law.

Truly effective implementation requires a close working relationship among state education bureaucracies, local school systems, and parents to design and execute specialized programs tailored to the needs of children with disabilities. The attention of relevant parties to the pursuit of this working relationship was

Table 8-1 Decisions and Actions Taken in Institutional Arenas Affecting the Development of Policies to Implement Handicapped Rights in Public Education

Institutional Arena/Date	Decision/Action Taken
Federal Courts (1971–72)	Courts began to assert rights of disabled children to free and appropriate education in *PARC v. Commonwealth of Pennsyvlania* and *Mills v. BOE of District of Columbia*
Congress (1975)	Passed Education for All Handicapped Children Act (PL94-142), requiring a free and appropriate education for all disabled children in school districts receiving funds for handicapped education
Department of Health, Education and Welfare (HEW) (1975–77)	Bureau of Education in HEW undertook rulemaking efforts to create administrative regulations for PL94-142; regulations closely follow statute
HEW (1977)	Office of Civil Rights issued regulations for implementation of section 504, which included requirement that free and appropriate education be provided to handicapped children
Congress (1977–81)	Many oversight hearings conducted on implementation of PL94-142 in both houses; both successes and implementation problems recounted
Supreme Court (1979)	Ruled in *Southeastern Community College v. Davis* that section 504 does not require affirmative actions be taken in accommodations or that fundamental alterations be made in programs
Department of Education (DOE) (1979–80)	Developed department interpretation to clarify use of and procedures for the implementation of individualized education programs
DOE (1980–81)	Carter administration announced intent to reconsider administration regulations for PL94-142 to clarify some issues
President (1981)	Reagan announced plan to merge most educational programs for disadvantaged students into a block grant
Congress (1981)	Created one small block grant but retained PL94-142 as categorical program

Table 8-1   (Continued)

Institutional Arena/Date	Decision/Action Taken
DOE (1982)	Undertook rulemaking activities to loosen administrative regulations for PL94-142; conducted regional hearings, where much negative reaction received
Congress—Senate Subcommittee on the Handicapped (1982)	Conducted oversight hearings on proposed revisions to PL94-142 regulations; many subcommittee members reacted critically
Congress—Senate (1982)	Senator Weicker, on floor of Senate, proposed amendment to Supplemental Appropriations Act of 1982 to express sense of Senate that regulatory changes in PL94-142 be delayed; provision passed
Congress—House (1982)	Representative Biaggi introduces H. R. 558 expressing House position that regulatory changes proposed for PL94-142 should not be made by DOE
Congress—House Subcommittee on Select Education (1982)	Conducted oversight hearings on proposed changes in PL94-142 regulations and on H. R. 558; subcommittee, and later full Committee on Education and Labor, voted to approve H. R. 558
DOE (1982)	Under intense pressure, DOE abandoned plans to revise PL94-142 regulations
Supreme Court (1982)	Ruled in *Board of Education v. Rowley* that PL94-142 requires equal access to education but not necessarily equal opportunity or outcome
Supreme Court (1984)	In *Smith v. Robinson*, Court ruled that since PL94-142 has no provision about the award of attorneys' fees, such fees need not be awarded by virtue of the statute
Congress (1985–86)	Considered and passed law to amend PL94-142 so that attorneys' fees can be awarded to prevailing parties other than the government
Supreme Court (1985)	Ruled in *Town of Burlington v. DOE* on payment of education costs of child removed from public schools unilaterally by parents

distracted during the early 1980s as efforts to redesign both laws and administrative regulations were undertaken by the Reagan administration. With the programs and regulations largely intact, and thus the direction and objectives of implementation clear, implementation again focuses on developing and delivering appropriate services to children with disabilities.

9
Employment Rights and Opportunities for Disabled Persons

Compared to other public policies for disabled persons, those dealing with employment have the longest history. Federal government involvement began just after World War I, in response to the number of disabled soldiers who returned home from the battlefield. From this time, the vocational rehabilitation (VR) program, funded primarily by the federal government and operated by the states, has grown dramatically in terms of expenditures, clients served, and types of services rendered. Long-term congressional support of the program has been based upon several underlying premises. First, VR aids physically handicapped persons, many of whom became disabled as the result of workplace accidents and military service to the nation. Second, the VR program has consistently defended itself as cost-effective; that is, the costs of rehabilitation have been argued to be less, overall, than the tax revenues derived from disabled persons who become employed as the result of the program. And third, employing handicapped persons means that society has fewer persons to support through social welfare programs.

What is interesting to note about these rationales for the VR program is that they evaluate the program largely from the vantage of society, not the disabled person. The program has been defended more on the basis that it is cost-effective for society than by how the lives of individuals can be enhanced through the opportunity of employment. Until the 1970s, VR operated on the assumption that employment was an achievable goal for many handicapped individuals, but in no sense was employment opportunity seen as a right. By the 1970s, however, it was generally recognized that VR alone would not offset the full range of barriers that impede the employment of persons with disabilities (Berkowitz 1987, 175). This recognition served as one stimulus to the development of disability rights programs in the area of employment.

The Benefits of and Impediments to Employment

Given the benefits derived from employment, it is not surprising that handicap advocacy groups have long supported VR programs. In addition to financial remuneration, employment provides disabled persons with other rewards, including the satisfaction of being self-supporting, enhancement of self-esteem, and the opportunity to leave restricted settings and participate in mainstream society. In the words of one advocate, employment is the "great equalizer"; it allows persons with disabilities to demonstrate their abilities and participate with others on an equal footing (Milk 1980, 127).

Despite the multitude of advantages available through employment, the movement of disabled citizens into the work force has been a slow process. The snail's pace of handicapped employment has persisted despite the sixty-year history of the VR program. One major impediment has been widespread perceptions about and attitudes toward handicapped persons, many of which are negative and presume that handicaps preclude the possibility of effective work performance. Research studies have documented that workers and employers have concerns about and misconceptions of handicapped workers (Schroedel and Jacobsen 1978; Pati, Adkins, and Morrison 1981). Seifert (1981) found workers to have very limited knowledge and information about disabilities, negative or paternalistic reactions toward disabled persons, low assessment of their productivity potential, and preference for social distance from handicapped workers.

For their part, employers have been shown to be reluctant to actively hire individuals with disabling conditions, because, in the words of one analyst, "employers, more often than not, appear more inclined to judge handicapped persons on the basis of disability rather than on what they are capable of performing" (Jamero 1979, 38). The reluctance of employers to hire persons with disabilities is rooted in common myths and misunderstandings, which include the ideas that the employment of disabled persons will increase insurance and worker compensation costs, cause higher absenteeism among employees, reduce productivity, harm the morale and productivity of nonhandicapped workers, and require costly accommodation measures (Nathanson 1981; Stroman 1982; Mithaug 1979; Lublin 1976).

Misconceptions about disabled persons in the workplace are illustrated in a study conducted by the Canadian Chamber of Commerce, which polled its members on reasons why they had not considered the possibility of hiring handicapped workers (Pacquette 1976). Among the responses given were that the firm (1) had no job they could handle, (2) never thought of hiring them, (3) considered it too dangerous and costly in terms of insurance premiums, (4) had buildings that were unsuitable, (5) would experience high absenteeism and turnover rates, and (6) possessed fears about reduced productivity. These attitudes have been slow in changing, despite studies that show disabled workers to perform at levels equal to or higher than other employees (E. I. Dupont 1982; Pati 1981; Lucas 1975; Ellner and Bender 1980).

Social attitudes toward disabled persons as workers form a backdrop against which policies to advance employment opportunities must operate. The misperceptions—coupled with low employment expectations of disabled persons and significant problems in transportation to work—have had a powerfully negative impact on their employment potential. Overcoming these obstacles requires changes in employee and employer attitudes and positive steps to accommodate disabled workers in performance of job tasks. Expanding accommodation efforts was the primary objective behind rights-oriented legislation passed by Congress to remove employment discrimination against and enhance job opportunities for persons with disabilities.

Employment Protection Laws for Disabled Persons

Federal laws providing employment protections for handicapped individuals date back to 1948, when Congress amended the Civil Service Act to include the provision that no potential or current member of the federal work force should be discriminated against on the basis of physical handicap.[1] Through this measure, Congress articulated a commitment to remove discriminatory practices against physically disabled workers in its own work force. There is little evidence, however, that this and other largely symbolic provisions in the Civil Service Act worked to significantly expand the work opportunities of persons with disabilities.

A far more important set of employment protections was included in Title V of the Rehabilitation Act of 1973 as "miscellaneous" amendments. We have examined one of these, section 504, in some detail, including development of the requirement for reasonable accommodation in employment, as articulated in the administrative regulations promulgated by the Department of Health, Education, and Welfare (HEW). In addition to section 504, which places requirements on recipients of federal financial assistance and programs conducted by federal agencies, two other sections of Title V concerned employment of handicapped citizens. Section 501 requires the agencies of the federal government to take affirmative action in employing qualified disabled persons. The provision created an Interagency Committee on Handicapped Employees (ICHE), charged with reviewing the adequacy of hiring, placement, and advancement practices of the federal government in regard to disabled persons. The section also required all federal agencies to submit to the Civil Service Commission (CSC) an affirmative action plan for hiring and advancement of handicapped workers.

Through section 503, Congress placed an affirmative action requirement upon those persons and organizations who have contracts or subcontracts with the federal government in excess of $2,500. The law requires contractors to take affirmative action to employ, and advance in employment, qualified handicapped persons. It also provides that handicapped persons, who believe a contractor has failed to comply with affirmative action provisions, may file a complaint with the Department of Labor (DOL), which will then conduct an investigation.

Congress passed another law in 1974 relevant to a particular class of disabled persons, veterans of military action in the Vietnam era. The primary purpose of PL93-508, the Vietnam Era Veterans' Readjustment Assistance Act (VEVRAA), is to increase the educational benefits available to veterans of military service in the post–Korean War period. Included in this bill is a provision, section 402, that requires those with federal contracts and subcontracts in excess of $10,000 to take affirmative action to employ, and advance in employment, disabled veterans. This provision mirrors section 503 of the Rehabilitation Act of 1973, and in fact, disabled veterans are entitled to coverage under both provisions. Section 403 of the veterans law requires federal agencies to include in their affirmative action programs a separate section for employment of disabled veterans. Section 403 thus parallels and reiterates section 501 of the Rehabilitation Act of 1973. Congress passed the VEVRAA over the veto of President Gerald Ford, who argued that the increased benefits provided by the legislation were excessive and a burden on American taxpayers.

Section 501: Affirmative Action in Federal Agencies

Responsibility for implementing section 501 was initially vested in the U.S. Civil Service Commission, which was to be assisted, according to the statute, by ICHE. CSC, in consultation with the newly created ICHE, moved quickly to commence policy execution, preparing and issuing in early 1974 *Federal Personnel Manual* Letter 306-5 concerning affirmative action in the employment of persons with disabilities.[2] These instructions specified reporting requirements, outlined agency-wide and field activity affirmative action program plans, and required specific statistical data.[3] These instructions represented the first set of implementation policies prepared as a result of the disability rights provisions of the Rehabilitation Act of 1973.

During the early years of policy implementation, section 501 generated changes within the employment practices of federal agencies. Complying with

CSC regulations, federal agencies devised and began to activate affirmative action plans for hiring workers with disabilities and reported relevant statistical data.[4] Assessing preliminary implementation experiences in its 1975 report to Congress, CSC noted: "Overall, we have observed a considerable increase in the interest and commitment to the program among agencies. One major accomplishment has been the development of an awareness by nonhandicapped persons toward the capabilities, employment problems, and needs of handicapped individuals."[5]

Implementation of section 501 across federal agencies was, however, uneven, as CSC itself acknowledged in 1975 in reference to affirmative action plans: " . . . we found a wide range of quality in the plans. Some agencies displayed a keen interest in developing and implementing strong programs with ideas and methods that went beyond the suggested model. Other agencies submitted plans that can be classified as barely meeting minimum requirements."[6] In the same 1975 report, CSC identified a problem to be long associated with implementation of section 501, insufficient resources: "One serious problem area, common to several agencies, involves the allotment of new resources or the reordering of existing resources needed to do the job."[7]

In 1977, CSC undertook formal rulemaking with regard to the discrimination complaint procedures available to handicapped persons through section 501.[8] The approach taken by CSC was to add discrimination on the basis of handicap to the procedures, designed for discrimination complaints based on race, sex, color, and national origin. A few variations were required, however, because while the section 501 mandate required affirmative action, it neither explicitly prohibited discriminatory practice nor provided specific remedies, as did other civil rights laws. One area of divergence between complaint procedures for disabled persons and those for other parties experiencing discrimination concerned back pay. CSC judged that section 501's affirmative action mandate did not provide sufficient authority to require back pay as a remedy for discrimination.

During the public comment period on the complaint procedure rules, which was extended for an extra three months, eighty-five comments were received.[9] They both supported the notion of nondiscrimination in civil service rules governing federal employees and made a variety of suggestions for clarification. CSC reviewed the comments, concurred that more detail would be helpful for implementation, and added several sections to the final complaint procedure regulations, issued in March 1978.[10] A section defining the term "qualified handicapped person" was added to the final rules. With respect to employment, such a person is one who (1) "with or without reasonable accommodation, can perform the essential functions of the position in question without endangering the health and safety" of himself or other workers, (2) meets the experience and/or education requirements of the position, and (3) meets the criteria for appointment under one of the special appointing authorities for handicapped persons.[11]

In response to public comments, CSC added a section to the regulations on reasonable accommodation.[12] This section mirrored that in the section 504 coordination rules, requiring reasonable accommodation unless it can be demonstrated that accommodation causes an undue hardship on the program or operation. Examples of accommodations were listed and, like HEW regulations, included making facilities accessible, job restructuring, modified work schedules, and acquisition of new technology usable by handicapped persons. Also like the HEW rules, the hardship test for "unreasonableness" was undefined but made reference to size and type of operation and the nature and cost of accommodations.

Again reacting to public comments, CSC added sections describing allowable employment criteria, preemployment inquiries, and physical access to buildings.[13] With regard to employment criteria, the regulations prohibited tests that screen out qualified handicapped persons. The regulations set strict limits on the use of medical examinations as part of preemployment evaluation, and in terms of physical access, agencies were required to comply with the Architectural Barriers Act. Finally, the regulations outlined the appropriate steps in processing complaints about discrimination based on mental or physical handicap.

Transfer of Implementation Authority to EEOC

Responsibility for implementing section 501 did not long remain with CSC.[14] In 1978, as one of several plans for reorganizing the executive branch, President Jimmy Carter proposed consolidating federal fair employment programs into the Equal Employment Opportunity Commission (EEOC). The authority to undertake reorganization, subject to congressional approval, was contained in legislation passed in 1977.[15] Included in Reorganization Plan No. 1 of 1978 was the shift of implementation responsibility for section 501 from CSC to EEOC.[16] In outlining his reorganization plan, Carter noted the fragmented nature of equal employment programs and argued that "fair employment is too vital for haphazard enforcement."[17]

The House Government Operations Committee examined and approved the reorganization plan, arguing that it would be "beneficial to those whose rights are being protected" and would "reduce the impact on the business community that has resulted from the proliferation of governmental units administering related programs.''[18] The plan was approved by Congress when the House of Representatives defeated a resolution of disapproval by a vote of 39 to 356.[19]

EEOC was the logical place to consolidate employment fairness actions of the federal government.[20] The origins of EEOC date back to the Civil Rights Act of 1964, which, through section 715, created the Equal Employment Opportunity Coordinating Council for the purpose of developing and implementing enforcement of equal employment policies. Executive Order 12067, issued by President Carter, transferred the functions of the coordinating council to EEOC and charged the agency with coordination and enforcement of employment opportunity programs throughout the federal government.[21]

The complaint procedure regulations, devised by CSC for section 501 and subsequently transferred to EEOC in 1978, remain basically unchanged in 1989. Only two significant changes have been made. One revoked a part of the section 501 regulations (promulgated in 1978), which prohibited the use of back pay as a remedy for discrimination on the basis of handicap.[22] This revocation resulted from the 1978 amendments to the Rehabilitation Act of 1973, which, through section 505, made available to individuals complaining of handicapped discrimination the same remedies as provided to other protected classes through Title VII of the Civil Rights Act of 1964.

The other regulatory change concerned a modification in 1981 to clarify the use of inquiries about disabilities as part of preemployment evaluation.[23] The revision recognized that gathering information on handicapped conditions may be important to implementing affirmative action in the hiring, placement, and promotion of persons with disabilities. The regulations, while allowing the collection of this information, required that it be kept confidential, except for purposes directly related to affirmative action measures, safety of workers, and investigation of compliance.

Implementation Experiences

The consolidation of equal opportunity in employment programs in a single agency, EEOC, worked to focus greater attention on the employment practices of the federal government. EEOC issued instructions to federal agencies for implementing section 501 in December 1979 in the form of a management directive. The directive instructed agencies to analyze handicap employment data for the agencies' work forces to establish goals and timetables for hiring persons with disabilities, to implement a special recruitment program for handicapped workers, and to survey and report on facility accessibility and barrier removal.[24]

To assess the impact of the transfer of section 501 responsibility to EEOC, the House Subcommittee on Employment Opportunities held an oversight hearing on federal enforcement of equal employment activities in August 1980, about eighteen months after EEOC was expanded and charged with central responsibility for implementing fair employment programs.[25] Primary attention at the hearing was given to discrimination problems related to race and sex; far less consideration was given to discriminatory practices against persons with mental or physical disabilities. The vice chairman of EEOC testified about activities being undertaken to implement the commission's new responsibilities and acknowledged that affirmative action in employment had not been a priority in many federal agencies.[26] With regard to section 501, the vice chairman argued that "for the first time agencies are beginning to deal with the issue of hiring and recruiting handicapped individuals at the Federal level and with a sense of priority."[27]

Significant implementation problems identified at the oversight hearing concerned the powers available to EEOC to enforce compliance activities and how enforcement power was to be shared with the Merit Systems Protection Board.[28] To achieve its mandate to enforce fair employment, the vice chairman stated that EEOC "must act not only as both mentor and monitor but as prodder and policeman"; he also noted that the "policeman" powers of the commission were as yet unclear.[29]

Despite the higher visibility of equal employment programs and their consolidation into a different agency, the progress achieved for disabled workers was not immediate. The annual report filed by EEOC for fiscal year 1981 showed an actual decline in the number of disabled workers, which the agency argued was a statistical phenomenon "rather than the result of decreased agency efforts to employ disabled veterans or handicapped persons."[30] There was better news for persons with "targeted" disabilities (including those with blindness, deafness, paralysis, convulsive disorders, and mental disabilities); their representation in the federal work force increased slightly during the fiscal year.

When the Reagan administration took office in 1981, implementation practices, not yet routinized, were jolted as the priority to reduce the regulatory impact of the federal government was set as a primary administration objective. The House Subcommittee on Employment Opportunities conducted a series of hearings in 1981, both in the nation's capital and in other cities, concerning equal employment opportunity and affirmative action. A report issued by the subcommittee, synthesizing and evaluating testimony given at the hearings, was critical of the new administration's approach to affirmative action.[31] The subcommittee also stated its concern about the administration's position, articulated by William Bradford Reynolds at a subcommittee hearing, that it would no longer insist upon or support the use of numerical formulas or timetables to provide preferential treatment in employment where no clear evidence of discriminatory action was evident.[32] This movement away from statistical-type remedies became the primary means by which the Reagan administration sought to redefine the direction of the affirmative action programs pursued by the federal government. The move was perceived by many legislators and most civil rights advocates as harmful to achieving the goal of equal employment opportunity.

Concerns about EEOC's role in enforcing employment opportunity continued through the early 1980s, as witnessed by testimony presented before the House Subcommittee on Employment Opportunities in 1983.[33] Several witnesses criticized the reduction in EEOC manpower that had been activated by the Reagan administration in the name of budget cuts. By 1983, agency personnel had declined by over ten percent, demonstrating, at least to civil rights groups, a reduced commitment to implementation of fair employment in the federal government. These groups also argued that EEOC had not been sufficiently aggressive in its enforcement actions, particularly in using litigation to push for compliance.

Overview of Section 501 Implementation

The evidence to date suggests mixed ratings for the federal government in implementing affirmative action in federal employment of persons with disabilities. Consolidation of affirmative action and fair employment programs in EEOC initially worked to increase the visibility of these programs in federal agencies. Some agencies have devised meritorious programs to increase employment of disabled citizens and other groups that previously have experienced discrimination in employment. On a less positive note, implementation shortcomings are evident. Many federal agencies have moved very slowly to implement affirmative action programs, with limited personnel and resources being devoted to these functions. Questions remain about the legal sanctions available to EEOC in enforcing fair employment, as well as the political feasibility of one federal agency taking strong sanctions against another.

The mixed results of EEOC in pursuing an effective affirmative action program, one which includes persons with disabilities, is highlighted by the agency's annual report for 1986.[34] Data presented in the report document that persons with targeted disabilities continue to be underrepresented in the federal work force. EEOC estimates that while 5.9 percent of the entire American work force experienced some form of targeted disability, the representation of this group in the federal government is just above 1 percent.

Even more instructive is the agency's report on on-site program reviews conducted during fiscal year 1986. During this time, EEOC conducted 174 on-site reviews of affirmative action programs for handicapped persons at federal agency field installations, including operations of the Departments of Agriculture, Air Force, Army, Health and Human Services, Interior, and Treasury. The on-site reviews focused on four areas: program management, special recruitment programs, data collection, and facility accessibility. Among the review findings are the following:[35]

1. One hundred sixty-two agencies (ninety-three percent) had designated a handicapped program coordinator, most of whom were of sufficient grade to have access to top administrators.

2. Thirty-seven percent of the installations were found to be from basically to fully accessible to handicapped persons.

3. Most program coordinators spent only ten percent of their time on programs for handicapped persons; only fourteen percent had been given adequate training; and only twenty-five percent of the coordinators had responsibilities in affirmative action for handicapped persons included in their job descriptions.

4. Fifty-five percent of reviewed installations had clearly delineated hiring goals.

These findings suggest that while the federal government has made progress, it has also encountered delays and problems in pursuing affirmative action in its own work force to increase the employment opportunities of disabled individuals.

Section 503: Affirmative Action by Government Contractors

While section 501 directs affirmative action in employment toward the organs of the federal government, section 503 aims requirements outward toward those public and private agencies that contract with the federal government. Contracting is defined within the law as the provision of supplies or services to, or the use of real or personal property by, the federal government. As compared to the slow rulemaking activity for section 504, that for section 503 was more rapid. The Department of Labor, given responsibility for implementation of section 503, issued administrative rules in June 1974.[36] Arguing that "notice of proposed rulemaking and delay in the effective date would be contrary to the public interest in view of the need for prompt implementation," DOL issued the regulations for section 503 in final form with an immediate effective date.[37] Interested persons were, however, invited to provide the agency with comments on the rule contents.

The regulations required contractors to take positive actions to employ qualified handicapped individuals. They stipulated that contractors review employment practices in light of affirmative action requirements and undertake outreach and "positive recruitment" efforts. The regulations listed possible outreach efforts: (1) internal communication to management of new affirmative action policies; (2) development of procedures to ensure compliance with such policies; (3) periodic informing of employees of contractor's commitment to engage in affirmative action; (4) enlisting the assistance of public and private recruiting sources; (5) recruiting in educational institutions that train handicapped persons; (6) establishing contacts with appropriate social service and VR agencies; (7) reviewing employment records to determine availability of promotable handicapped persons; and (8) using appropriate media for advertising affirmative action policies. It was not incumbent upon agencies, according to the rules, to undertake all of the positive recruitment steps; instead, the scope of efforts should "depend upon all the circumstances, including the extent to which existing employment practices are adequate and the contractor's size and resources."[38]

In terms of compliance responsibilities for affirmative action, the regulations created a three-tiered system of requirements for contractors based on dollar amount and contract length. Those with contracts in excess of $50,000 were given the greatest duties to create affirmative action programs.

Similar to the administrative regulations later issued for section 504, those for section 503 required contractors to engage in reasonable accommodation to the physical and mental limitations of an employee, unless such action would impose an undue economic hardship for the contractor. Specification of "undue" hardship was not clearly defined in the rules, although they allowed consideration of business necessity, financial cost and expense, and resulting personnel problems in determining the extent of contractor obligations to accommodate persons with disabilities.

It is useful to recognize that the approach to affirmative action taken by DOL was not a punitive one, based on rigid goals, quotas, or sanctions. Instead, the approach sought "a working relationship in which the employer will take the handicapped person's condition into account, and facilitate employment wherever possible, by making adjustments so that the handicapped may work as effectively as non-handicapped employees" (Ellner and Bender 1980, 18). As will become clear in discussions to follow, this "facilitative" approach to affirmative action differed from approaches used in equal opportunity programs for racial minorities and women.

Congress made changes to the VR program through the Rehabilitation Act Amendments of 1974. These amendments were largely clarifying and, as described in chapter four, were stimulated by concerns of the officials in HEW who had begun drafting section 504 regulations. The 1974 law changed and broadened the definition of handicapped persons beyond reference to employment and extended program authorization. DOL issued a proposal for revised regulations in August 1975 to reflect both the 1974 amendments to the Rehabilitation Act and comments received about the regulations released in 1974.[39]

Following the law, DOL changed the definition of "handicap" from reference to employability to any impairment that substantially limits a person's major life functions. The regulations also added a definition of "qualified handicapped person," a key phrase left undefined in the original regulations but now defined as an individual who, with the provision of reasonable accommodation, was otherwise qualified for the job in question.

DOL, responding to public comments and reactions, proposed to abandon its three-tiered approach to affirmative action requirements (based upon contract amount and length of contract), noting that "contractors have commented that the existing clause is confusing and imprecise."[40] In its place, the proposed rules added a requirement that firms with contracts in excess of $50,000 or with more than fifty employees prepare and maintain, at their place of business, an affirmative action program. No longer would contractors be required to file copies of their affirmative action plans with DOL; in practice, the agency had found it difficult to process and review the large number of plans that had been submitted.[41] The affirmative action section was also expanded to include more discussion of what is expected of contractors in fulfilling their affirmative action mandate.

The revised section 503 regulations were issued by DOL in final form in April 1976; at the same time, they were redesignated in a new area of the federal code of regulations, reflecting the transfer of section 503 within DOL to its Office of Federal Contract Compliance Programs (OFCCP).[42] This office was created in the mid-1960s, when responsibility for contract compliance was shifted to DOL through an executive order issued by Lyndon Johnson.[43]

The Role of OFCCP in Implementing Section 503

As part of its initiative to enhance the civil rights activities of the federal government through reorganization and consolidation of offices, the Carter administration moved, in 1978, to expand the role of OFCCP and mark it as the central bureaucratic mechanism for overseeing federally mandated affirmative action programs for contractors. Through Executive Order 12086, President Carter transferred the equal employment programs for federal contractors, residing in eleven different federal agencies, to DOL and its OFCCP.[44] The order also expanded the responsibilities of OFCCP, requiring it to issue regulations, undertake investigations, and perform other actions in order to effectively pursue equal employment opportunities among federal contractors. With the consolidation of responsibilities in OFCCP, the agency was charged with implementing not only section 503, but also section 402 of the VEVRAA and Executive Order 11246.[45] This executive order, issued in 1965, provides for affirmative action in employment practices by federal contractors to advance the job opportunities of those previously discriminated against on the basis of race, sex, and national origin.

The move by Jimmy Carter to consolidate equal employment opportunity programs in OFCCP was in large measure a response to a task force appointed in 1977 to review OFCCP and recommend means to develop a plan for improvement. The task force issued a preliminary report in September, much of which was critical of the current equal employment activities of OFCCP.[46] One major problem identified with OFCCP's activities was fragmentation of implementation responsibility: ''. . . the overriding defect in the administration of the Federal Contract Compliance Program lies in its fragmented enforcement structure, and the need to improve and strengthen its regulatory scheme.''[47] The task force report was particularly critical of the enforcement of Executive Order 11246, given the agency-based approach of its implementation. In light of this assessment, it was not surprising that the report strongly recommended that responsibility and authority be removed from individual federal agencies and consolidated into DOL.

The task force also reviewed the role of OFCCP in implementing section 503 of the Rehabilitation Act and section 402 of the VEVRAA. While the implementation of these programs was seen as more effective than that for Executive Order 11246, some problems were identified. These included inappropriate goals and timetables, insufficient guidance on evaluating the affirmative action programs of contracts, no procedure for conducting comprehensive compliance reviews, and inadequate data collection to measure program effectiveness.[48] The task force report also recommended a proactive approach to evaluating compliance through on-site reviews, rather than relying only on complaints to identify discriminatory practices.

Insight into OFCCP's implementation efforts, and the consequences of the expanded mandate on agency operations, were reflected in hearings on employment opportunities for disabled persons held by the Senate Committee on

Labor and Human Resources in June 1979.[49] At the hearings the director of OFCCP reported that the agency, given its new mandate, was proceeding to move beyond complaints to compliance reviews as a means to assess compliance with section 503. As a first step toward creating a compliance review system, OFCCP, in 1978, conducted a pilot study of contractors of different sizes to assess their compliance with current rules and regulations for section 503.[50] The results of the pilot study were not encouraging. Of the three hundred contractors examined:

1. Ninety percent were found to be in noncompliance with some aspect of the regulations.

2. Twenty-five percent did not have an affirmative action plan.

3. Fifty-seven percent did not give disabled persons the opportunity to identify themselves as handicapped.

4. Fifty-three percent did not review job descriptions or other dimensions of personnel policies that could be discriminatory.

5. Forty-four percent had no outreach program to recruit persons with disabilities.

6. Seventeen percent had made no reasonable accommodation for disabilities.

7. Fifty-three percent had not properly disseminated information on their affirmative action program.

8. Twenty-eight percent did not post the government's affirmative action notice.

The director acknowledged that these findings were distressing and that they had encouraged the agency to take a new and more proactive policy of compliance reviews. He concluded by arguing: "OFCCP believes in an aggressive but fair enforcement of the section 503 program. Through consolidation and the direct compliance reviews we have implemented in the last two years, we believe that we can considerably strengthen the administration of the section 503 program in the future."[51] Other analysts concurred with the weak performance of OFCCP through 1978, with one arguing that "the administrative enforcement record of the OFCCP demonstrates a singular lack of aggressiveness and effectiveness in protecting the employment right of the handicapped.''[52]

The Policy Environment Shifts

In 1979, DOL initiated rulemaking efforts to consolidate regulations for section 503 and section 402 of the VEVRAA of 1974 into the section of federal code containing the regulations for Executive Order 11246. This move would centralize OFCCP regulations for federal contractors into one place in the code. After a period of public comment, the consolidating regulations were issued in final form near the end of the Carter administration in late 1980.[53]

One interesting development during this round of rulemaking was consideration of changing the affirmative action regulations for section 503 to require contractors to use numerical goals to remedy discrimination. Goals and timetables were used, at this time, as part of affirmative action programs for women and minorities. It was decided, however, that prescribing goals for handicapped employment would be administratively impossible given the breadth, diversity, and varying intensities of disabling conditions. Whereas race and sex characteristics are generally easy to determine, such is not the case for handicaps, which demonstrate great variation. Given this recognition, it was decided not to employ numerical goals as part of affirmative action requirements for implementing section 503; instead, the existing approach, focusing on employer self-evaluation of employment practices, was retained.[54]

Like many other regulations issued at the twilight of the Carter administration, those issued by OFCCP were delayed by the Reagan administration almost immediately upon its assumption of office.[55] The purpose of the delay was to enable the administration to review the rules in terms of their regulatory impact pursuant to Executive Order 12291, which prescribed a cost-benefit examination of all new regulations. This delay marked the beginning of a protracted period of regulation writing, as the Reagan administration worked to modify OFCCP regulations for federal contractors. The effort to review and modify OFCCP contractor regulations clearly resulted from the new policy environment surrounding the new Reagan administration. A key organizing principle of the new administration, regulatory relief, was pursued in several contexts related to civil rights and antidiscrimination policy, including OFCCP regulations governing affirmative action requirements placed on contractors with the federal government.

In the summer of 1981, OFCCP issued two notices of rulemaking related to regulations for enforcing affirmative action requirements of government contractors. In one notice, issued in August 1981, OFCCP published a proposed revision of the regulations to consolidate provisions of Executive Order 11246, section 503 of the Rehabilitation Act of 1973, and section 402 of the VEVRAA as they apply to federal contractors. This move continued the consolidating effort begun during the Carter administration. In introducing the proposed revisions, which would lessen compliance requirements of federal contractors, DOL stated that:

> a number of OFCCP's procedures may not have been productive in encouraging voluntary compliance, and may have led to unnecessary confrontation between contractors acting in good faith and representatives of the government. Consistent with executive Order 12291, today's proposal attempts to reduce substantially compliance burdens of federal contractors without unnecessarily infringing protection of minorities, women, veterans, and the handicapped.[56]

The policy objective of reducing federal regulations, a hallmark of the Reagan administration, is clearly evident in this introductory statement.

Included within OFCCP's proposed regulations relevant to section 503 were provisions related to affirmative action plans. One provision raised the threshold level at which contractors are required to develop and maintain written affirmative action programs, from those with 50 employees and contracts totaling $50,000 or more (under existing regulations), to those with 250 employees and contracts of $1 million or greater. A second provision allowed contractors with between 250 and 499 employees to devise abbreviated affirmative action plans. Still another component of the regulations provided that OFCCP could defer compliance reviews if contractors successfully completed an on-site compliance review and were found to have an acceptable affirmative action plan in force. These provisions were justified on the bases that they compensated for inflation that had occurred since the original rules were issued and that they would relieve paperwork requirements placed on contractors.

From this point onward, the initiative to revise the administrative regulations for section 503 became caught up in a much larger political battle concerning affirmative action policies for women and minorities. The battle focused on, among other things, the plan of the Reagan administration to ease up on some affirmative action requirements placed on federal contractors. At the forefront here was the administration's plan to abandon numerical guidelines and statistical formulas as mechanisms for enforcing Executive Order 11246.[57] The administration justified its regulatory reforms on the grounds that they would facilitate more effective relations with federal contractors. After three years of political controversy and debate, and as the result of strong opposition, the Reagan administration abandoned its regulatory reform initiatives with regard to affirmative action programs. Lost in this abandonment were the less controversial regulatory revisions proposed for section 503 and section 402 of the VEVRAA.

Continuing Concerns about Enforcement

While concerns about regulatory reforms abated, Congress and interest groups continued scrutiny of OFCCP and its enforcement of affirmative action programs. Interest groups representing women and minorities remained convinced that OFCCP's enforcement activities were insufficient, reflecting more an interest to reduce regulatory activity than a commitment to equal employment opportunity. In the summer of 1984, the House Subcommittee on Employment Opportunities, the watchdog over OFCCP affirmative action efforts, held an oversight hearing.[58] Appearing at the hearing were three retired and rather disgruntled former employees of OFCCP, who chronicled problems with other affirmative action procedures. Among the problems identified was reliance on self-monitoring in order to ascertain compliance: "Contrary to expressions of some officials of the current administration, affirmative action works. OFCCP has studies to prove that it does work. Self-monitoring by contractors is certainly a noble gesture, but it was tried. . . . It was concluded that this method does not work."[59] Another witness argued that self-monitoring was unlikely to lead to self-reports of noncompliance, and in this way, he argued, "I see the burden of affirmative action delegated to the individual worker through the complaint process."[60]

The frustration of the subcommittee, after hearing testimony about reports being buried and problems anticipated with the self-monitoring system, was voiced by its chairman: "I'm almost inclined to believe that we're dealing with an agency that is actually involved in discriminating rather than protecting those who are discriminated against. Maybe the public would be better off if we didn't have the agency."[61] In response, the acting director of OFCCP, while affronted by the chairman's remarks, described recent enforcement activities, stating that the agency had conducted more compliance reviews than ever before.[62]

Evidence on the Impact of Section 503

A picture of the impact of section 503, during the first decade of its implementation, is provided by a research study sponsored by OFCCP "to discover the prevalence of current accommodation effort and the types and costs of accommodations currently being provided, to explore the related practices that

209

firms have found conducive to successful accommodation, and to understand the decision-making process involved'' (Berkeley Planning Associates 1982).[63] The findings of this study, conducted in the early 1980s, provide evidence on the impact of federal laws to advance the employment opportunities by changing the policies and attitudes of federal contractors.

One component of the study was a mail survey that queried contractors on the extent and types of accommodations made for workers with disabilities. While two-thirds of the contractors reported employing handicapped individuals, one-third reported making some accommodations. These accommodations, however, were made for fewer than ten percent of handicapped workers; the data do not indicate what percent of workers needed or would benefit from some form of accommodation in the workplace. The report also showed a positive relationship between contractor size, measured by number of employees, and the extent of accommodations taken.

A broad range of accommodations was made by federal contractors, according to study results. The most frequent forms included orienting supervisors and coworkers to provide necessary assistance, modifying work schedules, assigning tasks to other workers, adjusting work spaces and surfaces, and removing architectural barriers. Another component of the contractor survey examined accessibility modifications performed by the firms. Results indicated that about seventy-five percent of contractors provided parking or curb cuts, sixty-four percent had ramped entrances, sixty-seven percent had clear access to offices where applications are made, and sixty-two percent had access throughout the whole facility. A smaller percentage of firms had audible and visual alarm systems, braille markings, and lowered telephones and drinking fountains.

Still another hotly debated issue concerned the cost of making accommodations. In the author's words, ''a striking finding of this study was that accommodations rarely involved much expense'' (Berkeley Planning Associates 1982, 28). No cost outlays were required in over half of the accommodations, and an additional thirty percent of accommodation packages cost $500 or less. The report, however, noted that most contractors underestimated accommodation costs, since they counted only out-of-pocket expenses when calculating cost figures; they neglected the costs of planning, implementation time, and work undertaken by plant maintenance staff.

One final question examined in the mail survey, and in a related survey of disabled workers employed by contractors, concerned the impact of accommodations on workers. The study concluded that accommodations function to bring disabled workers up to company productivity standards but otherwise confer no special advantages (Berkeley Planning Associates 1982, 32–33). Accommodations were found to generate both benefits and costs to nondisabled workers. Twenty-nine percent of contractors reported that some nondisabled workers benefited from accommodations undertaken for handicapped workers, while nineteen percent said that workers suffered some form of inconvenience as the result of accommodations.

An overall assessment of these survey data presents a picture of reasonable accommodation that has both positive and negative dimensions. On the positive side, the survey results indicate that many federal contractors have begun to recognize the needs of disabled workers and to perform accommodations that enhance their employability and performance. In further good news, the costs of accommodation, often a psychological stumbling block, were found typically to be rather small, representing minor fiscal impact on the accommodating business concern. The downside is that many firms have yet to commence making modifications or accommodating the full range of disabled persons within the firm. Ultimately, one's assessment of federal contractor compliance is determined by a perception of how fast section 503 should and can be reasonably implemented. It seems clear that section 503 has been a major stimulus to reasonable accommodation by federal contractors, and from this vantage point, one might rate implementation favorably. On the other hand, if one judges implementation in terms of the extent to which it has reached its ultimate objective—providing full employment opportunities to all disabled workers—the survey results indicate that substantial work remains to be done.

Section 504: Employment Requirements for Recipients of Federal Financial Assistance

Central to the employment practices area of the section 504 coordination rules, issued by HEW in 1978, was the organizing principle of reasonable accommodation. This stipulation required recipients of federal financial assistance to make accommodations to work settings to enhance the employability of persons with disability.[64] Such accommodations were required of employers only for "otherwise qualified" handicapped workers and only when they do not impose an undue economic hardship. The regulations defined an otherwise qualified handicapped worker as one "who, with reasonable accommodation, can perform the essential functions of the job in question."[65] Thus, ability to perform "essential functions" was the disability-related criterion imposed to determine when accommodation must be activated. As we shall see, regulations for the other employment provisions of the Rehabilitation Act use somewhat different definitions of "qualified handicapped worker."

211

Dual Mandates and Conflicting Signals

By the late 1970s, an outpouring of reactions from employers signaled a significant problem for implementation of employment protections for handicapped individuals: conflicting guidelines for policy execution arising from sections 503 and 504. The problem resulted from the facts that (1) many employers served as both contractors and recipients of federal assistance, thus requiring compliance with both sections, and (2) the regulations for sections 503 and 504 were not completely consistent. For example, an employer might be both a vendor of office supplies under a federal contract and a participant in a job training program. In cases such as this, it was asked, when the section 503 and 504 regulations differ, which set should be followed? Inconsistencies in the administrative regulations for these sections thus caused what has been termed the "503/504 flap" (Zimmer 1981, 52).

Areas of inconsistency between the two sets of regulations included definitions of qualified handicapped persons, reasonable accommodation, collective bargaining agreements, use of preemployment medical exams and medical information, and affirmative action (Zimmer 1981, 54–57). A listing of the regulatory differences is presented in table 9-1.

In order to alleviate some of the confusion about conflicts in the section 503 and 504 responsibilities of employers, OFCCP and DOL took two actions in 1980. First, as part of its own administrative regulations for implementing section 504, DOL stipulated that contractors who are in compliance with section 503 shall also be deemed in compliance with section 504.[66] In this way, section 503 regulations were given precedence. This position was taken because section 503 requires that affirmative action be taken in employment, whereas section 504 stipulates the less strict position of prohibiting discrimination.

In a second action, OFCCP issued a proposed regulation that would modify the administrative rules for section 503 and section 402 of the VEVRAA to make them both more consistent with DOL's rules for section 504.[67] The primary action taken in the proposed rules was to change the language of the section 503 regulations to more closely parallel that in the section 504 rules. Thus, the proposed rules included changes that (1) included the "essential features of the job" language in defining a qualified handicapped person, (2) provided a definition of reasonable accommodation, (3) delineated in greater detail the types of employment covered by the regulations, and (4) restricted the use of preemployment medical examinations.

Unfortunately, these regulatory changes, initiated near the end of the Carter administration, to enhance the consistency between sections 503 and 504 were not removed, since the Reagan administration did not pursue finalization of the revised regulations. As described previously, the new administration instead

Table 9-1 Differences in Administrative Regulations Promulgated for Sections 503 and 504 of the Rehabilitation Act of 1973*

Definition of Qualified Handicapped Person

503: Defined as person capable of performing a particular job with reasonable accommodation to the handicap.

504: Defined as individual who, with reasonable accommodation, can perform the "essential functions" of the job.

Reasonable Accommodation

Both 503 and 504 require reasonable accommodation be made to handicapped workers if they do not cause undue economic hardship. However, the language of 503 regulations implies more flexibility for employers in determining whether financial costs and impacts on business necessity create hardship and thus eliminates accommodation requirements.

Collective Bargaining Agreements

503: Employers are instructed to consult with bargaining agents to determine whether accommodations and other compliance efforts conflict with collective bargaining agreements.

504: Specifically states that compliance regulations will in no way be reduced in terms of collective bargaining agreements.

Preemployment Medical Examinations

503: Employers not prohibited from giving a comprehensive medical exam prior to employment, provided the exam does not discriminate against handicapped persons who should be hired with reasonable accommodation.

504: Except under special circumstances, an employer is prohibited from conducting a preemployment physical exam unless employee has been offered a job and only when other new employees in same job classification are given same exam.

Medical Information

503: Must be kept confidential.

504: Must be collected on separate form, not commingled with other personnel information, and kept confidential.

Affirmative Action

503: Contractors have responsibility to take affirmative action to employ, and advance in employment, qualified handicapped persons.

504: Prohibits discrimination in employment and suggests (but does not require) affirmative action as a means to end discriminatory practices.

*Adapted from analysis presented in Zimmer, *Employing the Handicapped* (1981, 54–58).

pursued a program of regulatory revisions aimed at reducing some of the compliance burdens exerted upon federal contractors (section 503) and recipients of federal funds (section 504). Caught up in wider battles about affirmative action policy, the regulations to enhance consistency between sections 503 and 504 were neglected and eventually abandoned with other proposed regulatory reforms.

Court Interpretation of Section 504 and Employment

In the early 1980s, two significant questions remained pertaining to the reach of employment protections afforded by section 504 (Rothstein 1984, 127). One dealt with whether protections extended to all of an employer's programs or only to those directly receiving federal financial assistance. The second question centered on whether requirements for reasonable accommodation in employment extend to employers receiving federal financial assistance for purposes other than employment. Decisions reached by the Supreme Court in 1984 addressed these issues, with one restricting the section 504 mandate and the other expanding it.

In one 1984 case, *Grove City College v. Bell*, examined previously in chapter five, the Court held that civil rights protections, including section 504, extend to the programs that receive federal financial assistance and not to the entire institution in which the program resides.[68] This ruling was seen as restricting the reach of nondiscrimination provisions, including those dealing with mental and physical handicap. The Civil Rights Restoration Act, passed by Congress in 1988, nullified this interpretation and replaced it with the institution-wide approach to enforcing nondiscrimination policies.

A second Supreme Court case in 1984 served to expand the section 504 mandate. In *Consolidated Rail Corporation v. Darrone*, the Court held that the primary objective of federal financial assistance need not be employment in order for section 504 requirements to be activated.[69] Thus, this ruling answered the question of whether section 504 applied to only those programs that received federal financial assistance for the purpose of employment (e.g., a job-training program) or to all programs regardless of focus on employment. The latter interpretation was taken by the Court, thus clarifying that reasonable accommodation provisions, as mandated by section 504, are relevant to all programs receiving federal financial assistance.

Assessment of Implementation of Employment Protections for Persons with Disabilities

Policies to prohibit discrimination against and advance the employment opportunities of persons with mental or physical disabilities are more complex than those for other policy areas given multiple mandates. Sections 501, 503, and 504 all deal with employment of disabled Americans and require actions by federal agencies, contractors with the federal government, and recipients of federal financial assistance. In some instances, multiple mandates have generated fragmentation of implementation authority and inconsistencies in regulatory requirements.

Implementation experiences for sections 501 and 503 show much the same pattern. In both cases, administrative regulations were issued without extensive fanfare or debate, certainly with less attention than those for section 504. Implementation in the early years, following promulgation of administrative regulations, was largely ineffectual, since both federal agencies and contractors were slow to recognize their responsibilities and undertake accommodations and other actions to increase the employment potential of disabled Americans.

In both cases, actions were taken during the Carter administration, as part of a broader effort to enhance enforcement of civil rights laws, to reorganize the administrative mechanisms responsible for enforcing equal opportunity programs. In the case of section 501, the separate equal opportunity programs of federal agencies were consolidated into a strengthened EEOC, while for section 503, a reinvigorated OFCCP was charged with more active pursuit of equal employment by federal contractors. Immediately following both reorganizational changes, there was evidence to suggest that more aggressive enforcement was being pursued and that more disabled citizens were finding employment opportunities.

These new efforts were blunted, however, as the Reagan administration took office and moved to reconsider and revise administrative regulations to reduce regulatory burdens on contractors and federal agencies. Much of the battle that ensued focused on affirmative action programs for women and minorities. The administration sought to eliminate the use of statistical and numerical measures in both determining discrimination and fashioning remedies to discriminatory action. It is apparent that the bitter battles over affirmative action captured substantial attention and resources within the agencies charged with implementing sections 501 and 503.

As with other disability rights policies, multiple arenas were involved in shaping the content and direction of policies to implement equal employment opportunities for disabled persons. The institutional decisions relevant to section 501 are listed in table 9-2 and those for section 503 in table 9-3. In both instances, we see Congress making refinements and administrative agencies devising and revising regulations to implement congressional mandates. Overall, these initial rulemaking efforts were far less controversial than those surrounding section 504. During the Carter administration, when the policy environment was favorable to civil rights policies, implementation authority

215

was shifted and vested in strengthened offices. The impact of this action was initially favorable, only to be countered by another shift in the policy environment when the Reagan administration assumed office in 1980. At this point, concerns about regulatory relief and limiting the impact of the federal government on both the private sector and subnational governments, eclipsed civil rights policies.

One particularly important arena in regard to the debate over setting a new direction for affirmative action policy was the Subcommittee on Employment Opportunities. This subcommittee was relentless in holding oversight hearings and probing into the actions of both DOL and EEOC with regard to potential changes in affirmative action policies and enforcement. These hearings put the administration's actions in the spotlight and offered civil rights groups and others in the legal community a chance to protest, in a major public forum, against changing affirmative action policies. It was repeatedly argued that studies showed current affirmative action and equal employment opportunity programs to be effective, and that regulatory revision was nothing more than partisan attack on the employment protections of women and various minorities, including persons with mental and physical disabilities.

Not only did the subcommittee hold repeated oversight hearings, it also instigated a significant staff investigation into the civil rights enforcement practices of EEOC. The findings of this report showed EEOC to have changed affirmative action policy by modifying internal procedures and practices, without subjecting these changes to outside review. This report had to be embarrassing to the Reagan administration and certainly contributed to decisions to abandon the regulatory reform initiative.

Another factor that weakened the regulatory reform effort in regard to equal employment opportunity programs was that the regulated clients, firms and businesses across the nation, were divided about whether regulatory changes were needed. At hearings and in other forums, many businessmen reported that they had become accustomed to existing affirmative action requirements and found they were able to live with them. While many corporate leaders condemned the practice of strict hiring or promotion quotas, they found existing affirmative action provisions were acceptable. Without strong support of the business community, the Reagan administration was hard put to brook the strong forces against regulatory reform.

Unfinished Business

The state of handicapped employment was measured in 1985 through a study sponsored jointly by the International Center for the Disabled and the National

Table 9-2   Decisions and Actions within Institutional Arenas Affecting the Development of Implementation Policy for Employment Policies for Federal Agencies

Institutional Arena/Date	*Decision/Action Taken*
Congress (1973)	Passed the Rehabilitation Act, including section 501, requiring affirmative action by federal agencies in employing persons with disabilities
U.S. Civil Service Commission (CSC) (1974)	Added sections to the *Federal Personnel Manual* to guide federal agencies in implementing section 501
CSC (1977–78)	Issued administrative regulations to implement section 501
President (1978)	Issued reorganization plan shifting the responsibility for section 501 coordination to a strengthened Equal Employment Opportunity Commission (EEOC)
Congress—House of Representatives (1978)	Defeated resolution of disapproval, thus accepting EEOC reorganization plan
EEOC (1978)	Redesignated CSC rules under EEOC
Congress (1978)	Added section 505 to the Rehabilitation Act providing the remedies of Title VII of the Civil Rights Act of 1964 to persons discriminated against on the basis of handicap
EEOC (1978)	Amended section 501 regulations to remove prohibition against back pay as remedy for discrimination
Congress—House Subcommittee on Employment Opportunities (1980–83)	Conducted oversight hearings on EEOC and its strengthened mandate to pursue EEO policies; during Reagan administration, subcommittee expressed concerns about enforcement policy
EEOC (1981)	Made minor revision of section 501 administrative regulations with regard to inquiries related to preemployment evaluations
Congress—House Subcommittee on Employment Opportunities (1985–86)	Conducted oversight hearings and a staff investigation related to EEOC enforcement of affirmative action policies for women and minorities

Table 9-3 Decisions and Actions within Institutional Arenas Affecting the Development of Implementation Policy for Employment Policies for Federal Contractors

Institutional Arena/Date	*Decision/Action Taken*
Congress (1973)	Enacted section 503 of the Rehabilitation Act, requiring federal contractors to take affirmative action to employ persons with disabilities
Department of Labor (DOL) (1974)	Issued final administrative regulations for section 503 without period for public comment
Congress (1974)	Enacted amendments to the Rehabilitation Act, expanding definition of handicapped persons
DOL (1975–76)	Revised section 503 regulations to reflect changes made by Congress in the Rehabilitation Act
Presidential Task Force (1977)	Appointed by DOL, task force reviewed the enforcement actions of Office of Federal Contract Compliance Programs (OFCCP) and identified many problems
Presidency (1978)	Carter issued Executive Order 12086, to strengthen OFCCP programs and consolidate EEO programs for contractors in single agency
OFCCP, DOL (1978)	Conducted pilot study of contractor compliance with section 503, many instances of noncompliance documented
Congress—Senate Subcommittee on Labor and Human Resources (1979)	Conducted oversight hearings that examined EEO activities of OFCCP; new actions taken by OFCCP to strengthen enforcement are reported
DOL (1979–80)	Undertook rulemaking to consolidate EEO regulations for contractors, including section 503, in federal code; final rules issued late in the Carter administration; also proposed regulatory changes to make section 503 regulations more consistent with those for section 504
DOL (1981–84)	New Reagan administration in 1981 suspended section 503 regulations issued by Carter administration; undertook new rulemaking to reduce compliance burdens on contractors; most attention given to weakening affirmative action programs for women and minorities (Executive Order 11246); regulatory changes eventually abandoned

Council on the Handicapped and conducted by the Louis Harris polling firm.[70] The study was based upon a telephone survey of one thousand disabled persons aged sixteen and over. Study findings related to employment demonstrate that the task of advancing the employment potential of persons with disabilities remains unfinished business. Of those surveyed, two-thirds between the ages of sixteen and sixty-four were not working, although sixty-six percent stated that they would like to have a job. The potential benefits of employment are demonstrated by a comparison of working and nonworking disabled persons. Those who have a job are better educated, have higher family incomes, are more satisfied with their lives, and are much less likely to consider themselves disabled.

As a follow-up to the survey of disabled citizens, a second study was commissioned by the same two organizations and the President's Committee on Employment of the Handicapped.[71] This study focused on employers and included interviews with four separate samples of managers: top managers, department heads and line managers, top managers in very small companies, and managers of equal employment opportunity (EEO) programs. The findings of this employer study echo and reiterate findings reported in several other small studies.

Employers reported that disabled workers are good workers and that they did their jobs as well as other employees. Second, employers stated that the costs of making accommodations were generally not very expensive and should not be considered a significant barrier to employing disabled workers. Despite these assessments, however, the report findings indicate that employment of handicapped individuals is moving slowly: only half of the EEO officers reported that their firms had hired disabled employees in the past year. Not surprisingly, federal contractors and large firms were more likely than other firms to have employed disabled citizens.

The survey of employers identifies several factors that inhibit the employment of greater numbers of handicapped workers. Many firms have not yet devised policies for hiring handicapped workers, and many top managers often display a low level of consciousness toward disabled people as a group. Here again is evidence of persistent myths and lack of understanding by employers about the potential talents and abilities of persons with disabilities.

The findings of both surveys indicate that aggressive efforts remain requisite to advancing the employment of handicapped Americans and that the most pivotal role in meeting this objective is held by firms and companies across the nation. In the words of two analysts: "The key to successful placement lies in combining the efforts of vocational rehabilitation agencies, educational and governmental institutions, professional agencies, and handicapped persons themselves. But the lock to which the key applies is the employer" (Ellner and Bender 1980, 54).

219

Ultimately, the success of implementation of all equal employment opportunity programs depends upon the actions of employers, most of whom are in the private sector. Their movement to actively consider, hire, and promote disabled workers is most likely to occur when biases and misconceptions about persons with disabilities are removed. Compliance requirements are one means of heightening, and hopefully improving, awareness of this potential group of workers. Potentially more useful, however, would be aggressive outreach programs to communicate the consistent findings that handicapped workers are productive and reliable and that required accommodations are typically inexpensive. A combined strategy of outreach activity and compliance programs and remedies for persistent discrimination appears the most effective means of increasing the job opportunities of persons with disabilities across the nation.

Implementing Disability Rights Policies
Comparisons, Contrasts, and Dilemmas

The Four Stages of Policy Implementation

Federal government policies to protect the rights and opportunities of persons with disabilities have moved through four interrelated and overlapping stages of implementation. These stages, defined by the implementation activities pursued during each, centered on the following: (1) fine-tuning of legislative mandates for disability rights; (2) development of administrative regulations to guide implementation; (3) an assault by the Reagan administration on administrative guidelines, as part of a campaign for regulatory relief; and (4) a quiet lull as implementation moves away from refinement to policy diffusion and execution.

The first stage was basically concerned with legislative passage and refinement of disability rights laws. During this period, commencing in 1968 and lasting roughly through 1975, Congress first enacted and then made revisions to public laws outlining the rights of disabled citizens. This process began with the passage of the Architectural Barriers Act in 1968 and included enactment of several laws with disability rights provisions: the Urban Mass Transportation Act (as amended in 1970), Federal-Aid Highway Act of 1973 (and as amended in 1974), Rehabilitation Act of 1973, and Education for All Handicapped Children Act (1975). By the mid-1970s, major federal laws had been created specifying rights and protections for persons with disabilities in access to public buildings and transportation facilities, public education, and employment.

In most instances, Congress tinkered with and modified disability rights laws soon after they were enacted, in response to identified deficiencies and preliminary implementation problems. The Architectural Barriers Act, for example, was amended in 1970 to include urban mass transit projects, after Congress heard complaints that federally financed subway systems were not being constructed so as to be accessible to physically disabled persons. The Rehabilitation Act of 1973 was amended the year following its passage in response

221

to early problems encountered in drafting regulations for section 504. These legislative amendments created a new and expanded definition of handicapped persons covered by the act and provided some much-needed legislative history. Representing a somewhat different pattern, the Education for All Handicapped Children Act (PL94-142) was added to an existing categorical program as a means to mandate service delivery to all disabled children of school age.

Stage two of implementing disability rights laws, roughly covering the period from 1973 to 1980, centered on development of administrative regulations to guide policy implementation by federal, state, and local authorities. By and large, creation of administrative rules was a slow and difficult process, given that legislative statutes offered more in the way of symbolic promises than in concrete mechanisms for policy activation. The one exception in this regard was PL94-142, where several organizing and operating principles were included as statutory provisions, providing clearer insight into legislative intent.

The politics of implementation "heated up" dramatically during this second stage as interested parties came to understand either the magnitude of benefits they could receive through the new laws (program beneficiaries) or the potential behavioral modifications and costs that would be incurred through regulatory compliance (regulated clients). Groups representing disabled Americans, except those representing disabled veterans and parents of handicapped children, were not heavily involved during legislative passage and consideration. However, as these groups grew in number and strength and recognized the import of the new disability rights laws, they increasingly became active participants during administrative rulemaking. Those to be regulated by the new laws—including local school systems, public transit authorities, and corporations under contract to the federal government—also sought to participate actively in and influence the direction of administrative rulemaking.

The results of regulation writing yielded, by the late 1970s, administrative regulations for all of the disability rights laws. In many cases, significant compromises were made between the opposing parties, with, for example, reasonable accommodation in the section 504 rules, mandating accommodations, but only so long as they did not impose undue economic hardship. In the case of educational services, the free and appropriate education for handicapped children mandate was matched with authorization of increased federal funds to help cover the mandate's cost.

Presumably, the third stage of implementation would have focused on policy diffusion and execution, as the guidelines and operating procedures contained in the administrative regulations were communicated to implementing authorities, who, in turn, would commence or continue execution of public programs. While diffusion and execution did begin, the primary focus of the third stage returned to policy refinement. This occurred because of a change in the political environment resulting from the election of Ronald Reagan, who campaigned for office with a platform of regulatory reform. His election created a change in the policy environment, one where federal regulatory action was considered excessive and where regulatory "relief" was a hallowed objective.

Given this policy prescription, the Reagan administration moved during the third implementation stage to reconsider and revise the administrative regulations governing disability rights policies as one means of pursuing regulatory relief. Regulations issued late in the Carter administration were suspended, and other administrative rules were "opened" by new heads of executive agencies for the purpose of review and revision. What followed was nothing short of an orchestrated plan by the Reagan administration to revise policies to implement disability rights. The approach of these assaults was to loosen existing regulatory provisions, or suspend them altogether, in an effort to reduce the cost and effort required for compliance. If promulgated and issued in final form, these regulatory changes would have reduced the costs of compliance but, at the same time, weakened or eliminated some of the basic rights and protections recently granted to persons with disabilities.

What ensued in the early years of the Reagan administration, as a result of its regulatory relief initiative, was battle after battle over modifications in administrative regulations. The battles were fought in many arenas, as further discussed below, and generally resulted in defeats for the administration. Efforts to change rules for section 504 and PL94-142 were altogether abandoned by the administration in the wake of major political controversy, and regulations for complying with the Architectural Barriers Act and other laws dealing with accessibility were modified less than originally intended. The administration won few clear victories in its effort to pursue regulatory reform of disability rights policies. It may have been more effective in reducing regulatory impact, in a less visible fashion, through enforcement activities. In this regard, it has been widely charged that the Reagan administration was less aggressive and more selective in enforcing civil rights policies than previous administrations.

During the Reagan administration's second term, implementation of disability policies entered a fourth stage. It was a quiet one, compared to the two preceding phases, and the lull in political skirmishes allowed for greater attention to policy diffusion and execution. Up to this point, implementation efforts in the field, often hampered by policy changes and confusing policy signals from above, were far overshadowed by battles "at the top" to redirect implementation policies.

The wounds of battle are as yet unhealed. Interest groups representing disabled citizens remain both skeptical of the Reagan administration's commitment to enforcing disability rights policies and vigilant to further efforts to redirect implementation policy. The regulated clients—including school systems, transit authorities, state and local governments, and many corporations—have accepted a basic responsibility to accommodate handicapped persons; in this regard, the world has changed substantially in twenty years. At the same time, regulated groups remain concerned about compliance costs, which leads them to continue pressures for greater financial assistance in attaining compliance.

Finally, not all attention currently focuses on policy execution. Some advocates continue to call for clearer implementation policies with greater coverage of disabled persons. The National Council on the Handicapped (1988, 19), for example, in assessing the current status of disability rights policies, contends:

> Existing nondiscrimination laws, such as Section 504 of the Rehabilitation Act of 1973, are extremely important and have engendered much progress. In an overall context, however, our Nation's laws provide inadequate protection from discrimination for people with disabilities. Current statutes are not comparable in their scope of protection against discrimination to those afforded racial, ethnic, and religious minorities and women under civil rights laws.

In response to this finding, the council recommends passage of new legislation, the Americans with Disabilities Act, for the purpose of pulling together and strengthening nondiscrimination policies for persons with disabilities. The council is not alone in calling for more extensive nondiscrimination protections. Most policy actors, however, seem to prefer the current lull in policy issues related to disability to another round of contentious battle for new nondiscrimination laws and policies.

Implementation of Disability Rights: Comparison and Contrasts

With case descriptions of implementation of disability rights in four policy areas—barrier removal, public transportation, public education, and employment—it is possible to compare and contrast implementation experiences. This comparison is undertaken within the rubric of the theoretical framework outlined in the second chapter and applied within the case chapters. Primary attention is given to the conception of implementation policies being created and revised through repeated interactions of interested parties within institutional arenas.

The primary actors participating in the determination of implementation policies were legislators, administrative personnel in executive agencies, and interest groups affected by disability rights policy. Each set of actors played expected roles: legislators sought to ensure that implementation policies accurately reflected legislative intent, while administrative personnel worked to devise policies that mirrored legislative intent, policy preferences of agency leaders, and existing administrative practice within the agency. Interest groups acted to affect policy decisions that would either enhance the flow of benefits they received or reduce the incidence of regulatory sanctions and costs. While this depiction at first appears to resemble traditional models of policy formations, including the triangular conception of policy formation by "subgovernments," the actual situation is far more complex. A more detailed examination of the policy actors indicates that their aspirations, and their interrelations, are far more fluid than the three-sided "subgovernment" depiction.

Policy Entrepreneurs and Legislative Enactment

Unlike many other public policies, laws prohibiting discrimination against persons with disabilities were clearly initiated by a small set of policy entrepreneurs in Congress. Except in handicapped education, there was no ground swell of pressure from interest groups, as was the case with other civil rights laws, and there was no extensive media attention to the plight of persons with disabilities. Instead, policy innovation resulted from three factors: (1) the diligent efforts of policy entrepreneurs; (2) a political environment that had grown to accept an active role of the federal government in civil rights; and (3) acceptance of the symbolic need to help persons with disabilities.

In each policy context, the origins of public laws to protect the rights and opportunities of disabled Americans can be traced to a small set of legislators and their key staff members. For the Architectural Barriers Act, Senator E. L. Bartlett (D-AL) played a key role in initiating legislative action, motivated in part by the efforts of his legislative aid, Hugh Gallagher, who was physically handicapped as the result of polio. Bartlett was also motivated by the findings of a study commission, cosponsored by the Easter Seal Society and the President's Committee on Employment of the Handicapped, which documented the extensive mobility barriers encountered by physically disabled persons. The origins of section 504 have been traced to Senator Hubert Humphrey and Representative Charles Vanik, who introduced bills in Congress to amend the Civil Rights Act to include protections for persons with disabilities. While this strategy produced little result, it set the groundwork for section 504 to be included, quietly and without fanfare, in the Rehabilitation Act as the legislation was being marked up by staff members from the Senate Committee on Labor and

Public Welfare and the House Committee on Education and Labor. And the early effort to enhance the access of handicapped persons to public transit was fostered by Representative Mario Biaggi, who, serving as a policy entrepreneur, offered an amendment to the Urban Mass Transportation Act to require that special efforts be undertaken in transit systems to serve physically handicapped persons.

An exception to this pattern of quiet parentage of disability rights laws by dedicated policy entrepreneurs is offered in the case of the Education for All Handicapped Children Act (PL94-142). This law resulted from the long-term efforts of several interest groups, representing the parents of handicapped children, to push the federal government to a more active position in funding special education and in requiring, as a condition of receiving funds, that all disabled children be provided a free education tailored to their special learning needs and capabilities. The case of educational rights policies typifies Polsby's (1984) notion of an ''incubated'' innovation. Interest groups and their patrons in Congress worked persistently to set the groundwork for legislative action by clarifying the needs of disabled children and lobbying legislators to support their cause.

The other disability rights laws fit neither the acute nor incubated innovation types posited by Polsby (1984). Instead, they are best characterized as innovations by ''guardianship,'' whereby a small set of policy entrepreneurs, recognizing the problems or plight of some group, undertake efforts to create public laws to assist them. Guardians must first become convinced a target group needs some form of public sector assistance, and then they apply political resources in such a way as to gain sufficient support to enact public laws to assist this group.

The ability of guardians and other policy entrepreneurs to successfully open a policy window (Kingdon 1984), so as to provide an opportunity for legislative consideration, is strongly affected by the prevailing political and policy environment. If the political environment is such that proposals move against a prevailing consensus on appropriate forms of public sector activity, or if the policy environment is such as to militate against a set of instrumental practices, then entrepreneurs are unlikely to achieve legislative success. Despite the fact that several disability rights laws were enacted during Republican administrations, the prevailing political environment in Congress was favorable toward civil rights policies. Congress, as the result of great turmoil and debate, had passed the Civil Rights Acts of 1964 and 1968, culminating many years of civil protest. By the late 1960s and early 1970s, when disability rights laws were passed, much of the nation had begun to accept the notion of the federal government's leading the way in civil rights issues. Also by this time, the federal government had in place several executive orders requiring affirmative action by employers to advance the employment opportunities of minorities and women. In this way, disability rights were seen as almost a natural extension of ongoing civil rights policy.

Even if the political environment is favorable or benign, legislation can be stopped if it violates the current policy environment, that is, beliefs about the appropriate mechanisms for executing public policies. This potential obstacle was removed during legislative consideration by the way the laws were initially written: they stressed symbolic protections and sidestepped difficult questions and issues of implementation. The transportation laws called for ''special efforts'' to help physically handicapped persons; section 504 was simply a broad statement of a nondiscrimination position; and the Architectural Barriers Act stipulated ''enhanced access'' to public facilities. At the symbolic level, there was little basis to disapprove of the values articulated in proposed laws, and there was little negative reaction, yet, from the regulated clients. Thus, in a benign political environment, with difficult questions about policy implementation absent from debate, the disability rights policies became public law. The exception to this pattern, again, is PL94-142, where the political environment was generally favorable to federal support of education, and where political support was strong enough to overcome concerns about the implementation procedures and expenditures mandated by the legislation.

The importance of policy entrepreneurs was greatest during the period of legislative enactment of disability rights laws. At this point, many of the groups representing handicapped persons were relatively young and lacked adequate skills and resources to be major players in legislative consideration.[1] During phases of policy implementation, however, these groups had grown in strength, encouraged that some level of government had finally recognized their needs and abilities and undertaken measures to enhance their opportunities in mainstream society. A source of support for some handicapped groups was federal funding, provided so that the groups could conduct outreach efforts to inform handicapped citizens about disability rights programs. While undertaking outreach activities, the groups spread information about disability rights, formed large networks with constituents and local organizations, and fostered efforts to monitor and advocate public policies.

Program Beneficiaries

It is important to recognize that the interest groups involved in disability rights, both program beneficiaries and regulated clients, were not constant across policy areas. Interest groups representing persons with disabilities tended to direct attention and resources on policy areas of most direct salience to their own members. Thus, in terms of accessibility to public facilities, groups representing persons with physical disabilities, including the Paralyzed Veterans of America and regional affiliates, often took the lead in monitoring and lobbying for implementation policy. They were joined by coalitions such as the American Coalition of Citizens with Disabilities (ACCD), which served as umbrella representatives of other disability groups. Much the same groups were concerned about public transit policy, again given that accessibility problems were greatest for physically handicapped persons.

In battles over implementation policy for rights to public education, a somewhat different set of interest groups played key roles; very relevant here were the activities of such groups as the Council for Exceptional Children, the National Association for the Deaf, and, again, ACCD. For section 504 policies, and particularly in the fight with the Reagan administration over weakening the legal linchpin of antidiscrimination provisions, one group, the Disability Rights Education and Defense Fund, assumed a primary role in fighting for retention of existing implementation policies and regulations for section 504.

In the early years of disability rights policies, there was some proclivity for insular action and protective behavior on the parts of program beneficiaries. For example, groups representing physically disabled persons, which have the longest history of organized action, did not immediately embrace groups representing mentally handicapped individuals. The former, not unlike their nonhandicapped peers, sometimes had stereotypical views of mental illness and were concerned that hard-won benefits would be harmed by inclusion of a different class of disability into public policies. The view of nondisabled persons that the ''handicapped'' are a homogeneous group—with consistent concerns, needs, and aspirations—is not an accurate description.

Increasingly, however, there has developed a community of interest among the full range of groups representing persons with different types of disabilities. They have come to realize that despite differences between their constituents, there is often a strong political advantage to be gained from united efforts to pursue policy goals. This was particularly evident during battles with the Reagan administration over reform of administrative regulations for disability rights laws. The administration's attack was so widespread, affecting newly won rights across practically all areas of disability policy, that the groups arose together and, more than ever before, pursued a unified response.

Not only have groups representing program beneficiaries grown in strength, they have also become more skilled and politically sophisticated. One manifestation of their new sophistication has been the increased use of lawyers and legal analysts to supplement staffs versed in advocacy techniques. Legal analysis has allowed handicapped groups to more accurately track the development of new laws and administrative regulations. The implications of the technical language of laws and regulations can be great, and with legal analysts, the groups could assess the meaning and likely impacts of new or changed provisions. Once legal analysis was undertaken, then advocates could communicate the implication of legal or regulatory changes to their field networks as a means of stimulating advocacy activities.

Yet despite this unity and sophistication, there is little question but that several handicapped groups were considerably weaker by the mid-1980s, as compared to their vitality in the late 1970s. By the midpoint of the Reagan administration, such groups as ACCD and Mainstream, Inc., once extremely active in both program monitoring and advocacy, had diminished somewhat in size, influence, and activities undertaken. This pattern of relative decline, mirrored by many other handicapped groups across the nation, resulted neither from reduced interest in implementation policy nor satisfaction with policy outcomes. Instead, their waning strength results from a persistent shutoff of the federal funds that previously had financed a large proportion of disability groups' budgets.[2] Withdrawal of these funds, supplied so that disability groups could engage in outreach and educational programs, was a purposeful strategy on the part of the Reagan administration, which recognized that the groups conducting outreach efforts were also those that were the strongest advocates of aggressive implementation and enforcement of disability rights protections.

Regulated Clients

It is only natural, given assumptions of rational self-interest, that those organizations expected to change behaviors and incur costs in order to advance disability rights would take action to affect the direction of implementation policy. The policy cases examined within this book indicate that the regulated clients tended to be policy specific. That is, in contrast to the emerging coalitions among handicapped groups, no one set of regulated clients has fought disability rights policies and their implementation across the board. In accessibility policy, the regulated clients were widespread—with program accessibility (through section 504) mandated for recipients of federal financial assistance and with architectural accessibility (through the Architectural Barriers Act) required for public buildings built or leased with federal funds. The regulated interests in public transportation, urban transportation authorities, were a much smaller set of parties; this set of actors was well organized around professional and technical values. In public education, state education agencies and local school systems were also well organized through national lobbying groups, whose growth mirrored the increased federal presence in public education. The regulated clients in employment included federal contractors, recipients of federal funds, and the agencies of the federal government.

It should be clearly stated that the regulated clients were not totally unconcerned about the needs of disabled persons or ''anti-handicapped'' in their views. Certainly, many actors in both the public and private sectors were as guilty as the rest of society of ignoring the needs and capabilities of persons with disabilities. And they were not, as a whole, enthusiastic about bearing extensive costs in order to accommodate handicapped needs. Their greatest complaint, however, seemed to be that the federal government, in a relatively short period of time, had enacted expansive mandates that were perceived as requiring extensive costs and behavioral changes. Except for public education, the antidiscrimination policies were not accompanied by federal funds to cover compliance costs. And unlike other civil rights laws, rights and protections for disabled persons often required positive actions to overcome discrimination, actions that engender costs. The big gripe of the regulated clients was that the federal government neither helped fund accommodations nor allowed compliance timetables that would spread costs over a long period of time.

Regulated clients often played both visible and sophisticated roles in affecting the development of implementation policies. One example is that of the American Public Transit Association (APTA), which was heavily involved in efforts to convince the Department of Transportation (DOT) to employ means other than full-accessibility criteria to implement transportation policies for handicapped citizens. Examination of the rulemaking dockets for the DOT regulations for handicapped transportation shows a constant barrage of comments, analyses, reports, and other information being submitted by the transit association.[3] Ultimately, when APTA was unable to convince DOT to weaken or abandon its full-accessibility policy, it turned to another arena, the federal courts, to press its case. Similar sorts of tactical interventions in the administrative process were made by other interest groups representing regulated clients.

In some instances, the set of regulated clients within a specific policy area acted relatively in concert, united in their stance for or against various implementation policies. In other instances, the regulated parties were less unified, in which case their political power was less influential. The work of APTA and other regional transit authorities represents an example of strong and concerted effort by a set of clients to press for changes in transportation policy and practices. In contrast, the position of federal contractors on directions for affirmative action policy in employment manifested much more diversity of opinion. Some contractors articulated a preference for less federal government influence over employment practices, while others voiced basic acceptance of existing affirmative action policies.

230

Policy Entrepreneurs and Issue Networks in Implementation

The role of policy entrepreneurs for disability rights programs changed somewhat as policies moved from legislative consideration and passage to implementation. While legislators played the prime role as guardians of disability rights policies during consideration and passage of public laws, they moved to share the entrepreneur position with disability interest groups during implementation. Both the guardian legislators (assisted by committee and subcommittee staffs) and key interest groups performed the task of monitoring administrative agencies and initiating legislative and administrative policy changes. In several instances, a strong working relationship developed between congressional staffs and the handicapped interest groups most involved in disability rights policy.

This pattern of legislator-handicapped group connection suggests a dual system of constellations within what has been termed the "issue network." Kingdon (1984) and others have identified a single network of interested parties, including interest groups, legislators and their staffs, and administrative officials. The policy area being examined here suggests a bipolar formation of the issue network. On one side were the legislators who had sponsored disability rights laws and handicapped interest groups; their relationship was evident at oversight hearings. The other set of actors was composed of regulated clients, bearing costs as the result of policy implementation, joined on occasion by administrative officials and other legislators sympathetic to their position. These two groups—one oriented around program beneficiaries, the other around regulated clients—competed with each other to direct or redirect the flow of benefits and sanctions associated with policy implementation. In no sense was there a single cohesive network where all interested parties participated in "quiet" decisions and bargaining behind the scenes to the advantage of all involved. Instead, there was and will remain competition among these two sets of policy actors, each of which endeavors to push implementation policy in different directions.

Institutional Arenas and Implementation

The analyses of implementation experiences of different disability rights policies have documented the assertion articulated at the start of the book: implementation policy is the result of struggles among interested parties, pursued within multiple institutional arenas, to affect the direction of and strategies utilized in executing public programs. Current implementation policies—including program accessibility, reasonable accommodation and affirmative action in employment, and comparable service provision in public transportation—all evolved during a protracted period of policy refinement. These policies, therefore, are artifacts, emerging from interactions of self-interested parties within legally sanctioned institutions. In this way, the direction that implementation policies would take could not be predicted with certainty in advance; one had to wait to see how the game of affecting implementation was played out. Certainly the game is not over; while a lull in policy confrontations is now taking place, it is safe to conclude that the self-interested parties will continue efforts to influence the direction of implementation policy for disability rights.

Administrative Agencies as Arenas for Implementation

Since predominant attention in implementing disability rights policies has focused on policy refinement, administrative agencies have served as a primary arena for setting implementation policies. Administrators have worked to devise administrative regulations, often through the formal rulemaking process, and then have revised them in response to implementation experiences or changes in the political environment. With few exceptions, the organizations ultimately responsible for carrying out antidiscrimination mandates—generally state and local governments—have deferred to federal agencies, looking first for directions for implementing disability rights protections. Then, when initial regulations were challenged, both in the courts and by the new Reagan administration, authorities waited for the smoke to clear in order to determine to what standards they would be held accountable.

In their task of designing administrative regulations to guide implementation of disability rights, the administrative agencies were under pressure from various interested parties seeking to influence the content of regulations. Initially, administrators had a relatively free hand in crafting regulations, because beneficiaries and regulated clients paid little attention to antidiscrimination policies for handicapped persons. Thus, when the staff in the Office of Civil Rights in the Department of Health, Education, and Welfare (HEW) started drafting administrative rules for section 504, they acted relatively independently in crafting regulations in a strong civil rights mold. Only as the parameters of their plan for·implementation became known, however, did handicapped groups recognize the importance of section 504 to pursuing rights protections and did regulated clients comprehend the extent of required accommodations. From this point on, policy refinement remained highly charged and very political in nature.

The public officials charged with rulemaking for disability rights laws often found themselves at the vortex of pressures exerted from many directions.

232

First, they were bound by the statutory language of public laws and legislative history as expressed during hearings, floor debates, and committee deliberations. But as noted above, in the context of disability rights laws, the parameters set by Congress were, except for PL94-142, not particularly restrictive. Second, the rule drafters were subject to pressures from agency leaders and, in many circumstances, other actors in the presidential administration, including the Office of Management and Budget and the Executive Office of the president. Third, administrators were the object of continued pressures from regulated clients and program beneficiaries seeking to influence policy decisions.

While the ultimate responsibility for promulgating regulations and executing policy lay with the administrative agencies, their decisions about implementation policy were affected by ongoing political pressures and decisions made in other institutional arenas. The agencies were not immune from oversight pressures from Congress or the judicial decisions rendered by the federal courts, the former tending to increase the scope of disability rights mandates and the latter sometimes working to restrict their scope.

Congress as an Arena for Implementation

Congress in several instances served as an arena where interested parties sought to affect the direction of implementation policies. One role played by Congress was to revise laws so as to clarify intent about statutory objectives and mechanisms for implementation. For example, the legislature amended the Rehabilitation Act to expand the definition of handicapped persons covered by the act, when it recognized the existing definition made reference only to employment. Similarly, the Urban Mass Transportation Act was amended when Congress recognized that doubts remained about coverage of mass transit facilities. These refinement activities were limited, however, and represented rather modest statutory changes. Many of the most difficult questions remained in the administrative arena as agencies worked to devise and revise regulations. Congress played a much more important role in an oversight function, providing an important forum for policy entrepreneurs.

Despite the persistent belief that congressional oversight is insufficiently performed, this was not the case in regard to implementation practices associated with disability rights. As we have seen, various legislators, serving as "guardians" of handicapped interests, persistently called oversight hearings to examine implementation actions and efforts to revise administrative regulations. Early oversight efforts focused on delays in promulgation of final regulations and preliminary problems with implementation. The hearings worked as one source of pressures on the Ford and Carter administrations, first to issue final regulations and then to forcefully activate implementation.

During the Reagan administration's move to loosen the compliance burdens associated with the regulations for disability rights programs, hearings were frequently called by legislators worried about proposed regulatory reforms. For example, when the Reagan administration announced a different approach to affirmative action as implemented through sections 501 and 503 of the Rehabilitation Act of 1973 and other laws, the House Subcommittee on Employment Opportunities called hearing after hearing to pursue its oversight function. Hearings were called as soon as the subcommittee caught wind that regulatory changes were being internally considered by the Equal Employment Opportunity Commission or the Department of Labor's Office of Federal Contract Compliance Programs (OFCCP). Oversight hearings were also scheduled and staff investigations commissioned when legislators perceived administrative agencies were changing internal practices associated with enforcement of disability rights programs. In other areas, including rights for handicapped children, the Senate Subcommittee on the Handicapped and the House Subcommittee on Select Education both performed key oversight activities.

Oversight hearings also served to focus publicity and attention on implementation practices and regulatory reform activities. Subcommittee members, and especially those entrepreneurs who had championed rights and protections for persons with disabilities, used oversight hearings to chastise administrators, and sometimes the presidential administration more broadly, for inadequate performance or rulemaking delays. During battles with the Reagan administration, the hearings shed light on the administration's policy decisions and strategies being taken to redirect implementation toward leaner and weaker compliance requirements. The hearings also provided a forum for groups representing disabled persons to express their concerns, needs, and evaluations of implementation policies and experiences. Disability interest groups often had a difficult time directing public attention to their concerns, especially those relating to the regulatory relief initiatives, and congressional hearings provided them with a useful public forum.

In addition to publicly admonishing administrative agencies and calling for implementation changes, legislators sometimes took even stronger actions to affect policy decisions. One such action was the passage of resolutions that stated the sense of Congress that regulatory changes should not be made or allowed to take effect. In the case of changes in rules for implementing PL94-142, advocated by the Reagan administration in 1982, both houses of Congress passed legislative items opposing proposed regulatory changes. Another action was the formal communication by members of Congress, usually by letter, of displeasure with proposed changes in administrative rules. Thus, when

OFCCP was engaged in changing its regulations for affirmative action by federal contractors, legislators communicated their displeasure and concerns to the secretary of the Department of Labor.

The Reagan administration seems to have taken these expressions of congressional anger and concern quite seriously and in several cases dropped proposed changes in administrative regulations. In regulatory changes for section 504, OFCCP's rules for affirmative action for contractors, and the implementation of the Education for All Handicapped Children Act, the administration eventually backed away from revision of administrative regulations. It is not so clear, however, that the administration abandoned all efforts at implementation reforms, sometimes pursuing the same objectives through changes in internal procedures. Since administrative practice is less open to protracted scrutiny than formal rulemaking activities, it was to such practice that the Reagan administration turned its attention when rulemaking efforts were abandoned under political pressure.

The Courts as an Arena for Implementation

The federal courts represent still another institutional arena available for players to use in their efforts to influence implementation policies. By its nature, the court system is relatively more immune to partisan politics than Congress or executive agencies. Through lifetime appointments, judges do not face the periodic mechanism of accountability to which other governmental actors are subjected: regular elections. Because they are at least partially removed from immediate political pressures, the courts are generally not the first arena to become the center of disputes over implementation. Instead, interested parties turn to the courts when faced with unfavorable decisions reached in other arenas, including federal agencies and Congress.

Turning to the federal courts as a means of affecting policy changes can be a risky enterprise for interested parties, since case decisions can serve as important precedents for future policy questions. If a party loses a round in the courts, then the decision in the losing case may return to influence future policy debates. Still, the courts, because of their partial separation from ongoing political and policy environments, may represent the only arena in which otherwise popular policy decisions can be called into question and challenged. Generally, calls for reexamination must be based on questions related to the constitutionality of policies (often with reference to individual rights and equal protection provisions), the congruence between administrative regulations and legislative intent, or the appropriateness of administrative procedures used to devise regulations.

Many interested parties have sought to use the federal court system as an arena to reevaluate implementation policy. In some instances, aggrieved parties turned to the courts to press a claim against the government itself, arguing that policy decisions or enforcement actions were not legally justifiable. In other cases, the courts have been called upon to settle disputes among program beneficiaries and regulated clients, often as the former charged the latter with discrimination on the basis of handicap. In light of the relative ambiguity of the public laws that establish disability rights, it is not surprising that the federal courts were called upon many times to interpret the meanings and bounds of antidiscrimination policies for persons with disabilities.

The Supreme Court and other federal courts have issued several decisions that have served to restrict the scope of antidiscrimination policy. Two of these cases related to education and involved a dispute between a handicapped student and an educational institution. In its first major decision on section 504, the Supreme Court, in *Southeastern Community College v. Davis*, ruled that a college was not discriminating when it refused to alter fundamentally its nursing education program. While the Court recognized that the boundary point where actions become discriminatory is difficult to determine, it held that section 504 did not require the specialized instructional assistance sought by Davis. In the *Board of Education v. Rowley* decision, the Court ruled that an "appropriate" education, as stipulated by PL94-142, required basic access to educational services but not to service levels needed to raise the performance of handicapped students to their full potential.

Other cases within the judicial arena involved interactions between regulated clients and the government, with the former challenging either implementation policy broadly or its application to particular situations. As described in the chapter on public transportation, APTA directly challenged DOT's full-accessibility policy in the federal courts (*APTA v. Lewis*), arguing that the administrative regulations exceeded statutory intent. The federal circuit court concurred with the regulated clients, thus invalidating the full-accessibility approach as the model underlying implementation policy. In the *Grove City College v. Bell* case, significant to all civil rights policies, the Supreme Court upheld the claim that federal sanctions for identified discrimination should be levied on a program-specific, rather than institution-wide, basis. It took a new public law to overturn this interpretation.

This discussion should not imply that all decisions by the federal courts have been restrictive in nature; indeed, some have yielded interpretations that serve to expand the realm of antidiscrimination policy. For example, in *Consolidated Rail Corporation v. Darrone*, the Court interpreted section 504 protections in employment to extend to all programs receiving federal financial assistance, not just those specifically concerned with employment services and training. In a more recent case, discussed in more detail below, the Supreme Court has ruled that individuals with acquired immune deficiency syndrome (AIDS) are entitled to protection under the antidiscrimination protections of section 504.[4]

Different explanations might be offered for the often restrictive nature of federal court decisions. It could be argued that the conservative political environment and the antiregulatory policy environment that existed when many of the judicial decisions were reached worked to affect restrictive, rather than expansive, interpretations of nondiscrimination laws. It can also be argued that the conservative makeup of the federal judiciary (reflecting appointments made during the Reagan administration) and the basically conservative composition of the Supreme Court also affected court decisions. While these factors undoubtedly had some impact, an even stronger influence may have been the tendency of jurists to seriously consider statutory language and legislative history when evaluating administrative regulations and enforcement policies. Since disability rights laws were generally more symbolic than precise as to intent or administrative practice, the appropriate direction and strategies for implementation were open to differing perspectives. When these policies have been questioned, the courts have tended to take rather strict constructionist views and to strike down policies or claims that do not have clear statutory grounding.

It is interesting that, in some cases, Congress has reacted quickly and negatively to court decisions by changing public laws to clarify its intent; in this way, judicial decisions have served to stimulate the legislative agenda. Thus, when the Supreme Court struck down the award of legal fees to parties prevailing in disputes centered on protections afforded by the Education for All Handicapped Children Act (*Smith v. Robinson*), Congress reacted the next year by amending the act so as to instruct that attorneys' fees can be awarded to parties prevailing in section 504 actions. Congress has similarly reacted to the *Grove City* decision by passing the Civil Rights Restoration Act of 1988.

The Politics of Implementation

The pattern of policy refinement taking place as part of implementation of disability rights laws closely resembles the pluralist politics commonly associated with the legislative process. This pattern makes sense, considering that important decisions guiding policy execution are made as part of the administrative process of implementation. Program beneficiaries and regulated clients recognize the policymaking decisions made by administrative authorities, their own stakes in these decisions, and the necessity of exerting political pressure to affect decision making. Given the tendency of Congress to enact relatively vague guidelines, with the expectation that administrative agencies will "fill in the details," vast amounts of policymaking authority have been vested in the agencies. This authority has, in turn, enhanced the position of administrative authorities in both setting and implementing public policies. From this perspective, the policy-refining activities that take place as part of implementation actually represent a second stage of policymaking, one that takes place outside of the legislative branch but within the broad parameters of legislative intent established by Congress. The parameters, however, are quite broad, providing administrative authorities with substantial discretion and flexibility in designing mechanisms and objectives for activating public programs.

Implementation as Interest Group Politics

The politics of policy refinement in disability rights generally resembles what James Q. Wilson (1980, 368) has termed "interest group politics." Regulatory policies concerning disability rights were not of broad concern to the general public or the full set of actors in the policy process, nor were such policies given extensive media attention. Debates and struggles over economic policy, inflation, budget deficits, and welfare programs all received, with few exceptions, far greater attention by policymakers and the media than handicapped rights.

Despite occasional instances of media attention and public interest, such as that surrounding the full-accessibility approach to handicapped transportation, disability rights policies have remained the concern of a limited set of policy actors, including entrepreneurs, interest groups representing beneficiaries and regulated clients, and administrative agencies charged with implementation. For the most part, the struggles waged to affect the direction of implementation can be characterized as group politics played by a relatively small set of interested parties. To this day, the general public does not understand such important policies as reasonable accommodation, program accessibility, and others that serve as the cornerstones of antidiscrimination policies designed to protect persons with disabilities.

One might have expected professional and technical specialists to have played a more significant role in policy refinement, given that the rehabilitation community includes specialists in both medical treatment and rehabilitation engineering (see, for example, Tanenbaum 1986). Generally, however, specialists played a small role, except in the development of the American National Standards Institute standards for physical accessibility. Yet even these standards were debated and challenged. The Architectural and Transportation Barriers and Compliance Board (ATBCB), for example, added "scoping" requirements to accessibility standards, stipulating that the timing and extent of accommodations were as important as their technical design and construction. Scoping requirements were not so much technical as political and allocative; they defined the level of action and attendant costs for achieving compliance with accessibility regulations. The pattern of policy refinement in accessibility policy, therefore, was clearly based on political conflict and compromise, and not on the application of professional, technical, or scientific knowledge. This pattern is to be expected, in light of the fact that most accommodations performed to achieve regulatory compliance require (or were perceived to require) some degree of cost, and when resource allocations are involved, political rather than technical values are likely to predominate.

Implementation as Symbolic Politics

Not only is implementation of disability rights policies representative of interest group politics, it is also an example of symbolic politics. Throughout debates about implementation, symbols were frequently used by interested parties as resources to influence the direction of policy execution. As Edelman (1964), Cobb and Elder (1983b), and others have argued, symbols serve multiple purposes within the political process: "Symbols serve to link the individual to the larger political order and to synchronize the diverse motivations of different individuals, making collective action possible" (Cobb and Elder 1983b, 1). Symbols thus act to focus and crystallize political debates and serve as a rallying point for proponents of particular public policies. As political resources, symbols work to connect related policy preferences among individuals so as to heighten political interest and commitment. The impact of symbols, as they are employed as political resources, however, varies across individuals, since they evoke different meanings, experiences, and reactions (Scheingold 1974; Cobb and Elder 1983b).

This study of disability rights policies has demonstrated the use of symbols to advance policy objectives during both legislative consideration and implementation. The original symbol, employed frequently by proponents of disability rights, was that of "goodwill" toward handicapped Americans. By the second half of the twentieth century, traditional conceptions of disabled persons had moved to a relatively more enlightened position. Advances in medical science provided greater understanding about the causes of disabilities and their treatment, helping to break down common myths and fears about handicapped persons. Media depictions of traditional forms of treatment, including the isolation of disabled individuals from society and their frequent placement in institutional settings, generated pressures for more humane treatment of this class of citizens. And as the family and other community systems ebbed as means of supporting persons with disabilities, pressures grew for greater public support of handicapped citizens (Scotch 1984). All of these factors contributed to the power of the ''goodwill'' symbol as a resource for pressing legislators and administrators to action.

The goodwill symbol was usually evoked by coupling a description of problems and difficulties in the lives of disabled persons with implicit or explicit appeals to equity, for example, arguing that disabled Americans deserve the same opportunities as those afforded to nondisabled people. Use of the goodwill symbol is illustrated in a statement made by a representative of the Council for Exceptional Children, testifying about legislation that would become the Education for All Handicapped Children Act:

> But despite the tremendous strides realized through the refinement of both national and State policy toward liquidation of this Nation's last islands of extreme neglect, we find the Bureau of Education for the Handicapped reporting in 1975 to Congress that only 55 percent of our school-age handicapped children and a meager 22 percent of pre-school-aged handicapped children are receiving the public education programs which they so desperately require if they are to take their rightful place alongside their nonhandicapped peers in adulthood . . . it is time for the Congress to take one more step to get that schoolhouse door open, and keep it open, once and for all.[5]

Appeals such as this, to equalize the educational opportunities for handicapped children, served as strong symbols that contributed to the passage of PL94-142. A similar example of the goodwill symbol was used in reference to erection of man-made barriers that impede the mobility of disabled Americans:

> Because of the obstacles we have put in their way, the handicapped today are a hidden population. Only the most intrepid risk the dangers and suffer the discomforts and humiliations they encounter when they try to live a normal, productive life. Most of the handicapped are out of sight. Will we continue to put them out of mind. . . . These people live among us. They have hopes, talents, ambitions like the rest of us.[6]

Similar symbols of goodwill and equity were also used persistently to affect the development and execution of implementation policy.

The goodwill symbol was closely associated with another potent symbol of the late 1960s and early 1970s: civil rights. Disability rights laws and their implementation followed on a protracted period of public and legislative debate about civil rights, first for racial minorities and then for women. The success of the black civil rights movement proved an inspiration for disabled citizens, the hidden minority, who saw the payoff of concerted efforts to press for anti-discrimination laws. The language of the civil rights movement is clear in the rhetoric used by disabled advocates to press first for disability rights laws and, subsequently, for their aggressive enforcement.

The goodwill and civil rights symbols have remained powerful, although their strength has ebbed somewhat from that of earlier periods. Their diminished status has resulted from the development of new and conflicting symbols. Certainly one of these is the symbol of large public costs, which, like increased taxation, tends to generate unfavorable public reactions. The negative impact of high public costs is accentuated when coupled to assertions that expenditures are being (1) made for a relatively small class of beneficiaries and (2) mandated by the federal government without reference to local preferences or fiscal capacity. As but one example of the use of cost symbols is the following editorial, printed in the *Chicago Tribune* in the fall of 1978, in response to the full-accessibility regulations proposed by DOT:

> There's one good thing to say about the $1 billion estimated cost for making Chicago area public transportation facilities accessible to passengers in wheelchairs. The price tag is so far beyond the realm of possibility that it should force eager federal agencies to rethink their goal. . . . Even if the proposed changes prompted every one of these individuals to use public transportation, the estimated cost of providing it would work out to more than a half million dollars per person. . . . It defies common sense to spend more money to provide transportation for a few hundred people than the total cost of the entire [Chicago Transit Authority] from 1890 to the present.[7]

As can be seen from this editorial, the goodwill symbol of aiding persons with disability, a symbol very important to passage of disability rights laws, had given way to a new symbol: irresponsible spending mandated by the federal government. Throughout this period, cost estimates for accommodations, often in the billions of dollars, swirled around public forums, creating outcries about excessive mandates and impossible spending targets. Often such estimates were excessive, but nonetheless, they served to generate a broad discontent with handicapped transportation policy. As the full-accessibility mandate was rescinded, in response to the Supreme Court decision that it exceeded statutory intent, the uproar subsided, with the general public losing interest in transportation policy for handicapped citizens.

Related to symbolic politics is the strategic use of organizing and operating principles, which work to structure the development of and debates about implementation policy. In this way, the principles serve as a form of symbol. One fundamental organizing principle used in developing administrative regulations for section 504 was that of "balanced competing equities." This principle acknowledged that implementation of antidiscrimination policy represented benefits to some and costs to others, and that cost considerations were not appropriate for determining discrimination but could legitimately be used in fashioning remedies:

> . . . ending discriminatory practices and providing equal access to programs may involve major burdens on some recipients. Those burdens and costs, to be sure, provide no basis of exemption from section 504 or this regulation: Congress' mandate to end discrimination is clear. But it is also clear that factors of burden and cost had to be taken into account in the regulation prescribing the actions necessary to end discrimination and to bring handicapped persons into full participation in federally financed programs and activities.[8]

This "balanced equities" symbol was important, for it signaled a moderate approach to accommodating the needs of persons with disabilities, one that recognized the needs and limitations of both regulated clients and program beneficiaries.

Including the equity symbol within the administrative regulations for section 504 was clearly a political move intended to disarm regulated clients, diffuse their wrath, and prevent them from using a fairness symbol to retaliate against required accommodations. Had a full-compliance approach been developed for section 504, one that stipulated accommodations without recognizing cost limitations, then the regulated clients might have seized the opportunity to employ a fairness symbol, holding up the regulations as an example of overaggressive action by the federal government. Instead, administrative agencies have been able to employ the "balanced equity" symbol to ward off moves to weaken section 504 protections, under the claim that they are unfair to regulated clients and do not consider their needs and constraints.

Key operating principles, including reasonable accommodation and program accessibility, similarly were used as symbols in political debates about implementation policy. While the handicapped community was not fully pleased with these equity-based principles, which tempered required accommodations in light of cost considerations, they were able to invoke them as symbols during struggles over the direction of implementation policy. With these symbols, handicapped citizens communicated that (1) legal limits were already in place to protect regulated parties and (2) they already had compromised with regulated parties by accepting a balanced approach to implementation. In these ways, organizing and operating principles have been utilized as symbolic resources in struggles to design implementation policies to protect the rights of persons with disabilities.

Regulations: Forms and Impacts

The regulations used to execute disability rights laws are basically of two types: crosscutting requirements and crossover sanctions (Advisory Commission on Intergovernmental Relations 1984). The first type concerns mandates, such as the antidiscrimination policy of section 504, which apply broadly across governmental programs to all recipients of federal financial assistance. Crosscutting requirements are not unlimited mandates; they do not apply to all persons and organizations in the nation, but instead only to those that receive federal financial assistance. Section 503 of the Rehabilitation Act of 1973, which requires federal contractors to take affirmative action to employ persons with disabilities, is another example of a crosscutting regulation. Crossover sanctions, on the other hand, are regulations that mandate actions as a condition of receiving financial assistance through a specific federal program. PL94-142 established a crossover mandate by requiring recipients of federal special education funds to provide a free and appropriate education to each handicapped child.

Both types of regulations have costs and benefits, but crosscutting requirements have the advantage of widespread application, since they are coupled to a broad range of federal programs. The breadth of coverage afforded by crosscutting regulations, however, also creates implementation problems. To be applicable to a wide range of public programs, crosscutting regulations are often stated in sweeping and general terms, relying more on bold and symbolic language than on clear-cut objectives (Schuck 1980, 87). General language can serve as a hindrance to implementation, as authorities scramble to comprehend the meaning and implications of sweeping crosscutting regulations.

Effective enforcement monitoring of compliance with crosscutting regulations is made very difficult, if not impossible, by the number of governmental programs and implementing authorities involved in enforcement. The customary means to implement and enforce crosscutting regulations is for each federal agency to devise its own compliance offices and set of regulations for implementation. Following this pattern, each agency of the federal government has its own section 504 program.

The proliferation of offices and programs for implementing crosscutting regulations can lead to conflicting regulations, turf battles among agencies, and major problems of coordination. Recognizing this problem in the section 504 case, presidents have issued executive orders granting lead ''coordination responsibility'' to specific agencies, first to HEW and then to the Justice Department. In much the same way, Congress has created new administrative bodies to enhance coordination in regulatory enforcement across federal agencies. Often such bodies are composed of representatives of the executive agencies affected by the policy in question. As one example, Congress established ATBCB to coordinate implementation of the Architectural Barriers Act; membership on the board was composed of representatives of most cabinet-level departments.

The creation of coordinating bodies, either by designating one agency as the lead coordinator or by establishing a new administrative body to perform coordination tasks, does not, in itself, answer all problems related to fragmentation and coordinated enforcement. Often the coordinating body finds itself in turf battles with individual agencies. An example of such struggles is the tension that existed between ATBCB and the U.S. Postal Service over the requirements for accessibility modifications in leased property. Settling differences between the coordinating bodies and individual agencies has proved difficult and time-consuming, given that it is not always clear what powers the coordinating authorities have to coerce other executive agencies and commissions to comply with guidelines and policies.

Crossover sanctions have the advantage of targeted focus; they are linked to specific programs and monitored by specific agencies. Their disadvantage is that they work only in one programmatic area; protections activated and enforced in one area do not spill over into other public policies. Compared to crosscutting requirements, the crossover regulations for PL94-142, for example, have been activated more rapidly and have generated greater impact on the handicapped community. Few turf battles have emerged and state and local authorities were quick to recognize, if not enthusiastically embrace, their new responsibilities to educate handicapped children across the nation. These findings suggest a positive relationship between the targeted-ness of regulations and the speed and effectiveness of their enforcement.

Statutory Provisions and Policy Implementation

A final point about the politics of implementation is a straightforward one, but one that nonetheless bears mention: the statutory language of public laws affects the clarity of legislative intent, the ease with which administrative regulations can be promulgated, and the speed with which the legislative intent can be translated into strategies to achieve policy objectives. Disability rights laws present two extremes with regard to the clarity and specificity of statutory language. As we have seen, PL94-142's mandate for a free and appropriate education for handicapped children was clearly spelled out in the public law, including reference to such operating principles as individualized education programs and education in least restrictive environments. At the other extreme was section 504, a few words articulating a policy of nondiscrimination on the basis of handicap.

Compared to section 504, the PL94-142 mandate was activated with fewer headaches concerning legislative intent and with faster compliance by regulated clients. Because compliance activities were clearly drawn and communicated, regulated clients moved expeditiously to satisfy compliance requirements. Research studies, reviewed in chapter eight, demonstrated that within a few years of passage, PL94-142 was effecting significant and beneficial changes in the education of handicapped children. Much of the success of the free and appropriate education mandate was derived from the precise language in PL94-142, which described mechanisms to be utilized and objectives to be pursued in implementation. In contrast, vague legislative mandates, such as that presented in section 504, generate ambiguity, which subsequently must be worked out during rulemaking and through implementation experiences. Because the full bounds and implications of section 504 were not specified in the law, these determinations were left to administrators, and oftentimes to the courts, and implementation was slowed in the process.

Equity Approaches and Implementation of Disability Rights

The development and implementation of civil rights policies require that significant choices be made regarding which equity approach will be pursued. Close examination of the equity basis of disability rights policies shows that multiple equity approaches, or paradigms, are utilized, and that this multiplicity of approaches tends to confuse policy implementation. At least three such equity paradigms have been articulated with regard to policies used to execute disability rights laws: equity as equal treatment, equal access, and equal outcome.

Notions of *equal treatment* are pervasive in American civil rights policies. This approach, developed within the context of racial discrimination, requires that all persons be evaluated by neutral rules and standards, regardless of personal characteristics. The solution to discrimination using an equal treatment approach is to employ ''blind justice,'' whereby decision makers reach decisions without any reference to the personal characteristics that give rise to discrimination. More formally, this approach is known as the neutrality principle (Bell and Burgdorf 1983, 153). A second equity approach is that of *equal access*. Policies based on this approach endeavor to remove obstacles that detract from the ability of protected classes to consume public services and take advantage of social opportunities. An even more far-reaching notion of equity is that based on *equal outcomes*, meaning that the intent of public policies is to equalize specified conditions or situations of protected classes with those of nonprotected individuals. This equalization is sought through various instruments of public policy, oftentimes with the application of the regulatory powers of the state. Achieving equal outcomes customarily requires the provision of unequal treatment to disadvantaged persons in order for their positions to be significantly enhanced.

It has been generally recognized that the equal treatment approach is not workable, for the most part, in the context of disability rights. Simple application of the neutrality principle will not tear down the physical barriers that impede the mobility of handicapped persons, nor will it alone allow persons with disabilities to overcome their handicaps. But while the equal treatment paradigm has generally been rejected as a model for ending discrimination based on disability, policymakers have not clearly decided whether the equal access or equal outcome model is more appropriate. Ongoing questions about equity approach have been embedded within debates about specific implementation strategies.

Because the boundary between the equal access and equal outcome approaches is not always clear, decision makers often equivocate between the two. In fact, the approach most often used to implement disability rights policies falls somewhere between the equal access and equal outcome paradigms. Administrative regulations for disability rights policies—including section 504, the Architectural Barriers Act, PL94-142, and others—tend to go beyond rudimentary notions of equal access. Thus, accessibility standards require more than basic access to public buildings; they stipulate several sorts of modifications that allow persons with disabilities to function within such buildings. As another example, reasonable accommodations in employment can require significant, not token or rudimentary, changes in structures and practices in order that persons with disabilities can become meaningfully employed.

These policies fall short, however, of mandating equal outcomes. The potent policy measures required to achieve equal outcomes, often involving a substantial redistribution of resources and opportunities, have generally not been politically acceptable within the American political culture; public laws have seldom mandated the sweeping actions needed to achieve equal outcomes within a short time frame. Within the context of disability rights, policymakers recognized the political backlash that would be unleashed if requisite accommodations entailed unlimited costs. Therefore, the mandate to pursue accommodations was tempered with a "reasonable" cost constraint, which served to overrule the need for expensive accommodations. In much the same way, the current regulations for handicapped transportation couple a cost cap to the mandate to provide to disabled customers services that are comparable to those available to other transit patrons.

The fact that most handicapped policy mandates fall somewhere between the equal access and equal outcome paradigms causes problems for and questions about implementation. The fundamental question concerns the extent to which public and private organizations across the nation are required to accommodate the needs of persons with disabilities. Handicapped groups often argue that the public laws that lay the groundwork for disability rights policies do not acknowledge cost considerations as a legitimate reason for backing away from accommodations. Regulated clients articulate the opposite theme, that if there are no such limits, then the mandate will be too expensive, represent unwarranted federal government intrusion in the conduct of private and state and local government affairs, and potentially generate massive resistance.

Judicial decisions arising from disability rights protections have centered on issues related to which equity approach is appropriate in light of statutory provisions. In the *Southeastern Community College v. Davis* case, the Supreme Court held that "neither the language, purpose, nor history of section 504 reveals an intent to impose an affirmative action obligation on all recipients of federal funds."[9] Thus, from the Court's perspective, a commitment to nondiscrimination on the basis of handicap cannot be construed to imply or require that significant affirmative action remedies be taken.

In the *Board of Education v. Rowley*, the Court addressed the question of how far school districts must go to satisfy the mandate to provide handicapped students with a free and appropriate education. The Court held in this case that the free and appropriate education mandate was not unlimited and that this mandate is satisfied when "the State provides personalized instruction with sufficient support services to permit the handicapped child to benefit educationally from that instruction."[10] Clearly, the Court here articulated an equal access paradigm and overruled an interpretation that a free and appropriate education requires services to maximize a handicapped child's educational performance.

Often, then, policy debates about strategies and objectives for implementation of disability rights revolve around differing perspectives about the appropriate equity approach to be used in implementation. As would be expected, handicapped groups generally push for interpretations that favor an equal outcome approach, while regulated clients, seeking to minimize regulatory impacts, prefer an equal access approach. Debates about which approach is most appropriate will continue into the future, because of differences in the decision premises of affected parties and ambiguities in both statutes and administrative regulations. Until such time as policymakers clarify basic issues about equity approaches, thereby elucidating the bounds of disability rights mandates, policy debates will continue and affected parties will continue to use the full range of institutional arenas to affect the direction of implementation policies.

Relating Disability Rights and Civil Rights

Despite common public perceptions, disability rights laws and policies remain, in many ways, separate from other civil rights policies, which protect against discrimination based on race, sex, religion, and national origin. The first attempt to create a disability rights law was undertaken by Senator Hubert Humphrey and Representative Charles Vanik; their approach was a simple one, namely to add handicapped persons to the classes of persons protected by the Civil Rights Acts of 1964 and 1968. This move, had it been successful, would have forged a close relationship between civil rights and disability rights groups. Instead, disability rights laws emerged separately from other civil rights laws, partially because of a lack of enthusiasm by traditional civil rights groups to accept disabled citizens into the civil rights movement.

Civil rights groups representing racial and other minorities recognized that overcoming discrimination based on handicap was different in certain respects from overcoming other forms of discrimination. These groups were not sure of the impact of linking hard-won civil rights protections to disabled persons, particularly to those with mental impairments. Policy entrepreneurs representing disabled Americans, while unable to include handicapped discrimination in the Civil Rights Act, were more successful in initiating separate legislative provisions that focused directly on disabled persons and their needs. Often, the language of existing civil rights laws and policies were borrowed and placed within disability rights laws. Yet despite similarities in statutory language and appeals to fairness, disability groups remained in many ways outside of the broader civil rights movement.

Over time, legislative amendments to disability rights laws have forged greater consistency between these and other civil rights laws. Thus, when the legal remedies available through section 504 were questioned, including whether individuals have a private right of action, the Rehabilitation Act was amended to provide handicapped persons the same remedies as those afforded by Title VII of the Civil Rights Act. Later, when it was apparent that the federal courts would not award legal fees to parties prevailing in suits based on PL94-142, Congress amended the Education for All Handicapped Children Act to specifically provide for the award of such fees.

Questions of Implementation Continue

Despite the current lull in struggles of affected parties to influence the direction of disability rights policies, several significant implementation questions remain, many of which concern the bounds of coverage. One boundary issue arose from the "Baby Doe" case, where life-sustaining medical procedures were withheld from a severely handicapped newborn infant by decision of the parents. A second boundary question placed on the policy agenda concerned a new and virulent disease, AIDS. Both of these cases raised questions about the appropriate role of the public sector in protecting the rights of new classes of disabled citizens.

Protecting Handicapped Infants

A dramatic case, surrounded by emotion, conflicting values, and political controversy, served to raise an issue related to the boundaries of persons protected by section 504. This case revolved around an infant born in 1982 in a Bloomington, Indiana, hospital. Upon birth, this infant, known only as "Baby Doe," was found to have Down's syndrome and an incompletely formed esophagus. Evaluating the child's condition, parents and attending doctors decided to withhold medical treatment and nourishment. Representatives of the local hospital contacted the county circuit court, which conducted an emergency hearing on the case. After receiving testimony from the child's parents, attending doctors, and other medical personnel, the special judge ruled that the parents had the right to make decisions about the infant's medical care.[11] This decision was affirmed by the Indiana Supreme Court, and while appeals were being drawn up, the infant died.

The Baby Doe case generated widespread media coverage and criticism from civil rights and handicapped groups. The fundamental question centered on whether parents have the right to make life and death decisions about newborn, handicapped children. Among those concerned about the case was President Reagan, who ordered the Department of Health and Human Services (HHS) to instruct health care providers that failure to medically treat handicapped infants is a violation of federal law, specifically of section 504 of the Rehabilitation Act of 1973. In response, HHS issued a notice to health care providers stating that

> under Section 504, it is unlawful for a recipient of Federal financial assistance to withhold from a handicapped infant nutritional sustenance or medical or surgical treatment required to correct a life-threatening condition, if: (1) the withholding is based on the fact that the infant is handicapped, and (2) the handicap does not render the treatment or nutritional sustenance medically contraindicated.[12]

Seldom during the Reagan administration had such forceful and aggressive action been taken with regard to the nondiscrimination protections of section 504.

Congress, similarly concerned about the Baby Doe case, considered legislation to protect severely handicapped newborn infants in the aftermath of the Baby Doe case. Despite initial bipartisan concerns about the implications of the case, controversy grew within Congress about the means with which to protect handicapped children. Most concerns surrounded federal government intrusion into parental decisions about their children and the administration of health care facilities. The American Medical Association (AMA) came to the forefront as chief critic of many provisions of the child protection legislation, arguing: "The intent of this bill is to encourage governmental intervention into medical treatment decisions involving handicapped infants. We believe such government intervention intrudes on the rights and responsibilities of parents, families, physicians, and institutions."[13]

After a year of political wrangling, Congress passed the Child Abuse Amendments of 1984 (PL98-457).[14] The law (1) required states to establish procedures for reporting cases of medical neglect, (2) specified that withholding life-sustaining procedures from disabled infants constitutes medical neglect, unless the treatment would only prolong the process of dying, and (3) authorized grants to aid states in setting up procedures for preventing medical neglect of severely handicapped infants. While important determinations about treatment of disabled infants were left to medical authorities, the law clarified the federal government's view of treatment of Baby Doe cases and created state-level procedures to guard against neglect of handicapped babies.

While Congress debated child protection legislation, HHS issued an interim rule, following on its notice to health care providers, requiring hospitals to post, in a conspicuous position, a notice advising of the applicability of section 504 to handicapped infants.[15] It also noted the availability of a toll-free telephone hot line to report suspect violations, including failures to treat and feed severely handicapped infants. The regulation, issued without a period of public comment, was invalidated by the U.S. district judge for the District of Columbia on the grounds that it was "arbitrary and capricious" and that there was inadequate justification for waiving the public comment period as required by the Administrative Procedures Act.[16] The judge also questioned whether HHS had considered the possibly disruptive effects of the twenty-four hour hot line or the "sudden descent of Baby Doe squads" on the care of handicapped infants.[17]

Continuing with its intention to issue Baby Doe rules, HHS issued proposed regulations in July 1983.[18] The revised regulations added provisions regarding the role of state child protective service agencies, retained the hot line number for reporting infant neglect cases, and allowed for a sixty-day comment period. Almost seventeen thousand comments were received in response to the proposed regulations, with over ninety-seven percent of them supportive.[19] The final regulations, issued in December 1983, (1) encouraged health care providers to create Infant Care Review Committees to assist in creating health care policies for handicapped infants and make decisions in specific cases, (2) required posting of notices pertaining to the treatment of disabled children, and (3) stipulated that state child protection agencies establish written rules to ensure they utilize their full authority to prevent medical neglect of infants.[20]

The medical community remained dissatisfied with federal regulations that it perceived as unwarranted federal government intrusion into the decisions of parents and medical authorities. The regulated clients—the American Hospital Association, the AMA, and other medical organizations—took their case to the federal courts in an effort to have the regulations overturned. The medical community's claim was tested in the case *Bowen, Secretary of Health and Human Services v. American Hospital Association.*[21] The Supreme Court decision in this case held that the administration had presented no evidence that would justify federal government intervention in child abuse prevention, traditionally a state rather than federal function. The Court also noted that in none of the cases of child neglect cited in the administrative record did any hospital refuse to provide medical treatment when so requested.

The medical community was pleased with the Supreme Court decision on the Baby Doe regulations, with one representative stating: "The administration has been trying for three years to make this into a federal case and to make a record that there is a problem in care of newborns that justifies a federal role and the court flatly said no."[22] The disabled community and civil rights groups were dissatisfied with the judicial decision, and some groups have vowed to return to Congress for stronger legislation protecting severely disabled infants.

Protecting Persons with Infectious Diseases

By the middle 1980s, a new and frightening health problem was recognized in the United States: the spread of a deadly disease that works to break down the immune system of victims, so that they become susceptible to many other types of disease. In light of the disease's very debilitating effects and the fears and apprehensions surrounding its communication, the question soon arose as to whether AIDS victims are a protected class under section 504.

Wrestling with this issue, HHS requested the Justice Department in 1986 to render an opinion as to whether those with AIDS are entitled to protection under section 504. The Justice Department opinion drew a major distinction between the "disabling effects" of the disease and the ability of victims to transmit it. According to this ruling, an employer could not legally dismiss an

AIDS sufferer on the basis of having the disease itself but could legally undertake dismissal on the basis of fear of contagion (Cooper 1986).

The Justice Department opinion was overturned through a Supreme Court
case heard in 1986 and decided the following year. The case involved a woman
suffering not from AIDS but from recurrent tuberculosis (*School Board of Nassau County, Florida v. Arline*).[23] The central issue in the case was whether contagious diseases fall within the realm of disabilities covered by section 504 of
the Rehabilitation Act. In the majority opinion in the *Arline* case, Justice William Brennan argued that "few aspects of a handicap give rise to the same level
of public fear and misapprehension as contagiousness."[24] The Brennan opinion
also articulated the position that contagiousness is not a legitimate reason to ne-
gate disability rights protections as outlined in section 504:

> The fact that *some* persons who have contagious diseases may pose a serious
> health threat to others under certain circumstances does not justify excluding
> from the coverage of the Act *all* persons with actual or perceived contagious dis-
> eases. . . . We conclude that the fact that a person with a record of physical im-
> pairment is also contagious does not suffice to remove that person from coverage
> under section 504.[25]

Clearly, the Supreme Court opinion in the *Arline* case did much to strike
down the Justice Department's interpretation and extended antidiscrimination
protections to persons suffering from AIDS. At the same time, however, *Arline*
represents only a partial victory for civil rights groups, because the case did not
rule on whether persons who test positive for the disease but do not manifest
disease symptoms are protected by section 504. The Court sidestepped this vital question in *Arline*: "The case does not present, and we therefore do not
reach, the question of whether a carrier of a contagious disease such as AIDS
could be considered to have a physical impairment, or whether such a person
would be considered, solely on the basis of contagiousness, a handicapped
person as defined by the Act."[26] The question about the protection of nonsick
carriers will undoubtedly arise in subsequent section 504 cases. It also demonstrates the perplexing problems of setting boundaries for protected classes
under section 504.

The question of legal protections for persons with AIDS was given major
consideration by a commission created by President Reagan to advise him on
public policy to deal with the epidemic. A key finding of the commission's
1988 report, one championed by its chairman, James D. Watkins, is that the
nation should create a tough law barring discrimination against persons in-
fected with the AIDS virus (Boodman 1988). In this regard, the commission
argued that "persons with HIV [human immunodeficiency virus] infection

should be considered members of the group of persons with disabilities, not as a separate group unto themselves.''[27] As a remedy, the commission argued strongly for new and stronger legislative protections for all Americans with disabilities: ''For the long term, federal legislation which clearly provides comprehensive anti-discrimination protection for all persons with disabilities, including those with HIV infection, is needed.''[28] Following this recommendation, the commission pointed to the Americans with Disabilities Act, authored by the National Council on the Handicapped, as an appropriate legislative model.

Two specific recommendations of the presidential commission are worth noting. First, the commission stated that federal antidiscrimination law should be expanded to cover the private as well as public sector. Such a move would greatly expand the reach and impact of federal laws designed to enhance and protect the rights of persons with disabilities. Second, the commission argued that it did not intend for antidiscrimination legislation ''to invoke affirmative action for persons with HIV infection. In other words, no one would be required to hire an individual with HIV infection based on that status.''[29]

Tragic Choices

Creating policies to implement disability rights often requires that ''tragic choices'' be made, that is, choices about which handicapped persons will be assisted by public policies and which will be left to their own devices. Tragic choices are necessitated by the fact that societies face practically unlimited needs yet finite resources to use in satisfying needs (Calabresi and Bobbitt 1978). Ultimately, tragic choices are distributive ones, which signal how public authorities will disperse public resources so as to relieve the suffering and problems of constituents. Limited resources mean that some needs will remain unsatisfied, while others will only be partially fulfilled. It is through the value decisions implicit in tragic choices that societies define themselves, their purposes, and their aspirations (Calabresi and Bobbitt 1978, 17). Tragic choices are, therefore, not static but, instead, are dynamic and focus on two types of decisions about resource allocations: how much of a scarce good will be produced and who shall receive the good.

In the disability rights context, tragic choices imply decisions about the mechanisms employed to end discrimination, the extent of remedial action and accommodation required, and the boundaries set on which individuals are entitled to rights protections. We have examined each of these questions in some detail, including (1) how compromises have been fashioned in selecting mechanisms for policy implementation, (2) how a balanced equity approach has been utilized in defining the extent of required accommodation actions, and (3) how difficult questions about bounding the classes protected by disability rights policies have been answered.

These decisions about implementation, which structure and distribute rights protections for persons with disabilities, are not stagnant; they have mutated several times in their short history and will undoubtedly continue to do so. In this way, disability rights policies, like most other public policies, are dynamic and evolutionary instead of stable and predictable: "Policies are continuously transformed by implementing actions that simultaneously alter resources and objectives. . . . It is not policy design but redesign that occurs most of the time" (Majone and Wildavsky 1984, 170, 172). Resources and objectives change for several reasons, not the least of which is the motivations and aspirations of parties affected by public policies.

The natural tension between regulated clients and program beneficiaries is played out as they both endeavor to affect the direction of and responsibilities mandated by implementation. Neither side is likely to stay satisfied for long with existing policies, and each new question—whether about including a new group under nondiscrimination protections or requiring a new form of accommodation—will resurrect struggles between the opposing groups. Given the scope of benefits and costs associated with disability rights policies, the politics of implementation is likely to remain of the interest group politics mold described by Wilson (1980). The political struggles between these groups is, as argued many times throughout this book, rooted in multiple decision-making arenas within the American political system.

Within the context of disability rights, the problem is not that tragic choices must be made but that the choices are not clearly or consistently made. The failure of Congress to unambiguously specify its intent for various disability rights policies has thrust major choices of the tragic nature to other governmental authorities and has stimulated ongoing political struggles between regulated parties and those receiving rights protections. These struggles will continue as implementation policies are further refined and applied in specific contexts. Given this perspective, it becomes apparent that studying implementation requires more than a comparison of program goal statements with outcomes achieved in the field. This "black box" approach misses information crucial to understanding implementation: how, and for what reasons, various tragic choices have been made. Only by tracing the ongoing political processes of setting and resetting implementation objectives and practices, processes as common to the executive branch as to the legislative branch, can analysts accurately assess implementation experiences and the tragic choices that underlie them.

Abbreviations

ABA	Architectural Barriers Act
ACCD	American Coalition of Citizens with Disabilities
AIDS	acquired immune deficiency syndrome
AMA	American Medical Association
ANSI	American National Standards Institute
APTA	American Public Transit Association
ATBCB	Architectural and Transportation Barriers Compliance Board
BEOG	Basic Education Opportunity Grants
CBO	Congressional Budget Office
CSC	Civil Service Commission
DOD	Department of Defense
DOE	Department of Education
DOJ	Department of Justice
DOT	Department of Transportation
DREDF	Disability Rights Education and Defense Fund
EEO	equal employment opportunity
EEOC	Equal Employment Opportunity Commission
EHA	Education of the Handicapped Act
ESEA	Elementary and Secondary Education Act
GAO	General Accounting Office
GSA	General Services Administration
HEW	Department of Health, Education, and Welfare
HHS	Department of Health and Human Services
HIV	human immunodeficiency virus
HUD	Department of Housing and Urban Development
ICHE	Interagency Committee on Handicapped Employees
IEP	individualized education program
LEA	local education agency
NACUBO	National Association of College and University Business Officers
NEA	National Education Association
OCR	Office of Civil Rights

Abbreviations

OFCCP	Office of Federal Contract Compliance Programs
OMB	Office of Management and Budget
SEA	state education agency
UCPA	United Cerebral Palsy Association
UMTA	Urban Mass Transportation Administration
USPS	U.S. Postal Service
VEVRAA	Vietnam Era Veterans' Readjustment Assistance Act
VR	vocational rehabilitation

| Notes

Chapter 1. Disability, Public Policy, and Implementation

1. A note on terminology is useful at the very outset of this book. Individuals in the handicapped community currently prefer to refer to themselves as "persons with disabilities." It is felt that this term implies human individuality ahead of a handicapping condition. They also prefer that the words "disabled" and "handicapped" be used as adjectives instead of nouns. While sympathizing with their quest for individuality, the term "persons with disabilities" can be linguistically awkward when used repeatedly. Thus, I use the terms "disabled person," "handicapped individual," and others as synonymous with "person with disability." I have, however, tried to avoid using "disabled" or "handicapped" as nouns. I hope that no persons with disabilities will be offended by this usage. For more discussion of these linguistic issues, see Goldman (1987, 12–14).

2. For a comprehensive review of research studies through the late 1970s on attitudes toward persons with disability, see the compendium prepared by Schroedel (1979).

3. It should be noted that some literary depictions are not only accurate but also provide useful insights into the life experiences of persons with disabilities. Bower (1980) has edited an interesting text with literary extracts intended for use by students and others wishing to learn about and emotionally experience the handicap experience.

4. The International Center for the Disabled and the National Council on the Handicapped, *Bringing Disabled Americans into the Mainstream* (Washington, D.C., 1986). This study of one thousand persons with disabilities was conducted in November and December of 1985 by Louis Harris and Associates. It should be noted that when a disabled person was unavailable for an interview, or unable to be interviewed, a proxy was chosen who knew most about that person. About seventeen percent of the interviews were conducted with proxies. The use of proxies has caused some persons to question the validity of survey findings. While this approach raises some questions about validity, this study remains the only comprehensive survey of the disabled community in

257

America, and for this reason, it is reviewed here. It is the author's judgment that the proxy method has not generated substantial inaccuracies.

5. For a thorough examination of the development of federal disability policies, see Berkowitz (1987).

6. For a brief description of federal laws related to handicapped rights, see U.S. Department of Education (1980).

7. For a detailed discussion of changing conceptions of disability, see Stone (1984).

8. In addition to the growing number of studies of specific public programs, interest in implementation is illustrated by the number of general texts and readers that have been published on the topic of policy implementation. General texts include Mazmanian and Sabatier (1983), Ripley and Franklin (1986), Nakamura and Smallwood (1980), Hargrove (1985), Edwards (1980), Bardach (1977), Williams (1980), and Larson (1980). Edited readers on the implementation topic include Williams et al. (1982), Williams and Elmore (1976), Nelson and Yates (1978), Mazmanian and Sabatier (1981), and Palumbo and Harder (1981).

9. For a discussion and comparison of methodologies employed in implementation studies, see Yin (1982).

10. Elmore (1981) and Lipsky (1978) are among those who argue that micro or "bottom up" studies are more likely to yield accurate explanations of implementation outcomes than are more traditional "top down" approaches.

11. Among the writers who have included administrative and organizational variables—such as staff skills and commitment, communication, and organizational structure—as key determinants of policy implementation are Edwards (1980), Williams (1980), Van Horn and Van Meter (1976), Van Meter and Van Horn (1975), and Dunsire (1978).

Chapter 2. An Institutional Approach to the Study of Policy Implementation

1. Nakamura and Smallwood (1980) use the term "environments" to describe settings similar to those termed "arenas" in this analysis.

2. For other discussions of the nonlinear, often circular nature of policymaking and implementation, see Smith (1973) and Alexander (1985).

3. Among the important works dealing with congressional oversight and the reluctance of legislators to engage in oversight are Aberbach (1979), Berry (1977), Davis (1969), Ethridge (1985), Fiorina (1981), Harris (1964), Ogul (1976, 1981), and Rosenthal (1981).

4. These constellations of actors have received different names, including "subgovernments" (Freeman 1965), "cozy triangles" (James 1974; Davidson 1977), "policy community" (Kingdon 1984), and "community of policy experts" (Walker 1981). All authors are concerned about the set of actors who specialize in specific policy areas.

5. Thrasher (1983) presents an interesting discussion of how implementers often need resources from outside the organization to effectively perform implementation.

This need leads to the formation of interpersonal exchanges, often organized through networks.

6. Organizing principles defined here bear resemblance to what Edelman (1964, 6) terms "referential symbols," which are defined as "economical ways to referring to the objective elements in objects or situations: the elements identified in the same way by different participants."

7. It is interesting that there is some discrepancy among analysts about the categorization of particular policies within policy types. Most analysts characterize disability rights laws and their implementation as regulatory activity, while Ripley and Franklin (1986) would classify these laws and their enforcement as redistributive policy. Within this book, the regulatory classification will be used.

8. For discussion of regulatory mandates placed upon the federal government and the issue of regulatory enforcement, see Durant (1985), and Wilson and Rachal (1977), and U.S. Advisory Commission on Intergovernmental Relations (1989).

9. These arguments about the behavior of regulatory agencies draws upon James D. Thompson's classic work, *Organizations in Action* (1967).

10. The varied behavioral responses of regulatory agencies may also explain, at least in part, the "life cycle" perspectives on regulatory agencies in particular (Bernstein 1955) and bureaucratic agencies more generally (Downs 1967).

Chapter 3. Federal Laws to Assist Persons with Disabilities

1. Blind citizens and their representatives were one of the first handicapped groups to organize and work collectively to advance their own position. For this reason, the first disability-related facilities in many states were those that served blind, and often deaf, individuals.

2. The origins of federal efforts to remove architectural barriers that impede the mobility of handicapped persons is described in Senate Committee on Environment and Public Works (1979), *Architectural Barriers in Federal Buildings: Implementation of the Architectural Barriers Act of 1968*, 96th Cong., 1st sess., Committee Print, Serial 96-8.

3. U.S. Department of Health, Education, and Welfare (1967), 2.

4. Ibid., 2.

5. Katzmann (1986, 21) argues that Gallagher and Bartlett would have preferred the bill to have been considered by the Committee on Labor and Public Welfare. However, many on this committee wanted to wait for the final report of the National Commission on Architectural Barriers to Rehabilitation of the Handicapped before taking action. To avoid delay, the bill was designed with repeated reference to "public buildings" so that it would be considered by the Committee on Public Works, a committee that expressed interest in considering accessibility legislation.

6. Senate Committee on Public Works, Subcommittee on Public Buildings and Grounds (1967), *Hearings on Accessibility of Public Buildings to the Physically Handicapped*, 90th Cong., 2d sess., 3.

7. Ibid., 3.

8. Ibid., 27.

9. Ibid., 44–45.

10. Ibid., 52–58. This turf dispute about responsibility for implementation of a new policy initiative is indicative of what Holden (1966) has termed "bureaucratic imperialism."

11. U.S. Senate (1967), *Design and Construction of Public Buildings Financed with Federal Funds to Be Accessible to the Physically Handicapped*, 90th Cong., 1st sess., S. Rept. 538.

12. House Committee on Public Works, Subcommittee on Public Buildings and Grounds (1968), *Hearings on Building Design for the Physically Disabled*, 90th Cong., 2d sess.

13. Ibid., 4.

14. House Committee on Public Works (1968), *Design and Construction of Buildings Financed with Federal Funds to Be Accessible to the Physically Handicapped*, 90th Cong., 2d sess., H. Rept. 1532.

15. Ibid., 4.

16. House Committee on Public Works (1968), *Design and Construction of Buildings Financed with Federal Funds to Be Accessible to the Physically Handicapped*, 90th Cong., 2d sess., H. Rept. 1787.

17. "Statement by the President upon Signing the Bill for the Elimination of Architectural Barriers to the Handicapped in Public Buildings," *Public Papers of the President: Lyndon Johnson 1968–69* (Washington, D.C.: Government Printing Office, 1968), 88.

18. Section 504, Rehabilitation Act of 1973, PL93-112.

19. Section 7(6), Rehabilitation Act of 1973, PL93-112.

20. Section 111(a), Rehabilitation Act of 1974.

21. For legislative consideration of the Rehabilitation Act of 1972 (vetoed) and 1973 (enacted) see the following hearings: Senate Committee on Labor and Public Welfare, Subcommittee on the Handicapped (1972), *Hearings on the Rehabilitation Act of 1972*, 92d Cong., 2d sess., pts. 1 and 2; House Committee on Education and Labor, Subcommittee on Select Education (1972), *Hearings on Vocational Rehabilitation Services to the Handicapped*, 92d Cong., 2d sess.; and Senate Committee on Labor and Public Welfare, Subcommittee on the Handicapped (1973), *Hearings on the Rehabilitation Act of 1973*, 93d Cong., 1st sess.

22. As was the case in 1972, little discussion surrounded the antidiscrimination provision of the 1973 bill. One exception was a statement by John Nagle, National Federation of the Blind, who argued: "The Civil Rights Provisions in S.7 brings the disabled within the law when they have been so long outside the law. It establishes that because a man is blind or deaf or without legs, he is not less a citizen, that his rights of citizenship are not revoked or diminished because he is disabled" (*Hearings on the Rehabilitation Act of 1973*, 282).

23. A chapter of the Rand Report is included in House Committee on Education and Labor, Subcommittee on Select Education (1974), *Hearings on Financial Assistance for Improved Educational Services for Handicapped Children*, 93d Cong., 1st sess., pt. 1, 7–49.

24. For a detailed discussion of this case and its implications, see Lippman and Goldberg (1973).

25. *Pennsylvania Association for Retarded Children v. Commonwealth of Pennsylvania*, 334 F. Supp. 1257 (ED Pa 1971); 343 F. Supp. 279 (ED Pa 1972).

26. *Mills v. Board of Education of the District of Columbia*, 348 F. Supp. 866 (DDC 1972).

27. House Committee on Education and Labor, Subcommittee on Select Education (1973), *Hearings on Education of the Handicapped Amendments*, 93d Cong., 1st sess.

28. Senate Committee on Labor and Public Welfare, Subcommittee on the Handicapped (1973), *Hearings on Education of the Handicapped Act, 1973*, 93d Cong., 1st sess., 177.

29. Senate Bill S. 6, "Education for All Handicapped Act," considered by the Committee on Labor and Public Welfare, Subcommittee on the Handicapped, 93d Cong., 1st sess., 1973, 2.

30. Senate Committee on Labor and Public Welfare, Subcommittee on the Handicapped (1975), *Hearings on Education for All Handicapped Children Act, 1975*, 94th Cong., 1st sess., 160.

31. House Committee on Education and Labor, Subcommittee on Select Education (1974), *Hearings on Financial Assistance for Improved Educational Services for Handicapped Children*, 93d Cong., 2d sess., 51–52.

32. Ibid., 90.

33. Ibid., 293.

34. House Committee on Education and Labor, Subcommittee on Select Education (1975), *Hearings on Extension of Education of the Handicapped Act*, 94th Cong., 1st sess., 18.

35. Ibid., 139.

36. "Statement on Signing the Education for All Handicapped Children Act of 1975," *Public Papers of the President: Gerald R. Ford 1975*, Paper No. 707 (Washington, D.C.: Government Printing Office, 1975), 1935. In reluctantly signing the bill, President Ford stated: "Unfortunately this bill promises more than the Federal Government can deliver, and its good intentions could be thwarted by the many unwise provisions it contains."

37. For a detailed analysis of the origins and provisions of PL94-142, see Jones (1981), Martin (1979), Cremins (1983), Levine and Wexler (1981), and Ballard, Ramirez, and Weintraub (1982).

Chapter 4. From Symbolic Gestures to Implementation Guidelines: The Saga of Section 504

1. Scotch (1984) contends that HEW's Rehabilitative Services Administration and Office of General Counsel were also considered for drafting regulations for section 504. OCR was assigned the charge because of its familiarity and experience with civil rights laws similar to section 504.

2. For a detailed discussion of the development of HEW's OCR, see Rabkin (1980); OCR's role in school desegregation is described in Radin (1977).

3. These discussions between the HEW staff and the staff of the Senate Subcommittee on the Handicapped are described in Scotch (1984) and Katzmann (1986).

4. At hearings on the Rehabilitation Act Amendments of 1974, Senator Alan Cranston praised the somewhat unusual extent of executive branch-congressional discussions: "I do wish to note that the period since September 26, 1973, when the Rehabilitation Act of 1973 was enacted, has been characterized by what I consider to have been an unusual, and highly valuable, period of consultation between the legislative and executive branches with respect to the implementation of the new public law." Senate Committee on Labor and Public Welfare, Subcommittee on the Handicapped (1974), *Hearings on the Rehabilitation Act Amendments of 1974*, 93d Cong., 2d sess., 12.

5. For a more detailed discussion of the statutory authority of section 504 and the legislative guidance provided by the Rehabilitation Act Amendments of 1974, see Engebretson (1979).

6. U.S. Senate (1974), *Rehabilitation Act Amendments of 1974*, 93d Cong., 2d sess., S. Rept. 93-1297, 39.

7. Ibid., 39–40.

8. The outside consultant's analysis is reported in David M. O'Neill, "Discrimination against Disabled Persons: The Costs, Benefits, and Inflationary Impact of Implementing Section 504 of the Rehabilitation Act of 1973 Covering Receipt of HEW Financial Assistance," *Federal Register*, May 17, 1976, 20312–80. The conclusion of the report stated: "We found that in all cases there was evidence for pecuniary benefits that provide substantial offsets to the pecuniary cost involved. Indeed, even if non-pecuniary benefits are not added, the balance of benefits and costs appears in favor of implementation of the regulation."

9. 41 *Federal Register* 17871.

10. U.S. Senate, *Rehabilitation Act Amendments of 1974*; and House Committee on Education and Labor, Subcommittee on Select Education, and Senate Committee on Labor and Public Welfare, Subcommittee on the Handicapped (1975), *Joint Oversight Hearings on the Proposed Extension of the Rehabilitation Act*, 94th Cong., 1st sess.

11. *Joint Oversight Hearings on the Proposed Extension of the Rehabilitation Act*, 144.

12. 419 F. Supp. 922 (DDC 1976).

13. Senate Committee on Labor and Public Welfare, Subcommittee on the Handicapped (1976), *Hearings on Rehabilitation of the Handicapped Programs, 1976*, 94th Cong., 2d sess., pt. 3, 1490. Statement by Martin Gerry, director of HEW's OCR.

14. Ibid., 1502–3.

15. 41 *Federal Register* 29296–311.

16. 41 *Federal Register* 29548–67.

17. 42 *Federal Register* 22676–702.

18. Ibid., 22676.

19. The public comments presented in this chapter were submitted in response to HEW's notice of proposed rulemaking for section 504. Comments are included in the official rulemaking docket originally maintained by HEW but now on file in the De-

partment of Education (given the subsequent breakup of HEW and creation of a cabinet-level department responsible for education) at the national office in Washington, D.C.

20. 42 *Federal Register* 22686.

21. Such steps to remove obstacles to participation should not, however, be considered affirmative action, which concerns extra actions to overcome pervasive discrimination in the past. Affirmative action goes beyond removal of architectural barriers and would include such activities as outreach and recruiting efforts to increase the number of disabled persons in the work force. In *Southeastern Community College v. Davis*, the Supreme Court ruled that affirmative action cannot be required in the context of section 504 unless it is specifically provided for in the authorizing statute (which it is not). For more discussion on this point, see Bell and Burgdorf 1983, 149–58.

22. 41 *Federal Register* 20296.

23. Ibid.

24. 41 *Federal Register* 29550.

25. 42 *Federal Register* 22680.

26. Ibid., 22678.

27. Ibid., 22681.

28. Ibid.

29. Ibid., 22689.

30. Ibid., 22692–93.

31. 42 *Federal Register* 32264.

32. 43 *Federal Register* 2132–39.

33. Berry (1984, 35) makes a similar claim about early rulemaking in the food stamp program, where administrators "enjoyed great latitude in making critical decisions. There was no obvious congressional preference in many of the issues they faced. Nor was there any great congressional interest."

Chapter 5. A Conservative Reaction to Section 504 Regulations: The Politics of Rollback

1. Senate Committee on Labor and Human Resources, Subcommittee on the Handicapped (1978), *Hearings on the Rehabilitation Amendments of 1978*, 95th Cong., 2d sess., 772–73.

2. House Committee on Education and Labor (1978), *Comprehensive Rehabilitation Services Amendments of 1978*, 95th Cong., 2d sess., H. Rept. 95-1149.

3. *Congressional Record*, September 20, 1978, 15567.

4. U.S. House of Representatives (1978), *Comprehensive Rehabilitation Services Amendments of 1978*, 95th Cong., 2d sess., H. Rept. 95-1780, 102.

5. Interview with Pat Wright and Arlene Mayerson, DREDF, March 6, 1987.

6. 45 *Federal Register* 72995.

7. 99 S. Ct. 2361 (1979).

8. 42 *Federal Register* 22684.

9. 99 S. Ct. 2361 (1979), 2369.

10. Ibid.

11. Ibid., 2370.

12. Ibid.

13. For analysis of the legal implications of the *Davis* decision, see Cook and Laski (1980), Olenick (1980), Butler (1980), Houston (1979), Forsyth (1981), and Gerse (1982).

14. Vice President Bush announced lists of regulations for review at several points in early 1981 (Behr and Omang 1981). The list of "midnight" and existing regulations targeted for regulatory review are found in a press release by the vice president, contained in House Committee on Energy and Commerce (1981), *Hearings on the Role of OMB in Regulation*, 97th Cong., 1st sess., 391–409.

15. This Congressional Research Service analysis by a legislative attorney is presented in Jones (1982). The analysis compares drafts of section 504 regulations for recipients of federal funds prepared by (1) OMB (in its own draft dated January 4, 1982, and in reactions to the DOJ draft), (2) DOJ (dated January 27, 1987), and (3) the original HEW rules, issued in January 1978. Because the OMB and DOJ regulations were never published or officially released, the following discussion relies on the CRS analysis and other secondary documents.

16. 46 *Federal Register* 13193–96.

17. Ibid., 13193–94.

18. It should be noted that the legality of Executive Order 12291 has been questioned on the grounds that the cost-benefit principle may exceed the scope of presidential authority, despite a DOJ ruling that the order was legal. See Jones (1982, 33–42); House Committee on Energy and Commerce (1981), *Presidential Control of Agency Rulemaking—An Analysis of Constitutional Issues That May Be Raised by Executive Order 12291*, 97th Cong., 1st sess., Committee Print 97-0; and Shane (1981).

19. 45 *Code of Federal Regulations* S.85.51.

20. Ibid.

21. 45 *Code of Federal Regulations* S.85.32.

22. 45 *Code of Federal Regulations* S.85.53.

23. 45 *Code of Federal Regulations* S.85.56.

24. 45 *Code of Federal Regulations* S.85.58.

25. The effort of the Reagan administration to eliminate ATBCB is described in chapter six. We see here that OMB, recognizing the administration's plan to do away with ATBCB, wanted no regulations tied directly to the board.

26. The effort to design uniform guidelines for accessibility in federal facilities, as mandated by the Architectural Barriers Act (ABA) of 1968, was initiated by OMB in 1981. The lead agencies for implementing the ABA—Department of Housing and Urban Development, Department of Defense, General Services Administration, and the Postal Service—engaged in efforts to design accessibility rules at the same time ATBCB was considering revisions of its accessibility rules.

27. Federal regulations for section 504 implementation in education are found in HEW's (and now DOE's) departmental regulations, and not in the coordinating ones that HEW released in 1978. Because HEW was itself responsible for education, it did

not include a section on this topic in its coordination rules. Once shifted to DOJ, however, provisions relevant to education were appropriate for the coordination regulations.

28. Interview with Arlene Mayerson and Pat Wright, DREDF, March 6, 1987, in Washington, D.C.

29. A copy of this letter from Vice President George Bush to DREDF, informing them that the administration was abandoning efforts to revise the section 504 coordination regulations, is on file with the author.

30. 48 *Federal Register* 55996–56005.

31. Ibid., 56002.

32. Ibid., 55997.

33. Ibid., 56003.

34. 49 *Federal Register* 7792–93.

35. Ibid.

36. As justification for differences in 504 regulations for federally assisted and federally conducted programs, DOJ also mentions the *American Public Transit Association v. Lewis* case. This case is examined in chapter seven, which deals with section 504 as it applies to public transportation.

37. 662 F.2d 292 (5th Cir. 1981).

38. House Committee on the Judiciary, Subcommittee on Civil and Constitutional Rights (1982), *Hearings on Authorization Request for the Civil Rights Division of the Department of Justice*, 97th Cong., 2d sess., 154.

39. Ibid., 258.

40. Ibid.

41. For reasons unknown, this hearing before the Judiciary Committee's Subcommittee on Civil and Constitutional Rights, held on May 6, 1983, was never published. This information was given to the author in a telephone conversation with a staff person of the subcommittee. Therefore, I must rely on news reports of this hearing in regards to testimony presented before the subcommittee.

42. See n. 41 and Thornton (1983).

43. Ibid.

44. Senate Committee on Labor and Human Resources, Subcommittee on the Handicapped (1983), *Hearings on Enforcement of Section 504 of the Rehabilitation Act: Institutional Care and Services for Retarded Citizens*, 98th Cong., 1st sess.

45. Ibid., 146.

46. Ibid.

47. Ibid., 3.

48. Ibid.

49. Ibid., 153.

50. Ibid., 143.

51. Ibid., 321.

52. Senate Committee on the Judiciary (1985), *Hearing on the Nomination of William Bradford Reynolds to Be Associate Attorney General of the United States*, 99th Cong., 1st sess.

53. Despite the Senate's rejection of Reynolds's nomination to the post of associate

attorney general in 1985, he received a different promotion in 1987, to the position of counselor to the attorney general. This counselor position did not require Senate approval.

54. 104 S. Ct. 1211 (1984).

55. Ibid., 1221.

56. House Committee on Education and Labor, and Committee on the Judiciary, Subcommittee on Civil and Constitutional Rights (1985), *Joint Hearings on the Civil Rights Restoration Act of 1985*, 99th Cong., 1st sess., 1–2.

57. Ibid., 120.

58. Ibid., 150.

59. Ibid., 237.

60. Ibid., 238.

Chapter 6. Barrier Removal and Facility Access for Disabled Persons

1. The origins of and changes in the ABA are described in Senate Committee on Environment and Public Works (1979), *Architectural Barriers in Federal Buildings: Implementation of the Architectural Barriers Act of 1968*, 96th Cong., 1st sess., Committee Print, Serial 96-8.

2. 34 *Federal Register* 12828–29.

3. Senate, *Architectural Barriers in Federal Buildings*, 17.

4. Not included within the definition of "buildings" were those leased buildings that were not constructed or altered under federal government guidance or supervision.

5. 34 *Federal Register* 12829.

6. Legislative consideration of the Rehabilitation Act of 1972 is reflected in the following hearings: Senate Committee on Labor and Public Welfare, Subcommittee on the Handicapped (1972), *Hearings on the Rehabilitation Act of 1972*, 92d Cong., 2d sess., pts. 1 and 2; House Committee on Education and Labor, Subcommittee on Select Education (1972), *Hearings on Vocational Rehabilitation Services to the Handicapped*, 92d Cong., 2d sess.

7. "Memorandum of Disapproval of Nine Bills," *Public Papers of the President: Richard M. Nixon*, October 27, 1972 (Washington, D.C.: Government Printing Office), 377.

8. *The Rehabilitation Act Amendments of 1974*, PL93-516, 93d Cong., 2d sess., enacted December 7, 1974.

9. House Committee on Public Works and Transportation, Subcommittee on Investigations and Review (1975), *Hearings on the Effectiveness of the Architectural Barriers Act of 1968 (Public Law 90-480)*, 94th Cong., 1st sess. See statement made by Senator James Cleveland, 2–3.

10. U.S. General Accounting Office (1975).

11. A similar set of deficiencies are identified by Farber (1975). See also Ebert (1982) and Goldman (1983).

12. House, *Hearings on the Effectiveness of the Architectural Barriers Act of 1968*, 2.

13. Ibid., 35.

14. Ibid., 71–74.

15. With passage of the 1976 amendments to the ABA, USPS became the fourth standard-setting agency, joining GSA, HUD, and DOD.

16. 42 *Federal Register* 9038–39, 49485–86.

17. Under the 1969 GSA rules, accommodations were required in property only if the property was constructed or altered in accordance with plans and specifications of the United States. Accommodation was thus not required for leased facilities not constructed under government supervision. The 1978 GSA rules corrected this omission, applying accommodation required to property leased by the federal government after January 1, 1978.

18. 43 *Federal Register* 16478–80.

19. Ibid., 16479.

20. Ibid.

21. Senate Committee on Labor and Human Resources, Subcommittee on the Handicapped (1977), *Hearings on Rehabilitation Extension Amendments of 1977*, 95th Cong., 1st sess., 423.

22. Ibid.

23. Ibid., 209–10.

24. U.S. House of Representatives (1978), *Comprehensive Rehabilitation Services Amendments of 1978*, 95th Cong., 2d sess., H. Rept. 95-1780.

25. 45 *Federal Register* 12168–71.

26. House Committee on Education and Labor, Subcommittee on Select Education (1980), *Oversight Hearing on the Architectural and Transportation Barriers Compliance Board*, 96th Cong., 2d sess.

27. U.S. General Accounting Office (1980).

28. 45 *Federal Register* 55010–64.

29. The legal opinion of ATBCB's general counsel is contained in a memorandum distributed to board members and dated October 23, 1980. The memorandum is included in House Committee on Education and Labor, Subcommittee on Select Education (1981), *Oversight Hearings on the Architectural and Transportation Barrier Compliance Board*, 97th Cong., 1st sess.

30. Approved minutes, ATBCB meeting, January 6, 1981, on file in ATBCB's office, Washington, D.C., 29.

31. Ibid., 29.

32. 46 *Federal Register* 4270–304.

33. In its own accessibility rules (1979), USPS stated that accessibility changes in leased property were required only when new leases were negotiated or existing ones were renegotiated with new terms. The rules exempted accessibility changes for extensions of existing leases. These rules were obviously less stringent than those proposed and adopted by ATBCB.

34. Approved minutes, ATBCB meeting, May 5, 1981.

35. Approved minutes, ATBCB meeting, July 10, 1981, 7.

36. The vote split in this context is interesting. When ATBCB was reconstituted by Congress in 1978, eleven public members were added to the board, previously com-

posed of ten federal agency representatives. This gave the public members a one-person majority. This majority gave way to an equal position in 1980, when HEW was split into two new agencies, the Department of Education and the Department of Health and Human Services, both of which were granted a position on the board. On the vote to rescind the minimum guidelines, all eleven agencies voted as a bloc to rescind, being joined by one public representative. The remaining public representatives voted as a bloc against rescinding the minimum guidelines.

37. Approved minutes, ATBCB meeting, July 10, 1981, 15.

38. Ibid., 16.

39. 46 *Federal Register* 39764.

40. Comments were among those received by ATBCB in response to its rescission notice published in August. They are maintained as rulemaking docket 81-G-1, on file at ATBCB's office, Washington, D.C.

41. Ibid.

42. *Congressional Record*, August 1, 1981, S9031.

43. Approved minutes, ATBCB meeting, September 22, 1981.

44. 46 *Federal Register* 47745.

45. House Committee on Education and Labor, Subcommittee on Select Education (1981), *Oversight Hearing on the Architectural and Transportation Barriers Compliance Board*, 97th Cong., 1st sess., 1.

46. Ibid., 11.

47. Ibid.

48. Ibid., 35.

49. Ibid., 57.

50. Ibid., 15–16.

51. Ibid., 16.

52. Approved minutes, ATBCB meeting, December 1, 1981.

53. 47 *Federal Register* 3939–51.

54. Ibid., 3951.

55. House Committee on Appropriations, Subcommittee on the Department of Transportation and Related Agencies Appropriations (1982), *Hearings on Department of Transportation and Related Agencies Appropriations for 1983*, 97th Cong., 2d sess., pt. 3, 474.

56. Ibid., 493.

57. Ibid.

58. "Physically Handicapped Win Long Wrestling Match," *Washington Post*, May 25, 1982.

59. 47 *Federal Register* 33863–69.

60. 48 *Federal Register* 19610–29.

61. 49 *Federal Register* 31528–625. It is interesting to note that the Vice Presidential Task Force on Regulatory Relief claimed the change in the minimum accessibility guidelines as part of its deregulation campaign and claimed that $250 million would be saved. See Vice Presidential Task Force on Regulatory Relief (1982).

62. 49 *Federal Register* 31529.

63. 566 F. Supp. 367 (1983).

64. 744 F.2d (1984).

65. 51 *Federal Register* 13122–23.

66. 52 *Federal Register* 4325–56.

67. U.S. Architectural and Transportation Barriers Compliance Board (1987), "Report Submitted to the President and Congress of the United States for Fiscal Year 1987," Washington, D.C., 6–15.

Chapter 7. Access, Mobility, and Public Transportation

1. U.S. Urban Mass Transportation Administration (1973).

2. U.S. Urban Mass Transportation Administration (1978).

3. Katzmann (1986) has provided a very thorough description and examination of transportation policy for persons with disabilities. For more on early legislation, see Reed (1977).

4. Prior to laws passed in the 1970s, the courts recognized that transit carriers have responsibility to transport disabled and elderly persons (Mitchell 1976).

5. House Committee on Public Works, Subcommittee on Public Buildings and Grounds (1970), *Hearings on Design and Construction of Federal Facilities to Be Accessible to the Physically Handicapped*, 91st Cong., 1st sess.

6. Provisions of the Urban Mass Transportation Assistance Act of 1970, 49 U.S.C. 1612a.

7. Ibid.

8. For hearings on the Federal-Aid Highway Act of 1973, see House Committee on Banking and Currency, Subcommittee on Housing (1972), *Hearings on Urban Mass Transportation*, 92d Cong., 2d sess.; and Senate Committee on Public Works, Subcommittee on Transportation (1973), *Federal-Aid Highway Act of 1973*, 93d Cong., 1st sess.

9. House Committee on Public Works, Subcommittee on Public Buildings and Grounds (1972), *Hearing to Consider Accommodations for Handicapped on Metro System*, 92d Cong., 2d sess.

10. House, *Hearings on Urban Mass Transportation*, 58–59.

11. 39 *Federal Register* 39901.

12. A summary of comments made at the informal hearings are provided in 40 *Federal Register* 8316.

13. Ibid., 8314–20.

14. Ibid., 8314.

15. 41 *Federal Register* 18234, 18236–41.

16. Ibid., 18234.

17. Ibid., 18234.

18. Ibid., 18236.

19. 43 *Federal Register* 2132–39.

20. 43 *Federal Register* 2135.

21. Interview with Robert Ashby, deputy assistant general counsel for regulations and enforcement, DOT, September 1986. This perspective is also stated by Katzmann (1986, 103–5).

22. 43 *Federal Register* 25016–63.

23. Ibid., 25031.

24. Ibid., 25017.

25. The history of the Transbus and its sponsorship by DOT is a fascinating story in itself. The department originally embraced the plan, backed away, recommited itself, and then quietly abandoned this technological development to enhance the accessibility of physically disabled persons to public transit buses. The saga of Transbus is related in Katzmann (1986, 132–42.).

26. "A Preliminary Analysis of the Economic Impact Statement Submitted with the Department of Transportation's Notice of Proposed Rulemaking under Section 504 of the Rehabilitation Act of 1973," Office of Planning and Policy Analysis, APTA, June 1978 (included in DOT's rulemaking docket 56a).

27. This and other comments listed in this section were drawn from submissions to DOT's rulemaking docket 56a, maintained for the full accessibility rules issued in 1979. The docket is maintained by DOT in Washington, D.C.

28. U.S. Urban Mass Transportation Administration, *Technical Report of the National Survey of Transportation Handicapped People* (Washington, D.C.: Government Printing Office, 1978).

29. It should be noted that the Ohio Public Transit Association favored a demand-responsive paratransit system, which, they argued, would better serve the needs of handicapped persons.

30. 44 *Federal Register* 31442–79.

31. Ibid., 31442.

32. Ibid., 31456.

33. The DOT rules contained many other provisions besides those related to program accessibility in urban mass transit systems. Requirements for accessibility in other transit systems were also described in the rules, as well as stipulations about reasonable accommodation in employment.

34. House Committee on Public Works and Transportation, Subcommittee on Surface Transportation (1976), *Hearings to Consider Amendments to the Urban Mass Transportation Act of 1964 to Provide Operating Assistance for Projects Located in Areas Other Than Urbanized Areas, to Provide for Mass Transportation Assistance to Meet the Needs of Elderly and Handicapped Persons, and for Other Purposes*, 94th Cong., 2d sess., 197.

35. Ibid., 331.

36. "Hindsight on Helping the Handicapped," *New York Times*, February 16, 1980.

37. Ibid.

38. U.S. Congressional Budget Office (1979).

39. Ibid., xiv, xvi.

40. House Committee on Public Works and Transportation, Subcommittee on Oversight and Review (1980), *Urban Mass Transportation Administration's Technology Development and Equipment Procurement Programs: Do We Know What We're Trying to Do?* 96th Cong., 2d sess., Committee Print 96-34.

41. Ibid., 15.

42. Ibid., 21.

43. The reports of these studies of the Transbus design commissioned by DOT are *Transbus: An Overview of Technical, Operational, and Economic Characteristics* (McLean, Va.: Mitre Corporation, 1979) and *NRC Transbus Study* (Washington, D.C.: National Academy of Sciences, 1979).

44. *Congressional Record*, May 25, 1980, 16695. An influential paper on the concept of service criteria is presented in Cannon (1978).

45. The legislative debates over full accessibility and local flexibility in 1980 are described in detail in Katzmann (1986, 63–73) and in *Congressional Record*, November 21, 1980, 30538–55; December 2, 1980, 31554–80; December 4, 1980, 32154–80.

46. *Congressional Record*, December 2, 1980, 31549.

47. Interview with Robert Ashby, deputy assistant general counsel for regulations and enforcement, DOT, September 1986.

48. 45 *Federal Register* 72996.

49. 46 *Federal Register* 40687.

50. 46 *Federal Register* 37488–94.

51. Ibid., 37492.

52. 48 *Federal Register* 49684.

53. U.S. General Accounting Office (1982).

54. *Congressional Record*, December 14, 1982, S14742.

55. 48 *Federal Register* 40684.

56. This impression is gained from a review and comparison of the rulemaking dockets for the 1979 full-accessibility rules (docket 56a) and the 1986 comparable service rules (docket 56b). Robert Ashby, deputy assistant counsel for regulation and enforcement, DOT, agreed with this assessment in an interview with the author in September 1986.

57. This and comments to follow were extracted from those submitted to DOT in response to the notice of proposed rulemaking published in September 1983. They are contained in the official rulemaking docket (56b) maintained at DOT.

58. 51 *Federal Register* 18994–19031.

59. *Regulatory Impact Analysis: The Department of Transportation's Regulation Implementing Section 504 of the Rehabilitation Act of 1973 in the Urban Mass Transit Program.* Washington, D.C.: U.S. Department of Transportation, December 1985. This analysis was required under rules for issuing major rules as defined by the Office of Management and Budget under the Reagan administration.

60. Ibid., x.

61. 51 *Federal Register* 18994–19031.

62. *Adapt, et al. v. Dole* (U.S. District Court, Eastern Pennsylvania District, 1988). It is interesting to note that the judge in this case did not concur with the plaintiffs that Congress has, through various public laws, legislated mainstreaming for disabled persons in public transportation.

63. For a review of studies on the use and application of paratransit, see Brattgard (1979); Bell and Bell (1979); Navin (1979); Fix, Everett, and Kirby (1985); and U.S. Urban Mass Transportation Administration (1979a, 1979b).

64. Among the studies that comparatively assess the cost of paratransit options, see DOT's (1985) regulatory impact statement for the 1986 regulations and Jackson (1982).

Chapter 8. Access to Public and Higher Education

1. 41 *Federal Register* 56966–98.

2. Ibid., 56966.

3. Ibid., 56977.

4. Ibid., 56986.

5. Ibid., 56977.

6. 42 *Federal Register* 42474.

7. Ibid., 42474–518.

8. 42 *Federal Register* 22681.

9. Ibid.

10. Ibid.

11. 42 *Federal Register* 22682.

12. Ibid., 22683–85.

13. Oversight hearings on the Education for All Handicapped Children Act include the following. Senate Committee on Labor and Human Resources, Subcommittee on the Handicapped: (1978) *Hearings on Education for All Handicapped Children Act, 1978*, 95th Cong., 2d sess.; (1979) *Oversight on Education for All Handicapped Children Act, 1979*, 96th Cong., 1st sess.; (1980) *Oversight on Education for All Handicapped Children Act, 1980*, 96th Cong., 2d sess., pt. 1; (1980) *Oversight on Education for All Handicapped Children Act, 1980*, 96th Cong., 2d sess., pt. 2. House Committee on Education and Labor, Subcommittee on Select Education: (1977) *Education for All Handicapped Children Act*, 95th Cong., 1st sess.; (1977) *Extension of the Education of the Handicapped Act*, 95th Cong., 1st sess.; (1979) *Oversight of Public Law 94-142: The Education for All Handicapped Children Act*, 96th Cong., 1st sess., pt. 1 and appendix; (1979) *Education and Rehabilitation Services for the Handicapped in Illinois*, 96th Cong., 1st sess.; (1979) *Oversight Hearing on Education of Handicapped Children*, 96th Cong., 1st sess.; (1980) *Field Hearings on the Education for All Handicapped Children Act*, 96th Cong., 2d sess.

14. House Committee on Education and Labor, Subcommittee on Select Education (1977), *Hearings on Implementation of Section 504, Rehabilitation Act of 1973*, 95th Cong., 1st sess., 7.

15. Ibid., 201.

16. Senate, *Oversight on Education for All Handicapped Children Act, 1980*, 99.

17. "Going Wrong with Handicapped Rights," *New York Times*, July 21, 1980. For more discussion on costs and potential backlash, see Martin (1979, 9–10, 46–55).

18. Senate, *Oversight on Education for All Handicapped Children Act, 1980*, 48.

19. House, *Oversight Hearing on Education of Handicapped Children*, 113.

20. Senate, *Oversight on Education for All Handicapped Children Act, 1979*, 9.

21. Ibid., 1–2.

22. U.S. General Accounting Office (1981), *Unanswered Questions on Educating Handicapped Children in Local Public Schools*, HRD-81-43 (Washington, D.C.: General Accounting Office), i.

23. U.S. General Accounting Office (1981), *Disparities Still Exist in Who Gets Special Education*, IPE-81-1 (Washington, D.C.: Government Printing Office).

24. U.S. General Accounting Office, *Unanswered Questions.*

25. U.S. Department of Education (1981), *To Assure the Free Appropriate Public Education of All Handicapped Children: Third Annual Report to Congress on the Implementation of Public Law 94-142* (Washington, D.C.: Office of Special Education and Rehabilitative Services, Department of Education).

26. U.S. Office of Civil Rights (1979), "OCR Says Mainstreaming on the Rise," *Education Daily*, October 26.

27. The results of the UCPA study were presented in testimony before the House Subcommittee on Select Education. See House, *Oversight of Public Law 94-142*, 14–30.

28. The results of the study by the National Committee for Citizens in Education were presented by Stanley Salett during an oversight hearing conducted by the Senate Subcommittee on the Handicapped. See Senate, *Oversight on Education for All Handicapped Children Act, 1980*, 529–59.

29. 46 *Federal Register* 5460–74.

30. 45 *Federal Register* 85082–84.

31. Comments are contained in the rulemaking docket created for responses to notice of intent to devise rules, interpretations, or policy statements as announced in 45 *Federal Register* 85082–84. The docket is maintained by DOE, Washington, D.C.

32. Senate Committee on Labor and Human Resources (1981), *Nomination*, 97th Cong., 1st sess., 35.

33. Senate Committee on Labor and Human Resources, Subcommittee on Education, Arts, and Humanities (1981), *Hearings on Elementary and Secondary Education Consolidation Act of 1981*, 97th Cong., 1st sess., 19.

34. Ibid., 26.

35. Ibid., 27–28.

36. Ibid., 57.

37. Ibid.

38. Ibid., 150.

39. 47 *Federal Register* 33836.

40. Ibid.

41. The *Los Angeles Times*, for example, carried a story on the hearing that DOE sponsored in Los Angeles on the proposed changes in regulations, with the headline "Parents Boo Reagan's Plan for Handicapped Children" (Savage 1982).

42. Senate Committee on Labor and Human Resources, Subcommittee on the Handicapped (1982), *Oversight Hearings on Education for All Handicapped Children Act, 1982*, 97th Cong., 2d sess., 1–2.

43. Ibid., 3.

44. Ibid., 54–55.

45. Remarks of Lowell Weicker, *Congressional Record*, August 10, 1982, 10066.

46. House Committee on Education and Labor, Subcommittee of Select Education (1982), *Oversight Hearings on Proposed Changes in Regulations for the Education for All Handicapped Children Act*, 97th Cong., 2d sess.

47. Ibid., 115–27. (The withdrawal of proposed regulatory changes was announced in 47 *Federal Register* 49871–72.)

48. Ibid., 127.

49. Ibid., 131.

50. Ibid., 134.

51. House Committee on Education and Labor (1982), *Regulations Concerning the Education of the Handicapped Act*, 97th Cong., 2d sess., H. Rept. 97–906, 1.

52. For an analysis of PL98-199, the Education of the Handicapped Act Amendments of 1983, see Weintraub and Ramirez (1985).

53. 49 *Federal Register* 48520–27.

54. 99 S. Ct. 2361 (1979). For more detailed discussions of this case and its implications, see Cook and Laski (1980), Olenick (1980), Butler (1980), Houston (1979), Forsyth (1981), and Gerse (1982).

55. 20 *Code of Federal Regulations* S.1401.

56. 102 S. Ct. 3034 (1982).

57. 483 F. Supp. (1980).

58. 632 F.2d (1980).

59. 102 S. Ct. 3034 (1982), 3042.

60. Ibid., 3047.

61. Ibid., 3048.

62. Ibid., 3049.

63. Ibid., 3051.

64. Ibid.

65. For a more detailed discussion of the *Rowley* case and its legal implications, see Kroll (1983), Henry (1983), Wenderoff (1983), Boettner (1983), Taylor (1983), Beyer (1983), Buturla (1982), and Mansfield (1982).

66. The *Smith v. Robinson* case is found in 104 S. Ct. 3457 (1984).

67. In a dissenting opinion, Justice William Brennan argued: "Congress will now have to take time to revisit the matter and until it does, the handicapped children of our country whose difficulties are compounded by discrimination and by other deprivations of constitutional rights, will have to pay the costs."

68. 105 S. Ct. 1996 (1985). For more detail on this case, see Motsco (1985) and Sommer (1984).

69. House Committee on Education and Labor (1985), *Commemorating the Accomplishments of Public Law 94-142, the Education for All Handicapped Children Act, on the 10th Anniversary of Its Enactment*, 99th Cong., 1st sess., H. Rept. 99-328, 2.

70. Ibid., 3.

71. This point was affirmed by the federal courts in *New Mexico Association for Retarded Citizens v. New Mexico* (678 F.2d 847, 10th Cir.). New Mexico was the only state that opted out of participating in the federally funded program to educate handicapped children. The New Mexico Association for Retarded Citizens sued the state, charging that it was not taking efforts to provide a free and appropriate education for handicapped children. The state argued that it was not bound by federal laws and regulations in this regard, given that it was not a participant in the handicapped education program. The state lost its case in federal court, where it was ruled that under sections 504 of the Rehabilitation Act of 1973, New Mexico was required to provide a free and appropriate education to handicapped children.

72. U.S. Commission on Education of the Deaf (1988), 20.

73. Ibid., 25.

Chapter 9. Employment Rights and Opportunities for Disabled Persons

1. The amendment to the Civil Service Act pertaining to physical disability was contained in PL617, 80th Cong., 2d sess., signed into law June 10, 1948.

2. These instructions were included as *Federal Personnel Manual* (FPM) Letter 306-5, issued by the U.S. Civil Service Commission in late January 1974.

3. U.S. Civil Service Commission (1974), *Employment of Handicapped Individuals in the Federal Government*, report prepared for the Senate Committee on Labor and Public Welfare and House Committee on Education and Labor (Washington, D.C.: Civil Service Commission), 4.

4. The U.S. Civil Service Commission instructions for implementing section 501, originally issued in FPM Letter 306-5, were updated in FPM 306-7 (February 1975) and FPM 306-8 (April 1975). The latter instructions were issued in response to passage of the VEVRAA of 1974.

5. U.S. Civil Service Commission (1975), *Employment of Handicapped Individuals in the Federal Government*, report prepared for the Senate Committee on Labor and Public Welfare and House Committee on Education and Labor (Washington, D.C.: Civil Service Commission), 13.

6. Ibid., 27.

7. Ibid.

8. 42 *Federal Register* 46541–44.

9. 43 *Federal Register* 12293–96.

10. Ibid.

11. Ibid., 12295.

12. Ibid.

13. Ibid.

14. I am indebted to Clayton Boyd (interviewed by telephone March 31, 1987) and Sharon Wilkin (interviewed by telephone June 10, 1987) both of EEOC, for their insights into implementation of section 501.

15. PL95-17 renewed power to the president to reorganize the executive branch for three years, subject to approval by both houses of Congress. This power had first been granted by Congress in 1949 but had lapsed in 1973.

16. Reorganization Plan No. 1 of 1978 was issued as 43 *Federal Register* 19807 and as House of Representatives Document No. 95-295.

17. 43 *Federal Register* 19807.

18. House Committee on Government Operations (1978), *Reorganization Plan No. 1 of 1978*, 95th Cong., 2d sess., H. Rept. 95-1069, 12.

19. The resolution of disapproval for the reorganization plan relevant to EEOC was contained in House Resolution 1049. The official transfer of responsibility for section

501 from CSC to EEOC through Executive Order 12106 was issued December 28, 1978 (44 *Federal Register* 1053). EEOC redesignated the CSC regulations for section 501, with a few technical revisions (43 *Federal Register* 60900–901). This action moved the section 501 regulations from 5 *Code of Federal Regulations* 713 to 29 *Code of Federal Regulations* 1613.

20. For a review of the origins of EEOC, see U.S. Equal Employment Opportunity Commission (1979).

21. 43 *Federal Register* 28967–69.

22. 45 *Federal Register* 51383–84.

23. 46 *Federal Register* 11218. Current federal regulations are found in 29 *Code of Federal Regulations* 1613.701–709.

24. Equal Employment Opportunity Management Directive EEO-MD-703 (December 6, 1979). This directive has been updated as follows: EEO-MD-706 (July 1, 1980), EEO-MD-708 (February 20, 1981), EEO-MD-709 (October 6, 1981), EEO-MD-711 (November 2, 1982), EEO-MD-712 (March 29, 1983), and EEO-MD-711A (October 4, 1983).

25. House Committee on Education and Labor, Subcommittee on Employment Opportunities (1980), *Oversight Hearing on the Federal Enforcement of Equal Employment Opportunity Laws*, 96th Cong., 2d sess.

26. Ibid., 3–12.

27. Ibid., 5.

28. The Merit Systems Protection Board was created as part of the reorganization of the civil service system achieved through the Civil Service Reform Act (PL95-454). The board's primary responsibility was to hear grievances by federal employees.

29. House, *Oversight Hearing on the Federal Enforcement of Equal Employment Opportunity Laws*, 7.

30. U.S. Equal Employment Opportunity Commission (1982), 18.

31. House Committee on Education and Labor, Subcommittee on Employment Opportunities (1982), *Report on Affirmative Action and the Federal Enforcement of Equal Employment Opportunity Laws*, 97th Cong., 2d sess., Committee Print, 1.

32. House Committee on Education and Labor, Subcommittee on Employment Opportunities (1981), *Oversight Hearings on Equal Employment Opportunity and Affirmative Action*, 97th Cong., 1st sess., pt. 1.

33. House Committee on Education and Labor, Subcommittee on Employment Opportunities (1983), *Oversight Hearings on the Federal Enforcement of Equal Opportunity Laws*, 98th Cong., 1st sess., 134.

34. U.S. Equal Employment Opportunity Commission (1986).

35. Ibid., 148–51.

36. 39 *Federal Register* 20566–71.

37. Ibid., 20566.

38. Ibid., 20567.

39. 40 *Federal Register* 39887–95.

40. Ibid., 39887.

41. Telephone interview with David Brigham, Office of Federal Contract Compliance Programs, DOL, June 10, 1987.

42. 41 *Federal Register* 16147–55.

43. OFCCP was created in response to Executive Order 11246 (30 *Federal Register* 13441), signed by Lyndon Johnson on September 24, 1965. This order abolished the President's Committee on Equal Employment Opportunity and delegated its functions to DOL.

44. David Brigham, OFCCP, June 10, 1987.

45. 42 *Federal Register* 46501–4.

46. Office of Federal Contract Compliance Programs (1977), *Preliminary Report on the Revitalization of the Federal Contract Compliance Program* (Washington, D.C.: U.S. Department of Labor, Employment Standards Administration).

47. Ibid., viii.

48. Ibid., xvii.

49. Senate Committee on Labor and Human Resources (1979), *Hearings on Equal Employment Opportunity for the Handicapped Act of 1979*, 96th Cong., 1st sess. The purpose of this hearing was to consider legislation to amend the Civil Rights Act of 1964 to include protection for handicapped persons. As with previous efforts to reform the Civil Rights Act, dating back to the early 1970s, this legislative initiative never moved close to passage.

50. Ibid., 97–98.

51. Ibid., 99.

52. "Protecting the Handicapped from Employment Discrimination in Private Sector Employment: A Critical Analysis of Section 503 of the Rehabilitation Act of 1973," *Tulane Law Review* 54 (1980): 717–56.

53. 45 *Federal Register* 86206–14.

54. David Brigham, OFCCP, June 10, 1987.

55. 46 *Federal Register* 9084.

56. 46 *Federal Register* 42968.

57. See, for example, the statements of William Bradford Reynolds, assistant attorney general for civil rights, and Malcom Lovell, under secretary of DOL, made at the following congressional hearing: House Committee on Education and Labor, Subcommittee on Employment Opportunities (1981), *Oversight Hearings on Equal Employment Opportunity and Affirmative Action*, 97th Cong., 1st sess., pt. 1, 134, 288.

58. House Committee on Education and Labor, Subcommittee on Employment Opportunities (1984), *Oversight Hearing on the OFCCP's National Self-Monitoring and Reporting System*, 98th Cong., 2d sess.

59. Ibid., 17. The question of the DOL studies on the effectiveness of affirmative action measures was a major irritation among legislators, as expressed at the hearings. Senator John Glenn (D-OH) described the delay and runaround he and other legislators had received from DOL in receiving two reports that assessed the impact of affirmative action on the employment of various minority groups. These studies were described in an article in the *New York Times*, which served to peak the interest of the legislators. According to this article, the studies documented that strong affirmative action efforts, including the use of quota-type methods, had been quite effective in increasing the representation of women and minorities in the work force. Given that this evidence might work against the administration's position, by loosening regulatory requirements

for affirmative action by contractors, the legislators presumed that the reports were purposively being buried.

60. Ibid., 33.

61. Ibid., 44.

62. Ibid., 45–47.

63. It should be noted that most study results are based on a mail survey of contractors, which had a twenty-percent response rate. The study's authors examined characteristics of nonrespondents and felt that there was no systematic bias in responses. However, many contractors admitted having few statistics on the extent of handicapped workers in their firms or stated that many workers were reluctant to identify themselves as handicapped. For these reasons, the authors argue that "the findings of this study may systematically underreport the actual hiring and accommodation of handicapped workers" (p. 16).

64. 42 *Federal Register* 2138.

65. Ibid., 2137.

66. 45 *Federal Register* 66706–23.

67. 45 *Federal Register* 86206–14.

68. 104 S. Ct. 112 (1984).

69. 104 S. Ct. 1248 (1984).

70. International Center for the Disabled and National Council on the Handicapped (1986).

71. International Center for the Disabled, National Council on the Handicapped, and President's Committee on Employment of the Handicapped (1987).

Chapter 10. Implementing Disability Rights Policies: Comparisons, Contrasts, and Dilemmas

1. These remarks are not meant to indicate that there were no strong and well-developed interest groups representing persons with disabilities at this time. Several groups, especially those representing blind, deaf, and physically impaired persons, have long histories and were active in the early political struggles over disability rights.

2. This perspective, that disability groups have been weakened by the result of reduced federal funding, was expressed to the author both by interest group representatives and by administrators within federal agencies.

3. These rulemaking dockets, inspected and reviewed by the author, are maintained on file and are open for public inspection at the offices of DOT in Washington, D.C.

4. *School Board of Nassau County, Florida v. Arline*, 108, U.S. ——— (1987).

5. Senate Committee on Labor and Public Welfare, Subcommittee on the Handicapped (1975), *Hearings on Education for All Handicapped Children Act, 1975*, 94th Cong., 1st sess., 308.

6. National Commission on Architectural Barriers to Rehabilitation of the Handicapped (1967), *Design for All Americans* (Washington, D.C.: Government Printing Office).

7. "On Mixing Buses and Wheelchairs," *Chicago Tribune*, September 13, 1978.

8. 42 *Federal Register* 22676.

9. 99 S. Ct. 2361 (1979), 2363.

10. 102 S. Ct. 3034 (1982), 3037.

11. "In the Matter of the Treatment and Care of Infant Doe, Declaratory Judgement," Cause No. GU 8204-00, Circuit Court for the County of Monroe, State of Indiana, April 12, 1982. A copy of this judgment is found in House Committee on Education and Labor, Subcommittee on Select Education (1982), *Hearings on Treatment of Infants Born with Handicapping Conditions*, 97th Cong., 2d sess., 73–76.

12. U.S. Department of Health and Human Services, Office of Civil Rights, "Notice to Health Care Providers. Subject: Discrimination against the Handicapped by Withholding Treatment or Nourishment," May 18, 1982. The notice is reprinted in House, *Hearings on Treatment of Infants Born with Handicapping Conditions*, 79–80.

13. House Committee on Education and Labor, Subcommittee on Select Education (1983), *Hearings to Amend the Child Abuse Prevention and Treatment and Adoption Reform Act of 1978*, 98th Cong., 1st sess., 370.

14. House of Representatives (1984), *Child Abuse Amendments of 1984*, 98th Cong., 2d sess., H. Rept. 93-1038.

15. 48 *Federal Register* 9630–32.

16. *American Academy of Pediatricians v. Heckler*, 561 F. Supp. 395 (DDC 1983). The Department of Health and Human Services acknowledged the invalidation of its interim rule in 48 *Federal Register* 17588.

17. For a detailed discussion of the Baby Doe case, see Kuzma (1984).

18. 48 *Federal Register* 30846.

19. 49 *Federal Register* 1623.

20. Ibid., 1622–54.

21. *Bowen, Secretary of Health and Human Services v. American Hospital Association*, ———, U.S. ——— (1987).

22. Statement made by Benjamin Heinemen, Jr., an attorney for AMA (Kamen 1986).

23. *School Board of Nassau County, Florida v. Arline*, 108, U.S. ——— (1987). This case was argued December 3, 1986, and decided March 3, 1987.

24. Ibid. (slip opinion, pp. 9–10).

25. Ibid., 10–11.

26. Ibid., 7–8.

27. Presidential Commission on the Human Immunodeficiency Virus Epidemic (1988), *Report of the Presidential Commission on the Human Immunodeficiency Virus Epidemic* (Washington, D.C.), 121.

28. Ibid.

29. Ibid., 123.

Select Bibliography

Aberbach, Joel D. 1979. "Changes in Congressional Oversight." *American Behavioral Scientist* 22 (May/June): 493–515.

Abraham, Henry J. 1986. *The Judicial Process*. 5th ed. New York: Oxford University Press.

"Abroad in the Land: Legal Strategies to Effectuate the Rights of the Physically Disabled." *Georgetown Law Review* 61 (1973): 1501–23.

Administrative Conference of the United States. 1983. *A Guide to Federal Agency Rulemaking*. Washington, D.C.: Administrative Conference of the United States.

Advisory Commission on Intergovernmental Relations. 1989. *Disability Rights Mandates: Federal and State Compliance with Employment Protections and Architectural Barrier Removal*. Washington, D.C.: Advisory Commission on Intergovernmental Relations.

———. 1984. *Regulatory Federalism: Policy, Process, Impact and Reform*. Commission Report. Washington, D.C.: Advisory Commission on Intergovernmental Relations.

Alexander, Ernest B. 1985. "From Idea to Action: Notes for a Contingency Theory of the Policy Implementation Process." *Administration and Society* 16, no. 4 (February): 403–26.

———. 1979. "Policy-Planning-Implementation." In *New Trends in Urban Planning*, ed. Dan Soen. Oxford, England: Pergamon.

Alexander, Jacquelyn, Deborah Bond, and Randall M. Soffer. 1979. "The Impact of P.L. 94-142 on Collective Bargaining at the Local School District Level." Paper presented at the Annual International CEC Convention, Dallas (April).

Altman, Barbara M. 1981. "Studies of Attitudes toward the Handicapped: The Need for a New Direction." *Social Problems* 28, no. 3 (February): 321–37.

Ashford, Norman, and William B. Bell. 1979. "Transportation for the Elderly and the Handicapped: An Overview from the Late 70s." *Transportation Planning and Technology* 5: 71–78.

Astracham, Boris. 1978. "Changing Institutional Direction: The Connecticut Mental Health Center." In *Innovation and Implementation in Public Organizations*, ed. Richard R. Nelson and Douglas Yates. Lexington, Mass.: Lexington Books.

Bachrach, Peter, and Morton S. Baritz. 1979. *Power and Poverty*. New York: Oxford University Press.

Baer, Judith A. 1983. *Equality under the Constitution: Reclaiming the Fourteenth Amendment*. Ithaca, N.Y.: Cornell University Press.

Select Bibliography

Bailey, Stephen K., and Edith K. Mosher. 1968. *ESEA: The Office of Education Administers a Law*. Syracuse, N.Y.: Syracuse University Press.

Ballard, Joseph, Bruce A. Ramirez, and Frederick J. Weintraub, eds. 1982. *Special Education in America: Its Legal and Governmental Foundations*. Reston, Va: Council for Exceptional Children.

Bardach, Eugene. 1977. *The Implementation Game*. Cambridge: MIT Press.

Bardach, Eugene, and Robert A. Kagan. 1982. *Going by the Book: The Problem of Regulatory Unreasonableness*. Philadelphia: Temple University Press.

Bayh, Birch. 1978. "Forward to the Symposium Issue on Employment Rights of the Handicapped." *DePaul Law Review* 27: 943–52.

Begg, Robert T. 1979. "Disabled Libraries: An Examination of Physical and Attitudinal Barriers to Handicapped Library Users." *Law Library Journal* 72 (Summer): 513–25.

Behr, Peter, and Joanne Omang. 1981. "White House Targets 27 More Regulations for Review." *Washington Post*, March 6, A1.

Bell, Christopher G., and Robert L. Burgdorf, Jr. 1983. *Accommodating the Spectrum of Individual Abilities*. Washington, D.C.: U.S. Civil Rights Commission.

Bell, William G., and Robert S. Bell. 1979. "Stockholm's Transport for Elderly and Handicapped: An Integrated Model." *Transportation Planning and Technology* 5: 79–86.

Berkeley Planning Associates. 1982. *A Study of Accommodations Provided to Handicapped Employees by Federal Contractors: Final Report*. Vol. 1, *Study Findings*. Washington, D.C.: U.S. Department of Labor, Employer Standards Administration.

Berkowitz, Edward D. 1979. *Disability Policies and Government Programs*. New York: Praeger.

———. 1987. *Disability Policy: America's Programs for the Handicapped*. Cambridge, England: Cambridge University Press.

Berman, Paul. 1978. "The Study of Macro- and Micro-Implementation." *Public Policy* 26, no. 2 (Spring): 157–84.

Bernstein, Marver H. 1955. *Regulating Business by Independent Commission*. Princeton, N.J.: Princeton University Press.

Berry, Jeffrey M. 1977. *Lobbying for the People: The Political Behavior of Public Interest Groups*. Princeton, N.J.: Princeton University Press.

———. 1984. *Feeding Hungry People: Rulemaking in the Food Stamp Program*. New Brunswick, N.J.: Rutgers University Press.

Beyer, Henry A. 1983. "A Free Appropriate Public Education." *Western New England Law Review* 5: 363–90.

Blennemann, Friedhelm, and Ewald Pajonk. 1979. "An Evaluation of Additional Costs for Making Transportation Accessible to the Handicapped." *Transportation Planning and Technology* 5: 105–14.

Boettner, Karl. 1983. "Attack on EHA: The Education for All Handicapped Children Act after *Board of Education v. Rowley*." *University of Puget Sound Law Review* 7 (Fall): 183–210.

Bogdan, Robert, and Douglas Biklen. 1981. "Handicapism." In *Rehabilitating People with Disabilities into the Mainstream of Society*, ed. Allen D. Spiegel and Simon Podair. Park Ridge, N.J.: Noyes Medical Publications.

Select Bibliography

Boodman, Sandra G. 1988. "Reagan Accepts AIDS Panel Report." *Washington Post*, June 28, A3.

Bowe, Frank G. 1978. *Handicapping America: Barriers to Disabled People*. New York: Harper and Row.

———. 1980a. "An Overview Paper on Civil Rights Issues of Handicapped Americans: Public Policy Implications." In *Civil Rights Issues of Handicapped Americans: Public Policy Implications*. Consultation sponsored by the U.S. Commission on Civil Rights, May 7–18. Washington, D.C.

———. 1980b. *Rehabilitating America: Toward Independence for Disabled and Elderly People*. New York: Harper and Row.

Bower, Eli M., ed. 1980. *The Handicapped in Literature: A Psychological Perspective*. Denver: Love Publishing.

Brattgard, Sven-Olof. 1979. "Vehicles and Systems for Transportation of Disabled." *Transportation Planning and Technology* 5: 87–98.

Brewer, Garry D., and James S. Kakalik. 1979. *Handicapped Children: Strategies for Improving Services*. New York: McGraw-Hill.

Brown, Lawrence, and Bernard J. Frieden. 1976. "Rulemaking by Improvisation." *Policy Sciences* 7, no. 4 (December): 455–88.

Browne, Angela, and Aaron Wildavsky. 1984. "Implementation as Mutual Evolution." In *Implementation*, Jeffery L. Pressman and Aaron Wildavsky, 206–31. 3d ed. Berkeley: University of California Press.

Bryner, Gary. 1981. "Congress, Courts, and Agencies: Equal Employment and the Limits of Policy Implementation." *Political Science Quarterly* 96, no. 3 (Fall): 411–30.

Buress, Charles. 1983. "Fending off Attacks on Rights of Disabled: 'We are Still Watching.'" *San Francisco Examiner*, May 25, F4.

Burgdorf, Robert L., Jr., 1980. *The Legal Rights of Handicapped Persons: Cases, Materials and Text*. Baltimore: Brookes Publishers.

Burgdorf, Robert L., Jr., and Christopher G. Bell. 1984. "Eliminating Discrimination against Physically and Mentally Handicapped Persons: A Statutory Blueprint." *Mental and Physical Disability Law Reporter* 8 (January/February): 64–75.

Burgdorf, Robert L., Jr., and Marcia Pearce Burgdorf. 1977. "The Wicked Witch Is Almost Dead: *Buck v. Bell* and the Sterilization of Handicapped Persons." *Temple Law Quarterly* 50: 995–1033.

Butler, Daniel P. 1980. "*Southeastern Community College v. Davis*, Section 504, and Handicapped Rights." *California Western Law Review* 16: 523–55.

Buturla, Richard J. 1982. "The Handicapped Child's Right to a Free Appropriate Education: Defining the Limits of Responsibility." *Villanova Law Review* 27: 566–94.

Calabresi, Guido, and Philip Bobbitt. 1978. *Tragic Choices*. New York: W. W. Norton.

Califano, Joseph. 1981. *Governing America*. New York: Simon and Schuster.

Cannon, Dennis M. 1978. "Design Criteria for Transportation for Disabled People." Northridge, Calif.: In-Transit Communications.

———. 1980. "A Funny Thing Happened on the Way to the Bus Stop: Transportation and the Handicapped." In *Civil Rights Issues of Handicapped Americans: Public Policy Implementation*. Consultation sponsored by the U.S. Commission on Civil Rights, May 13–16. Washington, D.C.

Select Bibliography

Cannon, Dennis M., and Frances Rainbow. 1980. *Full Mobility: Counting the Costs of Alternatives*. Washington, D.C.: American Coalition of Citizens with Disability.

Cater, Douglass. 1964. *Power in Washington: A Critical Look at Today's Struggle to Govern in the Nation's Capital*. New York: Random House.

Cater, Morrow. 1982. "Trimming the Disability Rolls—Changing the Rules During the Game?" *National Journal* 14, no. 36 (September 4): 1512–14.

Clark, Timothy B. 1978. "Access for the Handicapped—A Test of Carter's War on Inflation." *National Journal* 10 (October 21): 1672–75.

———. 1980. "Regulation Gone Amok: How Many Billions for Wheelchair Transit?" *Regulation*, March/April, 47–52.

———. 1981a. "Here's One 'Midnight Regulation' That's Slipped through Reagan's Net." *National Journal* 13 (February 7): 221–24.

———. 1981b. "How to Survive in Government." *National Journal* 13 (October 3): 1776.

———. 1981c. "If Reagan Wants to Tromp the Regulators, Here's OMB's Target List for Openers." *National Journal* 13 (January 17): 94–98.

———. 1986. "Disability Power." *National Journal* 18 (October 25): 595.

Cobb, Roger W., and Charles D. Elder. 1983a. *Participation in American Politics: The Dynamics of Agenda-Building*. 2d ed. Baltimore: Johns Hopkins University Press.

———. 1983b. *The Political Uses of Symbols*. New York: Longman.

Cohen, Marie Prince. 1980. "Discrimination on the Basis of Handicap: The Status of Section 504 of the Rehabilitation Act of 1973." *Iowa Law Review* 65: 446–67.

Congressional Quarterly. 1982. *Regulation: Process and Politics*. Washington, D.C.: Congressional Quarterly.

Cook, Timothy M., and Frank J. Laski. 1980. "Beyond *Davis*: Equality of Opportunity for Higher Education for Disabled Students under the Rehabilitation Act of 1973." *Harvard Civil Rights–Civil Liberties Law Review* 15: 415–73.

Cooper, Charles J. 1986. *Application of Section 504 of the Rehabilitation Act to Persons with AIDS, AIDS-Related Complex, or Infection with AIDS Virus*. Memorandum for Ronald E. Robertson, general counsel, Department of Health and Human Services, June 20. Washington, D.C.: U.S. Department of Justice, Office of Legal Counsel.

Cremins, James J. 1983. *Legal and Political Issues in Special Education*. Springfield, Ill.: Charles C. Thomas.

Daneke, Gregory A., and David J. Lemak. 1985. *Regulatory Reform Reconsidered*. Boulder, Colo.: Westview Press.

Davidson, Roger H. 1977. "Breaking Up Those 'Cozy Triangles': An Impossible Dream?" In *Legislative Reform and Public Policy*, ed. Susan Welch and John J. Peters, 30–53. New York: Praeger.

Davis, Kenneth Culp. 1969. *Discretionary Justice: A Preliminary Inquiry*. Urbana: University of Illinois Press.

Demkovich, Linda E. 1984. "Administration About-Face on Disability Could Be a Political Blessing in Disguise." *National Journal* 16, no. 17 (July 28): 823–25.

Derthick, Martha. 1972. *New Towns In-Town*. Washington, D.C.: Urban Institute.

Derthick, Martha, and Paul J. Quirk. 1985. *The Politics of Deregulation*. Washington, D.C.: Brookings Institution.

Select Bibliography

DeWitt, Karen. 1973. "Education Report: Handicapped School-Children Enmeshed in Debate on Federal Role in Education." *National Journal* 5, no. 6 (February 10): 199–205.

Disability Rights and Education Defense Fund. 1983. *Draft Analysis of DOL Revisions of Section 504*. Berkeley, Calif.: Disability Rights and Education Defense Fund.

Dodd, Lawrence C., and Richard L. Schott. 1979. *Congress and the Administrative State*. New York: John Wiley and Sons.

Downs, Anthony. 1967. *Inside Bureaucracy*. Boston: Little, Brown.

———. 1972. "Up and Down with Ecology—the 'Issue-Attention Cycle.'" *The Public Interest* 28 (Summer): 38–50.

Dunsire, Andrew. 1978. *Implementation in a Bureaucracy*. New York: St. Martin's.

E. I. DuPont de Nemours and Company. 1982. *Equal to the Task*. Wilmington, Del.: E. I. Dupont de Nemours and Company.

Durant, Robert F. 1985. *When Government Regulates Itself: EPA, TVA, and Pollution Control in the 1970s*. Knoxville: University of Tennessee Press.

Eads, George C., and Michael Fix. 1984. *Relief or Reform: Reagan's Regulatory Dilemma*. Washington, D.C.: Urban Institute.

Ebert, Constance J. 1982. "Accessibility Legislation for the Handicapped: Is It Enabling or Disabling?" *Journal of Legislation* 9: 118–26.

Edwards, George E., III. 1980. *Implementing Public Policy*. Washington, D.C.: Congressional Quarterly.

Edelman, Murray. 1964. *The Symbolic Uses of Politics*. Urbana: University of Illinois Press.

Education Turnkey Systems. 1981. *P.L. 94-142: A Study of the Implementation and the Impact at the State Level*. Final Report. Falls Church, Va.: Education Turnkey Systems.

Eisenberger, Myron G., Cynthia Griggins, and Richard J. Duval, eds. 1982. *Disabled People as Second Class Citizens*. New York: Springer.

Elliott, Timothy R., and Keith Byrd. 1982. "Media and Disability." *Rehabilitation Literature* 43, no. 11–12: 348–55.

Ellner, Jack R., and Henry E. Bender. 1980. *Hiring the Handicapped*. American Management Association Report. New York: Amacom.

Elmore, Richard F. 1982. "Backward Mapping: Implementation Research and Policy Decisions." In *Studying Implementation: Methodological and Administrative Issues*, ed. Walter Williams et al. Chatham, N.J.: Chatham House.

Engebretson, Mark F. 1979. "Administrative Action to End Discrimination Based on Handicap: HEW's Section 504 Regulation." *Harvard Journal on Legislation* 16: 59–89.

English, William R. 1971. "Correlates of Stigma toward Physically Disabled Persons." *Rehabilitation Research and Practice Review* 2: 1–17.

Ethridge, Marcus E. 1985. *Legislative Participation in Implementation: Policy through Politics*. New York: Praeger.

Farber, Alan J. 1975. "The Handicapped Plead for Entrance—Will Anyone Answer?" *Kentucky Law Review* 64: 99–113.

Select Bibliography

Fielding, Gordon J. 1982. "Transportation for the Handicapped: The Politics of Full Accessibility." *Transportation Quarterly* 36, no. 2 (April): 269–82.

Fiorina, Morris P. 1981. "Congressional Control of the Bureaucracy: A Mismatch of Incentives and Capabilities." In *Congress Reconsidered*, ed. Lawrence C. Dodd and Bruce J. Oppenheimer. 2d ed. Washington, D.C.: Congressional Quarterly.

Fix, Michael, Carol Everett, and Ronald Kirby. 1985. *Providing Public Transportation to the Disabled: Local Responses to Evolving Federal Policies.* Washington, D.C.: Urban Institute.

Forsyth, Thomas L. 1981. "Protections for the Handicapped in Federally Financed Programs and *Southeastern Community College v. Davis.*" *Southern California Law Review* 54: 1053–73.

Foster, Wayne K. 1980. *Impact of PL94-142 on Local Education Agencies: Administrator's Response.* Technical Report. Batesville: Arkansas College.

Freeman, J. Leiper. 1965. *The Political Process.* New York: Random House.

Gambitta, Richard A. L., Marilyn L. May, and James C. Foster, eds. 1981. *Governing through Courts.* Beverly Hills: Sage.

Gerse, Steven W. 1982. "Mending the Rehabilitation Act of 1973." *University of Illinois Law Review* 1982: 701–30.

Gliedman, John, and William Roth. 1980. *The Unexpected Minority: Handicapped Children in America.* New York: Harcourt, Brace, and Jovanovich.

Goffman, Erving. 1963. *Stigma: Notes on the Management of Spoiled Identity.* New York: Prentice-Hall.

Goggin, Malcolm L. 1987. *Policy Design and the Politics of Implementation: The Case of Child Health Care in the American States.* Knoxville: University of Tennessee Press.

Goldman, Charles D. 1983. "Architectural Barriers: A Perspective on Progress." *Western New England Law Review* 85, no. 3 (Winter): 465–93.

―――. 1987. *Disability Rights Guide: Practical Solutions to Problems Affecting Persons with Disabilities.* Lincoln, Nebr.: Media Publishing.

Goodrich, James A. 1981. "Optimizing under CETA: Program Design, Implementation Problems, and Local Agencies." In *Implementing Public Policy*, ed. Dennis J. Palumbo and Marvin A. Harder, 45–54. Lexington, Mass.: Lexington Books.

Gormley, William T., Jr. 1983. *The Politics of Public Utility Regulation.* Pittsburgh: University of Pittsburgh Press.

Green, Mark J., Beverly C. Moore, Jr., and Bruce Wasserstein. 1972. *The Closed Enterprise System: Ralph Nader's Study Group on Anti-Trust Enforcement.* New York: Grossman.

Grey Advertising. 1980. "Summary Report of a Survey of Transportation of Handicapped Users and Non-Users of Special Transportation Systems." Washington, D.C.: U.S. Department of Transportation, Urban Mass Transit Administration.

Guy, Jana H. 1979. "Accommodations for the Handicapped—What Is the Employer's Duty?" *Employee Relations Law Journal* 5, no. 3: 350–68.

Hammond, Thomas. 1986. "Agenda Control, Organizational Structure, and Bureaucratic Policies." *American Journal of Political Science* 30, no. 2 (May): 379–410.

285

Select Bibliography

Hargrove, Edwin C. 1985. *The Missing Link: The Study of the Implementation of Social Policy*. Washington, D.C.: Urban Institute.

Harris, Joseph P. 1964. *Congressional Control of Administration*. Washington, D.C.: Brookings Institution.

Harris, Robert M., and A. Christine Harris. 1977. "A New Perspective on the Psychological Effects of Environmental Barriers." *Rehabilitation Literature* 38 (March): 75–78.

Hartman, Chester A. 1984. *The Transformation of San Francisco*. Totowa, N.J.: Rowman and Allanhand.

Having, Marilyn, and Lee Meyerson. 1981. "Attitudes of College Students toward Sexual Behavior of Disabled Persons." In *Rehabilitating People with Disabilities into the Mainstream of Society*, ed. Allen D. Spiegel and Simon Podair. Park Ridge, N.J.: Noyes Medical Publications.

Heclo, Hugh. 1978. "Issue Networks and the Executive Establishment." In *The New American Political System*, ed. Anthony King, 87–124. Washington, D.C.: American Enterprise Institute.

Henry, Laura C. 1983. "Crippling the Education for All Handicapped Children Act." *Stetson Law Review* 12 (Spring): 791–813.

Heumann, Judith. 1980. "Social Services and Disabled Persons." In *Civil Rights Issues of Handicapped Americans: Public Policy Implications*. Consultation sponsored by the U.S. Commission on Civil Rights, May 13–16. Washington, D.C.

Hippolitus, Paul. 1985. *College-Bound Freshmen with Disabilities Preparing for Employment: A Statistical Profile*. Washington, D.C.: President's Committee on Employment of the Handicapped and the American Council on Education.

Holden, Matthew, Jr. 1966. "Imperialism in Bureaucracy." *American Political Science Review* 60 (December): 943–51.

Horowitz, Donald L. 1977. *The Courts and Social Policy*. Washington, D.C.: Brookings Institution.

Hourihan, John P. 1981. *Disability: The College's Challenge*. New York: Teachers College, Columbia University.

Houston, John R. 1979. "Defining the Rights of the Handicapped under Section 504 of the Rehabilitation Act of 1973: *Southeastern Community College v. Davis*." *Saint Louis University Law Journal* 24: 159–76.

Howard, Irving, Henry P. Brehm, and Saad Nagi. 1980. *Disability: From Social Problem to Federal Program*. New York: Praeger.

Hull, Kent. 1979. *The Rights of Physically Handicapped People*. New York: Avon.

Huntington, Samuel P. 1952. "The Marasmus of the ICC." *Yale Law Journal* 61 (April): 467–509.

Hyatt, Sheila K. 1981. "Litigating the Rights of Handicapped Children to an Appropriate Education: Procedures and Remedies." *UCLA Law Review* 29: 1–67.

Hyder, Masood. 1984. "Implementation: The Evolutionary Model." In *Policies into Practice: National and International Case Studies in Implementation*, ed. David Lewis and Helen Wallace. London: Heinemann Educational Books.

Ingram, Helen. 1977. "Policy Implementation through Bargaining: The Case of Federal Grants-in-Aid." *Public Policy* 25, no. 4 (Fall): 499–526.

Select Bibliography

International Center for the Disabled and the National Council on the Handicapped. 1986. *Bringing Disabled Americans into the Mainstream: A Nationwide Survey of 1,000 Disabled People*. Washington, D.C.

International Center for the Disabled, National Council on the Handicapped, President's Committee on Employment of the Handicapped. 1987. *Employing Disabled Americans*. Washington, D.C.

Isbell, Florence. 1977. "How the Handicapped Won Their Rights." *Civil Liberties Review*, November/December, 61–65.

Jackson, Raymond. 1982. "The Cost and Quality of Paratransit Services for the Elderly and Handicapped." *Transportation Quarterly* 36, no. 4 (October): 527–40.

Jamero, Peter M. 1979. "Handicapped Individuals in the Changing Workforce." *Journal of Contemporary Business* 8, no. 4: 33–41.

James, Dorothy B. 1974. *The Contemporary Presidency*. 2d ed. Indianapolis: Bobbs-Merrill.

Johnson, Charles A., and Bradley C. Cannon. 1984. *Judicial Policies: Implementation and Impact*. Washington, D.C.: Congressional Quarterly Press.

Jones, Charles O. 1977. *An Introduction to the Study of Public Policy*. 2d ed. North Scituate, Mass.: Duxbury.

Jones, Charles O., and Richard D. Thomas. eds. 1976. *Public Policy Making in a Federal System*. Beverly Hills: Sage.

Jones, Nancy Lee. 1982. *Analysis of Proposed Changes in Regulations Promulgated under Section 504 of the Rehabilitation Act of 1973*. Washington, D.C.: U.S. Library of Congress, Congressional Research Service.

Jones, Philip R. 1981. *A Practical Guide to Federal Special Education Law: Understanding and Implementing PL 94-142*. New York: Holt, Rinehart and Winston.

Kamen, Al. 1986. "Court Strikes Down 'Baby Doe' Rules." *Washington Post*, June 10, 1.

Katzmann, Robert A. 1980. *Regulatory Bureaucracy: The Federal Trade Commission and Antitrust Policy*. Cambridge: MIT Press.

———. 1986. *Institutional Disability: The Saga of Transportation Policy for the Disabled*. Washington, D.C.: Brookings Institution.

Kettl, Donald F. 1983. *The Regulation of American Federalism*. Baton Rouge: Louisiana State University Press.

Kingdon, John W. 1984. *Agendas, Alternatives, and Public Policies*. Boston: Little, Brown.

Kleinfield, Sonny. 1979. *The Hidden Minority: A Profile of Handicapped Americans*. Boston: Little, Brown.

Koch, Edward I. 1980. "The Mandate Millstone." *The Public Interest*. 61 (Fall): 42–57.

Kriegel, Leonard. 1969. "Uncle Tom and Tiny Tim: Some Reflections on the Cripple as Negro." *The American Scholar* 38, no. 4 (Autumn): 412–30.

Kroll, Shelley A. 1983. "Defining an Appropriate Education for Handicapped Children: *Board of Education v. Rowley*." *Syracuse Law Review* 34 (Fall): 1107–30.

Kurtz, Howard. 1985a. "Eliminating Job Goals Proposed." *Washington Post*, August 15, A1.

Select Bibliography

———. 1985b. "Reynolds' Nomination Voted Down." *Washington Post*, June 28, A1.

———. 1986. "Minority Hiring Battle Illustrates Policy Stalemate." *Washington Post*, January 11, A3.

Kurtz, Howard, and Peter Perl. 1985. "Brock May Lose Authority over Affirmative Action." *Washington Post*, October 11, A2.

Kuzma, Abigail Lawlis. 1984. "The Legislative Response to Infant Doe." *Indiana Law Journal* 59: 377–416.

Lander, Daryl A. 1979. "*Holland v. Boeing Co.*: Accommodating Handicapped Employees." *Williamette Law Review* 16: 153–63.

Lando, Mordechai E., Richard Cutler, and Edward Gamber. 1982. *The 1978 Survey of Disability and Work: Data Book*. Washington, D.C.: Social Security Administration, U.S. Department of Health and Human Services.

Larson, James S. 1980. *Why Government Programs Fail: Improving Polity Implementation*. New York: Praeger.

LaVor, Martin L. 1980. "Commentary; Section 504: Past, Present, and Future." *Archives of Physical Medicine and Rehabilitation* 61 (June): 36–40.

Levin, Martin A., and Barbara Ferman. 1985. *The Political Hand: Policy Implementation and Youth Employment Programs*. New York: Pergamon.

Levine, Erwin L., and Elizabeth Wexler. 1981. *PL94-142: An Act of Congress*. New York: Macmillan.

Linn, Brian J. 1978. "Uncle Sam Doesn't Want You: Entering the Federal Stronghold of Employment Discrimination against Handicapped Individuals." *DePaul Law Review* 27: 1047–88.

Lippman, Leopold D. 1972. *Attitudes toward the Handicapped: A Comparison between Europe and the United States*. Springfield, Ill.: Charles C. Thomas.

Lippman, Leopold D., and I. Ignacy Goldberg. 1973. *Right to Education: Anatomy of the Pennsylvania Case and Its Implications for Exceptional Children*. New York: Teachers College Press, Columbia University.

Lipsky, Michael. 1978. "Standing the Study of Public Policy Implementation on Its Head." In *American Politics and Public Policy*, ed. Walter D. Burnham and Martha D. Weinberg. Cambridge: MIT Press.

Litan, Robert E., and William D. Nordhaus. 1983. *Reforming Federal Regulation*. New Haven, Conn.: Yale University Press.

Livneh, Hanoch. 1982. "On the Origins of Negative Attitudes toward People with Disabilities." *Rehabilitation Literature* 43, no. 11–12: 338–47.

London, Alice L. 1986. "Transportation Services for the Disabled: A Complex Public Policy Issue." *GAO Review* 21, no. 2 (Spring): 21–27.

Lucas, Ronald E. 1975. "Why It's Good Business to Hire the Handicapped." *Occupational Hazards*, March, 61–62.

Lublin, Joann S. 1976. "Lowering Barriers: Pressured Companies Decide the Disabled Can Handle More Jobs." *Wall Street Journal*, January 27, 1.

McDermitt, George M., and Linda McDermitt, eds. 1979. *The Handicapped Experience: Some Humanistic Perspectives*. Baltimore: University of Baltimore.

Mace, Ronald. 1980. "Physical Facilities and the Handicapped." In *Civil Rights Issues of Handicapped Americans: Public Policy Implications*. Consultation sponsored by the U.S. Commission on Civil Rights, May 13–16. Washington, D.C.

Majone, Giandomenico, and Aaron Wildavsky. 1984. "Implementation as Evolution." In *Implementation*, Jeffrey L. Pressman and Aaron Wildavsky, 163–80. 3d ed. Berkeley: University of California Press.

Management Analysis Center. 1977. *Assessing State Information Capabilities under PL94-142*. Washington, D.C.: Management Analysis Center.

Mansfield, Stephen A. 1982. "Defining an 'Appropriaate Education' under the Education for All Handicapped Children Act of 1975." *Maine Law Review* 34: 79–110.

Martin, Reed. 1979. *Educating Handicapped Children: The Legal Mandate*. Champaign, Ill.: Research Press.

Mazmanian, Daniel A., and Paul L. Sabatier. 1981. *Effective Policy Implementation*. Lexington, Mass.: Lexington Books.

———. 1983. *Implementation and Public Policy*. Glenview, Ill.: Scott, Foresman.

Meier, Kenneth J. 1985. *Regulation: Politics, Bureaucracy, and Economics*. New York: St. Martin's.

Meyer, John R., and Jose A. Gomez-Ibanez. 1981. *Autos, Transit and Cities*. Cambridge: Harvard University Press.

Michaux, Louis Arthur. 1970. *The Physically Handicapped and the Community*. Springfield, Ill.: Charles C. Thomas.

Milbrath, Lester W. 1963. *The Washington Lobbyists*. Westport, Conn.: Greenwood.

Milk, Leslie B. 1980. "Out of Sight, Out of Mind, Out of Work." In *Civil Rights Issues of Handicapped Americans: Public Policy Implications*. Consultation sponsored by the U.S. Commission on Civil Rights, May 13–16. Washington, D.C.

Miller, Darvin L., and Marilee A. Miller. 1978. "The Handicapped Child's Civil Right as It Relates to the 'Least Restrictive Environment' and Appropriate Mainstreaming." *Indiana Law Journal* 54, no. 1: 1–28.

Miller, James C., III, and Jeffery A. Eisenach. 1981. "Regulatory Reform under Ronald Reagan." In *The Future under President Reagan*, ed. Wayne Valis. Westport, Conn.: Arlington House.

Mitchell, Thomas J. 1976. "Comment: Mass Transportation for the Handicapped and the Elderly." *Detroit College of Law Review* 2: 277–91.

Mithaug, Dennis E. 1979. "Negative Employer Attitudes toward Hiring the Handicapped: Fact or Fiction?" *Journal of Contemporary Business* 8, no. 4: 19–26.

Mitnik, Barry M. 1980. *The Political Economy of Regulation*. New York: Columbia University Press.

Montjoy, Robert S., and Laurence C. O'Toole, Jr. 1979. "Toward a Theory of Policy Implementation: An Organizational Perspective." *Public Administration Review* 39, no. 1 (September/October): 465–76.

Motsco, Martha A. 1985. "The *Burlington* Decision: A Vehicle to Enforce Free Appropriate Education for the Handicapped." *Akron Law Review* 19 (Fall): 277–94.

Murphy, Jerome T. 1971. "Title I of ESEA: The Politics of Implementing Federal Education Reform." *Harvard Educational Review* 1 (February): 35–63.

———. 1976. "Title V of ESEA: The Impact of Discretionary Funds on State Education Bureaucracies." In *Social Program Implementation*, ed. Walter Williams and Richard F. Elmore. New York: Academic Press.

Murphy, Michael J., Nancy T. Stark, and Betty L. Cheatham. 1981. *Beyond Paternalism: Local Governments and Rights of the Disabled*. Management Information Service Special Report. Washington, D.C.: International City Management Association.

Murphy, Russell D. 1971. *Political Entrepreneurs and Urban Poverty*. Lexington, Mass.: Lexington Books.

Nakamura, Robert T., and Frank Smallwood. 1980. *The Politics of Policy Implementation*. New York: St. Martin's.

Nathanson, Robert B. 1980. "Campus Interactions: Attitudes and Behaviors." In *Disability: The College's Challenge*, ed. John P. Hourihan. New York: Teachers College, Columbia University.

———. 1981. "The Disabled Employee: Separating Myth from Fact." In *Rehabilitating People with Disabilities into the Mainstream of Society*, ed. Allen D. Spiegel and Simon Podair. Park Ridge, N.J.: Noyes Medical Publications.

National Association of College and University Business Officers. 1981. *Management of Accessibility for Handicapped Students in Higher Education*. Washington, D.C.: NACUBO.

National Center for Law and the Deaf. 1982. *Legal Rights of Hearing-Impaired People*. Washington, D.C.: Gallaudet College Press.

National Council on the Handicapped. 1988. *On the Threshold of Independence*. Washington, D.C.: National Commission on the Handicapped.

National Education Association. 1978. *Education for All Handicapped Children: Consensus, Conflict, and Challenge: A Study Report*. Washington, D.C.: National Education Association.

National Federation of the Blind. 1979. *Why Section 504: Discrimination against the Blind in Employment: A Case Review*. Baltimore: National Center for the Blind.

National School Board Association. 1979. *A Survey of Special Education Costs in Local School Districts*. Washington, D.C.: National School Board Association.

Navin, Francis P. 1979. "Productivity of Vehicle Transport for the Elderly and Handicapped." *Transportation Planning and Technology* 5: 99–104.

Nelson, Richard R., and Douglas Yates. 1978. *Innovation and Implementation in Public Organizations*. Lexington, Mass.: Lexington Books.

Niskanen, William A., Jr. 1971. *Bureaucracy and Representative Government*. Chicago: Aldine-Atherton.

Noll, Roger G., ed. 1985. *Regulatory Policy and the Social Sciences*. Berkeley: University of California Press.

Noll, Roger G., and Bruce M. Owen, eds. 1983. *The Political Economy of Deregulation: Interest Groups in the Regulatory Process*. Washington, D.C.: American Enterprise Institute.

Ogul, Morris S. 1976. *Congress Oversees the Bureaucracy: Studies in Legislative Supervision*. Pittsburgh: University of Pittsburgh Press.

———. 1981. "Congressional Oversight: Structures and Incentives." In *Congress Reconsidered*, ed. Lawrence C. Dodd and Bruce J. Oppenheimer. 2d ed. Washington, D.C.: Congressional Quarterly Press.

Olenick, Donald J. 1980. "Accommodating the Handicapped: Rehabilitating Section 504 after *Southeastern.*" *Columbia Law Review* 80: 171–91.

Pacquette, Suzan. 1976. "Hiring the Handicapped: Fact and Fantasy." *The Labour Gazette*, April, 184–88.

Palumbo, Dennis J., and Marvin A. Harder. 1981. *Implementing Public Policy*. Lexington, Mass.: Lexington Books.

Pati, Gopal C. 1981. "Countdown on Hiring the Handicapped." In *Rehabilitating People with Disabilities into the Mainstream of Society*, ed. Allen D. Spiegel and Simon Podair. Park Ridge, N.J.: Noyes Medical Publications.

Pati, Gopal C., and John I. Adkins, Jr. 1980. "Hire the Handicapped—Compliance Is Good Business." *Harvard Business Review*, January/February, 14–21.

Pati, Gopal C., John I. Adkins, Jr., and Glenn Morrison. 1981. *Managing and Employing the Handicapped: The Untapped Potential*. Lake Forest, Ill.: Brace-Park/Human Resources Press.

Peltzman, Sam. 1976. "Toward a More General Theory of Regulation." *Journal of Law and Economics* 19 (August): 211–40.

Polsby, Nelson W. 1984. *Political Innovation in America: The Politics of Policy Initiation*. New Haven, Conn.: Yale University Press.

Presidential Commission on the Human Immunodeficiency Virus Epidemic. 1988. *Report of the Presidential Commission on the Human Immunodeficiency Virus Epidemic*. Washington, D.C.

Pressman, Jeffrey L., and Aaron Wildavsky. 1984. *Implementation*. 3d ed. Berkeley: University of California Press.

"Protecting the Handicapped From Employment Discrimination in Private Sector Employment: A Critical Analysis of Section 503 of the Rehabilitation Act of 1973." *Tulane Law Review* 54 (1980): 717–56.

Quirk, Paul J. 1981. *Industry Influence in Federal Regulatory Agencies*. Princeton, N.J.: Princeton University Press.

Rabkin, Jeremy. 1980. "Office for Civil Rights." In *The Politics of Regulation*, ed. James Q. Wilson. New York: Basic Books.

Radin, Beryl A. 1977. *Implementation, Change, and the Federal Bureaucracy: School Desegregation Policy in H.E.W., 1964–1968*. New York: Teachers College, Columbia University.

Reed, Gale Norton. 1977. "Equal Access to Mass Transportation for the Handicapped." *Transportation Law Journal* 9: 167–87.

Regens, James L., and Robert W. Rycroft. 1986. "Measuring Equity in Regulatory Policy Implementation." *Public Administration Review* 46, no. 5 (September/October): 423–31.

Rein, Martin, and Francine F. Rabinowitz. 1978. "Implementation: A Theoretical Perspective." In *American Politics and Public Policy*, ed. Walter D. Burnham and Martha D. Weinberg. Cambridge: MIT Press.

Research Triangle Institute. 1980. *A National Survey of Individualized Education Programs (IEPs) for Handicapped Children*. Research Triangle Park, N.C.: Research Triangle Institute.

Ripley, Randall B. 1975. *Congress: Process and Policy*. New York: W. W. Norton.

Ripley, Randall B., and Grace A. Franklin. 1986. *Policy Implementation and Bureaucracy.* 2d ed. Chicago: Dorsey.

Roach, Randy. 1978. "The Least Restrictive Environment Section of the Education for All Handicapped Children Act of 1975: A Legislative History and an Analysis." *Gonzaga Law Review* 13: 717–79.

Rodgers, Harrell R., Jr., and Charles S. Bullock III. 1972. *Law and Social Change: Civil Rights Laws and Their Consequences.* New York: McGraw-Hill.

Rosenthal, Alan. 1981. "Legislative Behavior and Legislative Oversight." *Legislative Studies Quarterly* 6 (February): 115–31.

Rosenthal, Stephen R., and Edith S. Levine. 1980. "Case Management and Policy Implementation." *Public Policy* 28, no. 4 (Fall): 381–413.

Rothstein, Laura F. 1984. *Rights of Physically Handicapped Persons.* Colorado Springs: Shepard's/McGraw Hill.

Roy Littlejohn Associates. 1978. *For a Study of Teacher Concerns with PL 94-142.* Final Report. Washington, D.C.: Roy Littlejohn Associates.

Rutherglen, George. 1983. *Major Issues in the Federal Law of Employment Discrimination.* Washington, D.C.: Federal Judicial Center.

———. 1985. *Major Issues in the Federal Law of Employment Discrimination: Supplement and Table of Authorities.* Washington, D.C.: Federal Judicial Center.

Sabatier, Paul, and Daniel Mazmanian. 1979. "The Conditions of Effective Implementation: A Guide to Accomplishing Policy Objectives." *Public Policy.*

Savage, David G. 1982. "Parents Boo Reagan's Plan for Handicapped Children." *Los Angeles Times*, September 24, 3.

Scheingold, Stuart A. 1974. *The Politics of Rights: Lawyers, Public Policy, and Political Change.* New Haven, Conn.: Yale University Press.

Schenck, Susan J., and William K. Levy. 1979. *IEPs: The State of the Art in Connecticut.* Hightstown, N.J.: Northeast Regional Resource Center.

Schipper, William, and William Wilson. 1978. *Implementation of Individualized Education Programming: Some Observations and Recommendations.* Washington, D.C.: National Association of State Directors of Special Education.

Schroedel, John G. 1979. *Attitudes toward Persons with Disabilities: A Compendium of Related Research.* Albertson, N.Y.: Human Resource Center.

Schroedel, John G., and Richard J. Jacobsen. 1978. *Employer Attitudes toward Hiring Persons with Disabilities.* Albertson, N.Y.: Human Resource Center.

Schroeder, Steven, and Edward Steinfeld. 1979. *The Estimated Cost of Accessible Buildings.* Washington, D.C.: U.S. Department of Housing and Urban Development, Office of Policy Development and Research.

Schuck, Peter H. 1980. "The Graying of Civil Rights Law." *The Public Interest* 60 (Summer): 69–93.

Schwartz, Gail. 1984. "Disability Costs: The Impending Crisis." *Business and Health*, May.

Schwartz, Terry A., et al. 1979. *The Relationship of Elementary Classroom Teachers' Perceptions of Job Satisfaction and Role in Implementing P.L. 94-142 to Their Degree of Alienation: Implications for In-Service Training.* Final Report. Charlottesville, Va.: Bureau of Educational Research.

Select Bibliography

Scotch, Richard K. 1984. *From Good Will to Civil Rights: Transforming Federal Disability Policy*. Philadelphia: Temple University Press.

Seifert, Karl H. 1981. "The Attitudes of Working People toward Disabled Persons, Especially in Regards to Vocational Rehabilitation." In *Rehabilitating People with Disabilities into the Mainstream of Society*, ed. Allen D. Spiegel and Simon Podair. Park Ridge, N.J.: Noyes Medical Publications.

Servedio, William. 1979. "Eliminating Mobility Barriers in Recreational Areas and Facililties." *Parks and Recreation* 14 (November): 69–72.

Shane, Peter M. 1981. "Presidential Regulatory Oversight and the Separation of Powers: The Constitutionality of Executive Order No. 12291." *Arizona Law Review* 23: 1235–65.

Siller, Jerome, et al. 1967. *Attitudes of the Nondisabled toward the Physically Disabled*. Studies in Reactions to Disability XI. New York: School of Education, New York University.

Simon, Pamela H. 1984. "Employment Discrimination—Analyzing Handicap Discrimination Claims: The Right Tools for the Job." *North Carolina Law Review* 62: 535–71.

Smith, Thomas B. 1973. "The Policy Implementation Process." *Policy Sciences* 4: 197–209.

Sommer, Susan L. 1984. "Securing the Right to Reimbursement under the Education for All Handicapped Children Act." *Yale Law and Policy Review* 3 (Fall): 277–94.

Spiegel, Allen D., and Simon Podair, eds. 1981. *Rehabilitating People with Disabilities into the Mainstream of Society*. Park Ridge, N.J.: Noyes Medical Publications.

Stanfield, Rochelle L. 1983. "Reagan Courting Women, Minorities, but It May Be Too Late to Win Them." *National Journal* 15 (May 28): 1118–23.

Stark, James H. 1982. "Tragic Choices in Special Education: The Effect of Scarce Resources on the Implementation of Pub. L. No. 94-142." *Connecticut Law Review* 14: 477–529.

Steinhauser, Larry, and Louis Vieceli. 1978. "Affirmative Action for the Handicapped." *Supervisory Management*, October, 34–37.

Stick, Robert S. 1976. "The Handicapped Child Has a Right to an Appropriate Education." *Nebraska Law Review* 55, no. 4: 637–82.

Stigler, George J. 1971. "The Theory of Economic Regulation." *Bell Journal of Economics and Management Science* 2 (Spring): 3–21.

Stone, Alan. 1982. *Regulation and Its Alternatives*. Washington, D.C.: Congressional Quarterly Press.

Stone, Clarence. 1980. "The Implementation of Social Programs: Two Perspectives." *Journal of Social Issues* 36, no. 4: 13–34.

Stone, Deborah. 1984. *The Disabled State*. Philadelphia: Temple University Press.

Straus, Robert. 1966. "Social Change and the Rehabilitation Concept." In *Sociology and Rehabilitation*, ed., Marvin V. Sussman. Washington, D.C.: American Sociological Association.

Stroman, Duane F. 1982. *The Awakening Minorities: The Physically Handicapped*. Washington, D.C.: University Press of America.

Tanenbaum, Sandra J. 1986. *Engineering Disability: Public Policy and Compensatory*

Technology. Philadelphia: Temple University Press.

Taylor, Patricia Y. 1983. "An 'Appropriate' Education for the Handicapped—*Board of Education v. Rowley.*" *Howard Law Review* 26: 1645–60.

Thomas, Richard D. 1984. "Implementing Federal Programs at the Local Level." *Political Science Quarterly* 94, no. 3 (Fall): 419–35.

Thompson, Frank J. 1981. *Health Policy and Bureaucracy: Politics and Implementation*. Cambridge: MIT Press.

Thompson, James D. 1967. *Organizations in Action*. New York: McGraw-Hill.

Thornton, Mary. 1983. "NAACP Office Asks Abolition of Justice's Civil Rights Division." *Washington Post*, May 7, A3.

Thrasher, Michael. 1983. "Exchange Networks and Implementation." *Policy and Politics* 11, no. 4: 375–91.

Thurer, Shari. 1981. "Disability and Monstrosity: A Look at Literary Distortion of Handicapping Conditions." In *Rehabilitating People with Disabilities into the Mainstream of Society*, ed. Allen D. Spiegel and Simon Podair. Park Ridge, N.J.: Noyes Medical Publications.

Tolchin, Susan J., and Martin Tolchin. 1983. *Dismantling America: The Rush to Regulate*. Boston: Houghton Mifflin.

Trautmann, Joanne. 1979. "Literary Treatments of the Handicapped." In *The Handicapped Experience: Some Humanistic Perspectives*, ed. George M. McDermitt and Linda McDermitt, 17–23. Baltimore: University of Baltimore.

Tucker, Bonnie P. 1979. "Section 504 of the Vocational Rehabilitation Act of 1973 and Postsecondary Education for the Deaf." *University of Colorado Law Review* 50: 341–60.

U.S. Commission on Education of the Deaf. 1988. *Toward Equality: Education of the Deaf*. Washington, D.C.: Government Printing Office.

U.S. Congressional Budget Office. 1979. *Urban Transportation for Handicapped Persons: Alternative Federal Approaches*. Washington, D.C.: Government Printing Office.

U.S. Department of Education. 1979. *Digest of Data on Persons with Disabilities*. Washington, D.C.: Office of Handicapped Individuals, U.S. Department of Education.

———. 1980. *Summary of Existing Legislation Relating to the Handicapped*. Washington, D.C.: Office of Special Education and Rehabilitative Services, U.S. Department of Education.

U.S. Department of Health, Education, and Welfare. 1967. *Design for All Americans*. Report of the National Commission on Architectural Barriers to Rehabilitation of the Handicapped. Washington, D.C.: Government Printing Office.

U.S. Department of Labor, Office of Federal Contract Compliance Programs. 1977. *Preliminary Report on the Revitalization of the Federal Contract Compliance Program*. Washington, D.C.: U.S. Department of Labor.

U.S. Department of Transportation. 1979. *NRC Transbus Study*. Washington, D.C.: National Academy of Sciences.

———. 1979. *Transbus: An Overview of Technical, Operational, and Economic Characteristics*. McLean, Va.: Mitre Corporation.

Select Bibliography

———. 1985. *Regulatory Impact Analysis: The Department of Transportation's Regulation Implementing Section 504 of the Rehabilitation Act of 1973 in the Urban Mass Transit Program.* Washington, D.C.: U.S. Department of Transportation.

U.S. Equal Employment Opportunity Commission. 1979. *Coordination of Federal Equal Employment Opportunity Programs: The First Year 1978–1979.* Washington, D.C.: U.S. Equal Employment Opportunity Commission.

———. 1982. *16th Annual Report—FY 1981.* Washington, D.C.: U.S. Equal Employment Opportunity Commission.

———. 1986. *Annual Report on the Employment of Minorities, Women, and the Handicapped Individuals in the Federal Government, Fiscal Year 1986.* Washington, D.C.: U.S. Equal Employment Opportunity Commission.

U.S. General Accounting Office. 1975. *Further Action Needed to Make All Public Buildings Accessible to the Physically Handicapped.* FPCD-75-166, July 15. Washington, D.C.: U.S. General Accounting Office.

———. 1980. *Making Public Buildings Accessible to the Handicapped: More Can Be Done.* FPCD-8-51. Washington, D.C.: U.S. General Accounting Office.

———. 1982. *Status of Special Efforts to Meet the Transportation Needs of the Elderly and Handicapped.* CED-82-66. Washington, D.C.: U.S. General Accounting Office.

———. 1985. *Implementation of Public Law 94-142 as It Relates to Handicapped Delinquents in the District of Columbia.* Report to the Ranking Minority Member, Committee on the District of Columbia, House of Representatives. Washington, D.C.: General Government Division, U.S. Government Accounting Office.

U.S. House of Representatives. 1970. *Accessibility to Physically Handicapped of Certain Public Facilities.* 91st Cong., 1st sess., H. Rept. 91-658.

———. 1976. *Public Buildings Cooperative Use Act of 1976.* 94th Cong., 2d sess., H. Rept. 1584.

———. 1978. *Comprehensive Rehabilitation Services Amendments of 1978.* 95th Cong., 2d sess., H. Rept. 95-1780.

———. 1984. *Child Abuse Amendments of 1984.* 98th Cong., 2d sess., H. Rept. 93-1038.

———. 1984. *Voting Accessibility for the Elderly and Handicapped Act.* 98th Cong., 2d sess., H. Rept. 98-582.

U.S. House of Representatives, Committee on Appropriations, Subcommittee on the Department of Transportation and Related Agencies Appropriations. 1982. *Hearings on Department of Transportation and Related Agencies Appropriations for 1983.* 97th Cong., 2d sess., pt. 3.

U.S. House of Representatives, Committee on Banking and Currency, Subcommittee on Housing. 1972. *Hearings on Urban Mass Transportation.* 92d Cong., 2d sess.

U.S. House of Representatives, Committee on Education and Labor. 1978. *Comprehensive Rehabilitative Services Amendments of 1978.* 95th Cong., 2d sess., H. Rept. 95-1149.

———. 1986. *Rehabilitation Act Amendments of 1986.* 99th Cong., 2d sess., H. Rept. 99-571.

———. 1986. *A Report on the Investigation of Civil Rights Enforcement by the EEOC.* 99th Cong., 2d sess., Committee Print 99-Q.

Select Bibliography

U.S. House of Representatives, Committee on Education and Labor, and Committee on the Judiciary, Subcommittee on Civil and Constitutional Rights. 1985. *Joint Hearings on the Civil Rights Restoration Act of 1985*. 99th Cong., 1st sess.

U.S. House of Representatives, Committee on Education and Labor, Subcommittee on Employment Opportunities. 1980. *Oversight Hearing on the Federal Enforcement of Equal Employment Opportunity Laws*. 96th Cong., 2d sess.

———. 1981. *Oversight Hearings on Equal Employment Opportunity and Affirmative Action*. 97th Cong., 1st sess., pt. 1.

———. 1982. *Report on Affirmative Action and the Federal Enforcement of Equal Employment Opportunity Laws*. 97th Cong., 2d sess., Committee Print.

———. 1983. *Oversight Hearings on the Federal Enforcement of Equal Opportunity Laws*. 98th Cong., 1st sess.

———. 1983. *Oversight Hearings on the OFCCP's Proposed Affirmative Action Regulations*. 98th Cong., 1st sess.

———. 1984. *Oversight Hearing on the OFCCP's National Self-Monitoring and Reporting System*. 98th Cong., 2d sess.

———. 1985. *Oversight Hearing on EEOC's Proposed Modification of Enforcement Regulations, Including Uniform Guidelines on Employee Selection Procedures*. 99th Cong., 1st sess.

———. 1985. *Oversight Review of Department of Labor's OFCCP and Affirmative Action Programs*. 99th Cong., 1st sess.

———. 1986. *Hearings on EEOC Policies Regarding Goals and Timetables in Litigation Remedies*. 99th Cong., 2d sess.

U.S. House of Representatives, Committee on Education and Labor, Subcommittee on Select Education. 1972. *Hearings on Vocational Rehabilitation Services to the Handicapped*. 92d Cong., 2d sess.

———. 1973. *Hearings on Education of the Handicapped Amendments*. 93d Cong., 1st sess.

———. 1974. *Hearings on Financial Assistance for Improved Educational Services for Handicapped Children*. 93d Cong., 2d sess., pt. 1.

———. 1975. *Hearings on Extension of Education of the Handicapped Act*. 94th Cong., 1st sess.

———. 1977. *Hearings on Implementation of Section 504, Rehabilitation Act of 1973*. 95th Cong., 1st sess.

———. 1980. *Oversight Hearing on the Architectural and Transportation Barriers Compliance Board*. 96th Cong., 2d sess.

———. 1981. *Oversight Hearings on the Architectural and Transportation Barriers Compliance Board*. 97th Cong., 1st sess.

———. 1982. *Hearings on Treatment of Infants Born with Handicapping Conditions*. 97th Cong., 2d sess.

———. 1983. *Hearings to Amend the Child Abuse Prevention and Treatment and Adoption Reform Act of 1978*. 98th Cong., 1st sess.

U.S. House of Representatives, Committee on Education and Labor, Subcommittee on Select Education; and U.S. Senate, Committee on Labor and Public Welfare, Subcommittee on the Handicapped. 1975. *Joint Oversight Hearings on the Proposed Extension of the Rehabilitation Act.* 94th Cong., 1st sess.

U.S. House of Representatives, Committee on Energy and Commerce. 1981. *Hearings on the Role of OMB in Regulation.* 97th Cong., 1st sess., 391–409.

————. 1981. *Presidential Control of Agency Rulemaking—An Analysis of Constitutional Issues That May Be Raised by Executive Order 12291.* 97th Cong., 1st sess., Committee Print 97-0.

U.S. House of Representatives, Committee on Government Operations. 1978. *Reorganization Plan No. 1 of 1978.* 95th Cong., 2d sess., H. Rept. 95-1069.

U.S. House of Representatives, Committee on Public Works. 1968. *Design and Construction of Buildings Financed with Federal Funds to be Accessible to the Physically Handicapped.* 90th Cong., 2d sess., H. Rept. 1532.

————. 1968. *Design and Construction of Buildings Financed with Federal Funds to Be Accessible to the Physically Handicapped.* 90th Cong., 2d sess., H. Rept. 1787.

U.S. House of Representatives, Committee on Public Works, Subcommittee on Public Buildings and Grounds. 1968. *Hearings on Building Design for the Physically Disabled.* 90th Cong., 2d sess.

————. 1970. *Hearings on Design and Construction of Federal Facilities to Be Accessible to the Physically Handicapped.* 91st Cong., 1st sess.

————. 1972. *Hearing to Consider Accommodations for Handicapped on Metro System.* 92d Cong., 2d sess.

U.S. House of Representatives, Committee on Public Works and Transportation, Subcommittee on Investigations and Review. 1975. *Hearings on the Effectiveness of the Architectural Barriers Act of 1968. (Public Law 90-480).* 94th Cong., 1st sess.

————. 1980. *Urban Mass Transportation Administration's Technology Development and Equipment Procurement Programs: Do We Know What We're Trying to Do?* 96th Cong., 2d sess., Committee Print 96-34.

U.S. House of Representatives, Committee on Public Works and Transportation, Subcommittee on Public Buildings and Grounds. 1976. *Hearings on Public Buildings Cooperative Use.* 94th Cong., 2d sess.

U.S. House of Representatives, Committee on Public Works and Transportation, Subcommittee on Surface Transportation. 1976. *Hearings to Consider Amendments to the Urban Mass Transportation Act of 1964 to Provide Operating Assistance for Projects Located in Areas Other Than Urbanized Areas, to Provide for Mass Transportation Assistance to Meet the Needs of Elderly and Handicapped Persons, and for Other Purposes.* 94th Cong., 2d sess.

U.S. House of Representatives, Committee on the Judiciary, Subcommittee on Civil and Constitutional Rights. 1982. *Hearings on Authorization Request for the Civil Rights Division of the Department of Justice.* 97th Cong., 2d sess.

U.S. Office of Personnel Management. 1982. *Handbook of Job Analysis for Reasonable Accommodation.* Washington, D.C.: Government Printing Office.

U.S. Postal Service. 1979. *Standards for Facility Accessibility by the Physically Handicapped.* Handbook RE-4. Washington, D.C.: Real Estate and Buildings Department, U.S. Postal Service.

Select Bibliography

U.S. Senate. 1967. *Design and Construction of Public Buildings Financed with Federal Funds to Be Accessible to the Physically Disabled*. 90th Cong., 1st sess., S. Rept. 538.

———. 1974. *Rehabilitation Act Amendments of 1974*. 93d Cong., 2d sess., S. Rept. 93-1297.

———. 1975. *Resolution of Support for a Barrier-Free Environment*. 94th Cong., 1st sess., S. Rept. 94-142.

U.S. Senate, Committee on Appropriations, Subcommittee on the Department of Transportation and Related Agencies Appropriations. 1982. *Hearings on Department of Transportation and Related Agencies Appropriations for Fiscal 1983*. 97th Cong., 2d sess., pt. 3.

U.S. Senate, Committee on Environment and Public Works. 1979. *Architectural Barriers in Federal Buildings: Implementation of the Architectural Barriers Act of 1968*. 96th Cong., 1st sess., Committee Print, Serial 96-8.

———. 1983. *Public Buildings Act of 1983*. 98th Cong., 1st sess., S. Rept. 98-289.

U.S. Senate, Committee on Labor and Human Resources. 1978. *Rehabilitation, Comprehensive Services and Development Disabilities Act of 1978*. Senate Report 95-890. 95th Cong., 2d sess.

———. 1979. *Hearings on Equal Employment Opportunity for the Handicapped Act of 1979*. 96th Cong., 1st sess.

U.S. Senate, Committee on Labor and Human Resources, Subcommittee on the Handicapped. 1977. *Hearings on Rehabilitation Extension Amendments of 1977*. 95th Cong., 1st sess.

———. 1978. *Hearings on the Rehabilitation Amendments of 1978*. 95th Cong., 2d sess.

U.S. Senate, Committee on Labor and Public Welfare, Subcommittee on the Handicapped. 1972. *Hearings on the Rehabilitation Act of 1972*. 92d Cong., 2d sess., pts. 1 and 2.

———. 1973. *Hearings on Education of the Handicapped Act, 1973*. 93d Cong., 1st sess.

———. 1973. *Hearings on the Rehabilitation Act of 1973*. 93d Cong., 1st sess.

———. 1974. *Hearings on the Rehabilitation Act Amendments of 1974*. 93d Cong., 2d sess.

———. 1975. *Hearings on Education for All Handicapped Children Act, 1975*. 94th Cong., 1st sess.

———. 1976. *Hearings on Rehabilitation of the Handicapped Programs, 1976*. 94th Cong., 2d sess.

———. 1983. *Hearings on Enforcement of Section 504 of the Rehabilitation Act: Institutional Care and Services for Retarded Citizens*. 98th Cong., 1st sess.

U.S. Senate, Committee on Public Works, Subcommittee on Public Buildings and Grounds. 1967. *Hearings on Accessibility of Public Buildings to the Physically Handicapped*. 90th Cong., 1st sess.

U.S. Senate, Committee on Public Works, Subcommittee on Transportation. 1973. *Federal-Aid Highway Act of 1973*. 93d Cong., 2d sess.

U.S. Senate, Committee on the Judiciary. 1985. *Hearing on the Nomination of William*

Select Bibliography

Bradford Reynolds to Be Associate Attorney General of the United States. 99th Cong., 1st sess.

U.S. Social Security Administration. 1981. *Characteristics of Social Security Disability Insurance Beneficiaries.* Washington, D.C.: U.S. Department of Health and Human Services.

U.S. Urban Mass Transportation Administration. 1973. *The Handicapped and Elderly Market for Transportation.* Executive summary. Washington, D.C.: Department of Transportation.

———. 1978. *Technical Report of the National Survey of Transportation for Handicapped People.* Washington, D.C.: Department of Transportation.

———. 1979a. *Elderly and Handicapped Transportation: Eight Case Studies.* Washington, D.C.: Department of Transportation.

———. 1979b. *Elderly and Handicapped Transportation: Local Government Approaches.* Washington, D.C.: Department of Transportation.

Van Horn, Carl E. 1979. *Policy Implementation in a Federal System.* Lexington, Mass.: Lexington Books.

Van Horn, Carl E., and Donald S. Van Meter. 1976. "The Implementation of Intergovernmental Policy." In *Public Policy Making in a Federal System*, ed. Charles O. Jones and Richard D. Thomas, 39–62. Beverly Hills: Sage.

Van Meter, Donald S., and Carl E. Van Horn. 1975. "The Policy Implementation Process: A Conceptual Framework." *Administration and Society* 6, no. 4 (February); 445–85.

Vice Presidential Task Force on Regulatory Relief. 1982. *Reagan Administration Achievements in Regulatory Relief: A Progress Report.* Washington, D.C.: Vice Presidential Task Force on Regulatory Relief.

Walker, Jack L. 1977. "Setting the Agenda in the U.S. Senate: A Theory of Problem Selection." *British Journal of Political Science* 7 (October): 423–45.

———. 1981. "The Diffusion of Knowledge, Policy Communities and Agenda Setting: The Relationship of Knowledge and Power." In *New Perspectives on Social Policy*, ed., John E. Tropman, Milan J. Dluhy, and Roger M. Lind, 75–96. New York: Pergamon.

Wegner, Judith W. 1984. "The Antidiscrimination Model Reconsidered: Ensuring Equal Opportunity without Respect to Handicap under Section 504 of the Rehabilitation Act of 1973." *Cornell Law Review* 69: 400–516.

Wehman, Paul, ed. 1981. *Competitive Employment: New Horizons for Severely Disabled Individuals.* Baltimore: Paul H. Brookes.

Weintraub, Frederick J., and Bruce A. Ramirez. 1985. *Progress in the Education of the Handicapped and Analysis of PL98-199.* Reston, Va.: Council for Exceptional Children.

Weiss, Janet A., and Judith E. Gruber. 1984. "Using Knowledge for Control in Fragmented Policy Arenas." *Journal of Policy Analysis and Management* 3, no. 2 (Winter): 225–47.

Wenderoff, Lori A. 1983. "*Board of Education v. Rowley*: Are Handicapped Children Entitled to Equal Educational Opportunities?" *California Western Law Review* 20 (Fall): 132–55.

West, William F. 1985. *Administrative Rulemaking: Politics and Processes*. Westport, Conn.: Greenwood Press.

White House Conference on Handicapped Individuals. 1977. *Final Report*. Washington, D.C.: Government Printing Office.

White, Lawrence J. 1981. *Reforming Regulation: Processes and Problems*. Englewood Cliffs, N.J.: Prentice-Hall.

Williams, Walter. 1976. "Implementation Problems in Federally Funded Programs." In *Social Program Implementation*, ed. Walter Williams and Richard Elmore. New York: Academic Press.

————. 1980. *The Implementation Perspective: A Guide for Managing Social Service Delivery Programs*. Berkeley: University of California Press.

Williams, Walter, and Richard F. Elmore, eds. 1976. *Social Program Implementation*. New York: Academic Press.

Williams, Walter, et al. 1982. *Studying Implementation: Methodological and Administrative Issues*. Chatham, N.J.: Chatham House.

Williamson, Oliver E. 1967. "Hierarchical Control and Optimum Firm Size." *Journal of Political Economy* 75, no. 2 (April): 123–38.

Wilson, James Q. 1980. "The Politics of Regulation." In *The Politics of Regulation*, ed. James Q. Wilson. New York: Basic Books.

Wilson, James Q., and Patricia Rachal. 1977. "Can Government Regulate Itself?" *The Public Interest* 36 (Winter): 3–14.

Wilson, Woodrow. 1887. "The Study of Administration." *Political Science Quarterly* 2 (June): 197–222.

Wright, William A. 1977. "Equal Treatment of the Handicapped by Federal Contractors." *Emory Law Journal* 26: 64–106.

Yates, Douglas. 1977. *The Ungovernable City*. Cambridge: MIT Press.

Yin, Robert K. 1982. "Studying the Implementation of Public Programs." In *Studying Implementation: Methodological and Administrative Issues*, ed. Walter Williams et al. Chatham, N.J.: Chatham House.

Zettel, Jeffrey J. 1982. "Implementing the Right to a Free and Appropriate Public Education." In *Special Education in America: Its Legal and Governmental Foundations*, ed. Joseph Ballard et al. Reston, Va.: Council for Exceptional Children.

Zimmer, Arno B. 1981. *Employing the Handicapped: A Practical Compliance Manual*. New York: Amacom.

Index

Aberbach, Joel D., 258 (n. 3)

Abzug, Bella, 132

Accessibility: section 504 provisions for, 75–76. *See also* Architectural Barriers Act of 1968; Uniform Federal Accessibility Standards

Acquired Immune Deficiency Disease, 251–53, 279 (n. 27)

Action League for Physically Handicapped Persons, 68

Actors: in policy implementation, 24–29, 227–31

Adams, Brock, 136, 156

Adapt v. Dole, 271 (n. 62)

Adkins, John I., Jr., 194

Administrative agencies: as arenas for implementation, 232–33

Administrative personnel: as policy actors, 26–27

Administrative Procedures Act, 250

Advisory Commission on Intergovernmental Relations, 38, 243, 259 (n. 8)

Agenda setting, 17, 30–32

Agriculture, U.S. Department of, 202

Air Force, U.S. Department of, 202

Alexander, Ernest B., 12, 258 (n. 2)

Alexander, Jacqelyn, 172

American Academy of Pediatricians v. Heckler, 279 (n. 16)

American Coalition of Citizens with Disabilities, 67, 99, 145, 147, 228, 229

American Council on Education, 185

American Medical Association, 250

American National Standards Institute

(ANSI), 76, 93, 110, 115, 122, 134, 137, 140, 184, 238

American Public Transit Association, 134–56 passim

American Public Transit Association v. Lewis, 94, 144, 146, 147, 155, 230, 236, 256 (n. 36), 270 (n. 26)

Americans Disabled for Accessible Public Transportation, 157

Americans with Disabilities Act, 224, 253

Architectural and Transportation Barriers Compliance Board, 38, 55, 93, 107–28 passim, 238, 244, 264 (n. 25, 26), 267 (n. 30, 33, 34, 35, 36), 268 (n. 40, 43, 52), 269 (n. 67)

Architectural Barriers Act of 1968: legislative history, 49–51; original administrative regulations, 108; early implementation experiences, 110–12; second round of administrative regulations, 112–17; congressional oversight, 114–15, 120–21; Reagan administration and regulatory reform, 117–24; politics of implementation, 124–28

Arenas. *See* Institutional arenas

Army, U.S. Department of, 202

Ashby, Robert, 269 (n. 21), 271 (n. 47, 56)

Association for Children and Adults with Learning Disabilities, 177

Association for Retarded Citizens, 177

Baby Doe case, 249–51

Bachrach, Peter, 32

Balanced competing equities, 34, 72–73, 79

Index

Ballard, Joseph, 261 (n. 37)

Banking, Housing and Urban Affairs, Senate Committee on, 147

Bardach, Eugene, 14, 16, 24, 37, 40, 258 (n. 8)

Baritz, Morton S., 32

Barrier Free Environments of Raleigh, North Carolina, 86

Bartlett, E. L., 50, 225, 259 (n. 5)

Basic Education Opportunity Grants, 102

Beard, Joseph, 178

Behr, Peter, 264 (n. 14)

Bell, Christopher G., 87, 245

Bell, Robert S., 271 (n. 63)

Bell, Terrel H., 60, 173–79 passim

Bell, William G., 271 (n. 63)

Bender, Henry E., 195, 203, 219

Berkeley Center for Independent Living, 85

Berkeley Planning Associates, 210

Berkowitz, Edward D., 193, 258 (n. 5)

Berman, Paul, 24, 36

Bernstein, M. H., 40, 256 (n. 10)

Berry, Jeffrey M., 13, 31, 41, 258 (n. 3), 263 (n. 33)

Beyer, Henry A., 274 (n. 65)

Biaggi, Mario, 131–32, 178

Biklen, Douglas, 6

Board of Education v. Rowley, 181–82, 191, 236, 247

Bobbitt, Philip, 253

Boettner, Karl, 274 (n. 65)

Bogdan, Robert, 6

Bond, Deborah, 172

Boodman, Sandra G., 252

Bowe, Frank G., 7, 48, 63

Bowen, Secretary of HHS v. American Hospital Association, 251, 279 (n. 21)

Bower, Eli M., 257 (n. 3)

Boyd, Clayton, 275 (n. 14)

Brattgard, Sven-Olaf, 217 (n. 63)

Brennan, William J., 252, 274 (n. 67)

Brigham, David, 276 (n. 41), 277 (n. 44, 54)

Browne, Angela, 36

Bryner, Gary, 42

Budget, Senate Committee on, 142

Buress, Charles, 97

Burgdorf, Robert L., Jr., 56, 57, 87, 245, 271 (n. 63)

Bush, George, 88, 96, 264 (n. 14), 265

(n. 29)

Butler, Daniel P., 264 (n. 13), 274 (n. 54)

Buturla, Richard J., 274 (n. 65)

Byrd, Keith, 5

Calabresi, Guido, 253

Califano, Joseph, 69–70, 78

Cannon, Bradley C., 27

Cannon, Dennis M., 140, 147, 271 (n. 44)

Carter, Jimmy, 86, 113–14, 126, 146, 198, 205

Catholic Conference, U.S., 104

Cherry v. Matthews, 68

Chicago Tribune, 241, 278 (n. 7)

Child Abuse Amendments of 1984, 250

Children's Defense Fund, 174

Civil and Constitutional Rights, House Subcommittee on, 99, 265 (n. 38, 41), 266 (n. 65)

Civilian Vocational Rehabilitation Act, 44

Civil Rights Acts, 65, 72, 199, 277 (n. 49)

Civil rights movements, 48–49

Civil Rights Restoration Act, 103–104, 214, 237

Civil Service Commission, U.S., 98, 196–99, 275 (n. 1–5, 19)

Civil Service Reform Act, 276 (n. 28)

Clark, Timothy B., 114, 140, 146, 158

Cleveland, James, 111, 266 (n. 9)

Cleveland, Max, 114

Cobb, Roger W., 30, 239

Commission on Education of the Deaf, 187, 275 (n. 72)

Comparable standards regulations in transportation, 148–52

Comprehensive Rehabilitation Services Amendments of 1978, 84

Congress: as arena for policy implementation, 233–35

Congressional Budget Office, 142, 143, 145, 147, 154, 270 (n. 38)

Congressional committees. *See* specific committee name

Congressional Quarterly, 37

Congressional Research Service, 89, 264 (n. 15)

Consolidated Rail Corporation v. Darrone, 214, 236

Consortium Concerned with the

Index

Developmentally Disabled, 177

Cook, Timothy, 100, 101, 264 (n. 13), 274 (n. 59)

Cooke, Charles M., Jr., 60

Cooper, Charles J., 252

Cooptation, 40–41

Coordination guidelines for section 504, 78

Council for Exceptional Children, 55, 59, 166, 228

Courts: as arena for policy implementation, 235–37

Craig, Roger, 116, 117, 118

Cranston, Alan, 119, 127, 144, 148, 149, 262 (n. 4)

Cremins, James J., 261 (n. 37)

Cutler, Richard, 3

Daneke, Gregory A., 38

Davidson, Roger H., 258 (n. 4)

Davis, Kenneth C., 258 (n. 3)

Defense, U.S. Department of, 51, 52, 93, 109, 110, 111, 121, 264 (n. 26), 267 (n. 15)

Derthick, Martha, 41

Disability: public perceptions and attitudes, 4–7; a profile of, 7–9. *See also* Handicapped person

Disability Rights Education and Defense Fund, 85, 86, 89, 95, 96, 97, 99, 103, 176, 228

Disabled American Veterans Association, 119

DOT and Related Agencies' Appropriations, House Subcommittee on, 268 (n. 55)

Downs, Anthony, 31, 35, 259 (n. 10)

Dunsire, Andrew, 258 (n. 11)

DuPont, E. I., 195

Durant, Robert F., 259 (n. 8)

Eads, George C., 31

Eastern Paralyzed Veterans Association, 157

Easter Seals Society, 51, 225

Ebert, Constance J., 266 (n. 1)

Edelman, Murray, 40, 239, 259 (n. 6)

Education: early programs for handicapped students, 46–47; section 504 provisions for, 77–78, 162–65; costs of educating handicapped children, 165–67. *See also* Education for All Handicapped Children Act

Education, U.S. Department of, 93, 94, 102, 170–80 passim, 190, 191, 258 (n. 6), 262 (n. 19), 264 (n. 27), 273 (n. 25, 31, 41)

Education, Arts, and Humanities, Senate Subcommittee on, 174, 273 (n. 33)

Education Act Amendments of 1972, 65, 72, 102

Education Act Amendments of 1974, 57–58

Education for All Handicapped Children Act (PL94-142): legislative history, 55–61; and section 504, 94; administrative rulemaking for, 161–62; implementation experiences, 165–72; students served, 169; regulatory reform under Carter, 172–73; proposed merger into block grant, 173–75; regulatory reform under Reagan, 175–79; judicial interpretation of, 181–84; assessment of implementation experiences, 186–92

Education of the Handicapped Act Amendments of 1983, 179

Education Turnkey Systems, 171

Edwards, Don, 103

Edwards, George E. III, 258 (n. 8, 11)

Eisenach, Jeffrey A., 31, 38

Elder, Charles D., 30, 239

Elementary and Secondary Education Act, 46–47, 174, 175

Elementary and Secondary Education Consolidation Act of 1981, 174

Elisburg, Donald, 114

Elliott, Timothy R., 5

Ellner, Jack R., 195, 219

Elmore, Richard F., 12, 258 (n. 8, 10)

Employment: section 504 provisions for, 73–75

Employment of disabled persons: vocational rehabilitation program, 44–45, 193; benefits of, 194; impediments to, 194–95; employment protection laws, 195–96; implementation of section 501, 196–202; implementation of section 503, 202–11; implementation of section 504, 211–14; assessment of implementation experiences, 213–20

Energy and Commerce, House Committee on, 264 (n. 14, 18)

Engebretson, Mark F., 262 (n. 5)

English, William R., 6

Environment. *See* Policy environment;

303

Index

Political environment
Environment and Public Works, Senate Committee on, 259 (n. 1), 266 (n. 1)
Equal Employment Opportunity Commission: responsibility for section 501 transferred to, 198–99, 200, 201, 215, 216, 217; implementation of section 501, 199–202
Equal Employment Opportunity Coordinating Council, 245–48
Equity approaches to implementation, 245–48
Erlenhorn, John, 85
Ethridge, Marcus E., 25, 258 (n. 3)
Everett, Carol, 129, 158, 271 (n. 63)
Executive Orders: No. 11246, 205, 207, 208, 277 (n. 43); No. 11821, 66; No. 11914, 67, 68; No. 12086, 205; No. 12250, 86, 146; No. 12291, 88, 89, 205, 264 (n. 18)

Federal-Aid Highway Act of 1973, 132, 134, 269 (n. 8)
Ferman, Barbara, 14, 24
Fielding, Gordon J., 139, 157
Fiorina, Morris P., 258 (n. 3)
Fix, Michael, 31, 129, 158, 271 (n. 63)
Ford, Gerald R., 61, 66–67, 196, 261 (n. 36)
Forsyth, Thomas L., 264 (n. 13), 274 (n. 54)
Foster, Wayne K., 171
Franklin, Grace A., 25, 258 (n. 8), 259 (n. 7)
Free and appropriate education, 61, 161–62
Freeman, J. Lieper, 258 (n. 4)
Full accessibility regulations in transportation: drafting by DOT, 136–44; congressional reactions, 144–45
Funk, Robert, 99

Gallagher, Hugh, 50, 225, 259 (n. 5)
Gamber, Edward, 3
Gambitta, Richard A., 22
General Accounting Office, 107, 110, 111, 114, 115, 124, 126, 127, 147, 155, 169, 266 (n. 10), 267 (n. 27), 271 (n. 53), 272 (n. 22, 23, 24)
General Services Administration, 50, 51, 52, 93, 107–27 passim, 264 (n. 26), 267 (n. 15, 16)
Gerry, Martin, 262 (n. 13)
Gerse, Steven W., 264 (n. 13), 274 (n. 54)
Glenn, John, 277 (n. 59)

Gliedman, John, 5
Goffman, Erving, 4
Goggin, Malcolm L., 36
Goldberg, I. Ignacy, 57, 261 (n. 24)
Goldman, Charles D., 257 (n. 1), 266 (n. 11)
Gomez-Ibanez, Jose A., 158
Goodrich, James A., 15
Government Operations, House Committee on, 198, 275 (n. 18)
Grant, Carol, 123
Gray, C. Boyden, 95, 118, 120, 121, 123
Green, Mark J., 40
Grove City College v. Bell, 102–104, 214, 236, 237
Gruber, Judith E., 24, 30

Handicapism, 6
Handicapped, Senate Subcommittee on, 65, 67, 68, 84, 100, 112, 165, 177, 191, 234, 260 (n. 21), 261 (n. 28, 29, 30), 262 (n. 4, 10, 13), 266 (n. 6), 263 (n. 1), 265 (n. 44), 267 (n. 21), 272 (n. 13), 273 (n. 42)
Handicapped Act Amendments of 1986, 184
Handicapped Children's Early Education Assistance Act, 47
Handicapped Children's Protection Act of 1986, 183
Handicapped infants: protection of, 249–51
Handicapped person: definition under section 504, 70–71; change in 504 definition, 84–85; proposed regulatory changes in definition, 90–91
Harder, Marvin A., 258 (n. 8)
Hargrove, Edwin C., 15, 20, 258 (n. 8)
Harris, Louis, 7, 219, 257 (n. 4)
Harris, Robert M., 258 (n. 13)
Hartman, Chester A., 13
Having, Marilyn, 6
Health and Human Services, U.S. Department of, 86, 101, 142, 146, 202, 249, 250, 251, 267 (n. 36)
Health, Education, and Welfare, U.S. Department of, 28, 51, 52, 53, 60, 64–70, 75, 80–94 passim, 108, 109, 114, 136, 137, 142, 152, 154, 161, 164, 165, 166, 190, 198, 211, 232, 243, 259 (n. 3), 261 (n. 1, 2), 262 (n. 19), 267 (n. 36), 264 (n. 27)
Heclo, Hugh, 27
Heinemen, Benjamin, Jr., 279 (n. 22)

Index

Henry, Laura C., 274 (n. 65)

Higher education: and section 504, 164; cost of implementation, 166, 172, 180

Hippolitus, Paul, 185

Holden, Matthew, Jr., 260 (n. 10)

Housing, House Subcommittee on, 269 (n. 8)

Housing and Urban Development, U.S. Department of, 13, 51, 52, 93, 107, 109, 110, 111, 116, 117, 121, 123, 127 (n. 26), 267 (n. 15)

Houston, John R., 264 (n. 13), 274 (n. 54)

Howard, James, 145

Humphrey, Hubert H., 53, 225

Huntington, Samuel P., 40

Implementation. *See* Policy implementation

Income support programs, 45–46

Individualized education plan, 62, 167, 169–70

Infectious diseases, 251–53

Ingram, Helen, 77

Institute for Rehabilitation and Disability Management, 4

Institutional arenas: roles in implementation, 22–27; and transportation policy, 152; and education policy, 188–92; roles in implementation, 231–37

Interagency Committee on Handicapped Employees, 195

Interagency Committee on the Handicapped, 98

Interest group politics, 39–40, 238–39

Interested publics, 25–26, 227–30

Interior, U.S. Department of, 109, 202

International Center for the Disabled, 7, 216, 257 (n. 4), 278 (n. 70, 71)

Investigations and Review, House Subcommittee on, 111, 126, 266 (n. 9)

Iron triangles, 225

Isbell, Florence, 7

Issue Networks, 27–28, 231; for section 504, 65, 79–80, 85–86; in transportation policy, 153–56; in education, 160

Jackson, Raymond, 271 (n. 64)

Jacobsen, Richard J., 194

Jamero, Peter M., 194

James, Dorothy B., 258 (n. 4)

Johnson, Charles A., 27

Johnson, Lyndon B., 52, 260 (n. 17), 277 (n. 43)

Jones, Nancy L., 89, 92, 264 (n. 15, 18)

Jones, Philip R., 261 (n. 37)

Judicial officials: as policy actors, 27

Judiciary, Senate Committee on, 101, 265 (n. 52)

Justice, U.S. Department of, 84–105 passim, 116, 119, 146, 151, 155, 251, 265 (n. 15, 36)

Kagan, Robert A., 37, 40

Katzmann, Robert A., 41, 50, 53, 66, 131, 132, 133, 157, 259 (n. 5), 262 (n. 3), 269 (n. 3, 21), 270 (n. 25), 271 (n. 45)

Kennedy, Edward, 174

Kettl, Donald F., 37, 40, 42

Kingdon, John W., 29, 30, 31, 32, 258 (n. 4)

Kirby, Ronald, 129, 158, 271 (n. 63)

Koch, Edward, 142

Kriegel, Leonard, 6

Kroll, Shelley A., 274 (n. 65)

Kurtz, Howard, 101

Labor, U.S. Department of, 49, 109, 196, 202, 203, 204, 205, 216, 218, 235

Labor and Human Resources, Senate Committee on, 205, 218, 273 (n. 32), 277 (n. 49)

Labor and Public Welfare, Senate Committee on, 53, 58, 225–26, 259 (n. 5), 275 (n. 3, 5), 278 (n. 5)

Lancaster, John, 141

Lando, Mordechai E., 3

Larson, James S., 258 (n. 8)

Laski, Frank J., 264 (n. 13), 274 (n. 54)

Least restrictive environment, 162, 167–68, 170

Legislators: as policy actors, 24–25

Lemak, David J., 38

Levin, Martin A., 14, 24

Levine, Erwin L., 61, 261 (n. 37)

Levy, William K., 170

Lippman, Leopold D., 57, 261 (n. 24)

Lipsky, Michael, 258 (n. 10)

Litan, Robert E., 41

Livneh, Hanoch, 5–6

Local option regulations in transportation, 146–48

Index

London, Alice L., 158, 159
Los Angeles Times, 273 (n. 41)
Lovell, Malcolm, 277 (n. 57)
Lublin, Joann S., 194
Lucas, Ronald E., 195

Mainstream, Inc., 229
Majone, Giandomenico, 36, 254
Management Analysis Center, 171
Mansfield, Stephen A., 274 (n. 65)
Martin, Reed, 261 (n. 37), 272 (n. 17)
Matthews, David, 66, 68, 69
Mayerson, Arlene, 103, 263 (n. 5), 265 (n. 28)
Mazmanian, Daniel A., 14, 33, 258 (n. 8)
Meier, Kenneth J., 37
Meisen, Walter, 111
Merit Systems Protection Board, 200, 276 (n. 28)
Metro Subway system (D.C.), 131, 133
Meyer, John R., 158
Milk, Leslie B., 294
Miller, James C., 31, 38
Mills v. Board of Education of District of Columbia, 57, 58, 181, 261 (n. 26)
Mitchell, Thomas J., 269 (n. 4)
Mithaug, Dennis E., 194
Mitnik, Barry M., 37, 40
Mitre Corporation, 271 (n. 43)
Montjoy, Robert S., 16, 24
Morrison, Glenn, 194
Motsco, Martha A., 274 (n. 68)
Murphy, Austin J., 120
Murphy, Jerome T., 15, 16, 29

Nakamura, Robert T., 27, 258 (n. 1, 8)
Nathanson, Robert B., 6, 194
National Academy of Sciences, 271 (n. 43)
National Advisory Committee on Handicapped Children, 59
National Association for the Advancement of Colored People, 100
National Association for the Blind, 26
National Association for the Deaf, 228
National Association of College and University Business Officers, 185
National Association of Retarded Children, 55
National Association of State Directors of Special Education, 171

National Association of the Physically Handicapped, 51
National Center for the Deaf, 89
National Commission on Architectural Barriers to Rehabilitation of the Handicapped, 50, 126, 259 (n. 5), 278 (n. 6)
National Committee for Citizens in Education, 172, 273 (n. 28)
National Council on the Handicapped, 219, 224, 253, 257 (n. 4), 278 (n. 70, 71)
National Education Association, 60, 177, 189
National Federation of the Blind, 51
National Paraplegic Association, 111
National School Board Association, 172
Navin, Francis P., 271 (n. 63)
Nelson, Richard R., 258 (n. 8)
New Mexico Association for Retarded Citizens v. New Mexico, 274 (n. 71)
New York Times, 142, 166, 277 (n. 59)
Niskanen, William A., Jr., 35
Nixon, Richard M., 54, 108, 266 (n. 7)
Noll, Roger G., 41
Nordhaus, William D., 41

Office of Civil Rights, HEW: drafting 504 regulations, 64–70, 78–82; contents of 504 regulations, 74–78
Office of Federal Contract Compliance Programs, DOL, 38, 204–18 passim, 234, 235, 276 (n. 41), 277 (n. 43, 46, 58)
Office of Management and Budget, 88–95 passim, 117, 122, 123, 127, 151, 264 (n. 14, 15, 25), 271 (n. 59)
Ogul, Morris S., 258 (n. 3)
Olenick, Donald J., 264 (n. 13), 274 (n. 54)
Omang, Joanne, 264 (n. 14)
O'Neill, David M., 262 (n. 8)
Open Doors for the Handicapped, 121
Operating Principles, 33–34
Organizing Principles, 17, 32–34; for section 504, 78–79; in transportation policy, 153
O'Toole, Laurence C., Jr., 16, 24
Oversight and Review, House Subcommittee on, 143, 145, 154, 270 (n. 40)
Owen, Bruce M., 41

Pacquette, Suzan, 194
Palumbo, Dennis J., 258 (n. 8)

Index

Paralyzed Veterans of America, 26, 51, 89, 122, 141, 228
Pati, Gopal C., 194, 195
Peltzman, Sam, 40
Pennsylvania Association for Retarded Children v. Commonwealth of Pennsylvania, 56–57, 58, 181, 261 (n. 25)
Peterson, Roger, 67
PL94-142. *See* Education for All Handicapped Children Act
Policy diffusion, 2
Policy entrepreneurs, 28, 225–27
Policy environment, 29–30, 156
Policy execution, 2
Policy implementation: definition, 1–2; as political process, 12–14; as administrative process, 14–15; as intergovernmental relations, 15–16; as game between rational actors, 16–17; a synthetic approach, 17–18; as dynamic process, 23–24; institutional model for study, 35–36
Policy implementation, disability rights policy: four stages of, 221–24; comparison and contrasts, 224–31; politics of, 237–43; and regulation, 243–44; and statutory provisions, 244–45; and equity approaches, 245–48; ongoing questions of, 248–53; tragic choices in, 253–54
Policy innovation: acute, 226; incubated, 226; by guardianship, 226
Policy refinement, 2
Policy window, 31, 226
Political environment, 18, 29–30, 156
Polsby, Nelson W., 31, 226
Postal Service, U.S., 93, 110–27 passim, 244, 264 (n. 26), 267 (n. 15, 33)
Presidential Commission on the Human Immunodeficiency Virus Epidemic, 279 (n. 27)
President's Committee on Employment of the Handicapped, 219, 225, 278 (n. 71)
Pressman, Jeffrey L., 14
Prewitt v. United States Postal Service, 99
Program accessibility, 75–76, 79, 93, 163
Program beneficiaries, 25–26, 222, 227–29
Public Buildings and Grounds, House Subcommittee on, 51, 111, 269 (n. 5, 9)
Public Buildings and Grounds, Senate Subcommittee on, 50, 259 (n. 6)

Public Buildings Cooperative Use Act of 1976, 111
Public Interest Law Center of Philadelphia, 85
Public Works, House Committee on, 260 (n. 14, 16)
Public Works, Senate Committee on, 259 (n. 5)

Quirk, Paul J., 41

Rabkin, Jeremy, 82, 261 (n. 2)
Rachal, Patricia, 259 (n. 8)
Radin, Beryl A., 27, 261 (n. 2)
Rainbow, Frances, 140, 147
Ramirez, Bruce A., 261 (n. 37), 274 (n. 52)
Rand Corporation, 55
Randolph, Jennings, 168
Reagan, Ronald, 83, 101, 117, 146, 190, 223, 249
Reasonable accommodation, 34, 73–75, 79, 91–93
Reed, Gale N., 269 (n. 3)
Regens, James L., 41
Regulated clients, 25–26, 222, 229–31
Regulation: types of, 38–39; politics of, 39–40; behavior of regulatory agencies, 40–41; aggressiveness of enforcement, 41–42; forms and impacts in disability rights, 243–44
Regulatory reform: Reagan administration plan for section 504, 88–95; politics of 504 reform, 95–96, 104–105; Reagan administration plan to revise accessibility regulations, 117–20, 121–24; Carter administration plans for PL94-142, 172; Reagan administration plans for PL94-142, 175–79
Rehabilitation Act Amendments of 1974, 65–67, 70, 204
Rehabilitation, Comprehensive Services, and Developmental Disabilities Amendments of 1978, 113
Related services in education of handicapped children, 162, 168, 170
Reorganization Plan No. 1 of 1978, 275 (n. 16)
Research Triangle Institute, 169
Reynold, William Bradford, 95, 99, 100, 101, 103, 119, 121, 122, 123, 200, 265 (n. 52,

53), 277 (n. 57)

Riegel, Donald, 148, 149

Ripley, Randall B., 25, 258 (n. 8), 259 (n. 7)

Roosevelt, Franklin D., 4

Rose, Mason, 117–22 passim

Rosenthal, Alan, 258 (n. 3)

Rose v. U.S. Postal Service, 122, 125, 127

Roth, William, 5

Rothstein, Laura F., 214

Roy Littlejohn Associates, 171

Rycroft, Robert W., 41

Sabatier, Paul, 14, 33, 258 (n. 8)

Salett, Stanley, 273 (n. 28)

Sargent, Francis, 59

Scheingold, Stuart A., 239

Schipper, William, 171

Schneck, Susan J., 170

School Board of Nassau County, Florida v. Arline, 252, 278 (n. 4, 23)

Schroedel, John G., 194, 257 (n. 2)

Schuck, Peter H., 243

Schwartz, Gail, 4

Schwartz, Terry A., 171

Scoping requirements: for accessibility, 115–16

Scotch, Richard K., 28, 53, 64, 66, 69, 81, 240, 261 (n. 1), 262 (n. 3)

Section 501, Rehabilitation Act of 1973: provisions, 195–96; original implementation policy by CSC, 196–98; responsibility for implementation transferred to EEOC, 198–99; implementation experiences, 199–202

Section 502, Rehabilitation Act of 1973, 108–10

Section 503, Rehabilitation Act of 1973: provisions, 196; original rulemaking by DOL, 202–204; role of OFCCP in implementation, 204–209; implementation experiences, 209–11

Section 504, Rehabilitation Act of 1973: legislative history, 52–55; OCR's responsibility for, 64–65; effect of Rehabilitation Act Amendments of 1974, 65–66; drafting regulations for, 66–70; content of regulations for federal aid recipients, 70–78; coordination guidelines for, 78; analysis of rulemaking, 78–82;

extending coverage to federal agencies, 84–85; Reagan administration effort to revise regulations, 88–96; regulations for federally conducted programs, 96–99; questions about enforcement, 99–101; judicial interpretation, 102–104, 214; influence on DOT's full accessibility regulations, 137–46; in higher education, 184–86; provisions regarding employment, 211; conflicts with section 503, 212–14

Section 505, Rehabilitation Act of 1973, 85

Seifert, Karl H., 194

Select Education, House Subcommittee on, 57, 114, 120, 126, 127, 166, 178, 179, 191, 234, 260 (n. 21, 23), 261 (n. 28, 31, 34), 262 (n. 10), 266 (n. 6), 267 (n. 26, 29), 268 (n. 45), 272 (n. 13, 14), 273 (n. 46), 279 (n. 11, 13)

Siller, Jerome, 6

Smallwood, Frank, 27, 258 (n. 1, 8)

Smith, Thomas B., 258 (n. 2)

Smith-Fess Act, 44

Smith-Sears Veterans' Rehabilitation Act, 44

Smith v. Robinson, 182–83, 191, 237, 274 (n. 66)

Social Security Act of 1935, 45

Soffer, Randall M., 172

Southeastern Community College v. Davis, 86–88, 91, 95–99, 105, 180, 190, 236, 247

Special efforts regulations in transportation, 133–36

Stanfield, Rochelle L., 97

Stark, James H., 187

Stigler, George J., 40

Stone, Alan, 42

Stone, Clarence, 36

Stone, Deborah, 45, 258 (n. 7)

Straus, Robert, 6

Stroman, Duane F., 194

Surface Transportation, House Subcommittee on, 141, 142, 145, 270 (n. 34)

Surface Transportation Act of 1980, 145

Surface Transportation Assistance Act of 1982, 148

Switzer, Mary, 50

Symbolic politics, 32–34, 239–42

Tanenbaum, Sandra J., 238

Targeted disabilities, 200, 201

Index

Taylor, Patricia Y., 274 (n. 65)

Thompson, Frank J., 24

Thompson, James D., 35, 259 (n. 9)

Thornton, Mary, 265 (n. 42)

Thrasher, Michael, 258 (n. 5)

Thurer, Shari, 5

Tolchin, Martin, 38

Tolchin, Susan J., 38

Town of Burlington v. Department of Education, 183–84, 191

Tragic choices, 253–54

Transbus, 138, 141, 143, 144, 271 (n. 43)

Transportation: needs of disabled persons, 129–30; early legislation concerning disability, 130–33; special efforts regulations, 133–36; full accessibility regulations, 136–44; congressional reactions to full accessibility, 144–45; unraveling of full accessibility regulations, 145–46; local option regulations, 146–48; comparable standards regulations, 148–52; politics of implementing handicapped policy for, 152–59

Transportation, Senate Subcommittee on, 269 (n. 8)

Transportation, U.S. Department of, 10, 94, 109, 133–57 passim, 230, 268 (n. 55), 270 (n. 25, 33), 271 (n. 43, 56, 57, 59, 64)

Trautmann, Joanne, 5

Treasury, U.S. Department of, 202

Undue economic hardship, 74–75

Uniform Federal Accessibility Standards, 93, 122

United Cerebral Palsy Association, 73, 170, 273 (n. 27)

Urban Mass Transportation Act of 1964, 131, 132

Urban Mass Transportation Administration, 130, 131, 133, 134, 135, 137, 152, 269 (n. 1, 2), 270 (n. 28), 271 (n. 63)

Van Horn, Carl E., 15–16, 21, 258 (n. 11)

Vanik, Charles, 43, 225

Van Meter, Donald S., 21, 258 (n. 11)

Veterans Administration, 109

Vice Presidential Task Force on Regulatory Relief, 83, 88, 95, 96, 117, 118, 120, 121, 127, 268 (n. 61)

Vietnam Era Veteran's Readjustment Assistance Act, 196, 205, 207, 208, 209, 212, 275 (n. 4)

Vocational rehabilitation program, 9, 44–45, 193

Walker, Jack L., 32, 258 (n. 4)

Watkins, James D., 252

Weicker, Lowell, 101, 177, 273 (n. 45)

Weintraub, Frederick J., 261 (n. 37), 274 (n. 52)

Weiss, Janet A., 24, 30

Wenderoff, Lori A., 274 (n. 65)

West, William, 81

Wexler, Elizabeth, 61, 261 (n. 37)

White, Lawrence J., 37, 38, 42

White House Conference on Handicapped Individuals, 3

Wildavsky, Aaron, 14, 36, 254

Wilken, Sharon, 275 (n. 14)

Williams, Harrison, 58, 68, 85, 144

Williams, James Q., 29, 39, 41, 238, 254, 259 (n. 8)

Williams, Walter, 258 (n. 8, 11)

Wilson, William, 171

Wilson, Woodrow, 13

Worker's Compensation, 45

Wright, Pat, 263 (n. 5), 265 (n. 28)

Yates, Douglas, 23, 258 (n. 8)

Yin, Robert K., 258 (n. 9)

Zettl, Jeffrey J., 169

Zimmer, Arno B., 212, 213n

Zorkinsky, Edward, 144